AF836296

Computer Bible Games
For Microsoft® Small Basic

A Computer Programming Tutorial

3rd Edition

By Philip Conrod & Lou Tylee

BibleByte Books

PO Box 701
Maple Valley, WA 98038

http://www.BibleByteBooks.com
http://www.BibleByteGames.com

Published by:
BibleByte Books (a division of Kidware Software LLC)
PO Box 701
Maple Valley, Washington 98038
1.425.413.1185
www.biblebytebooks.com

Printed in the United States of America

ISBN-13: 978-1-937161-06-4 (Printed Paperpack Edition)
ISBN-13: 978-1-937161-10-1 (Electronic Edition)

Copy Editor: Stephanie Conrod & Jessica Conrod
Book Cover Illustration by Kevin Brockschmidt

This guide was developed for the course, "Computer Bible Games for Microsoft Small Basic ," produced by BIBLEBYTE BOOKS, Maple Valley, Washington. It is not intended to be a complete reference to the Small Basic language. Please consult the Microsoft website for detailed reference information.

About The Authors

Philip Conrod was awarded with a Certificate in "Computer Programming for Business" from WarrenTech and a Bachelor's degree in Computer Information Systems from Regis University. Philip has authored, co-authored and edited numerous computer programming books for students of all ages. Philip has also held various Information Technology leadership roles in companies like Sundstrand Aerospace, Safeco Insurance, FamilyLife, Kenworth Truck Company, PACCAR Inc., and Darigold. Philip also serves as the President & Publisher of BibleByte Books & Kidware Software LLC. He makes his home with his lovely family in Maple Valley, Washington.

Lou Tylee holds BS and MS degrees in Mechanical Engineering and a PhD in Electrical Engineering. Lou has been programming computers since 1969 when he took his first Fortran course in college. He has written software to control suspensions for high speed ground vehicles, monitor nuclear power plants, lower noise levels in commercial jetliners, compute takeoff speeds for jetliners, locate and identify air and ground traffic and to let kids count bunnies, learn how to spell and do math problems. He has written several on-line texts teaching Visual Basic, Visual C# and Java to thousands of people. He taught a beginning Visual Basic course for over 15 years at a major university. Currently, Lou works as an engineer at a major Seattle aerospace firm. He is the proud father of five children and proud husband of his special wife. Lou and his family live in Seattle, Washington.

Acknowledgements

I want to thank my best friend Jesus, who has always been there by my side giving me wisdom and guidance. Without you, this book would have never been printed and published. I also want to thank my three wonderful daughters - Stephanie, Jessica and Chloe, who helped with various aspects of the book publishing process including software testing, book editing, creative design and many other more tedious tasks like finding all my errors. I could not have accomplished this without all your hard work, love and support.

Last but definitely not least, I want to thank my multi-talented co-author, Lou Tylee, for doing all the real hard work necessary to develop, test, debug, and keep current all the 'kid-friendly' applications, games and base tutorial text found in this book. Lou has tirelessly poured his heart and soul into so many previous versions of this tutorial and there are so many beginners who have benefited from his work over the years. Lou is by far one of the best application developers and tutorial writers I have ever worked with. Thanks Lou for collaborating with me on this book project.

Foreword

For over 20 years I have known Philip Conrod as a best friend, fellow Christian, and my personal IT guy for a variety of computer issues that have come my way. Philip's technological expertise mixed with his spiritual gifts of knowledge and teaching have given him not only a unique set of skills for working in the Information Technology field for over 30 years but also for serving Jesus in the church. He has saved his home church thousands of dollars in needed upgrades, understanding networks intricacies and teaching staff members needed computer skills.

The "other side" of Philip's gifts lie in his amazing ability to teach. Simply put, he makes the "hard concepts" easy to understand! Whether it's doctrinal, devotional or day to day living from the Bible, student after student have grown tremendously from Philip's teaching at New Community Church. Recently I was leading a group of young adults and asked "Which mentor has influenced you the most?" Not surprisingly, Philip Conrod's name quickly rose to the top! He has, for years been a favorite Sunday school teacher for many students in our church, including my own son.

Of course the highlight of each year is when a crowded house of teenagers and college graduates, of "Mr. Phil", play hours of computer games intertwined with Christian fellowship in his home every year for over 15 years. It is this very combination that makes Philip the perfect author for the *Computer Bible Games* series of programming books. Making the Bible fun, intriguing and filled with learning enables all of us to grow in our biblical knowledge. Sit back and be prepared to be challenged, captivated and without knowing it, grow in your knowledge and understanding of the Bible!

Ken B. Michell
Sr. Pastor
New Community Church
Maple Valley, Washington USA

www.newcommunitychurch.us

Reviews for Computer Bible Games For Microsoft Small Basic:

"Phil Conrod has a passion for writing tutorials and books aimed at beginner programmers and he's done an excellent job of covering all the fundamentals of Small Basic programming." - Vijaye Raji, Creator of Microsoft Small Basic

"Have your kids expressed interest in computers? Most children have, and will continue to do so, because we are in a technological world. There aren't many programming courses on the market today that cater to teaching children about computer programming. Fortunately, BibleByte Books & Computer Science for Kidsoffer two different "parent-friendly" middle school and high school computer programming curriculums for Microsoft Small Basic, Visual Basic Express, Visual C# Express, and Oracle-Sun Java. One curriculum is designed for Christian based homeschool programs while the other curriculum is designed for secular homeschooling. Both are self-study and self-paced tutorials and neither requires prior parental or student computer programming experience. The games are very, very simple. What's important here is the programming. With programming knowledge, your kids can program more complexity into their games and other programming projects. While learning how to program, there is a sense of accomplishment—a feeling of self-confidence. After taking this course, I wanted to learn more! Isn't that what we want for our kids? To instill a desire to learn even more? BibleByte Books & Computer Science for Kids does just that! With no previous programming experience, I found that their Computer Programming Tutorials made computer programming both fun and easy to learn. Their customer service was also very eager to answer any questions that I might have. This combination of curriculum and customer service makes their tutorials attractive to both the Homeschool parent and their beginning student programmer."
- Homeschool.com - Seal of Approval Product Review

"Third Day Games would be thrilled if every child who played our video games would learn how to develop Bible-based Christian video games themselves. BibleByte Books produces a wonderful Computer Science For Kids Curriculum that we believe will help train up the next generation of Christian game developershe games industry desperately needs talented game developers, who are also Christians, to help build the next generation of Bible-based Christian video games. Learning a computer programming language early in life will give your child a great head start in the wonderful field of computer programming and give them the opportunity to use their skills to further the Kingdom." - Bobby Wells, CEO, Third Day Games

"My son is 12 years old and is in the 7th grade. My son found this program extremely easy to use. The material in the Computer Science for Kids program was presented in a way that even a middle school or high school student who has never seen a computer before would be able to pick up and follow the self-paced tutorial guides with ease. There are more challenging exercises included that are intended for 7th through 12 graders, and he kept begging me to complete those as well. Of course I said yes. How often do I hear my son beg to do school work? I think the Computer Science for Kids tutorials are a great introduction to computer programming for middle school students." - Tere Scott

"Computer Science for Kids has great curriculum for children who are interested in learning how to program games. My children liked the curriculum because it was on game programming. All of us found that the curriculum was easy to use. The language of the text was easy to understand. The book was written with the child in mind, but as adult could use it and not feel that the exercises were too childish. We liked how the material was presented. The book starts off very simple. In each chapter you learn a new step while referring back to the previous steps. Some people might think that the curriculum is too slow, but by presenting the material the way the authors do you really learn the language. My children have also had fun doing the simple programs." - Karen Morris

"The program is a great introduction to more complex computer languages (i.e. C++, Java). I would especially recommend it for students 12+. If your child is interested in technology, it is also a program a parent can go through with him/her. The program was well-organized, starting out simple and gradually getting more complex, making it easy to follow and keep up. The theory was explained in clear language, making the world of computer programming reachable to anyone! The lessons do not just teach the computer language and program design, but also good habits! When the student gets the opportunity to design their own programs, the text explains and encourages important practices to keep. I enjoyed how this program made teaching computer science not just possible, but fun!" – Jannelle Nevels

"Computer Bible Games for Microsoft Small Basics IS designed for the beginner. The E-book (Textbook) is very through with instructions. My boys are very excited about this program. They have been working on it for a little over five weeks and they are still enthusiastic about it. That right there tells me that it's a keeper. It's been a bit of a challenge at times for them but that's a plus because they are working through the challenges. Their dad is there to help but he lets them figure things out. This is program is great because a parent who has little or no knowledge with computer programming will be able to teach their children using Computer Bible Games for Small Basics. The student textbook is spelled out so parents can learn along with their children. Would I recommend Computer Science for Kids? Absolutely! In fact we will be a returning customer." – Linda

"The tutorials are really well written and a good challenge to work through. We found the first few lessons extremely easy to whip through, as they were basics that we have already learned - how to open the program, open and save files, as well as how the program inherently works. But then things started to get more in-depth and the lessons took more time. I was actually quite amazed at how well my little man was able to grasp some seriously complex concepts that we haven't covered in other ways yet: order of operations, exponentials, and square roots - for example. What we like: Big's review of the program include the words "Awesome" and "Really Cool." I think he likes it. (I'm actually not very surprised at that!). He loves the challenge of learning complex concepts and master them, and making things that are actually workable. For me, I found the lessons extremely detailed and well-written. Each new lesson made sure to review the one before, which meant that we could keep things fresh in our memory, especially when we ended up breaking lessons into a few days long instead of trying to finish them all at once. I liked having everything laid out simply so that I could follow along, reading aloud and then explaining it again to BigKid so I could make sure he understood. We were able to copy and follow-along with the actual code from the lesson to type into his window and immediately see results. - Lisa Marie

"Laura has been able to work through this program completely independently, and has been enjoying it. She has been able to follow the instructions with no help at all from me, which is wonderful. She says that the lessons are a little hard to follow when they are introducing a new concept, but that the step by step instructions themselves are very easy to follow, so that eventually you can understand and begin to see the big picture. She was still able to follow the instructions, even without fully understanding the concept, until everything 'clicked'. This is important to me, because it helped her to work through the program and not get frustrated and want to just 'give up'. Every time she is able to create even a simple game, like the number guessing game, she calls us over to the computer to play her game. She thinks it is 'SO NEAT' to be able to create games on the computer, and is possibly interested in taking the second semester program when she finishes this one, in order to expand on her knowledge. We are very happy with this program so far, and Laura is enjoying it, and looking forward to finishing it, and actually making a REAL GAME!" – Erica B.

"If you own your own business, you either need computer skills or need to hire someone with computer skills. It also seems that all of us would be more valuable to employers if we had computer skills. So that is why I want all of my children to learn computer skills now and be able to use them as a tool to reach their potential in their careers in the future. This course is helping my kids head in the right direction. He loves it and we can't wait to tell you more about it. I am very excited for my family to have access to great programs through Computer Science For Kids." – Weiser Academy

"I love that this was made for Christian beginner homeschool students to learn programming with Small Basic. I had never even heard of Small Basic before we started this, and we are a Christian homeschooling family, so I thought this was perfect! It provides very clear step-by-step instructions on what to do. Issac and I are very happy with this program. It's very well thought out and thorough. I am very thankful for the opportunity to use it. I would definitely recommend Computer Bible Games to my friends." - Becca Carroll

"We asked "The Artist" how he liked taking the Computer Bible Games for Small Basic course. His response? "I like it...it's fun! It's teaching me how to create my own programs. At some point, I'd like to write my own computer games, and I think this is a good beginning." If I didn't make it clear earlier, I am NOT a techie. But I do like the way the class is formatted, and I did manage to pick up some programming education along the way. The important thing is that "The Artist" is enjoying learning computer programming, and is able to do so without a huge amount of parental support. He is looking forward to writing his own computer games, and his brothers are looking forward to playing them in the near future!" - Lori

"What I appreciated about this particular tutorial is that it is written in easy to understand language. I found the program to be very well organized. I loved the fact that we were taught in small steps. That was helpful for me as well as Josiah. We are going to use it again this summer. He is excited to be able to show his cousins and friends what he has created! I highly recommend this product. It's just plain fun! " - Rebeka

"First off let me say that this homeschool Momma, is totally clueless when it comes to computers, I can type and send an email, but that is about it. Before I give you our thoughts on Computer Bible Games for Microsoft Small Basic, let's first talk about customer service. In this day and age, we hear so much about customer no service! As Clark Howard would say. But in the case of Computer Science For Kids, the customer service was outstanding and I really do not think it had anything to do with us being on the TOS Review Crew. Philip Conrod (the author) was AMAZING and did not make me feel like a totally dork when I was clueless about how to get this set up on my computer. So here is our review... What the student liked... 1) It was fun! 2) It was easy! 3) I liked how you could do the programs & all the different variations. 4) I love the games! What the student did not like... 1) Mom would not let me spend more time each day playing with this! lol. Ya know, I had other school work to complete. What the homeschool Momma liked... 1) Easy to install (once I got the WinZip on board). 2) Simple for our son to understand and use. 3) AWESOME for me as a post-op homeschool Momma who spent her days during this review in a recliner recovering. This was a wonderful tool to get school moving along, so that my son could 'play' on the computer...hahaha...actually LEARN on the computer with Computer Bible Games for Microsoft Small Basic but it sure did not feel like learning, it was a fun time that he looked forward to each day. 4) This opened up a whole new world my son, this was all totally new to him. Yes we would buy this and use it again, and guess what? It's on sale!! What homeschool Momma can pass up a sale on curriculum?" - Moe, An Adoptive Mom

"My son, Nate, loves to be on the computer and has often said he'd like to program video games in the future, specifically, Bible games. He chose to work through the Computer Bible Games program. When he works on this, I have trouble getting him off the computer to do his other schoolwork. I count that as a success. Some time ago my boys had tried to learn programming through another course, but it was difficult for them to understand. This one is so much easier to follow. Nate created a "guess the number" game which we all enjoyed playing when he was finished. He showed a lot of creativity and ingenuity. I watched him create code for these games. I found it very interesting. I haven't programmed anything since I was in 8th grade, and it certainly didn't look this interesting. I can see why kids would think this was fun now and want to learn and create. I can see how much joy it brings him when he creates something and sees it working. This is a product I would highly recommend for your children if they are interested in learning how to program."
– Mrs. Bairen

"The E-Tutorial download provided to us is very clear and contains easy to follow instructions for the homeschool parent, such as myself, with no previous programming experience. I was extremely impressed with how well the authors did with the writing of this tutorial. It made me feel going in as though this was going to be "doable" for us…I almost expected to feel overwhelmed, but I did not. My student is a little below the recommended age level, but we were approved for the review because I made it a class for both of us. And truly, that works!! So if you and a child on the young"ish" side of the range (or a little bit below) are up to it, I could definitely say you can get through it, and not just adequately. At this point, I actually understand what we've been doing so far, and I've looked a little bit ahead, and still feel good about my understanding of the material and my ability to help her clearly understand it as well. Thanks to the authors for providing such a neat product for our students!!!" – Ellen B.

"We received a copy of Computer Bible Games for Microsoft Small Basic to review in our homeschool. When I heard about this opportunity, my husband and I were excited because our eldest son has an interest in computers and we thought this product might be a great fit for him. We were not disappointed. Computer Science for Kids takes Computer Bible Games for Microsoft Small Basic and makes the tedious process of learning a computer programming language user-friendly and fun. We thought this program was user-friendly and a great way for kids to learn more about how computer programming works. Our ten-year old was able to complete the tutorials with only a little assistance after the initial setup in the first couple of lessons. We were pleased with the tutorials and the results that were produced in such a short amount of time working with the curriculum. I would recommend this program for self-motivated students with a good eye for attention to detail.
- Jennifer A.

"Microsoft Small Basic was very easy to install and begin. I love that this is a self-study program. While I would love to understand the fine detail of computer programming...I really do not have the time to learn a completely new subject for me, and then teach it to him. Computer Science for Kids has made my job so much easier by writing directly to my student. The lesson notes are written very clearly and are well organized. My tester had no problem working independently. He is very impressed with Microsoft Small Basic and cannot wait to finish it and move on to the next course. Overall, the Bentz Test Laboratory was very impressed with Computer Science for Kids." - Mrs Bentz

"They are both really enjoying the programming, and can't wait until they hit the actual game building. My job: watch sometimes, be the guinea pig when needed, and ooh and ahh where appropriate. We love this! Seriously, it is completely self-led, and they are doing great. I love that they are learning programming, and can build on these basic skills as they progress. It's also a wonderful way for them to 'talk tech' with their dad. I imagine this will segue into dad teaching some things when they get into more complex languages. When they finish this book, I'll have them finish the other book, too. Then I plan on having them finish the tutorial they mistakenly began before getting the next level of the Bible programming books. They have some other neat programs available, too. These are perfect for the homeschooling kid who has an interest in programming." - Audra Marie

"As a parent and teacher, I really like how this curriculum is put together. It covers every step, from installing the software to color selections for the program. They explain things in ways that are simple enough for middle school and high school students to grasp and be able to follow as they work through the lessons. It is very thorough and explanatory. We are about half-way through it right now and Jonathan is loving it. Each step closer to the finished project he gets more excited. Overall, I would definitely recommend this course to any homeschooling family. It is perfect for the child who wants to learn more about computer program writing. My son loves it." - Elizabeth Yenca

"We used this program exclusively with Benjamin, who is 11. He was very, very, excited to be able to take a programming class. I think he was most excited that he got to work exclusively with Dad for this program. So this review is my observations of watching my husband work with my son, using the Microsoft Small Basic program and the Computer Bible Games Tutorial. I, Mom, was impressed at how much Ben learned and used during this review. He must have been hungry for computer knowledge, because he talked about it during the week and even went back to the programs he wrote and used them again and again. I would recommend this program to anyone. I think it is a great program for both kids who know a little about computer programming and kids who do not even realize computers need a specific language to work (like my daughter). We will be continuing with this course until the end of the book as Ben was really enjoying himself and looking forward to learning more. - Jill Clark

"We have enjoyed using Computer Bible Games for the last few weeks. So far I've learned some new things, and am realizing that I already knew a few of the basic lessons. My kids are enjoying learning about programming and are looking forward to completing the whole course. We worked together on each lesson and spent the necessary time needed for all of us to fully grasp the concept. The language of programming can take a little bit of time to get used to. My daughter (17) caught on pretty quick and wanted to zoom through the lessons, but my son (12) needed some extra time to understand. I think that once all of this truly "clicks" for him, he will be asking to continue on to the next level of programming. But really, learning to navigate through Microsoft Small Basic with Computer Science for Kids can start an exciting journey into the world of computer programming for my son and yours. We've had a lot of fun so far and know that there's more to come." - Mona Lisa

"Taylor has always been interested in computers and video games and we have had endless talks about appropriate content and using computers and video games for good. We have also chatted about how you can use your passion in something to create your career and actually get to do something you love for money. I can see Taylor being a computer programmer or video game designer and if this course helps to show him that this is the right path for him or not and help him get a jump start on basic programming knowledge then that is wonderful. I will say that even with Taylor's vast computer skills he did struggle with this some as he is not strong in Math at all. What I did find valuable even in his frustration was that he saw that you do need Math to do things in life that he did not think crossed over. I am hoping this helps spark him to try a little harder in Math. He always says he won't use the Math skills we are trying to learn, but if he wants to go into computer programming he now sees he will need these Math skills, that give this program an A+ right off the bat. All in all I think this is a valuable program that can be used as an elective credit. I think basic computer knowledge is a must for all in this day and age and this takes it one step further by teaching kids programming skills. Once you know programming the possibilities are endless. I think this would be an asset to any homeschool classroom." - Jenn Kasprzak

"Computer Science for Kids provides introductory programming lessons, which I think is a great skill to have! DH is the techie in the family and he has been interested in learning some programming. We felt it was a very thorough introduction to programming, but not too overwhelming to be enjoyed. I was relieved that the parents/teachers don't need to have any prior knowledge to teach this course. It is really all outlined very well in the lessons so that parents can teach as they learn, too. If your child has an interest in a programming career or is just curious about how technology works, Computer Science for Kids is a great way to begin learning. " - Sara

"This digitally downloaded e-book teaches students, step by step, how to use the Microsoft Small Basic computer language. The end goal is to program seven different Bible story inspired games. This e-book eases the student into the language. The author uses bold print to emphasize important vocabulary and there are lots of screen shots to illustrate. I really love that the author takes the approach of learning a foreign language. He mentions that we are "talking to the computer in its language" to get it to do what we want it to do. I also love that he takes time to clearly explain complicated concepts using simple language. I also tried my hand with the Small Basic. It was a very interesting experience. I've played around with HTML with this blog, but never programmed anything. One of the things I learned doing Computer Science for Kids, is that computers are very good at, well, computing. There is math, and the course explains how to do the math. Mostly it is basic concepts, but within the actual programming there are some very sophisticated concepts that used words from math, like variable. However because the author takes such time and effort to explain everything, those concepts go from a little intimidating to understandable. I would definitely recommend this course for any Middle School or High School student looking to experience the world of Computer Programming. I would also highly recommend this for any beginning adult who would like to try their hand at something new." - Holly

"I am very impressed with the ease of each lesson. They are very thorough and easily paced. It was not a problem at all to pick up where we left off in each lesson. Carter really enjoyed the program and we are both very anxious to continue working through the program. I'm excited to see him tell others that he is learning computer programming. Who knows what doors that has opened up for him and his future!" - Miranda

"In having some computer programming experience professionally, I give Computer Bible Games for Microsoft Basic a big thumbs up! The projects that are given to the students are incremental and can realistically be accomplished in a relatively short amount of time. They use an actual computing language. The tutorial as a whole is also great from a parent perspective in that it does come with completed code files for each project. You as the parent do not need to know anything about computer programming to be able to help your student figure out where they went wrong if their project does not do what it was supposed to do. Computer programming in general is also a great way to get your children to logically think things through one small step at a time, which helps them in organizational thinking, tackling the different steps in any new project, and may even be a great training ground for the step by step thinking needed for successful completion of higher level math courses. Computer Bible Games for Microsoft Basic is a great place to start." - Dr. Dawn Oaks

Table of Contents

4. Small Basic Program Design, Input Methods

5. Debugging, Decisions, Random Numbers

6. Small Basic Looping, Subroutines

7. More Small Basic Looping, Arrays

8. Small Basic Graphics, Mouse Methods

9. Timers, Animation, Keyboard Methods

10. Noah's Ark Project

11. Daniel and the Lions Project

12. Elijah and the Ravens Project

13. More Learning Games & Computer Bible Games

Appendix I. Small Basic Colors

Appendix II. Classic Small Basic Computer Games

More Programming Tutorials By BibleByte Books

Course Desription:

Computer Bible Games For Microsoft Small Basic consists of 13 chapters explaining (in simple, easy-to-follow terms) how to build a Small Basic application. Microsoft Small Basic is a wonderful programming environment for beginners. Small Basic is very easy and approachable for both kids and adults. The aim of this book is to teach you the fundamentals of programming with Microsoft Small Basic by using the free Microsoft Small Basic Development Environment. You will learn the features of the Small Basic language, and then use them to build applications running on the Microsoft Windows operating system. You learn about program design, text window applications, graphics window applications and many elements of the Small Basic language. Numerous examples are used to demonstrate every step in the building process. The tutorial also includes several detailed computer programs to illustrate the fun of Small Basic. Computer Bible Games For Microsoft Small Basic is presented using a combination of over 550 pages of course notes and actual Small Basic examples.

BibleByte Books also produces beginning programming tutorials for several other programming languages like Visual Basic, Visual C#, and Java. Please visit our website for more information on our beginning programming tutorials: http://www.BibleByteBooks.com. If you are learning Microsoft Small Basic after learning a different programming language, the final chapter of this tutorial can help you leverage your existing programming knowledge in that specific programming language to help you better understand Microsoft Small Basic.

By the time you complete this book; you will have a thorough understanding of Microsoft Small Basic and will have used it to build several applications and games that can be published on the internet.

System Requirements:

You will need the following hardware and software to complete the exercises in this book:

- Microsoft Windows 7 Operating System (or higher)
- Microsoft Small Basic 1.3 (or higher)
- Processor: 1 gigahertz (GHz) or faster (1.5 Ghz Recommended)
- RAM: 1 gigabyte (GB) (32-bit) or 2 GB (64-bit)
- Graphics card: Microsoft DirectX 9 graphics device with WDDM driver.
- Microsoft Mouse or compatible pointing device

Course Prerequisites:

To use the Computer Bible Games For Microsoft Small Basic Programming Tutorial, you should be comfortable working within the Windows operating system environment, knowing how to find files, move windows, resize windows, etc. No programming experience is needed. You will also need the ability to view and print documents saved in the Adobe Acrobat format. Finally, and most obvious, you need to have Microsoft Small Basic. This is a FREE product that can be downloaded from the Microsoft Small Basic website:

http://www.smallbasic.com

How To Take the Course:

The Computer Bible Games For Microsoft Small Basic Tutorial is a self-paced course. The suggested approach is to do one chapter a week for thirteen weeks. This assumes that you can dedicate 45-60 minutes a day reading through the tutorial chapter and completing the exercises. Each week's class should require about 3 to 6 hours of your time to grasp the concepts completely. Try to do each example as they are encountered in the tutorial. Work through all the programs. If you need any help, all completed programs are included in the BSB Code folder.

Installing and Using the Solution Files:

If you purchased this directly from http://www.computerscienceforkids.com you received an email with a special and individualized internet download link where you could download the compressed Program Solution Files. If you purchased this book through a 3rd Party Book Store, the solutions files for the Computer Bible Games For Microsoft Small Basic Tutorial are included in a compressed ZIP file that is available for download directly from our website at:

https://www.biblebytebooks.com/cbgsb-solutions

Complete the online web form at this webpage above with your name, shipping address, email address, the exact title of this book, date of purchase, online or physical store name, and your order confirmation number from that store. After we receive all this information we will email you a download link for the Program Solution Files and all multimedia files associated with this book.

Warning: If you purchased this book "used" or "second hand" you are not licensed or entitled to download the Program Solution Files. However, you can purchase the Download Only version of this book as an E-Tutorial at a discounted price which allows you access to the digital program solutions required for completing this tutorial.

Using Computer Bible Games For Microsoft Small Basic

The course notes and code for **COMPUTER BIBLE GAMES FOR MICROSOFT SMALL BASIC** are included in one or more ZIP file(s). Use your favorite 'unzipping' application to write all files to your computer. The course is included in the folder entitled **BeginSB**. This folder contains two other folders: **BSB Notes** and **BSB Code**. There's a chance when you copy the files to your computer, they will be written as '**Read-Only**.' To correct this (in **Windows Explorer** or **My Computer**), right-click the **BeginSB** folder and remove the check next to **Read only**. Make sure to choose the option to apply this change to all sub-folders and files. The **BSB Code** folder includes all projects developed during the course.

1

Introducing Small Basic

Preview

You are about to start a new journey. Writing programs that ask a computer to do certain tasks is fun and rewarding. Like any journey, you need to prepare before starting. In this first class, we do that preparation. You will learn why you might want to learn Small Basic. You will see the historical lineage of Small Basic. You will download and install the Small Basic development software that will help you create Small Basic programs. Once the preparation is done, you will run your first Small Basic application to check that you have prepared properly. Let's get started.

Why Learn Small Basic?

We could very well just ask the question – **Why Learn a Programming Language?** A programming language is used to provide instructions to a computer to do specific tasks. There are several reasons for doing this. First, if you know how to program, you will have a better understanding of just how computers work. Second, writing programs is good exercise for your thinking skills – you must be a very logical thinker to write computer programs. You must also be something of a perfectionist – computers are not that smart and require exact, perfect instructions to do their jobs. Third, computer programmers are in demand and make a lot of money. And, last, writing computer programs is fun. It's rewarding to see your ideas for a certain computer program come to life on the computer screen.

So, why learn **Small Basic**? One big reason is that it's free. Another reason for learning Small Basic is that it is one of the easiest languages to learn. Small Basic is a simple language. There are many built-in elements that make your work simpler and the language itself is very simple – only 15 reserved keywords. But, just because it is a simple language doesn't mean it lacks capabilities. You will see throughout these notes that you can build some fairly complex programs.

Because of its simplicity, you can learn to write Small Basic programs very quickly. But, just because you can write your first program quickly doesn't mean you'll learn everything there is to know about Small Basic. This course just introduces Small Basic. There's still a lot to learn – there's always a lot to learn. So, consider this course as a first step in a journey to becoming a proficient computer programmer.

And, once you've mastered Small Basic, you can move on to its more capable cousin **Visual Basic**, another Microsoft product used to develop applications with **GUI** (graphical user interfaces). These are applications with menus, toolbars, buttons, scroll bars, and other controls which depend on the computer mouse for input. Examples of GUI applications you may have used are word processors, spreadsheet programs and computer games. Our company, KIDware, offers several tutorials for the Visual Basic product.

A Brief History of Small Basic

We're almost ready to get started. But, first I thought it would be interesting for you to see just where the **Small Basic** language fits in the history of some other computer languages and, in particular, with Microsoft products

Most programming in these early days was done in such cryptic languages by engineers and mathematicians. Two professors at Dartmouth College wanted to explain programming to "normal" people and developed the **BASIC** (Beginner's All-Purpose Symbolic Code) language to help in that endeavor. BASIC was meant to be a simple language with just a few keywords to allow a little math and a little printing.

In the later 1960's, timeshare computing, where a user could sit at a terminal and interact with the computer, became popular. The primary language used in these interactive sessions was BASIC. The Dartmouth BASIC was not sufficient for the many applications being developed, so many extensions and improvements were made in the BASIC language. Many of the first computer games were written on timeshare terminals using BASIC. The first complete game I wrote in BASIC was on an HP-1000 Timeshare Basic system using a ASR-33 Terminal. Here is one such terminal:

These terminals allowed direct interaction with a mainframe computer. Your output was on paper and programs could be saved on a punched paper tape.

In the summer of 1969 (when man first set foot on the moon), my first programming job was using such a terminal to write BASIC programs for the US Navy. Coincidentally, that same year, Bill Gates and Paul Allen began writing BASIC programs at Lakeside School in Seattle using this same kind of teletype. Needless to say, the career paths of myself and Bill Gates diverged just a bit at this time. I went on to work as an engineer for several companies, continuing programming in Fortran and BASIC. Bill continued programming and starting little business ventures until the early winter of 1975 when this magazine appeared on the stands:

On the cover is an Altair 8800 computer. It must have been expensive – note the 'Save Over $1000' line. About all the computer could do was flash some lights according to a program written by the user. But, it was the first home computer. Bill Gates and Paul Allen saw the potential. They developed a BASIC language for the Altair computer and marketed it through their new company – Microsoft. Yes, the first product sold by Microsoft was the BASIC computer language. It sold for $350 and was distributed on a cassette tape.

Then, in the late 1970's and early 1980's, it seems there were computers everywhere with names like Radio Shack TRS-80, Commodore 64, Texas Instruments 99/4A, Atari 400, Coleco Adam, Timex Sinclair and the IBM PC-Jr. Stores like Sears, JC Penneys and even K Mart sold computers. One thing these machines had in common was that they were all programmed in some version of Microsoft's BASIC. Each computer had its own fans and own magazines. Users would wait each month for the next issue of a magazine with BASIC programs you could type into your computer and try at home. Our computers of choice were the Texas Instruments model:

And the TRS-80 Color Computer:

Like Microsoft's first product, our programs were distributed on audio cassette tapes. This was a fun and exciting time for the beginning programmer, but the fun times ended with the introduction of the IBM-PC in the early 1980's. Bigger and faster computers brought forth bigger languages and more complicated development environments. These new languages were expensive to purchase and difficult for the beginning programmer to grasp. Which brings us to **Small Basic**, which I would call a close relative of the early, original BASIC language. Small Basic was developed by Vijaye Raji, a developer at Microsoft, in 2008 in response to an article written in September 2006 by David Brin called, "Why Johnny can't code". It would be best to let Vijaye tell the story of how Small Basic was born. The following Small Basic History was copied with permission from Vijaye's Blog dated October 23, 2008 entitled "Hello World".

> "It all happened in August of 2007 when someone sent me a pointer to the article Why Johnny Can't Code and it got me thinking. After all, when I was a kid, I started programming in ZX Spectrum with a built in Sinclair

BASIC interpreter and did so until I ran into Turbo BASIC. To me that transformation was groundbreaking and was the single most important reason why I chose to write software for a living, for the rest of my life.

An informal poll along the corridors in Microsoft revealed that most developers within Microsoft had started programming in some variant of BASIC. It had all the good characteristics of a good beginner programming language - simplicity, minimal ceremony, instant gratification and ubiquity. It helped them "get" programming and assisted them with understanding the need for more advanced concepts.

When I asked them how they're going to teach programming to their children, they were stumped. Almost everyone wanted to, they just didn't know how. Some said KPL, Python and Ruby. Some said Alice and Scratch. But they all felt that none of these have the charm of BASIC. Of course there were some that took the Dijkstra's stand, but they were few.

Of the numerous programming languages, BASIC, from its inception in the 1960s has undergone some major transformations. Even among Microsoft's BASIC offerings, the language and the environment (VS) has been repeatedly updated to include more powerful features with every release. On the one hand this makes the language and the environment very powerful and capable, but on the other hand, it makes it daunting for a beginner.

That got me thinking as to why isn't there a "Small" variant of BASIC that brings the simplicity of the original language to the modern day. And after a year, here we are, announcing Small Basic. Small Basic is a project that will help make programming easy and approachable for beginners. Now, that's a pretty big claim - let's see how Small Basic does it.

Make programming approachable

Small Basic starts with a really simple programming language that gathers inspiration from the original BASIC language. It has no more than 16 keywords and is strictly imperative. There are no classes, scopes, generics, lambdas, etc. - just pure imperative code. The language is typeless and all variables are dynamic and global all the time. The code gets compiled to IL and runs on the .Net Framework.

It comes with a set of libraries that can be accessed from within a Small Basic program. Since the language itself is .Net based, new libraries can be created or the existing libraries modified using any .Net programming language.

Next, it combines the features of the language and the libraries into a very simple and friendly programming environment. This environment gives beginners, access to professional features like Intellisense(TM) and Instant context sensitive help. It makes writing programs and executing them a breeze."

The development of Small Basic was a several year project by Vijaye Raji to rekindle the exciting days when just about anyone could sit down at a computer and write a simple program using the BASIC language. Those of you who wrote programs on those old "toy" computers will recognize the simplicity of the Small Basic language and the ease of its use. And, you will also notice Small Basic is a great environment for writing and testing code, something missing in the early 1980's. Let's get started now. For those of you new to programming, I hope you can feel the excitement we old timers once had. For the old timers, I hope you rekindle your programming skills with this new product.

Let's Get Started

Learning how to use **Small Basic** to write a computer program (like learning anything new) involves many steps, many new terms, and many new skills. We will take it slow, describing each step, term, and skill in detail. Before starting, we assume you know how to do a few things:

- You should know how to start your computer and use the mouse.
- You should have some knowledge on working with your particular Windows operating system. In these notes, we used Windows Vista. If you are using another operating system, your screens may appear different than those shown here.
- You should know how to resize and move windows around on the screen.
- You should know how to run an application on your computer by using the **Start Menu** or some other means.
- You should know how to fill in information in dialog boxes that may pop up on the screen.
- You should know about folders and files and how to create and find them on your computer.
- You should know what file extensions are and how to identify them. For example, in a file named **Example.ext**, the three letters **ext** are called the extension.
- You should know how to click on links to read documents and move from page to page in such documents. You do this all the time when you use the Internet.
- You should know how to access the Internet and download files.

You have probably used all of these skills if you've ever used a word processor, spreadsheet, or any other software on your computer. If you think you lack any of these skills, ask someone for help. They should be able to show you how to do them in just a few minutes. Actually, any time you feel stuck while trying to learn this material, never be afraid to ask someone for help. We were all beginners at one time and people really like helping you learn.

Let's get going. And, as we said, we're going to take it slow. In this first class, we will learn how to install Small Basic and its documentation on your computer, how to load a Small Basic program, how to run the program, and how to stop the program. It will be a good introduction to the many new things we will learn in the classes to come.

Downloading and Installing Small Basic

To write and run programs using Small Basic, you need the **Small Basic** program. This is a free product that you can download from the Internet. This simply means we will copy a file onto our computer to allow installation of Small Basic.

Start up your web browser (Internet Explorer, Netscape or other). Small Basic has its own web site:

http://www.smallbasic.com

This web site has lots of useful programming information. As you become more proficient in your programming skills, you will go to this site often for answers to programming questions, interaction with other programmers, and lots of sample programs.

On the Small Basic web page, you should see a button on the top right side of the webpage that allows to download Small Basic:

Click the download button. This window will appear:

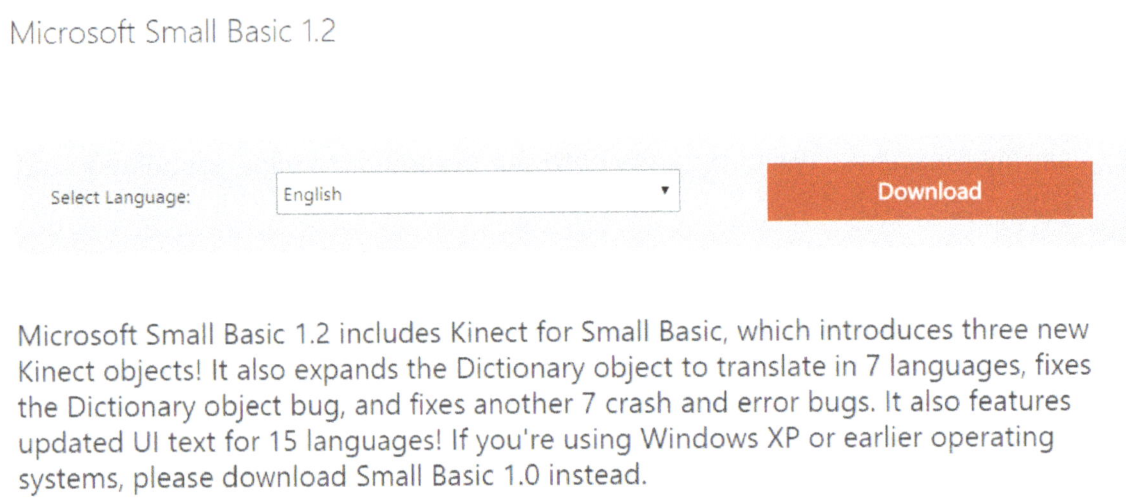

Click on the red **DOWNLOAD** button and the download of the installer begins. Depending on the Internet Browser version that you are using, you may see different types of download menu screens. On Interner Explorer 11 you will see a download bar at the bottom of you screen:

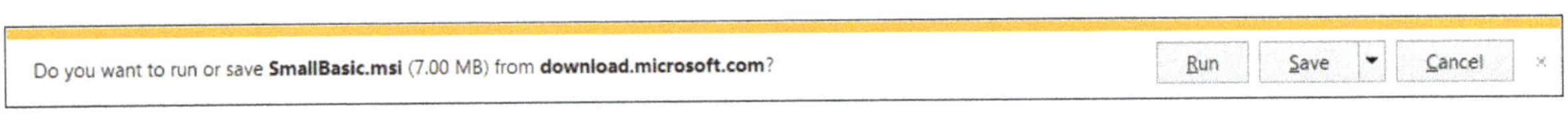

Click **Run** and the download of the installer begins.

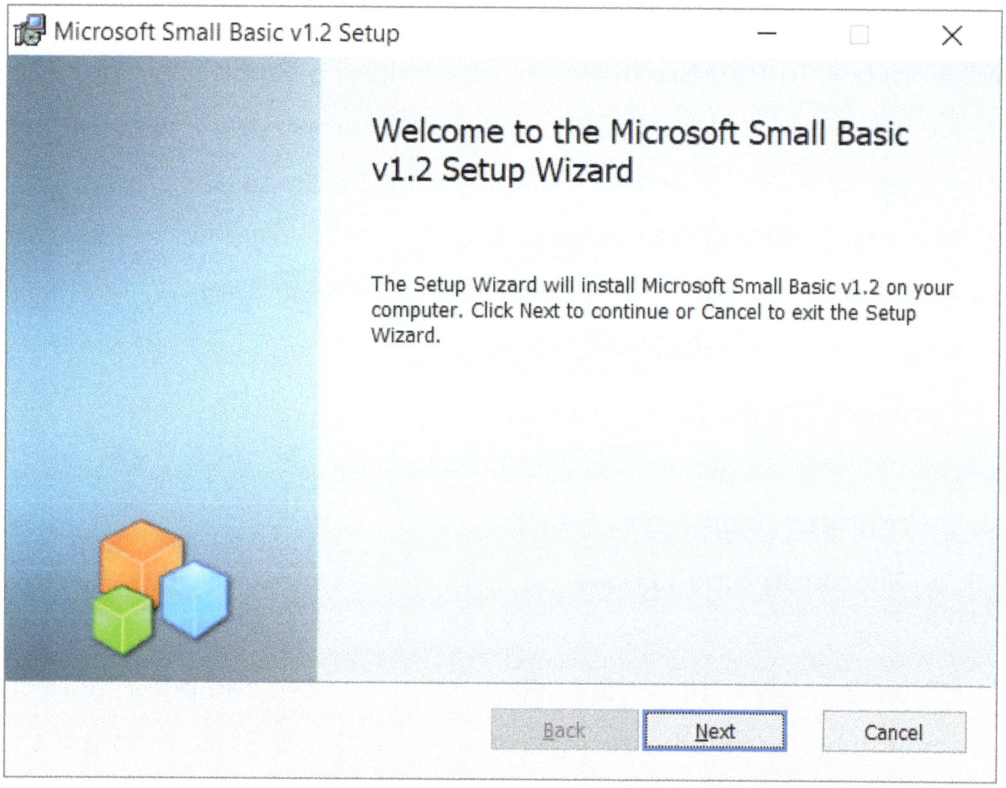

Click **Next** to start the installation process. Accept the licensing agreement. Then, for each screen afterwards, accept the default choice by clicking **Next**. When done you should see a screen announcing a successful installation.

Starting Small Basic

We'll learn how to start **Small Basic**, how to load a Small Basic program, and how to run a program. This will give us some assurance we have everything installed correctly. This will let us begin our study of the Small Basic programming language.

Once installed, to start Small Basic:

- Click on the **Start** button on the Windows task bar
- Select **Programs**, then **Small Basic**
- Click on **Microsoft Small Basic**

(Some of the headings given here may differ slightly on your computer, but you should have no trouble finding the correct ones.) The Small Basic program should start. Several windows will appear on the screen.

After installation and trying to start, you may see an error message that announces Small Basic cannot be started. If this occurs, try downloading and installing the latest version of the Microsoft .NET framework at:

http://msdn.microsoft.com/en-us/netframework/aa569263.aspx

This contains some files that Small Basic needs to operate and such files may not be on your computer.

With the installation of newer versions of Small Basic the start up screen below will appear right after you run Small Basic for the very first time:

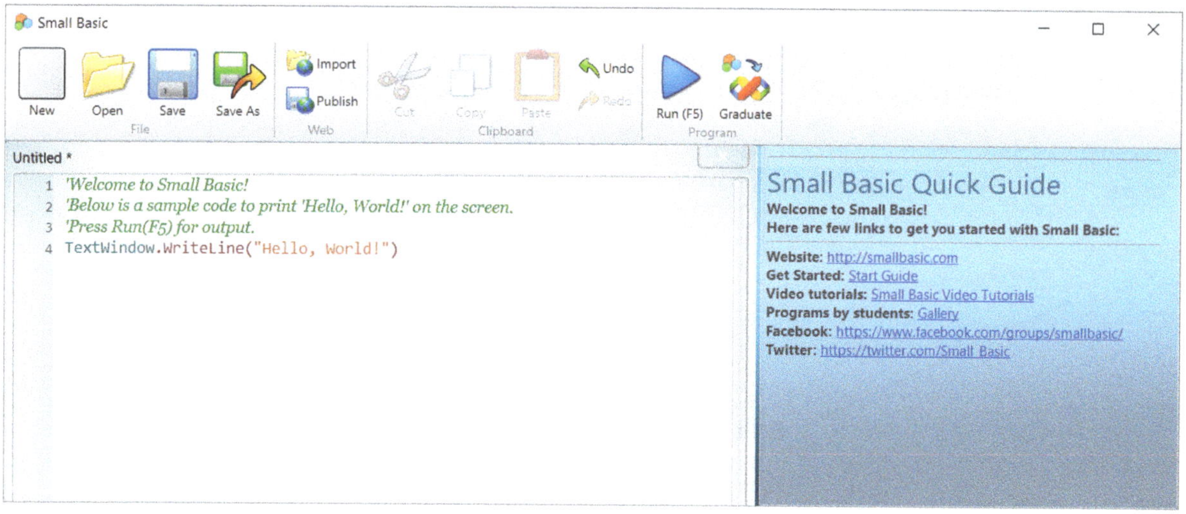

.Feel feel free to click on the Run button at the top right of the menu bar:

The following screen will run and type "Hello, World!" on your screen. Press any key to close the window.

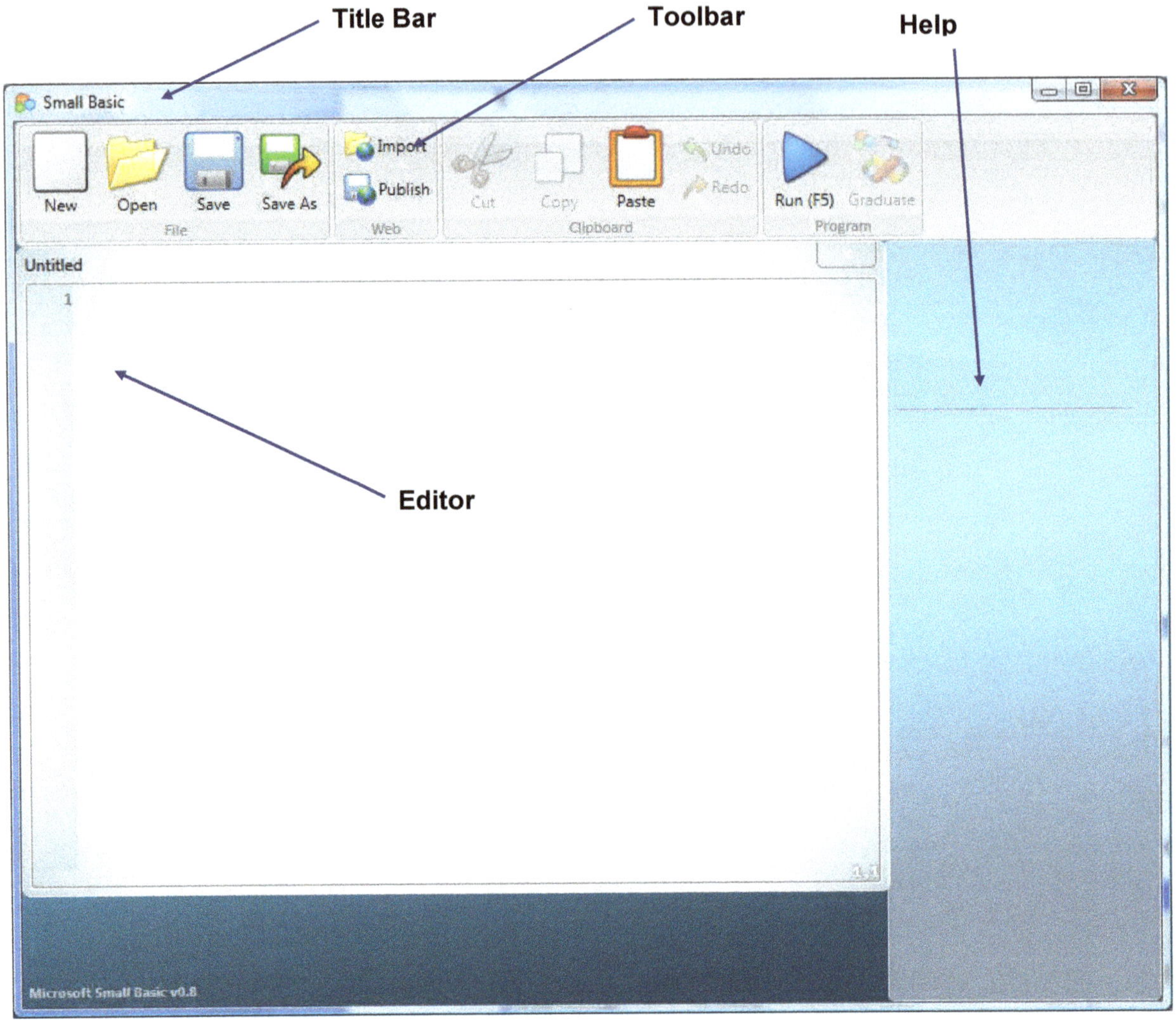

This window displays the **Small Basic Development Environment**. We will learn a lot more about this in Class 2. Right now, we're just going to use it to test our Small Basic installation and see if we can get a program up and running. There are many windows on the screen. At the top of the window is the **Title Bar**. The title bar gives us information about what program we're using and what Small Basic program we are working with. Below the title bar is a **Toolbar**. Here, little buttons with pictures allow us to control Small Basic. Almost all Windows applications (spreadsheets, word processors, games) have toolbars that help us do different tasks. This is the purpose of the Small Basic toolbar. It will help us do most of our tasks. In the middle of the screen is the **Editor**. This is where we will write our Small Basic programs. To the right is a **Help** area. Small Basic has great help features when writing programs. This area will display hints and tips while we write code.

Opening a Small Basic Program

What we want to do right now is **open a program**. Included with these notes are many Small Basic programs you can open and use. Let's open one now. Make sure **Small Basic** is running. We will open a program using the toolbar. Follow these steps:

- Click the **Open Program** button:

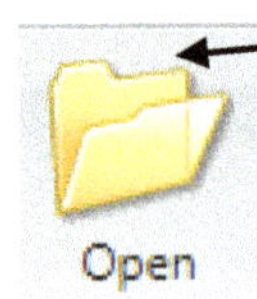

Open Program
Toolbar Button

An **Open Program** window will appear:

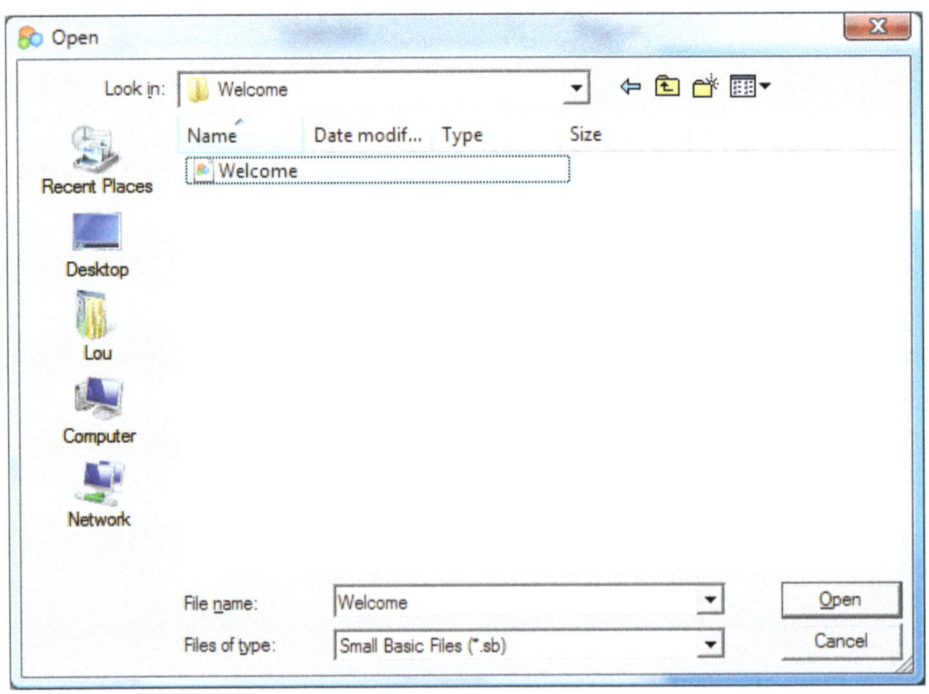

- Find the folder named **BeginSB** (stands for **Beginning Small Basic**). This is the folder that holds the notes and programs for this course. Open that folder.
- Find and open the folder named **BSB Code.** This folder holds all the programs for the course

Remember how you got to this folder. Throughout the course, you will go to this folder to open programs you will need. Open the program folder named **Welcome**. Note there is one file in **Welcome** named **Welcome**. Select that file and click **Open**. The Small Basic source code can have the file extention of .sb or .smallbasic. We have used the smaller .sb extention to make it faster for you to type.

This should appear in the Small Basic editor:

Welcome.sb - C:\BeginSB\BSB Code\Welcome\Welcome.sb

```
'
' Welcome Program
' Beginning Small Basic
' KIDware
' www.KIDwareSoftware.com
'
TextWindow.Title = "Welcome Program"
TextWindow.WriteLine("Welcome to Beginning Small Basic!")

```

You now finally see your first Small Basic program: We'll learn what these few lines of code do in the next class. Right now, we just want to see if we can get this program running.

Running a Small Basic Program

After developing a Small Basic program, you want to start or run the program. This gets the program going and allows the computer do its assigned tasks. We can run a program also using the toolbar. Look for a button that looks like the **Play** button on a VCR, CD player, or cassette tape player:

Run Program
Toolbar Button

- Click this button to run **Welcome** program (the program we opened previously).

You can also run a program by pressing the **<F5>** function key.

A window should open and you should see the following Welcome message:

If you've gotten this far, everything has been installed correctly. If you don't see the Welcome message, something has not been installed correctly. You should probably go back and review all the steps involved with installing Small Basic and Small Basic and make sure all steps were followed properly.

To stop this program, press any key or click the boxed **X** in the upper right corner of the window.

Stopping Small Basic

It's been a lot of work just to get to this point. We finally have our first Small Basic program running and now we're just going to stop it and move on. We'll dig into many more details in Class 2.

When you are done working with a Small Basic program, you want to leave the Small Basic environment. To stop Small Basic, click on the close button in the upper right hand corner of the main window. It's the button that looks like an **X**. Stop Small Basic now. Small Basic will close all open windows and you will be returned to the Windows desktop. You may be asked if you would like to save the program modifications (in case any were made):

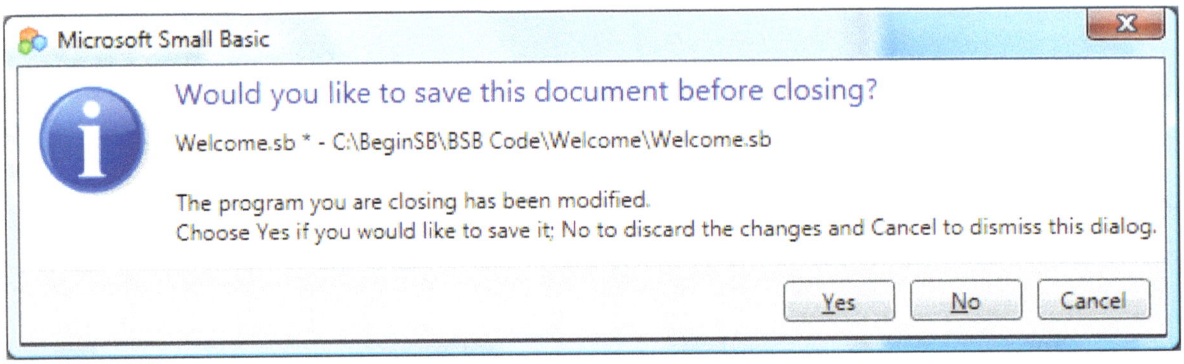

If you are asked such a question, answer **No** so the Welcome program remains unchanged.

Summary

We covered a lot of new material here. As we said earlier, you learned a lot of new words and concepts. Don't worry if you don't remember everything we talked about here. You will see the material many times again. It's important that you just have some concept of what goes into a Small Basic program. And you know how to start and stop the Small Basic environment.

In summary, we installed the Small Basic environment. Using Small Basic, we learned how to open a Small Basic program. We learned how to run a program. In the next class, you will learn (in detail) what each of these steps really means. And, you will begin to acquire the skills that allow you to start building your own Small Basic program. Using the **Welcome** program as an example, you will learn about important concepts related to a Small Basic program. Then, in Class 3, you will actually build your first program!

2

Small Basic Program Basics

Review and Preview

In the first class, we spent all of our time just preparing our computer for creating and running Small Basic programs. In this second class, we will look further into some of the tasks we have done. We will reexamine the Welcome program from Class 1. We will learn some of the basic rules for writing Small Basic programs. We will create and save a program using Small Basic. This will give us the skills needed to create our first Small Basic program in Class 3.

The Welcome Program (Revisited)

Start **Small Basic** and open the **Welcome** program we looked at in Class 1 Here's the code you will see in the editor:

```
'
'  Welcome Program
'  Beginning Small Basic
'
TextWindow.Title = "Welcome Program"
TextWindow.WriteLine("Welcome to Beginning Small Basic!")
```

A program is made up of many **statements**. Every line is a statement and every statement instructs the computer to do something.. Let's go through this code line by line to explain its structure and see what each line does.

The first several lines of the program are:

```
'
'  Welcome Program
'  Beginning Small Basic
'
'
```

These lines are **comments**. They simply provide some information about what the program is and provides some contact information. The comment begins with a single apostrophe (**'**). These lines are also known as a **program header**. It's a good idea to always put a header on your Small Basic programs to give someone an idea of what your program does and who wrote it. When running a program, Small Basic ignores any comments – their only use is provide explanation.

The first non-comment statement is:

```
TextWindow.Title = "Welcome Program"
```

Remember the Welcome program back in Class 1? When you ran the program, you saw this window:

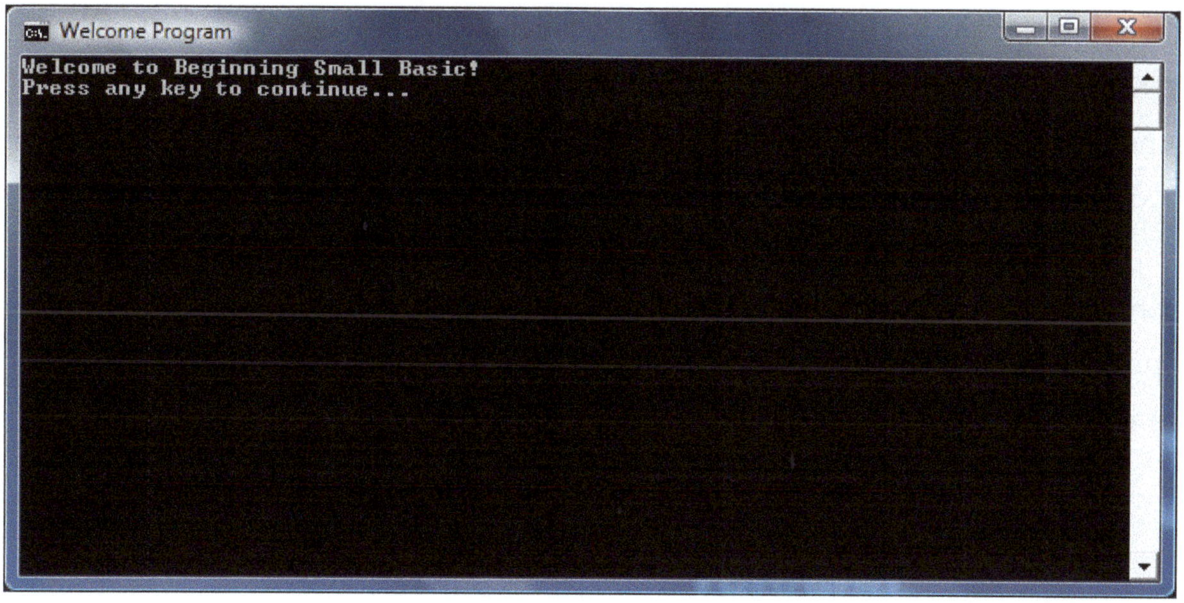

Notice the words **Welcome Program** in the title bar of the window. The above line of code displays that title. In this line, **TextWindow** is an **object** built into Small Basic – it is the window that displays the output of the program. Small Basic has a number of such objects available for our use. We will use the **TextWindow** object extensively in our first few programs. Objects have both **properties** and **methods**. Properties describe objects, while methods do things to objects. In this single line of code, we are setting the **Title** property of the **TextWindow** object to the text string "**Welcome Program**". The dot (**.**) and assignment operator (**=**) are punctuations that must be placed appropriately for the computer to understand your intent. This line of code literally says "set the **Title** property of the **TextWindow** object to **Welcome Program**."

The other statement in this short program is:

```
TextWindow.WriteLine("Welcome to Beginning Small Basic!")
```

Notice in the text window of the running program, there is a message that says **Welcome to Beginning Small Basic!** . The above line of code printed that message. This line of code uses the TextWindow **WriteLine** method to perform the task. We say the text "Welcome to Beginning Small Basic!" is passed to the **WriteLine** method – the input is placed in parentheses – which then results in the input text being written in the text window.

Though this is a very short, very simple program, it illustrates some major components in a Small Basic program. We want a program header and appropriate comments. Using properties and methods, we can display information using the built-in Small Basic object, the **TextWindow**.

Some Rules of Small Basic Programming

Let's look at the **Welcome** code one more time to point out some basic rules of Small Basic programming. Here's that code:

```
'
'  Welcome Program
'  Beginning Small Basic
'
TextWindow.Title = "Welcome Program"
TextWindow.WriteLine("Welcome to Beginning Small Basic!")
```

And, here's the rules:

- Small Basic code requires perfection. All keywords must be spelled correctly. If you type **WriteLne** instead of **WriteLine**, a human may know what you mean, but a computer won't.
- Small Basic is not case-sensitive, meaning upper and lower case letters are considered to be the same characters. That means **writeline** and **WriteLine** are the same. But, even though Small Basic is not case-sensitive, it is good practice to use accepted conventions.
- Small Basic ignores any "**white space**" such as blanks. We will often use white space to make our code more readable.
- To set an object property, we use this 'dot' convention:

  ```
  ObjectName.PropertyName = PropertyValue
  ```

  where **ObjectName** is the object, **PropertyName** the property and **PropertyValue** the value you want to establish.

* To invoke an object method, use this convention:

  ```
  ObjectName.MethodName(MethodInputs)
  ```

  where **ObjectName** is the object, **MethodName** the method and **MethodInputs** the inputs needed by the method.

We'll learn a lot more Small Basic programming rules as we progress.

Creating Small Basic Programs

In Class 3, we will begin learning the Small Basic language and start writing our own Small Basic programs. In preparation for this, you'll need to know how to create a new program with Small Basic. Let's do that now. What we'll do is re-create the **Welcome** program.

If it's not already running, start **Small Basic**. Click the **New Program** button in the toolbar:

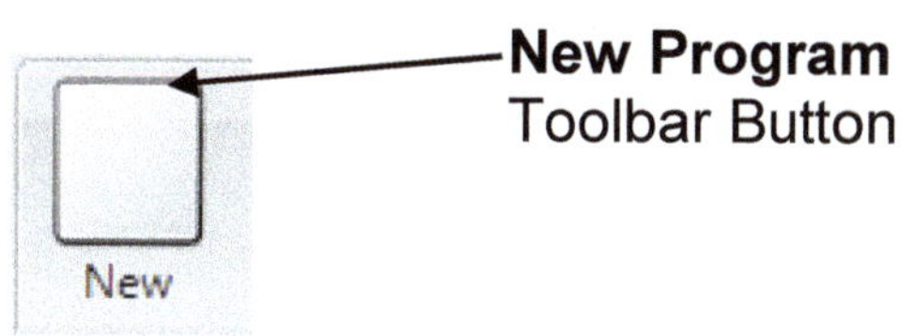

An empty editor will appear:

Click in this window and start typing in the code for the **Welcome** program.

Type one line at a time, paying close attention that you type everything as shown (pay attention to the rules seen earlier). After each line, press the <Enter> key. Here, again, is the code:

```
'
' Welcome Program
' Beginning Small Basic
'
TextWindow.Title = "Welcome Program"
TextWindow.WriteLine("Welcome to Beginning Small Basic!")
```

After typing the four comment lines and starting to type the first line of code you will notice this popup appears:

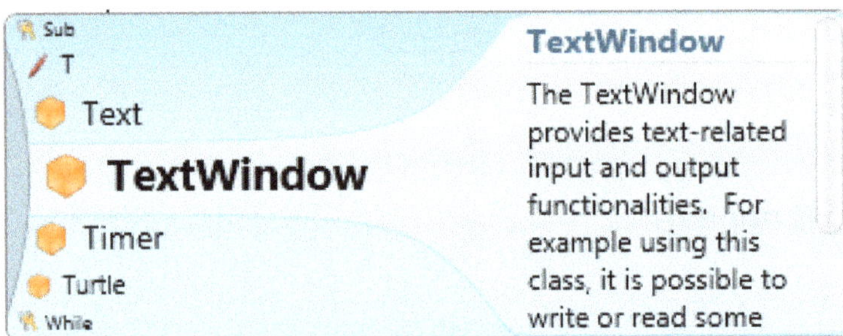

Small Basic has a feature called “intellisense” that helps you type your programs faster. When this list appears, you move through the list using the up/down arrow keys and make a selection by pressing <Enter>. It will appear for object names, properties and methods. Give it a try!

Also notice as soon as you type **TextWindow**, this appears in the help area of the Small Basic environment:

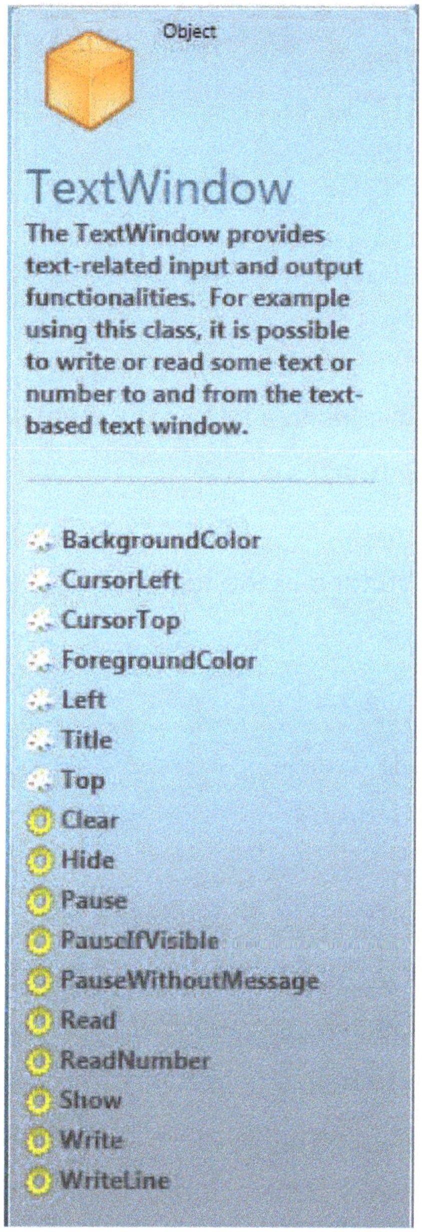

Small Basic provides "context-sensitive" help. The help area will always display information it deems is important to the user at the appropriate time. In this case, information concerning the properties (marked by painter's palette icon) and methods (marked by gear icon) for the TextWindow object are displayed. And, once you select a property or method, a help description for that selection appears. For example, once you type **Title**, you will see this help screen describing the property and how its used:

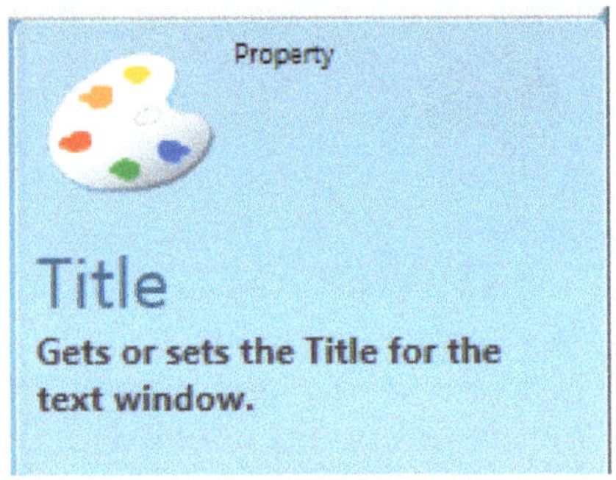

With intellisense and context-sensitive help, you always have on-line information to help with your programming tasks.

Notice these editing buttons in the toolbar:

If you've ever used a word processor, these tasks are familiar to you. When typing code, you can **Cut**, **Copy** and **Paste**. And you can **Undo** and **Redo** tasks. These tasks make typing code (especially long programs) much easier in the Small Basic environment. Another thing to notice is that the editor uses different colors for different things in the code. Comments, objects, method names and data used by objects are all colored differently. This coloring sometimes helps you identify mistakes you may have made in typing.

When done typing, you should see:

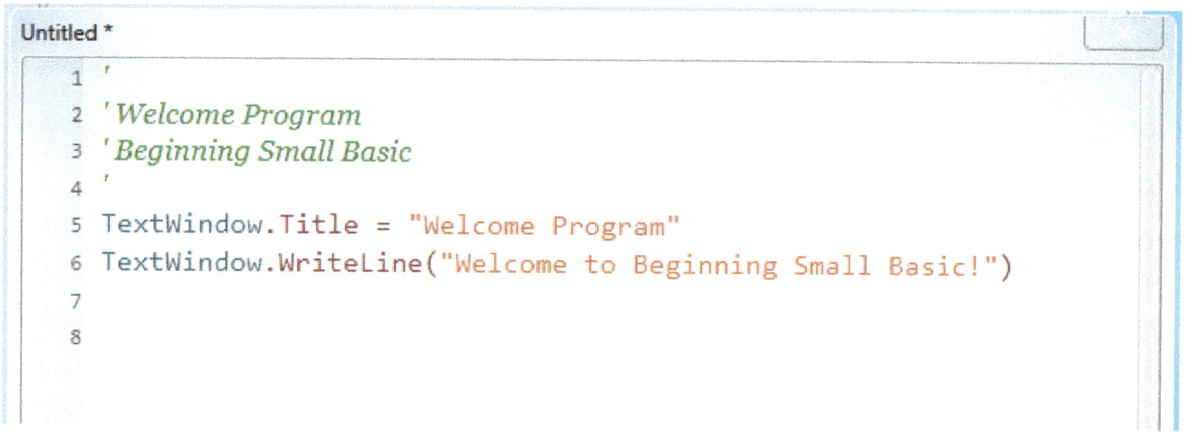

Try running your program. Use the toolbar run program button (or press <**F5**>). You should once again see the **Welcome to Beginning Small Basic!** Message:

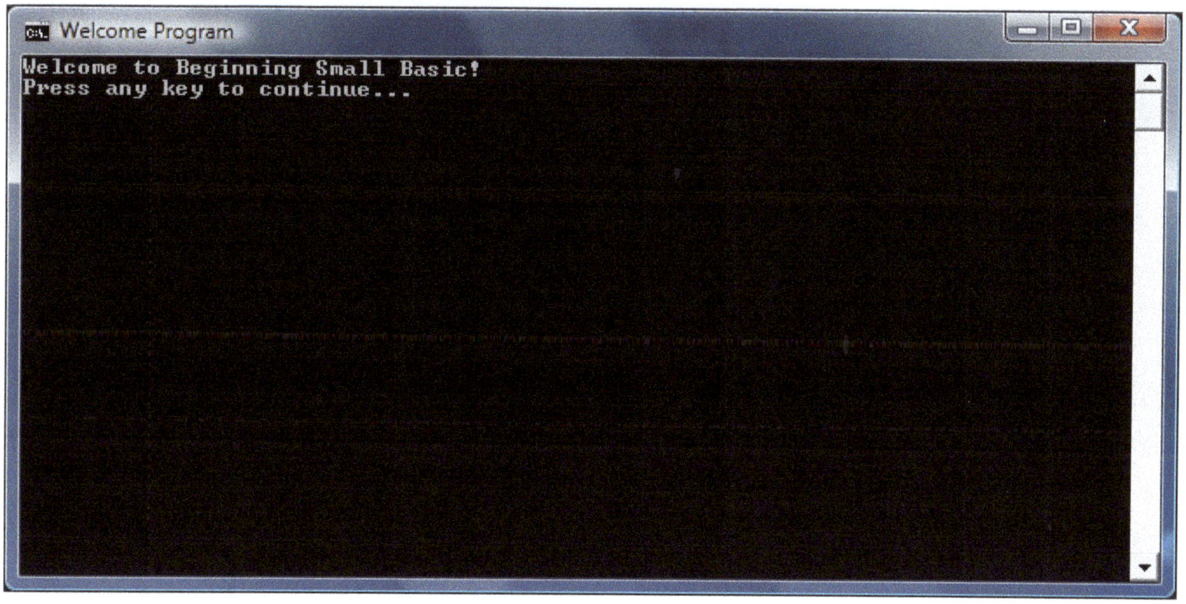

You should also see that it's really kind of easy to get a Small Basic program up and running.

Saving Small Basic Programs

Before leaving Small Basic, we need to discuss how to save programs we create. Each program should be saved in its own folder. You decide where you want to store this folder. There are two buttons on the toolbar used to save programs. To save a new program, click the **Save Program** button:

A dialog box will appear:

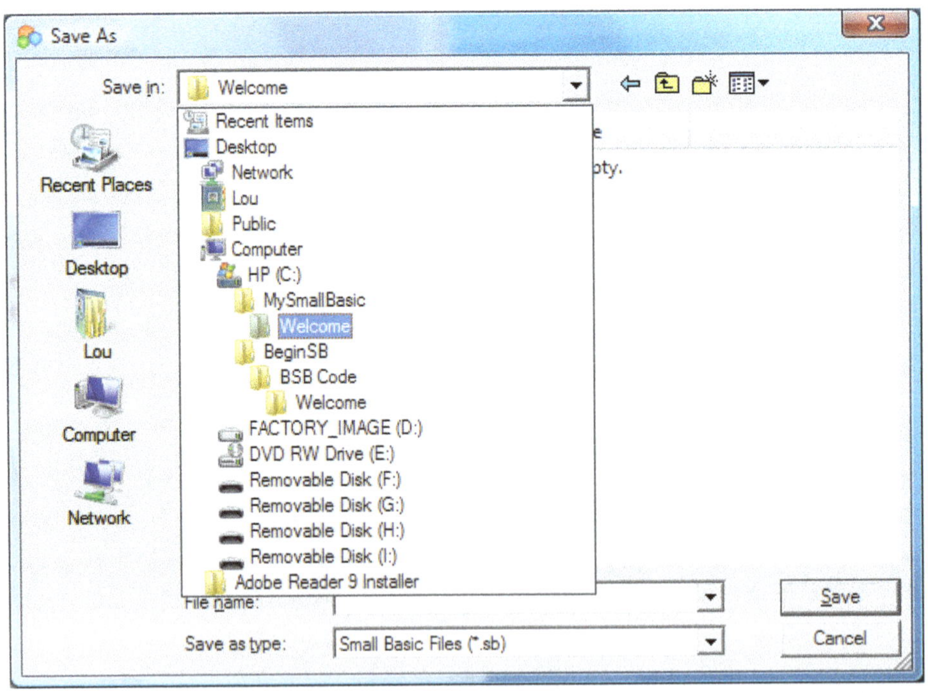

Create the folder you want to save the program in. In this example, I have created a folder named **Welcome** in a **MySmallBasic** folder.

Select a name for your program. Here I have selected **Welcome**:

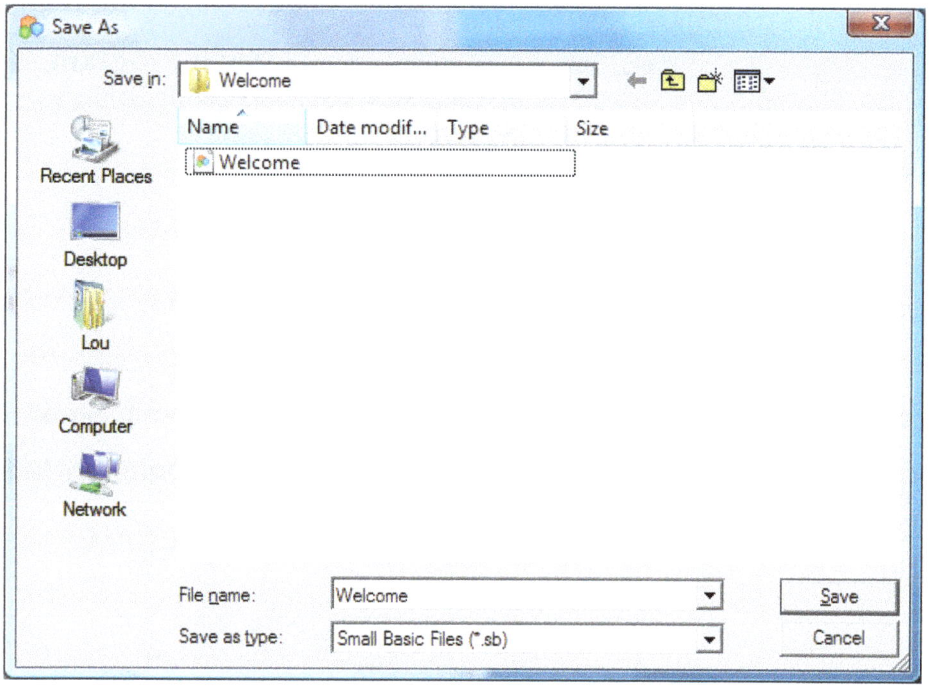

Click **Save** and the program is saved. From this point on, whenever you reopen this program and make modifications, if you click the **Save** toolbar button, the program will be automatically saved with the same name in the same folder. We suggest you do this occasionally while modifying a program.

If you wish to assign a different name to or create a different folder for the modified program, use the **Save As** toolbar button:

Save Program
Toolbar Button

Use the resulting dialog boxes to name and locate your program.

If you try to exit Small Basic and have not saved programs, Small Basic will pop up a dialog box to inform you of such and give you an opportunity to save files before exiting. An example dialog is:

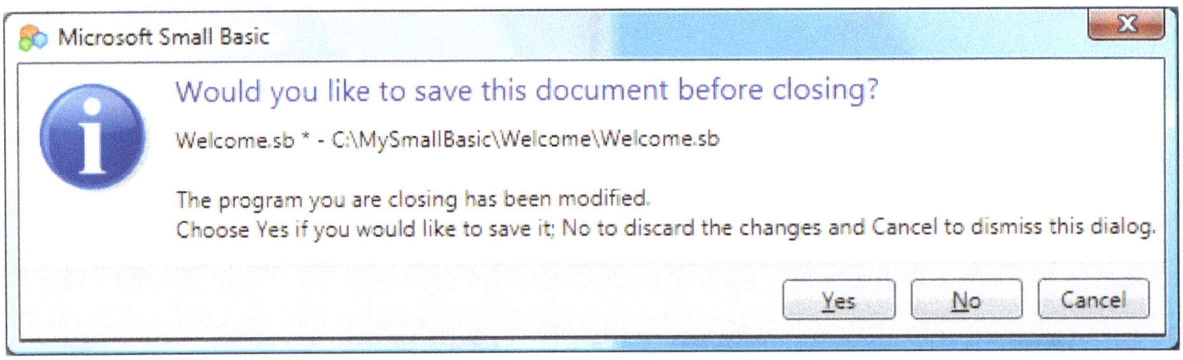

Make the appropriate choice.

Small Basic Files

When you save a Small Basic program in a particular folder, files other than the file listing your code are saved. These files are needed by the Small Basic environment to keep track of things.

Using My Computer or Windows Explorer in Windows, go to the folder containing the **Welcome** program you just built and ran. You should see the following files:

Name	Date modified	Type	Size
SmallBasicLibrary.dll	2/3/2010 11:56 PM	Application Extens...	238 KB
Welcome	3/19/2010 8:04 AM	Application	3 KB
Welcome.pdb	3/19/2010 8:04 AM	PDB File	12 KB
Welcome	3/19/2010 8:03 AM	Small Basic Progra...	1 KB

The file named **Welcome** with type **Small Basic Program** is the source code that appears in the editor of Small Basic. The **Welcome** file marked **Application** is a 'compiled' version of the code and is the 'executable' code. If you double-click this file, the Welcome program will run independent of the Small Basic environment. Try it if you like. Later we will learn how to use this file to let your friends run your programs on their computers or even on the Internet! The **Welcome.pdb** file is a database file with information needed by your program and lastly, **SmallBasicLibrary.dll** is called a run-time library. It contains files that help your program run.

We describe these files so you are aware of their presence. Do not modify or delete any of these files outside of the Small Basic environment.

Summary

After all the downloading and installing done in the first class, this second class must have seemed like a breeze. In this class, we looked at several important concepts that will let us start building our own Small Basic programs.

In this class, we studied the structure of a program, knowing it is built using objects, properties and methods. We learned how to use Small Basic to create and run a new program. We looked briefly at some of the rules used in writing Small Basic code and we saw how to save a program. In the next class, we finally get started learning the Small Basic language. And, we'll write and run our first Small Basic program.

3

Your First Small Basic Program

Review and Preview

In the first two classes, you've learned about the structure of a Small Basic program, some rules for typing code, and how to run a Small Basic program. Do you have some ideas of programs you would like to build using Small Basic? If so, great. Beginning with this class, you will start to develop your own programming skills. In each class to come, you will learn some new features of the Small Basic language. In this class, you will write your first Small Basic program. To do this, you first need to learn about some of the basic components of the Small Basic language. You will learn about variables, assignment statements and some simple operators.

Creating a Small Basic Program

Recall from Class 2 that a **Small Basic statement** does something. In the **Welcome** example, we saw a statement that printed some information ("Welcome to Beginning Small Basic!"). Each program we build in this class will be made up of many Small Basic statements for the computer to process. Creating a computer program using Small Basic (or any other language) is a straightforward process. You have a particular task you would like the computer to do for you. You tell the computer in a logical, procedural set of steps how to accomplish that task.

It's relatively easy to write out solution steps to a problem in our language (English, in these notes). The difficult part is you have to talk to the computer in its own language. It would be nice if we could just write "Hey computer, here's two numbers – add them together and tell me the sum." A human might understand these instructions, but a computer won't. Why? First, the computer needs to be told how to do tasks in very specific, logical steps. For this little addition example, the steps would be:

1. Give a value to the first number.
2. Give a value to the second number.
3. Add the first number to the second number, resulting in the sum, a third number.
4. Tell me the sum.

Next, we need to talk to the computer in its own language. We translate each solution step into a statement (or statements) in the computer's language. And, in this course, the computer's language is **Small Basic**. To be able to tell the computer how to do any task, you need to have a thorough understanding of the Small Basic language. Your understanding of Small Basic will allow you to translate your programming steps into a language the computer can understand.

Another thing to remember as you write Small Basic programs is that you need to be logical and exact. A computer will follow your instructions – even if they're wrong! So, as you learn Small Basic, we will emphasize the need to be exact. Once you write exact and logical Small Basic code, the computer is very good and fast at doing its job. And, it can do some pretty amazing things. Let's look at a couple of other examples of writing out a programming task as a series of steps to illustrate some things a computer can do.

What if the local school principal asks you to average the test scores of the 352 students in the school? Those steps are:

1. Determine the score of each student.
2. Add up the 352 scores to get a sum.
3. Divide the sum by 352 to get the average value.
4. Tell the principal the average.

Not too hard, huh? Notice here that the second step can be further broken down into smaller steps. To add up 352 scores, you would:

1. Start with the first score.
2. Add in the second score, then the third score, then the fourth score, etc.
3. Stop when all scores have been added.

In these steps, the computer would do the same task (adding a number) 352 times. Computers are very good at repeating tasks – we will see that this process of repetition is called **looping**. You will build code for this example in Class 7.

Computers are also very good at playing games with you (that's why video games are so popular). Have you ever played the card game "War?" You and another player take a card from a standard playing deck. Whoever has the 'highest' card wins the other player's card. You then each get another card and continue the comparison process until you run out of cards. Whoever has the most cards once the game stops is declared the winner. Playing this game would require steps similar to these:

1. Shuffle a deck of cards.
2. Give a card to the first player.
3. Give a card to the second player.
4. Determine which card is higher and declare a winner.
5. Repeat the process of giving cards to players until you are out of cards.

Things are a bit more complicated here, but the computer is up to the task. The first step requires the computer to shuffle a deck of cards. How do you tell a computer how to do this? Well, before this course is over, you will know how. For now, just know that it's a series of several programming steps. We will put the Small Basic program for such a specific task in its own area called a **subroutine**. This makes the program a little easier to follow and also allows use this code in other programs. Notice Step 4 requires the computer to make a **decision** – determining which card is higher. Computers are very good at making decisions. Finally, Step 5 asks us to repeat the handing out of cards – another example of **looping**. You will also build this program in Class 7.

If all of these concepts are not clear at the moment, that's okay. They will become clearer as you progress through this course. I just wanted you to have some idea of what you can do with Small Basic programs. Just remember, for every Small Basic program you create, it is best to first write down a series of logical steps you want the computer to follow in performing the tasks needed by your program. Then, converting those steps into the Small Basic language will give you your Small Basic program – it's really that simple. This class begins instruction in the elements of Small Basic. And, in subsequent classes, you learn more and more Small Basic, adding to your Small Basic vocabulary. We'll start slow. By the end of this course, you should be pretty good at "talking Small Basic."

Small Basic - The First Lesson

At long last, we are ready to get into the heart of a Small Basic program - the Small Basic language. In this class, we will discuss variables (name and type), assignments, arithmetic operations, and techniques for working with a particular type of variable called strings. In each subsequent class in this course, you will learn something new about the Small Basic language.

Variables

All computer programs work with information of one kind or another. Numbers, text, dates and pictures are typical types of information they work with. Computer programs need places to store this information while working with it. What if we need to know how much ten bananas cost if they are 25 cents each? We would need a place to store the number of bananas, the cost of each banana, and the result of multiplying these two numbers together. To store such information, we use something called **variables**. They are called variables because the information stored there can change, or vary, during program execution. Variables are the primary method for moving information around in a Small Basic program. And, certain rules must be followed in the use of variables.

Variable Names

You must **name** every variable you use in your program. Rules for naming variables are:

- Can only use letters, numbers, and the underscore (_) character (though the underscore character is rarely used).
- The first character must be a letter. It is customary, though not required, in Small Basic that this first letter be upper case
- You cannot use a word reserved by Small Basic (for example, you can't have a variable named **WriteLine** or one named **TextWindow**).

If a variable name consists of more than one word, the words are joined together, and each word after the first begins with an uppercase letter

The most important rule is to use variable names that are meaningful. You should be able to identify the information stored in a variable by looking at its name. As an example, in our banana buying example, good names would be:

Quantity	Variable Name
Cost of each banana	BananaCost
Number of bananas purchased	NumberBananas
Cost of all bananas	TotalBananaCost

As mentioned in an earlier class, the Small Basic language is not case sensitive. This means the names **BananaCost** and **bananacost** refer to the same variable. Try to be consistent in how you write variable names. And make sure you assign unique names to each variable. A nice feature of the Small Basic intellisense feature is that as you add variables to your program, the variable names are added to the list of choices available in the intellisense drop-down menu.

Variable Types

We need to know the **type** of information stored by each variable. Does it contain a number? Does the number have a decimal point? Does it just contain text information? Let's look at some variable types.

The first variable type is the **integer** type. This type of variable is used to represent whole, non-decimal, numbers. Examples of such numbers are:

1 -20 4000

Notice you write 4,000 as 4000 in Small Basic – we can't use commas in large numbers. In our banana example, **NumberBananas** would an **integer** type variable.

What if the variable you want to use will have decimal points. In this course, such variables will be of **floating** type (the decimal point being the thing that "floats"). All you need to know about floating type variables is that they are numbers with decimal points. Examples of such numbers:

-1.25 3.14159 22.7

In our banana example, the variables **BananaCost** and **TotalBananaCost** would be **floating** type variables.

The next variable type is a **string** variable. A **string** variable is just that – one that stores a string (list) of various characters. A string can be a name, a string of numbers, a sentence, a paragraph, any characters at all. And, many times, a string will contain no characters at all (an empty string). We will use lots of strings in Small Basic, so it's something you should become familiar with. Strings are always enclosed in quotes ("). Examples of strings:

"I am a Small Basic programmer"   "012345"   "Title   Author"

One last variable type is the **boolean** variable. It takes its name from a famous mathematician (Boole). It can have one of two values: **true** or **false**. Many languages have **true** and **false** as reserved words for use with Boolean variables. Small Basic does not have such reserved words. In Small Basic, we will use string values of "**true**" and "**false**" to provide a representation for boolean variables. We will see that such variables are at the heart of the computer's decision making capability. If wanted to know if a banana was rotten, we could name a boolean variable **IsBananaRotten**. If this was "true", the banana is indeed rotten.

With all the different variable types, we need to be careful not to improperly mix types. We can only do mathematical operations on numbers (integer and floating types). String types must only work with other string types. Boolean types are used for decisions.

Assignment Statement

The simplest, and most widely used, statement in Small Basic is the **assignment** statement. Such a statement appears as:

```
VariableName = VariableValue
```

Note that only a single variable can be on the left side of the assignment operator (**=**). Some simple assignment examples using our "banana" variables:

```
NumberBananas = 22
BananaCost = 0.27
IsBananaRotten = "false"
MyBananaDescription = "Yes, we have no bananas!"
```

The actual values assigned to variables here are called **literals**, since they literally show you their values.

You may recognize the assignment operator as the equal sign used in arithmetic, but it's not called an equal sign in computer programming. Why is that? Actually, the right side (**VariableValue** in this example) of the assignment operator is not limited to literals. Any legal Small Basic expression, with any number of variables or other values, can be on the right side of the operator. In such a case, Small Basic computes **VariableValue** first, then assigns that result to **VariableName**. This is an important programming concept to remember – "evaulate the right side, assign to the left side." Let's start looking at some operators that help in evaluating Small Basic expressions.

Arithmetic Operators

One thing computer programs are very good at is doing arithmetic. They can add, subtract, multiply, and divide numbers very quickly. We need to know how to make our Small Basic programs do arithmetic. There are four **arithmetic operators** we will use from the Small Basic language.

Addition is done using the plus (+) sign and **subtraction** is done using the minus (-) sign. Simple examples are:

Operation	**Example**	**Result**
Addition	7 + 2	9
Addition	3 + 8	11
Subtraction	6 - 4	2
Subtraction	11 - 7	4

Multiplication is done using the asterisk (*) and **division** is done using the slash (/). Simple examples are:

Operation	**Example**	**Result**
Multiplication	8 * 4	32
Multiplication	2 * 12	24
Division	12 / 2	6
Division	42 / 6	7

I'm sure you've done addition, subtraction, multiplication, and division before and understand how each operation works.

What happens if an assignment statement contains more than one arithmetic operator? Does it make any difference? Look at this example:

```
7 + 3 * 4
```

What's the answer? Well, it depends. If you work left to right and add 7 and 3 first, then multiply by 4, the answer is 40. If you multiply 3 times 4 first, then add 7, the answer is 19. Confusing? Well, yes. But, Small Basic takes away the possibility of such confusion by having rules of **precedence**. This means there is a specific order in which arithmetic operations will be performed. That order is:

1. Multiplication (*) and division (/)
2. Addition (+) and subtraction (-)

So, in an assignment statement, all multiplications and divisions are done first, then additions and subtractions. In our example (7 + 3 * 4), we see the multiplication will be done before the addition, so the answer provided by Small Basic would be 19.

If two operators have the same precedence level, for example, multiplication and division, the operations are done left to right in the assignment statement. For example:

24 / 2 * 3

The division (24 / 2) is done first yielding a 12, then the multiplication (12 * 3), so the answer is 36. But what if we want to do the multiplication before the division - can that be done? Yes - using the Small Basic **grouping operators** - parentheses **()**. By using parentheses in an assignment statement, you force operations within the parentheses to be done first. So, if we rewrite our example as:

24 / (2 * 3)

the multiplication (2 * 3) will be done first yielding 6, then the division (24 / 6), yielding the desired result of 4. You can use as many parentheses as you want, but make sure they are always in pairs - every left parenthesis needs a right parenthesis. If you nest parentheses, that is have one set inside another, evaluation will start with the innermost set of parentheses and move outward. For example, look at:

((2 + 4) * 6) + 7

The addition of 2 and 4 is done first, yielding a 6, which is multiplied by 6, yielding 36. This result is then added to 7, with the final answer being 43. You might also want to use parentheses even if they don't change precedence. Many times, they are used just to clarify what is going on in an assignment statement.

As you improve your programming skills, make sure you know how each of the arithmetic operators work, what the precedence order is, and how to use parentheses. Always double-check your assignment statements to make sure they are providing the results you want.

Some examples of Small Basic assignment statements with arithmetic operators:

```
TotalBananaCost = NumberBananas * BananaCost
NumberOfWeeks = NumberOfDays / 7
AverageScore = (Score1 + Score2 + Score3) / 3.0
```

Notice a couple of things here. First, notice the parentheses in the **AverageScore** calculation forces Small Basic to add the three scores <u>before</u> dividing by 3. Also, notice the use of "white space," spaces separating operators from variables. This is a common practice in Small Basic that helps code be more readable. We'll see lots and lots of examples of assignment statements as we build programs in this course.

String Concatenation

We can apply arithmetic operators to numerical variables. String variables can also be operated on. Many times in Small Basic programs, you want to take a string variable from one place and 'tack it on the end' of another string. The fancy word for this is **string concatenation**. The concatenation operator is a plus sign (**+**) and it is easy to use. As an example:

```
NewString = "Beginning Small Basic " + "is Fun!"
```

After this statement, the string variable **NewString** will have the value "Beginning Small Basic is Fun!".

Notice the string concatenation operator is identical to the addition operator. We always need to insure there is no confusion when using both. String variables are a big part of Small Basic. As you develop as a programmer, you need to become comfortable with strings and working with them.

Comments

You should always follow proper programming rules when writing your Small Basic code. One such rule is to properly comment your code. You can place non-executable statements (ignored by the computer) in your code that explain what you are doing. These **comments** can be an aid in understanding your code. They also make future changes to your code much easier.

To place a comment in your code, use the comment symbol, a single apostrophe ('). Anything written after the comment symbol will be ignored by the computer. You can have a comment take up a complete line of Small Basic code, like this:

```
' Set number of bananas
NumberBananas = 14
```

Or, you can place the comment on the same line as the assignment statement:

```
NumberBananas = 14 ' Set number of bananas
```

You, as the programmer, should decide how much you want to comment your code. We will try in the programs provided in this course to provide adequate comments.

Program Output

You're almost ready to create your first Small Basic program. But, we need one more thing. We have ways to name variables and ways to do math with them, but once we have results, how can those results be displayed? In this class, we will use the method seen in our little Welcome program, the Small Basic **WriteLine** method that works with the **TextWindow** object. What this method does is print a string result on a single line:

```
TextWindow.WriteLine(StringValue)
```

In this expression, **StringValue** could be a string variable that has been evaluated somewhere (perhaps using the concatenation operator) or a literal (an actual value). In the Welcome example, we used a literal:

```
TextWindow.WriteLine("Welcome to Beginning Small Basic!")
```

And saw that **Welcome to Beginning Small Basic!** was output to the text window.

What if you want to output numeric information? It's really quite easy. The **WriteLine** method will automatically convert a numeric value to a string for output purposes. For example, look at this little code segment:

```
NumberBananas = 45
TextWindow.WriteLine(NumberBananas)
```

If you run this code, a **45** will appear on the output screen. Go ahead and start Small Basic and try it. This is one fun thing about Small Basic. It is an easy environment to try different ideas.

I started a new program in Small Basic and typed these lines in the editor:

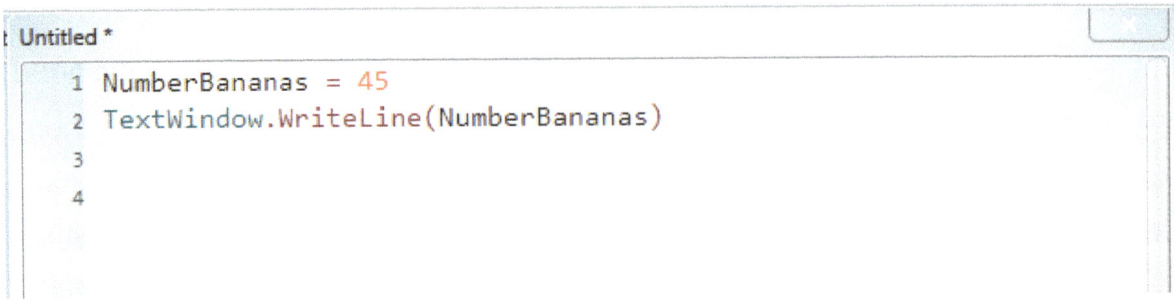

When I run this code, I see (I resized the window):

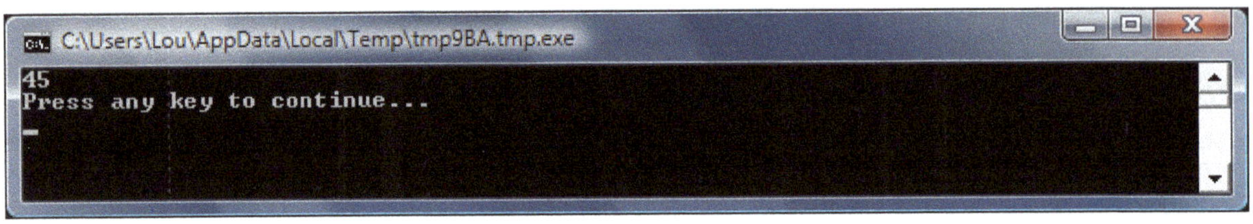

You can also combine text information with numeric information using the concatenation operator. For example, this code:

```
NumberBananas = 45
TextWindow.WriteLine("Number of Bananas is " + NumberBananas)
```

will print **Number of Bananas is 45** on the output screen:

The numeric data (**NumberOfBananas**) is converted to a string before it is concatenated with the text data.

So, it's pretty easy to output text and numeric information. Be aware one slight problem could occasionally arise though. Recall the concatenation operator is identical to the arithmetic addition operator. Look at this little segment of code:

```
NumberBananas = 32
NumberApples = 22
TextWindow.WriteLine("Pieces of fruit " + NumberBananas +
NumberApples)
```

You might think you are printing out the total number of fruit (numberBananas + numberApples = 54) with this statement. However, if you run this code, you will get **Pieces of fruit 3222**:

What happens is that Small Basic converts both pieces of numeric data to a string before the addition can be done. Then, the plus sign separating them acts as a concatenation operator yielding the 3222. To print the sum, we need to force the numeric addition by using parentheses:

```
NumberBananas = 32
NumberApples = 22
TextWindow.WriteLine("Pieces of fruit " + (NumberBananas +
NumberApples))
```

In this case, the two numeric values are summed before being converted to a string and you will obtain the desired output of **Pieces of fruit 54**:

So, we see the **WriteLine** method offers an easy-to-use way to output both text and numeric information, but it must be used correctly.

Notice one other thing about this example. The last line of code looks like it's two lines long! This is solely because of the word wrap feature of the word processor being used. In an actual Small Basic program, this line will appear as, and should be typed as, one single line. Always be aware of this possibility when reading these notes. Let's build a program.

Program – Sub Sandwich Party

Your family has decided to have a party. Two very long submarine sandwiches are being delivered and it is your job to figure out how much each person can eat. Sure, you could do this with a calculator, but let's use Small Basic!! This program is saved in the **Sandwich** folder in the course programs folder (**\BeginSB\BSB Code**).

Program Design

Assume you know the length of each submarine sandwich. To make the cutting easy, we will say that each person will get a whole number of inches (or centimeters) of sandwich (no decimals). With this information, you can compute how many people can be fed from each sandwich. If the total number is more than the people you have in your family, everyone eats and things are good. If not, you may have to make adjustments. The program steps would be:

1. Set a value for the number of inches a person can eat.
2. Determine length of both sandwiches.
3. Determine how many people can eat from each sandwich.
4. Increase or decrease the number of inches until the entire family can eat.

Let's translate each of these steps into Small Basic code as we build the program. Since this is your first program, we'll review many steps (creating a new program) and we'll type and discuss the code one or two lines at a time.

Program Development

Start **Small Basic**. Click the **New Program** button in the toolbar. A blank editor will appear. Immediately save the program as **Sandwich** in a folder of your choice.

First, type the following header information as a multi-line comment and add a title to the text window:

```
'
'  Sub Sandwich Program
'  Beginning Small Basic
'

TextWindow.Title = "Sub Sandwich Party"
```

We will use five variables in this program: one for how much each person can eat (**InchesPerPerson**), two for the sandwich lengths (**LengthSandwich1**, **LengthSandwich2**), and two for how many people can eat from each sandwich (**Eaters1**, **Eaters2**). These will all be numeric variables. Values for Eaters1 and Eaters2 must be whole numbers since you can't have a fraction of a family member. Set values for some of the variables (also include a comment about what you are doing):

```
'  set values
InchesPerPerson = 5
LengthSandwich1 = 114
LengthSandwich2 = 93
```

These are just values we made up, you can use anything you like. Notice we assume each person can eat 5 inches of sandwich.

Next, we compute how many people can eat from each sandwich using simple division:

```
'  determine how many people can eat each sandwich
Eaters1 = Math.Floor(LengthSandwich1 / InchesPerPerson)
Eaters2 = Math.Floor(LengthSandwich2 / InchesPerPerson)
```

We have used something not seen yet – the **Math.Floor** function. Small Basic provides a **Math** library that contains a large number of functions for our use (we will look at more of these in the next class). The Math.Floor function returns the whole number part of a decimal number – in this case it insures a whole number person is eating.

Also, notice when you start type the line computing Eaters1, the intellisense drop-down now includes added variables like **LengthSandwich1**:

Display the results using the **WriteLine** method:

```
'  write results
TextWindow.WriteLine("Letting each person eat " + InchesPerPerson
+ " inches")
TextWindow.WriteLine((Eaters1 + Eaters2) + " people can eat these
two sandwiches!")
```

Notice how each of the string concatenations works. Notice, too, that we sum the number of people before printing it.

The finished code in Small Basic should look like this:

```
'
'  Sub Sandwich Program
'  Beginning Small Basic
 TextWindow.Title = "Sub Sandwich Party"
'  set values
InchesPerPerson = 5
LengthSandwich1 = 114
LengthSandwich2 = 93
'  determine how many people can eat each sandwich
Eaters1 = Math.Floor(LengthSandwich1 / InchesPerPerson)
Eaters2 = Math.Floor(LengthSandwich2 / InchesPerPerson)
'  write results
TextWindow.WriteLine("Letting each person eat " + InchesPerPerson
+ " inches")
TextWindow.WriteLine((Eaters1 + Eaters2) + " people can eat these
two sandwiches!")
```

Double-check to make sure each line is typed properly.

Run the Program

Save your program (click the **Save** toolbar button). Run your program by clicking the **Run** toolbar button or it by pressing <**F5**>. If the program doesn't run, any errors encountered are listed below the editor. Double-check your code is exact – no misspellings, no missing quotes, no missing punctuation. When it runs, the text window should show this:

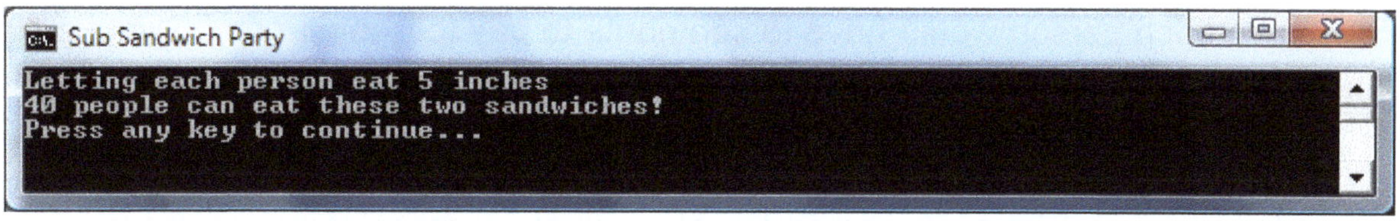

This says 40 people can eat from this particular set of sandwiches. Congratulations – you have written your very first Small Basic program!!

Other Things to Try

For each program in this course, we will offer suggestions for changes you can make and try. In this above run, we saw 40 people can eat. What if you need to feed more or less? Adjust the **InchesPerPerson** variable and determine the numbers of people who can eat for each value. After each adjustment, you will need to rerun the program. Assume the sandwiches cost so much per inch. Modify the program so it also computes the cost of the sandwiches. Determine how much each person would have to contribute to pay for their lunch. Give it a try!

Since we require each person to eat an whole number of inches, there might be leftover amounts in each sandwich. Can you figure out how to compute this amount? It's a neat little application of the **Remainder** function (returns the remainder when two whole numbers are divided) in the **Math** library. There are just a couple of code modifications. A new variable **InchesLeftOver** will be used to compute the leftover amount. Now, the code that computes that value:

```
' compute leftovers
InchesLeftOver = Math.Remainder(LengthSandwich1, InchesPerPerson)
+ Math.Remainder(LengthSandwich2, InchesPerPerson)
TextWindow.WriteLine("There are " + InchesLeftOver + " inches left
over.")
```

Add this code to your program and rerun. Do you see that there are a total of 7 inches remaining?

Can you see why in computing **InchesLeftOver**, we just don't add both sandwiches length together before using the remainder operator?

Summary

Again, congratulations are due for completing your first Small Basic program. You learned a lot about the Small Basic statements and assignments and how to do a little bit of arithmetic. You should be comfortable with starting a new program with Small Basic. In subsequent classes, we'll learn a little more Small Basic and write increasingly more detailed Small Basic programs.

4

Small Basic Program Design, Input Methods

Review and Preview

You should now be fairly comfortable with creating and running simple Small Basic programs. In this class, we continue learning new Small Basic topics to expand our programming knowledge. We'll look at some program design ideas, some mathematical functions and at ways to get input from users of your programs. And, we'll build a savings calculator program.

Program Design

You are about to start developing fairly detailed programs using Small Basic. We will give you programs to build and maybe you will have ideas for your own programs. Either way, it's fun and exciting to see ideas end up as computer programs. But before starting a program, it's a good idea to spend a little time thinking about what you are trying to do. This idea of proper **program design** will save you lots of time and result in a far better program.

Proper program design is not really difficult. The main idea is to create a program that is easy to use, easy to understand, and free of errors. That makes sense, doesn't it? Spend some time thinking about everything you want your program to do. What information does the program need? What information does the computer determine? Decide what programming steps you need to follow to accomplish desired tasks.

Make the Small Basic code in your methods readable and easy to understand. This will make the job of making later changes (and you will make changes) much easier. Follow accepted programming rules - you will learn these rules as you learn more about Small Basic. Make sure there are no errors in your program. This may seem like an obvious statement, but many programs are not error-free.

The importance of these few statements about program design might not make a lot of sense right now, but they will. The simple idea is to make a useful, clearly written, error-free program that is easy to use and easy to change. Planning carefully and planning ahead helps you achieve this goal. For each program built in this course, we will attempt to give you some insight into the program design process. We will always try to explain why we do what we do in building a program. And, we will always try to list all the considerations we make.

One other consideration in program design is to always build your program in stages. Don't try to build your entire Small Basic program and test it all at once. This just compounds the possibility of errors. We suggest always building your program in stages. Write a little code. Test that little bit of code making sure it works correctly. Slowly add more and more code. Run and test each code addition. Continue this approach until your program is complete. You will find that this "go slow" approach to creating a Small Basic program will make your programming task much simpler. Give it a try in programs we build.

Small Basic - The Second Lesson

We covered a lot of Small Basic in the last class. This was necessary to introduce you to many basic concepts so you could write your first program. In this briefer second lesson, we look at some mathematical functions.

Mathematical Functions

In Class 3, we saw the Small Basic arithmetic operators that allow us to perform the basics of addition, subtraction, multiplication and division. Like other computer programming languages, Small Basic also has the capability of doing very power mathematical computations. Small Basic's built-in mathematical **functions** (also called **methods**) are often used in these computations. We used a couple of these functions in the Sub Sandwich program (**Math.Floor** and **Math.Remainder**)

We don't expect you to be a mathematical genius to work through these notes, so we will only look at three mathematical functions. First, just what is a **function**? A function is a routine that computes some value for you, given some information. The format for using a function is:

```
FunctionValue = FunctionName(ArgumentList)
```

FunctionName is the name of the function and **ArgumentList** is a list of values (**inputs**, separated by commas) provided to the function so it can do its work. In this assignment statement, FunctionName uses the values in ArgumentList to compute a result and assign that result to the variable we have named **FunctionValue**.

How do you know what Small Basic mathematical functions exist, what type of information they provide and what the arguments are? Check various Small Basic references and the Microsoft Small Basic website. Or, just type the word **Math** in the Small Basic code window and the help area will display all the functions:

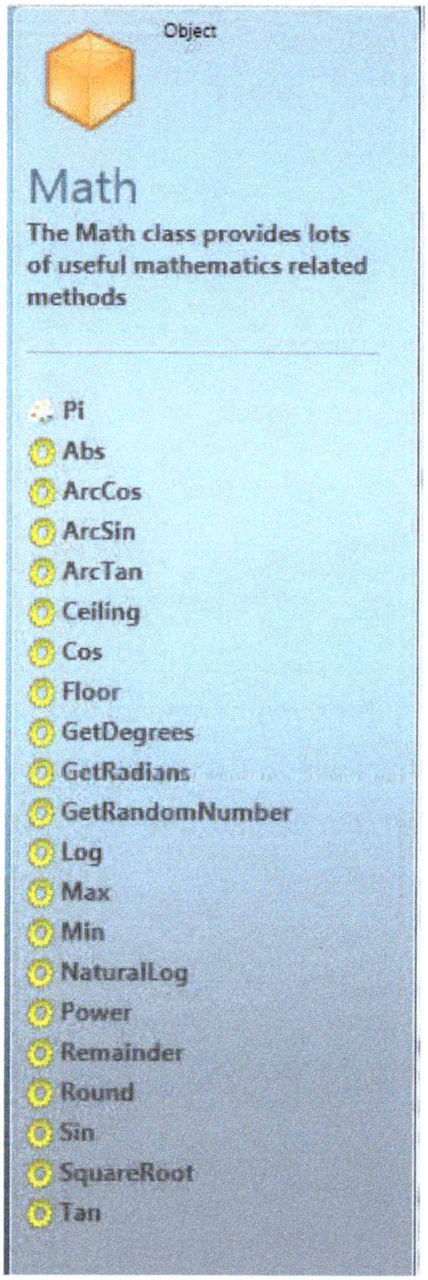

Then, choose a function name and the help window will tell you how to use it. Here is information on the first function we look at (**Abs**):

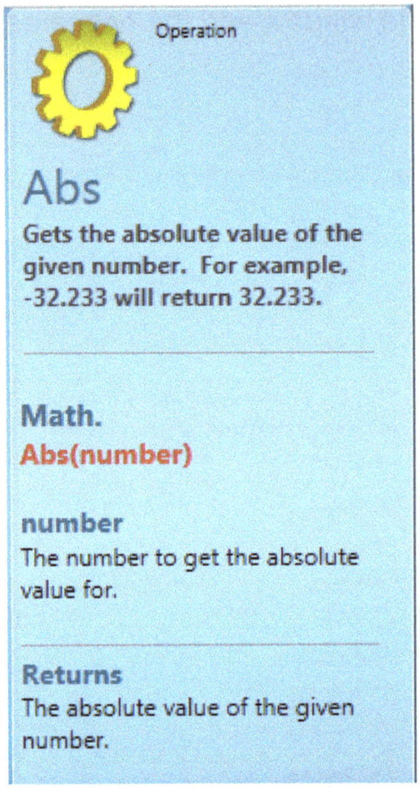

As mentioned, we will look at three mathematical functions here. The methods that support mathematical functions are implemented in the Small Basic class named **Math**. Hence, to refer to a particular function, you write **Math**, then a period, then the function name.

The first function we examine is the **absolute value** function. In math, the absolute value is the positive part of a number. The Small Basic function is:

```
Math.Abs(Argument)
```

where **argument** is number we want the absolute value of. The argument can be either an **int** or **double** type and the returned value will be the same type as the argument. Some examples:

Example	**Result**
`Math.Abs(7)`	7
`Math.Abs(-11)`	11
`Math.Abs(-3.14)`	3.14
`Math.Abs(72.1)`	72.1

Have you ever needed the **square root** of a number? A square root is a number that when multiplied by itself gives you the original number. For example, the square root of 4 is 2, since 2 times 2 is four. There's a button on your calculator (√) that will do this for you. In Small Basic, the square root function is:

```
Math.SquareRoot(Argument)
```

where **Argument** is number we want the square root of. The argument must be a non-negative number. Some examples:

Example	**Result**
`Math.SquareRoot(4)`	2
`Math.SquareRoot(36)`	6
`Math.SquareRoot(72.1)`	8.491

The last function we will use in this class is the **exponentiation** method. In exponentiation, a number is multiplied times itself a certain number of times. If we multiply a number by itself 4 times, we say we raise that number to the 4th power. The Small Basic function used for exponentiation is:

```
Math.Power(Argument1, Argument2)
```

Notice the **Power** function has two arguments. **Argument1** is the number we are multiplying times itself **Argument2** times. In other words, this function raises Argument1 to the Argument2 power. Some examples:

Example	**Result**
`Math.Power(4, 2)`	16
`Math.Power(-3, 3)`	-27
`Math.Power(10, 2)`	10000

In each example here, the arguments have no decimal parts. We have done this to make the examples clear. You are not limited to such values. It is possible to use this function to compute what happens if you multiply 7.654 times itself 3.16 times!! (The answer is 620.99, by the way.)

For the more mathematically inclined reader, you should know that there are many more Small Basic functions available for your use. You might want to look into using them. There are trigonometric functions and inverse trig functions, functions to convert from radians to degrees and vice versa, functions to find extreme values, functions for rounding, logarithm and inverse logarithm functions and a built-in value for pi. (If none of this means anything to you, don't worry – we won't be using them in this class).

Program Input Methods

In the example (Sub Sandwich Program) we built in the last class, we established variable values in code and ran the program to see the results. The results were printed by the Small Basic output method **WriteLine**. If we want to use different values, we need to change the code and rerun. This is a pain! It would be nice, in such a program, to allow a user to type in values while the program is running and have the computer do the computations based on the inputs. This way no code changes or recompiling would be needed to get a new answer. We need such capabilities in our programs.

The Small Basic language has two general methods that supports typed input. The methods are part of the **TextWindow** object we have been using. The first input method (**ReadNumber**) allows reading numeric (integer and floating) inputs. Its usage is:

```
ReturnedValue = TextWindow.ReadNumber()
```

where **ReturnedValue** is the number input by the user.

The other method (**Read**) returns a line of text (string information) input by the user. Its usage is:

```
ReturnedValue = TextWindow.Read()
```

where **ReturnedValue** is the text input by the user.

With either of these methods, the user types the requested input and presses the **<Enter>** key to have the computer accept the value.

Input Methods Example

Start **Small Basic**. Click the **New Program** button in the toolbar. A blank editor will appear. Immediately save the program as **InputExample** in a folder of your choice. Type these lines in the editor

```
TextWindow.WriteLine("What is your age?")
UserAge = TextWindow.ReadNumber()
TextWindow.WriteLine("You input " + UserAge)
```

In this code, we ask for a user to input their age, then write it in the text window.

Run the program (click the **Run** button or press <**F5**>). You should see:

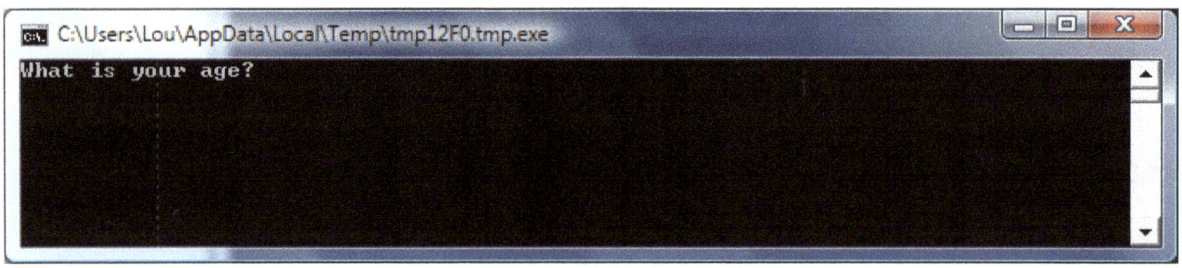

Notice how the prompt appears. Type in a value and press <**Enter**>. Once the number is input, it is assigned to the variable **UserAge** and the **WriteLine** method displays the entered value:

Notice the input value appears on a separate line after the prompting question. Most times, you would like this value to be on the same line as the prompt. This can be done by using a different **TextWindow** method. The **WriteLine** method appends a new line character to the output text, hence subsequent information goes to that new line. The Write method does not begin a new line. Modify the first line of code with the shaded changes (change the WriteLine method to Write and add a space after the question mark):

```
TextWindow.Write("What is your age? ")
```

Rerun the program. Now when you type your age, it appears next to the prompting question:

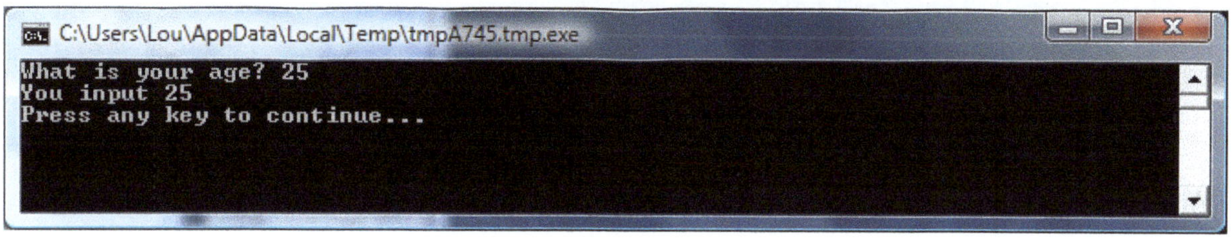

Run the program again and try to enter non-numeric characters – you won't be able to. The **ReadNumber** method only accepts numeric data (the digits 0 through 9, a leading minus sign, or a single decimal point).

Now, let's test the **Read** method (to input a string of text). Add these three lines of code that ask for a user's name in a manner similar to requesting the age:

```
TextWindow.Write("What is your name? ")
UserName = TextWindow.Read()
TextWindow.WriteLine("You input " + UserName)
```

Run the program again. Type your age, press <Enter> and you will see the prompt asking for your name:

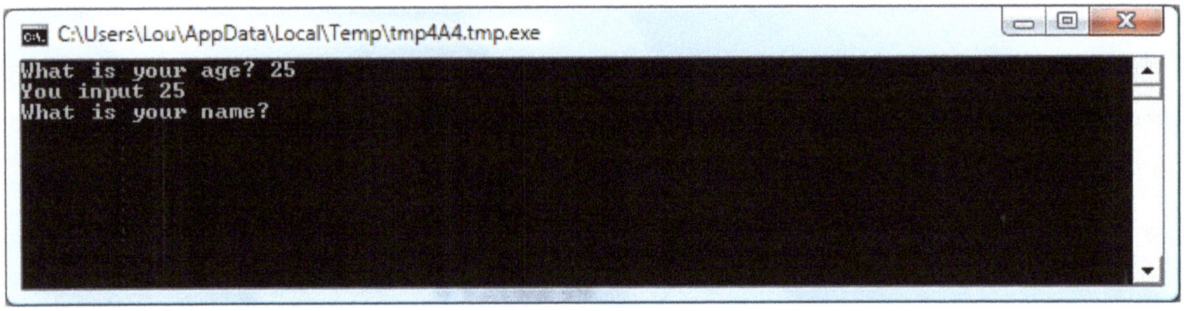

Enter a string (any characters at all can be typed) and press <Enter> to see:

It seems the input methods are working just fine. Did you notice how building a program in stages (adding a few lines of code at a time) is good? Always follow such a procedure. Before leaving this example and building another program, let's take a quick look at one other useful Small Basic concept. In the text window above, it would be nice if there was a blank line between each input request. This just makes your output appear a little cleaner, a quality of a well designed Small Basic program. To insert a blank line in the output, just use a **WriteLine** method with a blank argument:

```
TextWindow.WriteLine("")
```

Add the shaded line to the current code:

```
TextWindow.Write("What is your age? ")
UserAge = TextWindow.ReadNumber()
TextWindow.WriteLine("You input " + UserAge)
TextWindow.WriteLine("")
TextWindow.Write("What is your name? ")
UserName = TextWindow.Read()
TextWindow.WriteLine("You input " + UserName)
```

Run the program again and answer the prompts. Notice the new blank line.

This program has been saved in the **InputExample** folder in the course programs folder (**\BeginSB\BSB Code**).

Program – Savings Calculator

In this program, we will build a savings account calculator. We will input how much money we can put into an account each month and the number of months we put money in the account. The program will then compute how much we saved. This program is saved in the **Savings** folder in the course programs folder (**\BeginSB \BSB Code**).

Program Design

The steps needed to do this calculation are relatively simple:

1. Obtain an amount for each month's deposit.
2. Obtain a number of months.
3. Multiply the two input numbers together.
4. Output the product, the total savings.

We will use the **ReadNumber** method to get user input. The **WriteLine** and **Write** methods will be used to output the savings amount. We'll throw in an additional step to ask for the user's name (an example of using the **Read** method).

Program Development

Start **Small Basic**. Click the **New Program** button in the toolbar. A blank editor will appear. Immediately save the program as **Savings** in a folder of your choice.

First, type the following header information and code that adds a window title:

```
'
' Savings Program
' Beginning Small Basic
'

TextWindow.Title = "Savings Calculator"
```

We will use four variables in this program: one for the user's name (**YourName**), one for the deposit amount (**Deposit**), one for the number of months (**Months**) and one for the total amount (**Total**). Type these lines to initialize the variables:

```
YourName = ""
Deposit = 0.0
Months = 0
Total = 0.0
```

Now, we start the code, using the steps outlined under Program Design. At any time, after typing some code, you might like to stop and run just to see if things are going okay. That is always a good approach to take. First, ask the user his/her name using this code:

```
'  ask user name
TextWindow.Write("Hello, what is your name? ")
YourName = TextWindow.Read()
```

Next, determine how much will be deposited in the savings account each month:

```
TextWindow.WriteLine("")
' get deposit amount
TextWindow.Write("How much will you deposit each month? ")
Deposit = TextWindow.ReadNumber()
```

Notice the insertion of a blank line before printing the prompt. Finally, obtain the number of months:

```
TextWindow.WriteLine("")
' get number of months
TextWindow.Write("For how many months? ")
Months = TextWindow.ReadNumber()
```

With this information, the total deposit can be computed and displayed using a WriteLine method:

```
TextWindow.WriteLine("")
'  compute and display total
Total = Deposit * Months
TextWindow.WriteLine(yourName + ", after " + months + " months,
you will have $" + total + " in your savings.")
TextWindow.WriteLine("")
```

Save your program by clicking the **Save** button.

The finished code in the Small Basic editor should appear as:

```
'
'  Savings Program
'  Beginning Small Basic
'
TextWindow.Title = "Savings Calculator"
'   initialize variables
YourName = ""
Deposit = 0.0
Months = 0
Total = 0.0

'  ask user name
TextWindow.Write("Hello, what is your name? ")
YourName = TextWindow.Read()
TextWindow.WriteLine("")
' get deposit amount
TextWindow.Write("How much will you deposit each month? ")
Deposit = TextWindow.ReadNumber()
TextWindow.WriteLine("")
' get number of months
TextWindow.Write("For how many months? ")
Months = TextWindow.ReadNumber()
TextWindow.WriteLine("")
'  compute and display total
Total = Deposit * Months
TextWindow.WriteLine(yourName + ", after " + months + " months,
you will have $" + total + " in your savings.")
TextWindow.WriteLine("")
```

Run the Program

Run your program. If the program does not run successfully, try to find out where your errors are using any error messages that may appear. We will cover some possible errors in the next class.

When the program runs successfully, you will see:

Type in your name, a deposit amount and a number of months. Your total will be given to you in a nicely formatted string output. Notice how the name, deposit, months and total are all put together (concatenated) in a single sentence, along with a dollar sign ($). Make sure the answer is correct. Remember, a big step in program design is making sure your program works correctly! If you say you want to save 200 dollars a month for 10 months and your computer program says you will have a million dollars by that time, you should know something is wrong somewhere!

When I tried the program, I got:

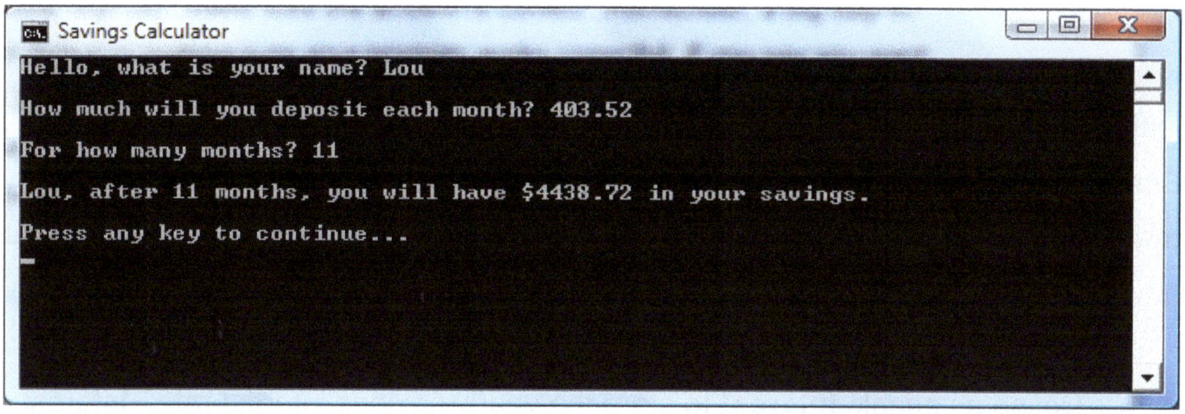

Notice if I deposit 403.52 (you don't, and can't, enter the dollar sign) for 11 months, the program tells me I will have $4438.72 in my savings account.

This program may not seem all that complicated. And it isn't. After all, we only multiplied two numbers together. But, the program demonstrates steps that are used in every Small Basic program. Valuable experience has been gained in recognizing how to read input values, do the math to obtain desired results, and output those results to the user.

Other Things to Try

Most savings accounts yield interest, that is the bank actually pays you for letting them use your money. This savings account program has ignored interest. But, it is fairly easy to make the needed modifications to account for interest - the math is just a little more complicated. We will give you the steps, but not show you how, to change your program. Give it a try if you'd like:

- Define a variable **Interest** to store the yearly savings interest rate. Interest rates are floating decimal numbers.
- Add additional statements to allow the user to input an interest rate.
- Modify the code to use Interest in computing **Total**. The code for that computation is (get ready - it's messy looking):

```
Total = 1200 * (Deposit * (Math.Power((1 + Interest / 1200),
Months) - 1) / Interest)
```

Make sure you type this all on one line – as often happens, the word processor has made it look like it is on two. As we said, this is a pretty messy expression, but it's good practice in using parentheses and a mathematical function (**Power**). The number '1200' is used here to convert the interest from a yearly value to a monthly value.

Now, run the modified program. Type in values for deposit, months, and interest. Make sure you get reasonable answers. (As a check, if you use a deposit value of 300, a months value of 14, and an interest value of 6.5, the total answer should be $4351.13. Note you'd have $4200 without interest, so this makes sense). Save your program.

I told a little lie, I didn't get $4351.13 in the above example with interest. I actually got $4351.1272052172923076923076923!!!:

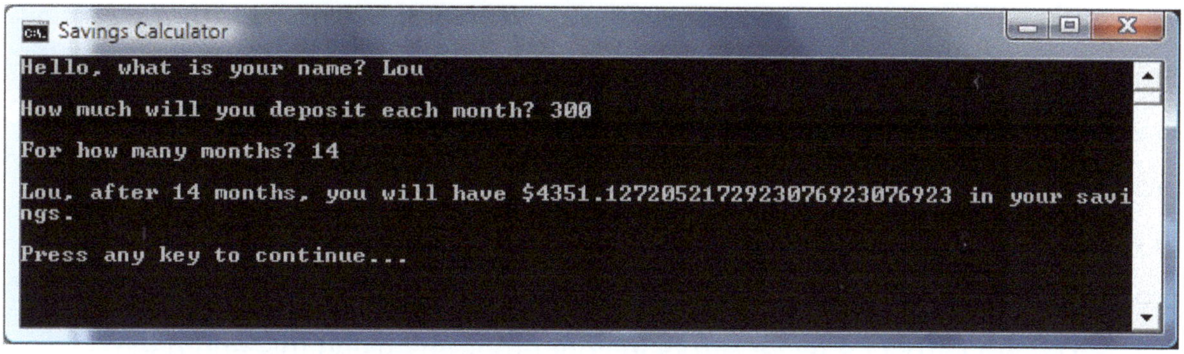

I rounded the answer. In such cases, the number should just be displayed with two numbers after the decimal. It is possible to do this using Small Basic but beyond the scope of our discussion at the moment.

Summary

Notice the programs are getting a little more detailed as you learn more Small Basic. In this class, you learned about proper program design, mathematical functions and how to add input capabilities to your Small Basic programs. You built a little savings account program. And, an important concept to remember as you continue through this course is to always try to build your programs a few lines of code at a time. A good mantra is "code a little, test a little." You will introduce fewer errors in your programs using this approach.

5

Debugging, Decisions, Random Numbers

Review and Preview

We continue our journey through the world of Small Basic. Hopefully, creating and running a Small Basic program is getting easier for you. In this class, you will examine how to find and eliminate errors in your programs, how you can make decisions using Small Basic, and look at a fun function, the random number generator. You will build a 'Guess the Number' game program.

Debugging a Small Basic Program

No matter how well you plan your program and no matter how careful you are in implementing your ideas in Small Basic code, you will make mistakes. Errors, or what computer programmers call **bugs**, do creep into your program. You may have already encountered a few in the programs we've built so far. Perhaps you spelled a keyword wrong, forgot a punctuation mark or misspelled a variable name. These are all examples of program bugs. You, as a programmer, need to have a strategy for finding and eliminating those bugs. The process of eliminating bugs in a program is called **debugging**. Unfortunately, there are not a lot of hard, fast rules for finding bugs in a program. Each programmer has his or her own way of attacking bugs. You will develop your ways. We can come up with some general strategies, though, and that's what we'll give you here.

Program errors, or bugs, can be divided into three types:

- **Syntax** errors
- **Run-time** errors
- **Logic** errors

Syntax errors occur when you make an error typing a line of Small Basic code. Something is misspelled or something is left out that needs to be there. Your program won't run if there are any syntax errors. **Run-time errors** occur when you try to run your program. It will stop abruptly because something has happened beyond its control. **Logic errors** are the toughest to find. Your program will run okay, but the results it gives are not what you expected. Let's examine each error type and address possible debugging methods.

Syntax Errors

Syntax errors are the easiest to identify and eliminate. The JCreator development environment is a big help in finding syntax errors. Syntax errors will occur as you're writing Small Basic code.

Start Small Basic. We'll type in a few snippets of code to see how different bugs are identified. Let's look at some typical errors. In the editor, type these two lines of code:

```
MyNumber = 7
TextWindow.WriteLine(MyNmber)
```

We've misspelled the assigned variable name (**MyNumber**) in the **WriteLine** statement.

Try running this and below the editor you will see the message:

Sorry, we found some errors... Close
2,22: The variable 'MyNmber' is used, but its value is not assigned. Are you sure you have spelled it correctly?

The 2,22 implies there is an error in Line 2, Column 22. It tells you it does not recognize the variable **MyNmber** and asks if you misspelled it. We did. Small Basic is pretty smart!

Correct that error, but misspell **WriteLine** as **WriteLne**:

```
MyNumber = 7
TextWindow.WriteLne(MyNumber)
```

Try running and Small Basic will tell you the problem:

Sorry, we found some errors...
2,12: Cannot find operation 'WriteLne' in 'TextWindow'.

Correct your error. But, change the first line as shown (leave out the assignment operator):

```
MyNumber  7
TextWindow.WriteLine(MyNumber)
```

Try running and you'll get this error message:

Sorry, we found some errors...
1,11: Unrecognized statement encountered.

You are being told this (line 1 again) is not a recognized statement and the problem is somewhere around Column 11. You should immediately see the problem and be able to fix it. Fix the error.

Let's try one other example. Change the second line by adding an additional parenthesis at the end of the **WriteLine** method:

```
MyNumber = 7
TextWindow.WriteLine(MyNumber))
```

Try running and you receive this message:

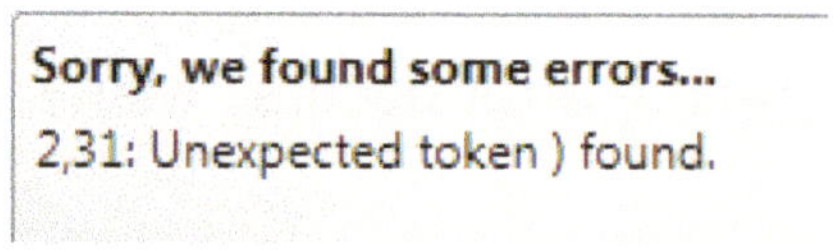

The problem is clear – you have one too many right parentheses.

So when you try to run with syntax errors, the Small Basic environment will kindly point out your errors to you so you can fix them. Note that syntax errors usually result because of incorrect typing, either misspellings, additions or omissions - another great reason to improve your typing skills, if they need it.

Run-Time Errors

Once you have written your code and eliminated all identified syntax errors, obtaining a successful compilation, you try to run your program. If the program runs, great! But, many times, your program may stop and tell you it found an error - this is a run-time error. You need to figure out why it stopped and fix the problem. At this writing, the Small Basic environment does not give you much useful information when a run-time error occurs. Many times, the program will just stop.

Let's look at a couple of examples. Type these lines in the editor:

```
MyNumber = 7
MyOtherNumber = 0
TextWindow.WriteLine(MyNumber / MyOtherNumber)
```

Yes, I know we'll get a divide by zero (a classic run-time error), but that's the point here – to illustrate potential errors. The program should not run, giving you some indication you are dividing by zero. If you run the program, it runs without error, printing a zero as the division result:

This needs to be corrected in future Small Basic versions.

Another common run-time error occurs when using one of Small Basic's built-in functions. Errors result if you use the wrong type or value as one of the arguments. Try these two lines of code:

```
MyNumber = -7
TextWindow.WriteLine(Math.SquareRoot(MyNumber))
```

We attempt to take the square root of a negative number (not allowed). When we run the program, we get some indication that something is wrong, but it is not very explicit:

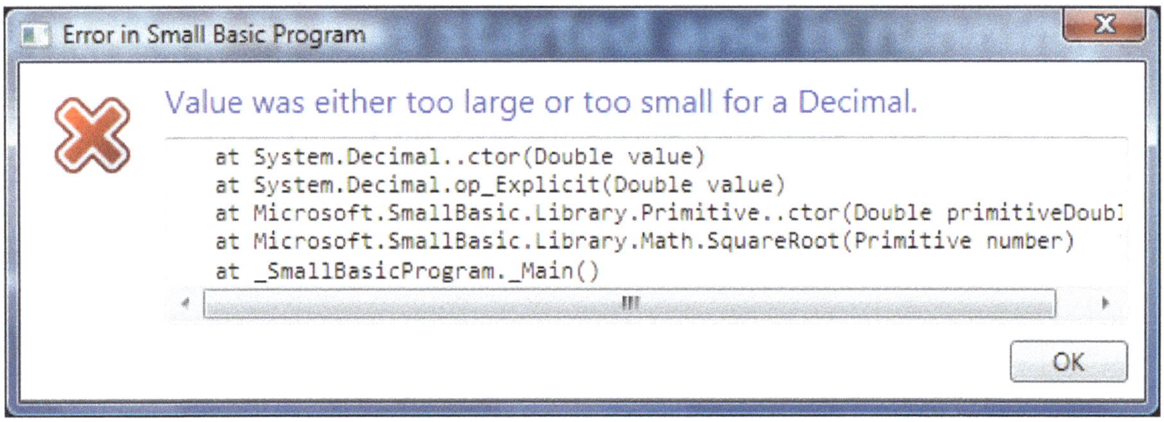

Click **OK** and the program just stops:

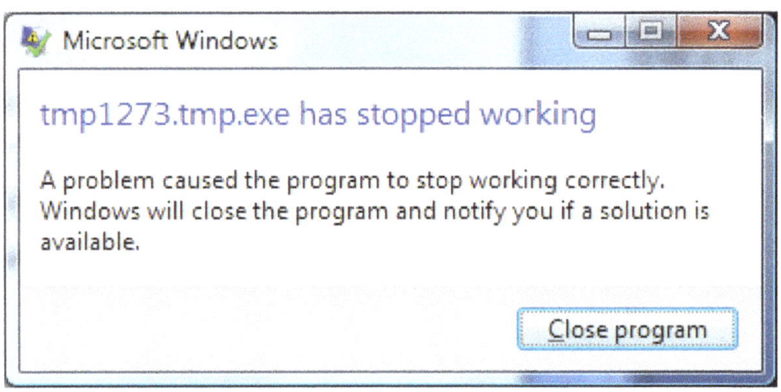

We've seen just a couple of possible run-time errors. There are others and you'll see them as you start building programs. And, unfortunately, the current Small Basic program is not very helpful in pointing out where errors are. Hopefully, this situation will change with future versions. One last thing about run-time errors. Small Basic will not find all errors at once. It will stop at the first run-time error it encounters. After you fix that error, there may be more. You have to fix run-time errors one at a time.

Logic Errors

Logic errors are the most difficult to find and eliminate. These are errors that don't keep your program from running, but cause incorrect or unexpected results. The only thing you can do at this point, if you suspect logic errors exist, is to dive into your program and make sure everything is coded exactly as you want it. Finding logic errors is a time-consuming art, <u>not</u> a science. There are no general rules for finding logic errors. Each programmer has his or her own particular way of searching for logic errors.

With the example we have been using, a logic error would be setting a variable to an incorrect value. Or, perhaps you add two numbers together when you should have subtracted. Logic errors are mistakes you have inadvertently introduced into your Small Basic code. And, unfortunately, these errors are not pointed out to you. Hence, eliminating logic errors is not always easy.

Advanced programming languages use something called a **debugger** that helps in the identification of logic errors. Using a debugger lets you examine variable values, stop your code wherever and whenever you want, and run your program line-by-line. Small Basic does not offer a debugger. So, for now, you need to learn to eliminate logic errors by paying close attention to your code. And, the best approach is to be so careful that you don't have any logic errors to worry about.

Small Basic - The Third Lesson

In the Small Basic lesson for this class, we learn about one of the more useful capabilities of a computer program - decision making. We will discuss expressions and operators used in decisions and how decisions can be made. We will also look at a new Small Basic mathematical function - the random number generator. Such a function is at the heart of every computer game.

Logical Expressions

You may think that computers are quite smart. They appear to have the ability to make amazing decisions and choices. Computers can beat masters at chess and help put men and women into space. Well, computers really aren't that smart - the only decision making ability they have is to tell if something is **true** or **false**. But, computers have the ability to make such decisions very quickly and that's why they appear smart (and because, unlike the True or False tests given in schools, computers <u>always</u> get the right answer!). To use Small Basic for decision making, we write all possible decisions in the form of **true or false?** statements, called **logical expressions**. We give the computer a logical expression and the computer will tell us if that expression is true or false. Based on that decision, we can take whatever action we want in our computer program.

Say in a computer program we need to know if the value of the variable **A** is larger than the value of the variable **B**. We would ask the computer (by writing some Small Basic code) to provide an answer to the true or false? statement: "A is larger than B." This is an example of a logical expression. If the computer told us this was true, we could take one set of Small Basic steps. If it was false, we could take another. This is how decisions are done in Small Basic.

To make decisions, we need to know how to build and use logical expressions. The first step in building such expressions is to learn about comparison operators.

Comparison Operators

In the Class 3, we looked at one type of Small Basic operator - arithmetic operators. In this class, we introduce the idea of a **comparison operator**. Comparison operators do exactly what they say - they compare two values, with the output of the comparison being either **true** or **false**. Comparison operators allow us to construct logical expressions that can be used in decision making.

There are six comparison operators. The first is the "**equal to**" operator represented by an equal (=) sign. This operator tells us if two values are equal to each other. Examples are:

Comparison	Result
6 = 7	false
4 = 4	true

There is also a "**not equal to**" operator represented by a **<>** (you need to type two characters to form this symbol). Examples of using this operator:

Comparison	Result
6 <> 7	true
4 <> 4	false

There are other operators that let us compare the size of numbers. The "**greater than**" operator (**>**) tells us if one number (left side of operator) is greater than another (right side of operator). Examples of its usage:

Comparison	Result
8 > 3	true
6 > 7	false
4 > 4	false

The "**less than**" operator (**<**) tells us if one number (left side of operator) is less than another (right side of operator). Some examples are:

Comparison	Result
8 < 3	false
6 < 7	true
4 < 4	false

The last two operators are modifications to the "greater than" and "less than" operators. The "**greater than or equal to**" operator (**>=**) compares two numbers. The result is true if the number on the left of the operator is greater than or equal to the number on the right. Otherwise, the result is false. Examples:

Comparison	**Result**
8 >= 3	true
6 >= 7	false
4 >= 4	true

Similarly, the "**less than or equal to**" operator (**<=**) tells us if one number (left side of operator) is less than or equal to another (right side of operator). Examples:

Comparison	**Result**
8 <= 3	false
6 <= 7	true
4 <= 4	true

Comparison operators have equal precedence among themselves, but are lower than the precedence of arithmetic operators. This means comparisons are done after any arithmetic. Comparison operators allow us to make single decisions about the relative size of values and variables. What if we need to make multiple decisions? For example, what if we want to know if a particular variable is smaller than one number, but larger than another? We need ways to combine logical expressions - logical operators can do this.

Logical Operators

Logical operators are used to combine logical expressions built using comparison operators. Using such operators allows you, as the programmer, to make any decision you want. As an example, say you need to know if two variables named A and B are both greater than 0. Using the "greater than" comparison operator (>), we know how to see if A is greater than zero and we know how to check if B is greater than 0, but how do we combine these expressions and obtain one result (true or false)?

Small Basic supports two logical operators. The first is the **And** operator. The format for using this operator is (using two logical expressions, **X** and **Y,** each either true or false):

X **And** Y

This expression is asking the question "are X and Y both true?" That's why it is called the And operator. The And operator will return a true value only if both X and Y are true. If either expression is false, the And operator will return a false. The four possibilities for **And** are shown in this **logic table**:

X	Y	X And Y
true	true	true
true	false	false
false	true	false
false	false	false

Notice the And operator would be used to solve the problem mentioned in the beginning of this section. That is, to see if the variables A and B are both greater than zero, we would use the expression:

A > 0 And B > 0

The other logical operator we will use is the **Or** operator. The format for using this operator is:

X **Or** Y

This expression is asking the question "is X or Y true?" That's why it is called the Or operator. The Or operator will return a true value if either X or Y is true. If both expressions are false, the Or operator will return a false. The four possibilities for **Or** are:

X	Y	X Or Y
true	true	true
true	false	true
false	true	true
false	false	false

The Or operator is second in precedence to the And operator (that is, And is done before Or), and all logical operators come after the comparison operators in precedence. Use of comparison operators and logical operators to form logical expressions is key to making proper decisions in Small Basic. Make sure you understand how all the operators (and their precedence) work. Let's look at some examples to help in this understanding.

In these examples, we will have two variables A and B, with values:

A = 14, B = 7

What if we want to evaluate the logical expression:

A > 10 And B > 10

Comparisons are done first, left to right since all comparison operators share the same level of precedence. A (14) is greater than 10, so A > 10 is true. B (7) is not greater than 10, so B > 10 is false. Since one expression is not true, the result of the And operation is false. This expression 'A > 10 And B > 10' is false. What is the result of this expression:

A > 10 Or B > 10

Can you see this expression is true (A > 10 is true, B > 10 is false; true Or false is true)?

There is no requirement that a logical expression have just one logical operator. So, let's complicate things a bit. What if the expression is:

A > 10 Or B > 10 And A + B = 20

Precedence tells us the arithmetic is done first (A and B are added), then the comparisons, left to right. We know A > 10 is true, B > 10 is false, A + B = 20 is false. So, this expression, in terms of Boolean comparison values, becomes:

true Or false And false

How do we evaluate this? Precedence says the And is done first, then the Or. The result of 'false And false' is false, so the expression reduces to:

true Or false

which has a result of true. Hence, we say the expression 'A > 10 Or B > 10 And A + B = 20' is true.

Parentheses can be used in logical expressions to force precedence in evaluations. What if, in the above example, we wanted to do the Or operation first? This is done by rewriting using parentheses:

(A > 10 Or B > 10) And A + B = 20

You should be able to show this evaluates to false (do the Or first). Before, without parentheses, it was true. The addition of parentheses has changed the value of this logical expression! It's always best to clearly indicate how you want a logical expression to be evaluated. Parentheses are a good way to do this. Use parentheses even if precedence is not affected. If we moved the parentheses in this example and wrote:

A > 10 Or (B > 10 And A + B = 20)

the result (true) is the same as if the parentheses were not there since the And is done first anyway. The parentheses do, however, clearly indicate the And is performed first. Such clarity is good in programming.

Comparison and logical operators are keys to making decisions in Small Basic. Make sure you are comfortable with their meaning and use. Always double-check any logical expression you form to make sure it truly represents the decision logic you intend. Use parentheses to add clarity, if needed.

Decisions - The If Statement

We've spent a lot of time covering comparison operators and logical operators and discussed how they are used to form logical expressions. But, just how is all this used in computer decision making? We'll address that now by looking at the Small Basic **If** statement. Actually, the If statement is not a single statement, but rather a group of statements that implements some decision logic. It is conceptually simple.

The If statement checks a particular logical expression. It executes different groups of Small Basic statements, depending on whether that expression is true or false. The Small Basic structure for this logic is:

```
If (Expression) Then
  ' Small Basic code to be executed if Expression is true
Else
  ' Small Basic code to be executed if Expression is false
EndIf
```

Let's see what goes on here. We have some logical **Expression** (enclosed by parentheses) which is formed from comparison operators and logical operators. **If** Expression is true, **Then** the first group of Small Basic statements is executed. **Else** (meaning Expression is not true, or it is false), the second group of Small Basic statements is executed. The If statement group is ended with an **EndIf** statement (all **If** statements require a matching **EndIf** statement). Whether Expression is true or false, program execution continues with the first line of Small Basic code after the EndIf statement.

The Else keyword and the statements between Else and EndIf are optional. If there is no Small Basic code to be executed if Expression is false, the If structure would simply be:

```
If (Expression) Then
  ' Small Basic code to be executed if Expression is true
EndIf
```

Let's try some examples.

Pretend a neighbor kid just opened a lemonade stand and you want to let the computer decide how much she should charge for each cup sold. Define a variable **Cost** (cost per cup in cents - our foreign friends can use some other unit here) and another variable **Temperature** (outside temperature in degrees F - our foreign friends would, of course, use degrees C). We will write an If/EndIf structure that implements a decision process that establishes a value for Cost, depending on the value of Temperature. Look at the Small Basic code:

```
If (Temperature > 90) Then
  Cost = 50
Else
  Cost = 25
EndIf
```

We see that if Temperature > 90 (a warm day, hence we can charge more), a logical expression, is true, the Cost will be 50, else (meaning Temperature is not greater than 90) the Cost will be 25. Not too difficult. Notice that we have indented the lines of Small Basic code following the If and Else statements. This is common practice in writing Small Basic code. It clearly indicates what is done in each case and allows us to see where an If structure begins and ends (with the EndIf statement). The Small Express environment will actually handle the indenting for you.

We could rewrite this (and get the same result) without the Else statement. Notice, this code is equivalent to the above code:

```
Cost = 25
If (Temperature > 90) Then
  Cost = 50
EndIf
```

Here, before the If/EndIf structure, Cost is 25. Only if Temperature is greater than 90 is Cost changed to 50. Otherwise, Cost remains at 25. Even though, in these examples, we only have one line of Small Basic code that is executed for each decision possibility, we are not limited to a single line. We may have as many lines of Small Basic code as needed in If/EndIf structures.

What if, in our lemonade stand example, we want to divide our pricing structure into several different Cost values, based on several different Temperature values. The If/EndIf structure can modified to include an **ElseIf** statement to consider multiple logical expressions. Such a structure is:

```
If (Expression1) Then
  ' Small Basic code to be executed if Expression1 is true
ElseIf (Expression2) Then
  ' Small Basic code to be executed if Expression2 is true
ElseIf (Expression3) Then
  ' Small Basic code to be executed if Expression3 is true
Else
  ' Small Basic code to be executed if Expression1, Expression 2,
and Expression3 are all false]
EndIf
```

Can you see what happens here? It's pretty straightforward - just work down through the code. If Expression1 is true, the first set of Small Basic code is executed. If Expression1 is false, the program checks to see if Expression2 (using the ElseIf) is true. If Expression2 is true, that section of code is executed. If Expression2 is false, Expression3 is evaluated. If Expression3 is true, the corresponding code is executed. If Expression3 is false, and note by this time,

Expression1, Expression2, and Expression3 have all been found to be false, the code in the Else section (and this is optional) is executed.

You can have as many ElseIf statements as you want. You must realize, however, that only one section of Small Basic code in an If/EndIf structure will be executed. This means that once Small Basic has found a logical expression that is true, it will execute that section of code then leave the structure and execute the first line of code following the EndIf statement. For example, if in the above example, both Expression1 and Expression3 are true, only the Small Basic statements associated with Expression1 being true will be executed. The rule for If/EndIf structures is: only the statements associated with the first true expression will be executed.

How can we use this in our lemonade example? A more detailed pricing structure is reflected in this code:

```
If (Temperature > 90) Then
  Cost = 50
ElseIf (Temperature > 80) Then
  Cost = 40
ElseIf (Temperature > 70) Then
  Cost = 30
Else
  Cost = 25
EndIf
```

What would the Cost be if Temperature is 85? Temperature is not greater than 90, but is greater than 80, so Cost is 40. What if this code was rewritten as:

```
If (Temperature > 70) Then
  Cost = 30
ElseIf (Temperature > 80) Then
  Cost = 40
ElseIf (Temperature > 90) Then
  Cost = 50
Else
  Cost = 25
EndIf
```

This doesn't look that different - we've just reordered some statements. But, notice what happens if we try to find Cost for Temperature = 85 again. The first If expression is true (Temperature is greater than 70), so Cost is 30. This is not the result we wanted and will decrease profits for our lemonade stand! Here's a case where the "first true" rule gave us an incorrect answer - a logic error.

This example points out the necessity to always carefully check any If/EndIf structures you write. Make sure the decision logic you want to implement is working properly. Make sure you try cases that execute all possible decisions and that you get the correct results. The examples used here are relatively simple. Obviously, the If/EndIf structure can be more far more complicated. Using multiple variables, multiple comparisons and multiple operators, you can develop very detailed decision making processes. In the remaining class programs, you will see examples of such processes.

Random Number Generator

Let's leave decisions for now and look at a fun concept - the random number. Have you ever played the Windows solitaire card game or Minesweeper or some similar game? Did you notice that every time you play the game, you get different results? How does this happen? How can you make a computer program unpredictable or introduce the idea of "randomness?" The key is the random number generator. This generator simply produces a different number every time it is referenced.

Why do you need random numbers? In the Windows solitaire card game, the computer needs to shuffle a deck of cards. It needs to "randomly" sort fifty-two cards. It uses random numbers to do this. If you have a game that rolls a die, you need to randomly generate a number between 1 and 6. Random numbers can be used to do this. If you need to flip a coin, you need to generate Heads or Tails randomly. Yes, random numbers are used to do this too.

Small Basic has a random generator of whole numbers (integers). The generator uses **GetRandomNumber** method of the Small Basic **Math** class. So, whenever you need a random integer value, use this method:

```
Math.GetRandomNumber(Limit)
```

This statement generates a random integer value that is between 1 and **Limit**. For example, the method:

```
Math.GetRandomNumber(5)
```

will generate random numbers from 1 to 5. The possible values will be 1, 2, 3, 4 and 5.

Let's see how this all works by building a quick application. Start **Small Basic**. Type this little code snippet:

```
'  Random Test
'  Beginning Small Basic
TextWindow.WriteLine("Random number " + Math.GetRandomNumber(10))
```

This code simply generates a random integer between 1 and 10 (**GetRandomNumber** uses a limit of 10) and prints it. Run the program. Some number should print in the text window. Here's my first run:

Stop the program and run it again. Most likely a different number will be printed; it could print the same number again, after all it is random. Continue stopping and running to see how each run results in a random result. The number printed should always be between 1 and 10.

So, the random number generator can be used to introduce randomness in a program. This opens up a lot of possibilities to you as a programmer. Every computer game, video game, and computer simulation, like sports games and flight simulators, use random numbers. A roll of a die can produce a number from 1 to 6. To use **GetRandomNumber** to roll a die, we would write:

```
DieNumber = Math.GetRandomNumber(6)
```

For a deck of cards, the random integers would range from 1 to 52 since there are 52 cards in a standard playing deck. Code to do this:

```
CardNumber = Math.GetRandomNumber(52)
```

If we want a number between 0 and 100, we would use:

```
YourNumber = Math.GetRandomNumber(101) - 1
```

Check the examples above to make sure you see how the random number generator produces the desired range of integers. Now, let's move on to a program that will use this generator.

Program - Guess the Number Game

As we mentioned in Class 1, discussing the history of Small Basic, back in the early 1980's, the first computers intended for home use appeared. Brands like Atari, Coleco, Texas Instruments, and Commodore were sold in stores like Sears and Toys R Us (sorry, I can't type the needed 'backwards' R). These computers didn't have much memory, couldn't do real fancy graphics, and, compared to today's computers, cost a lot of money. But, these computers introduced a lot of people to the world of computer programming. Many games appeared at that time and the program you will build here is one of those classics. This program is saved in the **Number** folder in the course programs folder (**\BeginSB\BSB Code**).

Program Design

You've all played the game where someone said "I'm thinking of a number between 1 and 10" (or some other limits). Then, you try to guess the number. The person thinking of the number tells you if you're right or wrong, low or high, or provides some other clue and, sometimes, you guess again. We will develop a computer version of this game here. The computer will pick a number between 1 and 10 (using the random number generator). You will try to guess the number. Based on your guess, the computer will tell you if you are correct, too low or too high and tell you the answer. You only get one chance to guess it!!

The steps needed to do play this game are:

1. Computer picks a number between 1 and 10.
2. Computer asks your guess.
3. Computer analyzes your guess and outputs the result.

We will use the **ReadNumber** input method to get user input. The **WriteLine** method will be used to output the result of your guess.

Program Development

Start **Small Basic**. Click the **New Program** button in the toolbar. A blank editor will appear. Immediately save the program as **Number** in a folder of your choice.

First, type the following header information and title information:

```
'
'  Number Program
'  Beginning Small Basic
'

TextWindow.Title = "Guess the Number Game"
```

We will use two variables in this program: one for the computer's number (**ComputerNumber**) and one for your guess (**YourGuess**).

Now, we start writing the code, following the steps listed in Program Design. Again, after typing some code, you might like to stop and run just to see if things are going okay. First, have the computer pick and print its random number:

```
'  get the computer's number between 1 and 10
ComputerNumber = Math.GetRandomNumber(10)
TextWindow.WriteLine("I'm thinking of a number between 1 and 10.")
'  get your guess
```

Notice how the number selected is between 1 and 10.

Next, you input your guess using the **ReadNumber** method:

```
'  get your guess
TextWindow.Write("What do you think it is? ")
YourGuess = TextWindow.ReadNumber()
```

With this information, your guess is next analyzed for correctness using a Small Basic **If** structure:

```
'  analyze guess and print results
If (YourGuess = ComputerNumber) Then
  '  you got it
  TextWindow.WriteLine("You got it!! That’s my number!")
ElseIf (YourGuess < ComputerNumber) Then
  '  too low
  TextWindow.WriteLine("You are too low!! My number was " +
ComputerNumber)
Else
  '  too high
  TextWindow.WriteLine("You are too high!! My number was " +
ComputerNumber)
EndIf
```

You should be able to see how this works. Save your program by clicking the **Save** button.

The finished code in the Small Basic editor should appear as:

```
'
'  Number Program
'  Beginning Small Basic
'
TextWindow.Title = "Guess the Number Game"
'  get the computer's number between 1 and 10
ComputerNumber = Math.GetRandomNumber(10)
TextWindow.WriteLine("I'm thinking of a number between 1 and 10.")
'  get your guess
TextWindow.Write("What do you think it is? ")
YourGuess = TextWindow.ReadNumber()
'  analyze guess and print results
If (YourGuess = ComputerNumber) Then
  '  you got it
  TextWindow.WriteLine("You got it!! That's my number!")
ElseIf (YourGuess < ComputerNumber) Then
  '  too low
  TextWindow.WriteLine("You are too low!! My number was " +
ComputerNumber)
Else
  '  too low
  TextWindow.WriteLine("You are too high!! My number was " +
ComputerNumber)
EndIf
```

Run the Program

Run the program. Eliminate any syntax, run-time or logic errors you may encounter. You should now see (I resized the text window a little):

Enter your guess and make sure the computer provides the correct analysis. Here's the results of my guess:

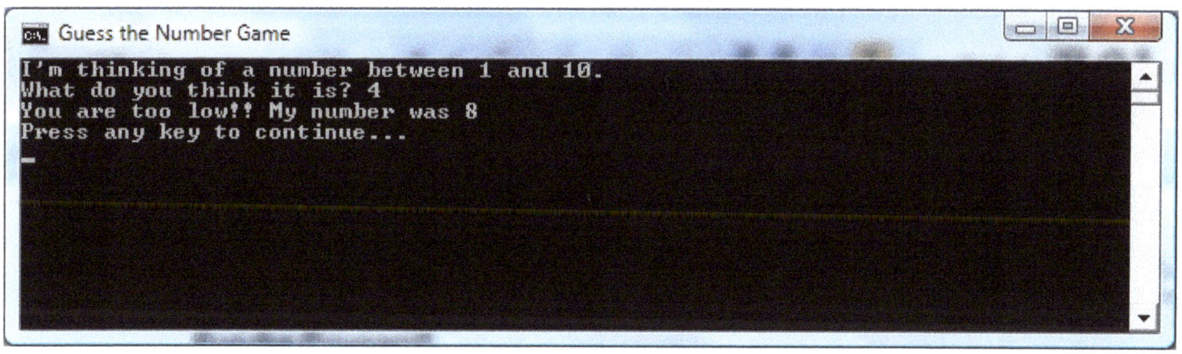

Run the program again and again until you know it can determine if a guess is correct, too low or too high. You should always thoroughly test your program to make sure all options work. Save your program if you needed to make any changes.

Other Things to Try

A good modification would be to offer more informative messages following a guess. Have you ever played the game where you try to find something and the person who hid the item tells you, as you move around the room, that you are freezing (far away), cold (closer), warm (closer yet), hot (very close), or burning up (right on top of the hidden item)? Try to modify the **Guess the Number** game to give these kind of clues. That is, the closer you are to the correct number, the warmer you get. To make this change, you will need the Small Basic **absolute value** function, **Math.Abs**. Recall this function returns the value of a number while ignoring its sign (positive or negative).

In our number guessing game, we can use **Math.Abs** to see how close a guess is to the actual number. One possible decision logic is:

```
If (YourGuess = ComputerNumber) Then
  ' Small Basic code for correct answer
ElseIf (Math.Abs(YourGuess - ComputerNumber) <= 1) Then
  ' Small Basic code when burning up - within 1 of correct answer
ElseIf (Math.Abs(YourGuess - ComputerNumber) <= 2) Then
  ' Small Basic code when hot - within 2 of correct answer
ElseIf (Math.Abs(YourGuess - ComputerNumber) <= 3) Then
  ' Small Basic code when warm - within 3 of correct answer
Else
  ' Small Basic code when freezing - more than 3 away
EndIf
```

I'm sure you noticed it was kind of a pain to only get one guess at the computer's number. A great modification to this program would be to add the capability of entering another guess, based on the computer's analysis. Then, you could see how many guesses it takes to "hone in" on the correct answer. To do this requires capability we haven't discussed yet in this course. But, don't worry, this idea of **looping** is covered in the next class. With looping, or the capability to repeat code, we will modify the Guess the Number game to allow repeated guesses until correct.

Adding the ability to enter improved guesses opens up a number of additional modifications you could make to this little game. One suggestion is to allow the user to input the upper range of numbers that can be guessed. That way, the game could be played by a wide variety of players. Use a maximum value of 10 for little kids, 1000 for older kids. Implement the "hot, warm, cold" If logic discussed above. Or, perhaps make the program into a math game, and tell the guesser "how far away" the guess is. I'm sure you can think of other ways to change this game. Have fun doing it.

Summary

In this class, you learned a lot of new material. You discovered there are three types of errors that try to attack your hard work: syntax errors, run-time errors and logic errors. You learned about a key part of Small Basic programming - decision making. You learned about logical expressions, comparison operators, logical operators, and If structures. And, you had fun with random numbers in the Guess the Number game. You are well on your way to being a Small Basic programmer.

6

Small Basic Looping, Subroutines

Review and Preview

The programs we build are becoming more detailed, especially with the capability to make decisions using the If structure. In this class, you learn about another very important programming concept – looping, which allows you to repeat blocks of code. You also learn about subroutines, which are self-contained blocks of code that accomplish given tasks. And, you will build a Lemonade Stand simulation as your program.

Small Basic - The Fourth Lesson

In the Guess the Number program built in Class 5, we noted it would be nice if we could continue to make guesses until we got the correct number. To do this requires the ability to repeat segments of code. In this Small Basic lesson, we learn how to add this looping capability to our Small Basic programs. We will also learn about subroutines, which allow us to write better, more compact programs.

Small Basic Loops

Many (in fact, most) Small Basic programs require repetition of certain code blocks. For example, as just noted, the Guess the Number game we built could really use it. Or, you may want to roll a die (simulated die of course) until it shows a six. Or, you might generate some math results until a value has been achieved. This idea of repeating code is called iteration or **looping**.

In Small Basic, one way of looping is with the **While** loop:

```
While (Expression)
  ' Small Basic code block to repeat while Expression is true
EndWhile
```

In this structure, all code between While and EndWhile is repeated **while** the given logical **Expression** is **true**.

Notice a while structure looks a lot like a simple **If** structure:

```
If (Expression) Then
  ' Small Basic code block to process if Expression is true
EndIf
```

What's the difference? In the If structure, the code block is processed just once if Expression is true. In the While structure, the code block is continually processed as long as Expression remains true.

Note a **While** loop structure will not execute even once if Expression is false the first time through. If we do enter the loop (Expression is true), it is assumed at some point Expression will become false to allow exiting. Once this happens, code execution continues at the statement following the EndWhile statement. This brings up a very important point about loops – if you get in one, make sure you get out at some point. In the While loop, if Expression is always true, you will loop forever – something called an infinite loop.

Let's look at a couple of examples. First, here is a loop that can be used in a rocket countdown. It repeats as long as (while) the variable **Counter** (starting at 10) is greater than or equal to 0:

```
Counter = 10
While (counter >= 0)
  TextWindow.WriteLine("Counter is " + Counter)
  Counter = Counter - 1
EndWhile
TextWindow.WriteLine("Blastoff!!")
```

Start Small Basic and type in this code. Run it and you will see:

Another example:

```
Rolls = 0
Counter = 0
While (Counter < 10)
  '  Roll a simulated die
  Roll = Roll + 1
  TextWindow.WriteLine("Roll Number " + Roll)
  If (Math.GetRandomNumber(6) = 6) Then
    Counter = Counter + 1
    TextWindow.WriteLine("That's " + Counter + " sixes!")
  EndIf
EndWhile
```

This loop repeats while the **Counter** variable remains less than 10. The counter variable is incremented (increased by one) each time a simulated die rolls a 6. The **Roll** variable tells you how many rolls of the die were needed to roll 10 sixes. Theoretically, it should take 60 rolls since there is a 1 in 6 chance of rolling a six. Type this code in the Small Basic editor and run it. You will see something like this:

In this case, it took 63 rolls. Because you are using random numbers, you will see different results.

As mentioned, if the logical expression used by a While loop is false the first time the loop is encountered, the code block in the While loop will not be executed. This may be acceptable behavior – it may not be. We can build a loop that will always be executed at least once. To do this we need to introduce the Small Basic **Goto** statement. A Goto allows you to transfer code execution to anywhere in your code. A Goto requires a **label**. A label is like a bookmark – it can be named anything you want. A label name is always followed by a colon. An example is:

```
MyLabel:
```

Anytime we want to transfer program execution to this label statement, we use a Goto:

```
Goto MyLabel
```

You do not write the colon in the Goto statement. Using these new concepts in a loop, we have what we'll call a **Goto loop**:

```
MyLabel:
  ' Small Basic code block to process
If (Expression) Then
  Goto MyLabel
EndIf
```

The code block repeats as long as **Expression** is true. Unlike the While loop, this loop is always executed at least once. Somewhere in the loop, Expression should be changed to false to allow exiting.

Let's look at examples of the **Goto** loop. What if we want to keep adding three to a **Sum** until the value exceeds 50. This loop will do it:

```
Sum = 0
SumLoop:
  Sum = Sum + 3
  TextWindow.WriteLine("Sum is " + sum)
If (Sum <= 50) Then
  Goto SumLoop
EndIf
```

Try this code in Small Basic and you should see:

Or, another dice example:

```
Sum = 0
Roll = 0
SumLoop:
  ' Roll a simulated die
  Die = Math.GetRandomNumber(6)
  Sum = Sum + Die
  Roll = Roll + 1
  TextWindow.WriteLine("After Roll #" + Roll + ", the sum is " +
Sum)
If (Sum <= 30) Then
  Goto SumLoop
EndIf
```

This loop rolls a simulated die (**Die**) while the **Sum** of the rolls does not exceed 30. It also keeps track of the number of rolls (**Roll**) needed to achieve this sum. Try this in Small Basic and you will see something like this (again, due to random numbers, your results will be different):

You need to decide which of the loop structures (While, Goto) fits your program. Recall the major difference is that a Goto loop is always executed at least once; a While loop may never be executed. And, make sure you can always get out of a loop. In both looping structures, this means that, at some point, the checking logical expression must become false to allow exiting the loop. When you exit a While loop, processing continues at the next Small Basic statement after the EndWhile. In a Goto loop, processing continues at the Small Basic statement after the If structure checking whether the loop should repeat.

If, at some point in the code block of a loop, you decide you need to immediately leave the loop, a **Goto** statement can also do this. You just need a label statement at the end of the loop. When the **Goto** statement is encountered, processing is immediately transferred to the labeled statement. As an example:

```
Sum = 0
Roll = 0
SumLoop:
  ' Roll a simulated die
  Die = Math.GetRandomNumber(6)
  If (die = 5) Then
    TextWindow.WriteLine("Rolled a 5 - we're stopping!")
    Goto EndLoop
  EndIf
  Sum = Sum + Die
  Roll = Roll + 1
  TextWindow.WriteLine("After Roll #" + Roll + ", the sum is " +
Sum)
If (sum <= 30) Then
  Goto SumLoop
EndIf
EndLoop:
```

This is a modified version (new code is shaded) of the dice example we just looked at. In this example, the Die value is added to the Sum, unless the die rolls a 5. In that case, the loop is immediately exited via a Goto statement. When I run this code in Small Basic, I get:

Some times, we may not want to leave a loop completely but only skip statements not yet executed in the loop and immediately return to the beginning of the loop. In a While loop, this means control returns to the While statement. In a Goto loop, control is returned to the label starting the loop. In either case, a Goto statement (you will need to add a label if using a While) will do the job. Let's try this with the dice example (modified code is shaded):

```
Sum = 0
Roll = 0
SumLoop:
  '  Roll a simulated die
  Die = Math.GetRandomNumber(6)
  If (Die = 5) Then
    TextWindow.WriteLine("Rolled a 5!")
    Goto SumLoop
  EndIf
  Sum = Sum + Die
  Roll = Roll + 1
  TextWindow.WriteLine("After Roll #" + Roll + ", the sum is " +
Sum)
If (sum <= 30) Then
  Goto SumLoop
EndIf
EndLoop:
```

In this case, if a 5 is rolled (Die = 5), that value is just not included in Sum and program control transfers to the SumLoop label. The big difference is that the loop continues. Running this in Small Basic, I got:

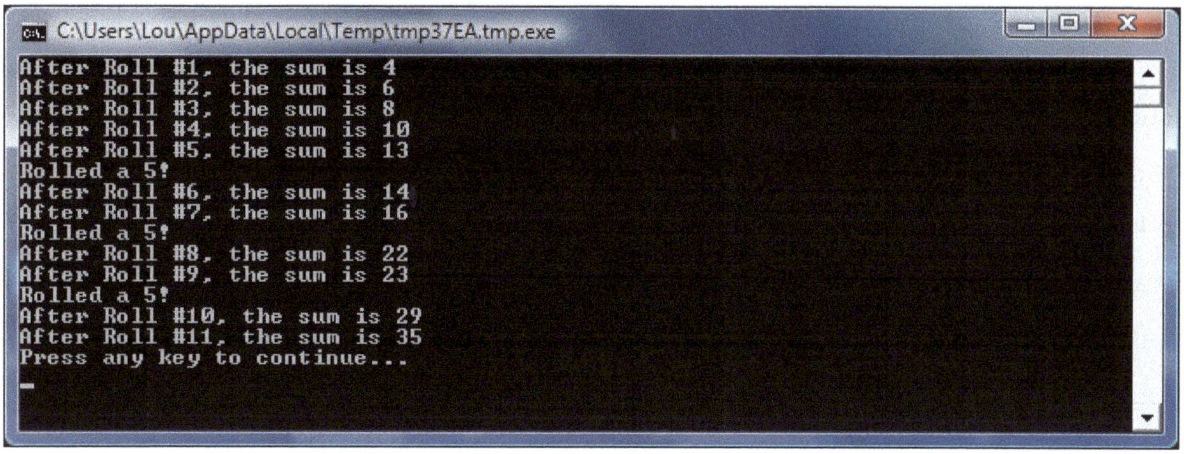

A Brief Interlude - Guess the Number Game (Revisited)

We'll return to our Small Basic lesson in a bit. But first, let's change the Guess the Number game from Class 5 so a user can have repeated guesses until getting the computer's number. It's a simple application of a **Goto** loop – we want to keep guessing as long as your guess does not equal the computer's number. Start Small Basic and open the Guess the Number game you built in Class 5. Resave the program (use the **Save As** toolbar button) as **Number2** in a folder of your choice. The modified code (changes are shaded) is:

```
'
'  Number Program
'  Beginning Small Basic
'
TextWindow.Title = "Guess the Number Game"
'  get the computer's number between 1 and 10
ComputerNumber = Math.GetRandomNumber(10)
TextWindow.WriteLine("I'm thinking of a number between 1 and 10.")

' Start Loop here
StartLoop:
'  get your guess
TextWindow.Write("What do you think it is? ")
YourGuess = TextWindow.ReadNumber()
'  analyze guess and print results
If (YourGuess = ComputerNumber) Then
  '  you got it
  TextWindow.WriteLine("You got it!! That’s my number!")
ElseIf (YourGuess < ComputerNumber) Then
  '  too low
  TextWindow.WriteLine("You are too low!!")
Else
  '  too high
  TextWindow.WriteLine("You are too high!!")
EndIf
If (YourGuess <> ComputerNumber) Then
  Goto StartLoop
EndIf
```

In this code, we have made a few changes. We have put the code asking for your guess and checking your guess within a loop (using the "not equals" operator in the If structure at the end). And, we have removed the display of the computer's number when you are too low or too high (that would make the game too easy). We have saved this modification in the **Number2** folder in the course programs folder (**\BeginSB\BSB Code**).

Once you have modified the code, run it. Here's one time I played:

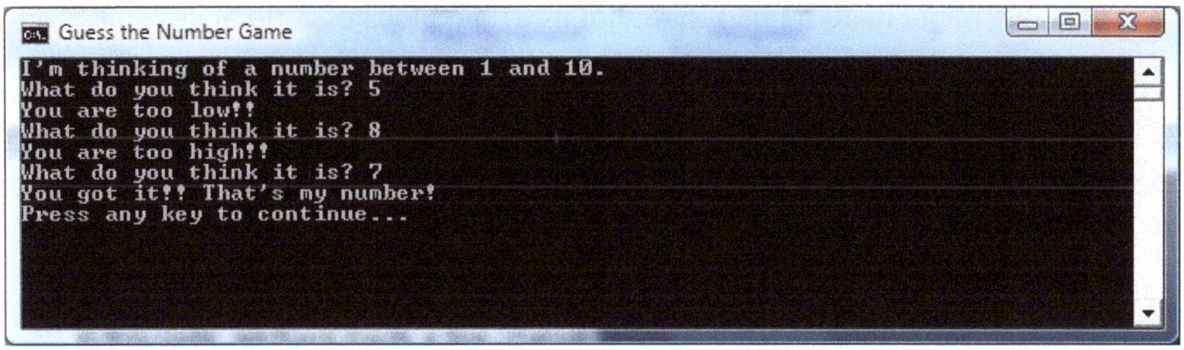

I think you will agree that this is a much better game. The loop has really improved this program. We often use our programming skills to improve programs we build. You can probably think of many more improvements. Maybe add another loop that, once one game ends, you are given the option to play again. With repeated guesses possible, you might like to extend the possible range for the computer's number (try it with 100). Maybe implement the "hot, warm, cold" logic outlined in Class 5. Have fun trying your own ideas!!

Now, back to the Small Basic lesson.

Small Basic - The Fourth Lesson

The interlude is over. We finish this class' Small Basic lesson with a look at a very important Small Basic programming concept – the subroutine.

Small Basic Subroutines

In the looping discussion, we saw how code in one particular block could be repeated until some desired condition was met. Many times in Small Basic programs, we might have a need to repeat a certain block of code at several different points in the program. Why would you want to do this? Say we had a game that requires us to roll 5 dice and add up their individual values to yield a sum. What if we needed to do this at 10 different places in our program? We could write the code, then copy and paste it to the 10 different places. I think you can see problems already. What if you need to change the code? You would need to change it in 10 different places. What if you needed to put the code in another place in your program? You would need to do another 'copy and paste' operation. There's a better way. And that way is to use a Small Basic **subroutine**.

A subroutine allows you to write the code to perform certain tasks just once. Then, whenever you need to access the code in your program, you can "call it.," providing any information it might need to do its tasks. Subroutines are the building blocks of a Small Basic program. Using subroutines in your Small Basic programs can help divide a complex application into more manageable units of code. Just think of a subroutine as a code block you can access from anywhere in a Small Basic program. When you call the subroutine, program control goes to that subroutine, performs the assigned tasks and returns to the calling program. It's that easy.

Let's see how to create and call a subroutine. Subroutines go at the end of your '**main'** program code. A subroutine named **MySubroutine** would have the form (starts with a **Sub** keyword and ends with **EndSub**):

```
Sub MySubroutine
  ' Code to be executed in the subroutine
EndSub
```

You execute, or call, this subroutine using:

```
MySubroutine()
```

The parentheses are needed to tell the computer you are executing a subroutine. When the subroutine is called, the corresponding code is executed until the **EndSub** line is reached. At this point, program execution returns to the 'main' code after the line calling the subroutine. A subroutine can access and use any variable you use in your main program. Likewise, your main program can use any variables defined in your subroutines. In computer talk, we say the variables in a Small Basic program have **global scope**.

Let's try to make this clearer by looking at a few of subroutine examples. We'll do the dice example of rolling five dice and computing their sum. The subroutine that accomplishes this task is:

```
Sub RollDice
  Die1 = Math.GetRandomNumber(6)
  Die2 = Math.GetRandomNumber(6)
  Die3 = Math.GetRandomNumber(6)
  Die4 = Math.GetRandomNumber(6)
  Die5 = Math.GetRandomNumber(6)
  SumDice = Die1 + Die2 + Die3 + Die4 + Die5
EndSub
```

This subroutine is named **RollDice** and the variable **SumDice** has the resulting sum.

Using this subroutine, any time you need the sum of five dice in your program, you would use:

```
RollDice()
A = SumDice
```

After this code is executed, the variable **Sum** will have sum of five dice. Let's try it. Start Small Basic and type this code (just the two lines above with an added WriteLine statement and the subroutine): Notice the subroutine is placed after the 'main' code:

```
RollDice()
A = SumDice
TextWindow.WriteLine("Sum of five dice is " + A)

Sub RollDice
  Die1 = Math.GetRandomNumber(6)
  Die2 = Math.GetRandomNumber(6)
  Die3 = Math.GetRandomNumber(6)
  Die4 = Math.GetRandomNumber(6)
  Die5 = Math.GetRandomNumber(6)
  SumDice = Die1 + Die2 + Die3 + Die4 + Die5
EndSub
```

Run the code. When I do it, I get:

Notice we also have access to Die1, Die2, Die3, Die4 and Die5 if we want any of the individual dice values.

Now, we will build a subroutine that, given the length (**RectangleLength**) and width (**RectangleWidth**) of a rectangle, prints out the area of the rectangle. Here's that subroutine (yes, I know it's a very simple one):

```
Sub RectangleArea
  TextWindow.WriteLine("Your rectangle has an area of " +
RectangleWidth * RectangleHeight)
EndSub
```

To use this subroutine, you supply a value for the length variable and the width variable, then call the subroutine. Try this code in Small Basic:

```
RectangleWidth = 13
RectangleHeight = 15
RectangleArea()

Sub RectangleArea
  TextWindow.WriteLine("Your rectangle has an area of " +
RectangleWidth * RectangleHeight)
EndSub
```

Run this program and you should see:

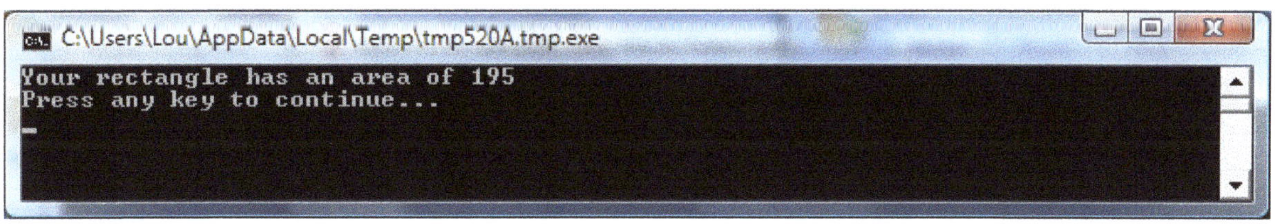

As you progress in your Small Basic programming education, you will become more comfortable with using subroutines and see how useful they are. In the remainder of this course, we will use subroutines when needed. Study each example to help learn how to build and use subroutines.

Program – Lemonade Stand

A very powerful use of computers is to do something called **simulation**. Before building an actual airplane, companies "build" the plane on a computer and simulate its performance. This is much cheaper and far safer than testing actual airplanes. Engineers simulate how a building might react to an earthquake to help them design better buildings. And, businesses use computers to simulate how decisions could affect their profits. Based on computer results, they decide how and where to invest their money. In this program, we will build a small business simulation. We will simulate the operation of the neighborhood kids' backyard lemonade stand. Based on the temperature, they set a selling price for their lemonade (the hotter it is, the more they can charge). They will then be told how many cups were sold and how much money was made. If the kids are too greedy, asking too much for their product, they won't sell as much. If they're too nice, they won't make as much money. It's a tough world out there! This program is saved in the **Lemonade** folder in the course programs folder (**\BeginSB\BSB Code**).

Program Design

Lemonade will be sold for five days (simulated days). On each day, the temperature is reported. Based on this temperature, a price is set for a cup of lemonade. You will be told how many cups of lemonade were sold and how much money was made. The steps to follow on each day:

1. Computer picks a random temperature.
2. Assign a price for each cup of lemonade.
3. Computer analyzes the information and computes number of cups sold.
4. Sales are computed and displayed.

The first step is a straightforward use of the random number generator. In the second step, we will use the **ReadNumber** method to get the price. Step 3 is the difficult one – how does the computer determine cups sold? In this program, we will give you the code to do this (code we made up) in the form of a subroutine you can use. This is something done all the time in programming – borrowing and using someone else's code. In this subroutine, you provide the temperature and the price and the subroutine computes the number of cups sold. Finally, the **WriteLine** method will be used to output the results of each day's sales.

Program Development

Start **Small Basic**. Click the **New Program** button in the toolbar. A blank editor will appear. Immediately save the program as **Lemonade** in a folder of your choice.

First, type the following header information and add a window title:

```
'
' Lemonade Stand
' Beginning Small Basic
'

TextWindow.Title = "Lemonade Stand"
```

We will use several variables in this program. Notice with good naming practice, you can see what each variable is. We keep track of the current day (**DayNumber**), the temperature (**Temperature**), the price set for a cup of lemonade (**CupPrice**), the number of cups sold (**CupsSold**), the amount of money made in one day (**DaySales**) and the current total sales (**TotalSales**). One note – we will assume the **CupPrice** is an whole number value in cents, while **DaySales** and **TotalSales** are in dollars. For our foreign readers, there are 100 cents in a dollar. Feel free to change the units to anything you want.

Now, we write the code, following the previously defined programming steps. First, initialize the **DayNumber** and TotalSales and begin a **While** loop over the five days of sales:

```
'  start loop of five days
DayNumber = 1
TotalSales = 0.0
While (DayNumber < 6)
  ' go to next day
  DayNumber = DayNumber + 1
EndWhile
```

Each day begins with the computer selecting a random temperature (degrees F, you can change this if you want) between 61 and 100 degrees:

```
  ' pick a random temperature between 61 and 100
  Temperature = Math.GetRandomNumber(40) + 60
```

Based on this, you set the price for each cup of lemonade:

```
  ' get price
  TextWindow.Write("How many cents are charged for a cup of
lemonade? ")
  CupPrice = TextWindow.ReadNumber()
```

With this information, the computer computes how many cups were sold and determines daily and total sales. The cups sold (**CupsSold**) will be computed in a subroutine named **GetSales**, with two inputs, **Temperature** and **CupPrice**. We will show you that subroutine soon. For now, just assume it is available so it can be called. The code to report sales is:

```
  ' get cups sold (from GetSales subroutine), provide sales report
  GetSales()
  DaySales = CupsSold * CupPrice / 100.0
  TotalSales = TotalSales + DaySales
  TextWindow.WriteLine("")
  TextWindow.WriteLine(CupsSold + " cups of lemonade were sold,
earning $" + DaySales + ".")
  If (dayNumber > 1) Then
    TextWindow.WriteLine("Total sales after " + DayNumber + " days
are $" + TotalSales + ".")
  EndIf
```

You should be able to see what's going on here. We find the **CupsSold**, compute daily and total sales and report the results. Notice that **TotalSales** are only displayed for the second through the fifth day (since, on the first day, daily and total sales are the same). Next, increment the **DayNumber**, close out the **While** loop:

```
  ' go to next day
  DayNumber = DayNumber + 1
EndWhile
TextWindow.WriteLine("")
TextWindow.WriteLine("The lemonade stand is now closed.")
```

The subroutine (**GetSales**) that computes the number of cups sold is placed after the final line of 'main' code. For this subroutine, we will just give you the code, so you can type it in. We will try to explain what's going on. Here is the complete subroutine. Type this in the editor, being careful to check that it is correct (note some lines are fairly long):

```
Sub GetSales
  '
  '  GetSales subroutine
  '  input temperature Temperature and price CupPrice
  '  output number of cups sold - CupsSold
  '
  '  find best price
  BestPrice = (Temperature - 60) * (46 - Math.GetRandomNumber(20))
/ 40 + 20
  ' find maximum sales
  MaxSales = (Temperature - 60) * (231 -
Math.GetRandomNumber(100)) / 40 + 20
  ' find sales adjustment
  Adjustment = 1.0 - Math.Abs((CupPrice - BestPrice) / BestPrice)
  If (Adjustment < 0.0) Then
    Adjustment = 0.0
  EndIf
  ' compute adjusted sales
  CupsSold = Math.Floor(Adjustment * MaxSales)
EndSub
```

Let me try to explain what I'm doing here. First, I assume there is a **BestPrice** (most that can be charged) for a cup of lemonade, based on the temperature (**Temperature**). More can be charged on hotter days. The equation used assumes this BestPrice ranges from 20 cents at 60 degrees to a random value between 45 and 65 cents at 100 degrees. Similarly, there is a maximum number of cups that can be sold (**MaxSales**) based on Temperature. More can be sold on hotter days. The equation used assumes MaxSales ranges from 20 cups at 60 degrees to a random value between 150 and 250 at 100 degrees. Before returning a number of cups, I compute an **adjustment** variable. This is used to adjust sales based on input price (**CupPrice**). If the "asking" price is more than the BestPrice, sales will suffer because people will think too much is being asked for the product. Sales will also suffer if too little is charged for lemonade! Why's that? Many people think if something doesn't cost enough, it may not be very good. You just can't win in the business world. So, adjustment is computed based on how far the set price (**CupPrice**) is from the **BestPrice**. Once the adjustment is found, it is multiplied times MaxSales to compute CupsSold:

```
CupsSold = Math.Floor(Adjustment * MaxSales)
```

You may not recognize the **Math.Floor** function being used here. This function converts the product (Adjustment * MaxSales) to a whole number. You can't sell a fraction of a cup! This brings up a good point. Many times, when using someone else's Small Basic code, you may see things you don't recognize. What do you do? The best thing is to consult some Small Basic reference (another Small Basic programmer, a textbook, the Microsoft website) and do a little research and self-study. This helps you learn more and helps you become a better Small Basic programmer.

Notice if you play this program as a game, you wouldn't know all the details behind the rules (how CupSales are computed). You would learn these rules as you play. That's what happens in all computer games – the games have rules and, after many plays, you learn what rules the programmers have included. If you can't follow all the math in the **GetSales** subroutine, that's okay. You don't really need to – just trust that it does the job. Actually, Small Basic programmers use subroutines all the time without an understanding of how they work (do you know how Small Basic finds the square root of a number?). In such cases, we rely on the subroutine writer to tell us what information is required (inputs) and what information is computed (outputs) and trust that the subroutine works. That's the beauty of subroutines – we get code without doing the work.

The finished code in the Small Basic editor should appear as (note the subroutine is at the end of the code:

```
'
'  Lemonade Stand
'  Beginning Small Basic
'
TextWindow.Title = "Lemonade Stand"
'  start loop of five days
DayNumber = 1
TotalSales = 0.0
While (DayNumber < 6)
  ' pick a random temperature between 61 and 100
  Temperature = Math.GetRandomNumber(40) + 60
  TextWindow.WriteLine("")
  TextWindow.WriteLine("Welcome to Day " + DayNumber + ", the
temperature is " + Temperature + " degrees.")
  ' get price
  TextWindow.Write("How many cents are charged for a cup of
lemonade? ")
  CupPrice = TextWindow.ReadNumber()
  ' get cups sold (from GetSales subroutine), provide sales report
  GetSales()
  DaySales = CupsSold * CupPrice / 100.0
  TotalSales = TotalSales + DaySales
  TextWindow.WriteLine("")
```

```
  TextWindow.WriteLine(CupsSold + " cups of lemonade were sold,
earning $" + DaySales + ".")
  If (dayNumber > 1) Then
    TextWindow.WriteLine("Total sales after " + DayNumber + " days
are $" + TotalSales + ".")
  EndIf
  ' go to next day
  DayNumber = DayNumber + 1
EndWhile
TextWindow.WriteLine("")
TextWindow.WriteLine("The lemonade stand is now closed.")

Sub GetSales
  '
  '  GetSales subroutine
  '  input temperature Temperature and price CupPrice
  '  output number of cups sold - CupsSold
  '
  '  find best price
  BestPrice = (Temperature - 60) * (46 - Math.GetRandomNumber(20))
/ 40 + 20
  ' find maximum sales
  MaxSales = (Temperature - 60) * (231 -
Math.GetRandomNumber(100)) / 40 + 20
  ' find sales adjustment
  Adjustment = 1.0 - Math.Abs((CupPrice - BestPrice) / BestPrice)
  If (Adjustment < 0.0) Then
    Adjustment = 0.0
  EndIf
  ' compute adjusted sales
  CupsSold = Math.Floor(Adjustment * MaxSales)
EndSub
```

Run the Program

Run the program. Eliminate any syntax, run-time or logic errors you may encounter. You may have to recheck your typing, especially in the subroutine. You should now see something like this in the text window:

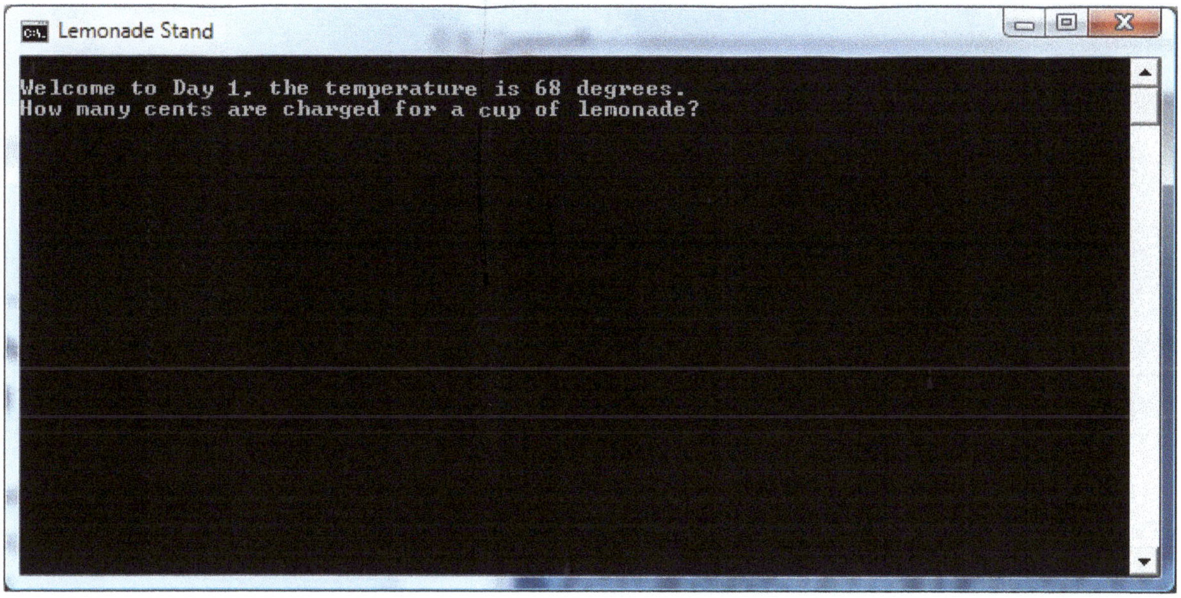

Enter a value for cup price (in cents) and you should see something like:

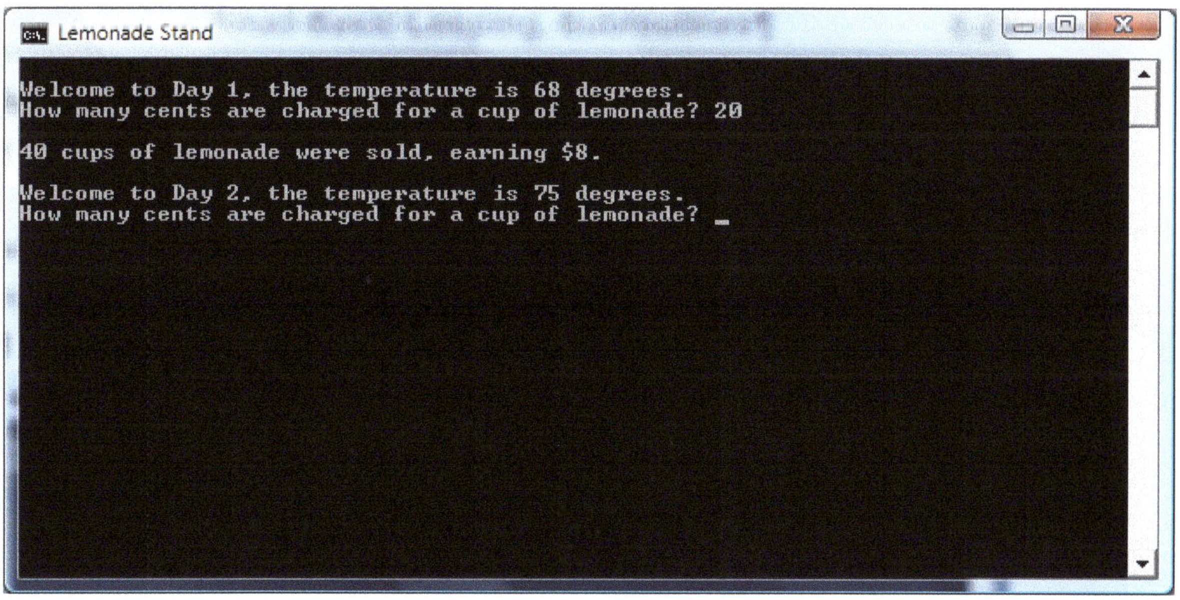

Continue playing until the lemonade stand has run for five days. Here's my try at five days:

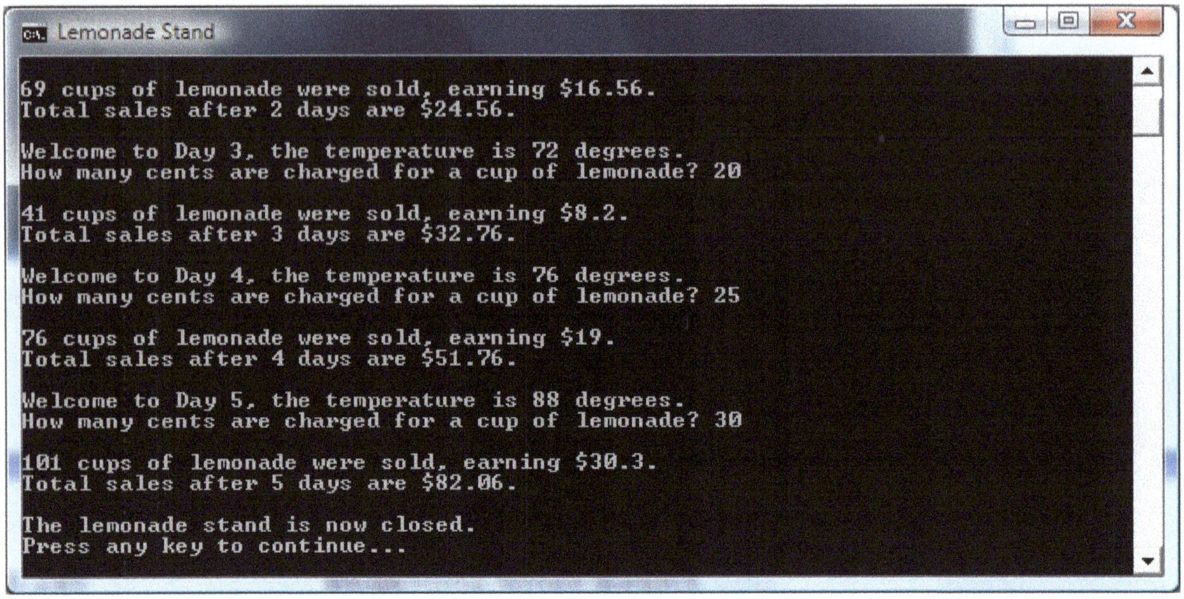

Try several runs to see if you can improve your playing skills. Save your program if you needed to make any changes.

Other Things to Try

You have the beginnings of a fun computer simulation. Can you think of changes you would like to make? Add more days, change the rules in **GetSales**? Why not add another loop so you can play it over and over again without having to rerun the application each time? We have some ideas.

To make lemonade, you need products: cups, lemons, sugar. These cost money and cut into your profit. A great modification would be to add the need for shopping into the simulation. You would need to figure out how much of each product is needed to make a cup of lemonade. Research at a grocery store would tell you the cost to make a cup of lemonade. Then, you can determine how much profit is made on sales. This gives the program more of a "real-world" flavor.

Add more randomness into the program. Maybe consider both temperature and weather conditions. Add a chance of precipitation into the computations. You wouldn't sell as much lemonade on a hot rainy day as you would on a hot clear day. Try these and any other ideas you have.

Summary

In this class, with the added capabilities of looping and subroutines, we greatly expanded our Small Basic programming skills. Being able to repeat blocks of code lets us build far more useful programs. We used this capability to allow multiple guesses in our Guess the Number game and the Lemonade Stand program was seen to be a fun computer simulation. In the next class, we'll study another looping method that gives us even more programming power.

7

More Small Basic Looping, Arrays

Review and Preview

In the last class, we introduced the idea of looping – repeating code blocks. In this class' Small Basic lesson, we look at another way to loop (the Small Basic **For** loop) and at a new way to refer to variables. And, as a program, we build a version of the card game War. We'll learn how to get the computer how to shuffle a deck of cards!

Small Basic - The Fifth Lesson

In this Small Basic lesson, we look at a technique for counting (another looping method) and ways to store large numbers of variables.

Small Basic For Loops

In an earlier class, we looked at two types of loops – the **While** loop and the **Goto** loop. In each of these, we loop (repeat code) until some particular condition is met, perhaps not knowing how many times the loop would be repeated. If we know how many times we want to loop, we call that counting. Small Basic offers a convenient way to do counting: the **For** loop.

A **For** loop has this structure:

```
For LoopCounter = StartValue To EndValue Step Increment
  ' Small Basic code to execute goes here]
EndFor
```

The **For** statement creates a loop (place where code is repeated) in which the variable **LoopCounter** (called the **loop index**) is initialized at **StartValue** and is then incremented (changed) by **Increment** each time the program executes the loop. The words "Step Increment" are optional. If they are omitted, an increment (Step) of one is assumed. The end of the loop is marked by the **EndFor** statement. The loop is repeated until LoopCounter reaches or exceeds **EndValue**. When the loop is completed, program execution continues after the EndFor statement. Each **For** statement in your Small Basic program must have a matching **EndFor** statement. The code between the For and EndFor should be indented. For loops can be nested (one loop in another), but that's beyond this class.

Let's look at a few For examples to see how they work. This loop will repeat 10 times:

```
For LoopCounter = 1 To 10
  TextWindow.WriteLine(LoopCounter)
EndFor
```

LoopCounter has a value of 1 the first time through loop, 2 the second time through, and repeats until LoopCounter has a value of 10 the final time through. Run this in Small Basic and you'll see:

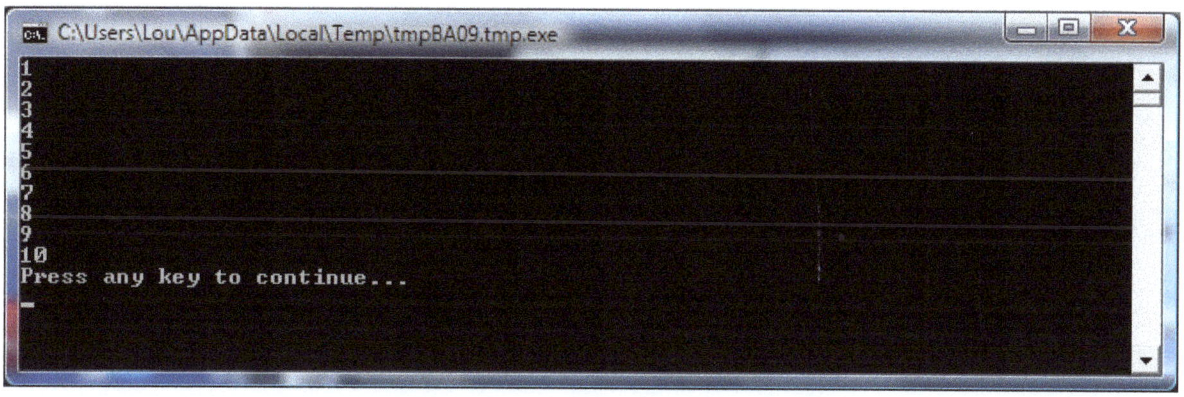

How about a rocket launch countdown? This loop will do the job:

```
For LoopCounter = 10 To 0 Step -1
  TextWindow.WriteLine(LoopCounter)
EndFor
```

Here LoopCounter starts at 10 and goes down by 1 (Step -1) each time the loop is repeated. Yes, you can have negative Step values. Running this in Small Basic shows:

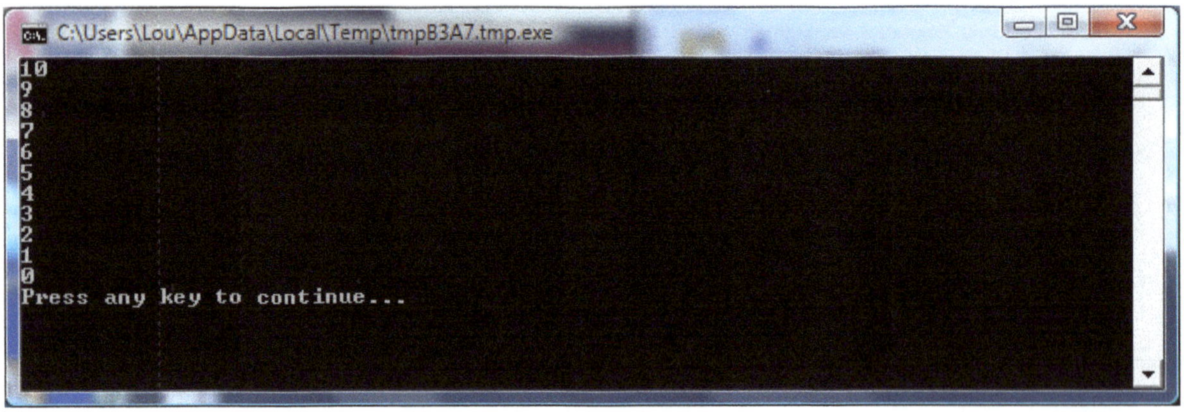

And, you can have increments that are not 1. This loop counts from 0 to 200 by 5's:

```
For LoopCounter = 0 To 200 Step 5
  TextWindow.WriteLine(LoopCounter)
EndFor
```

Run this in Small Basic and you get:

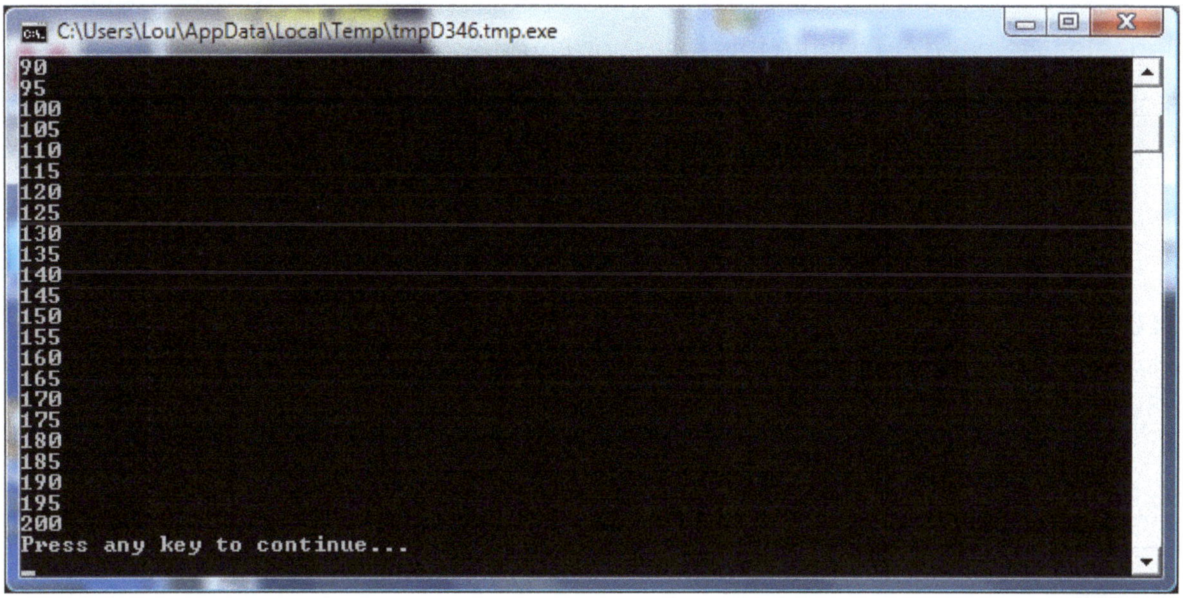

Study each of these examples so you have an idea of how the For loops work. Use them when you need to count. A very useful application of these loops is when working with a new type of variable – the array. We look at that now.

Variable Arrays

The local school principal has recognized your great Small Basic programming skills and has come for your help. Everyone (300 students) in the school has just taken a basic skills test. The principal wants you to write a program that stores each student's name and score. The program should rank (put in order) the scores and compute the average score. The code to do this is not that hard. The problem we want to discuss here is how do we define all the variables we need? To write this test score program, you need 300 variables to store student names and 300 variables to store student scores. We are required to create and set a value for every variable we use. We could use variables like this:

```
Student1
Student2
Student3
   .
   .
Student300

Score1
Score2
Score3
   .
   .
Score300
```

And, to get this information input, we could type code like this:

```
TextWindow.Write("Enter Student 1 Name - ")
Student1 = TextWindow.Read()
TextWindow.Write("Enter Student 1 Score - ")
Score1 = TextWindow.Read()
TextWindow.Write("Enter Student 2 Name - ")
Student2 = TextWindow.Read()
TextWindow.Write("Enter Student 2 Score - ")
Score2 = TextWindow.Read()
TextWindow.Write("Enter Student 3 Name - ")
Student3 = TextWindow.Read()
TextWindow.Write("Enter Student 3 Score - ")
Score3 = TextWindow.Read()
  .
  .
  .
TextWindow.Write("Enter Student 300 Name - ")
Student300 = TextWindow.Read()
TextWindow.Write("Enter Student 300 Score - ")
Score300 = TextWindow.Read()
```

This would work, but I don’t think you want to type all this code. Let’s look at another way.

Small Basic provides a way to store a large number of variables under the same name - **variable arrays**. Each variable in an array, called an **element**, must have the same data type, and they are distinguished from each other by an array index. For the student example, we could use two arrays:

```
Student[1]
Student[2]
Student[3]
   .
   .
Student[300]

Score[1]
Score[2]
Score[3]
   .
   .
Score[300]
```

We now have the student names stored in the **Student** array and the scores in the **Score** array. The numbers in brackets are the array **indices**.

We now have 300 **Student** variables and 300 **Score** variables available for our use. Each variable in an array is referred to by its name and index. For example, to assign the 150th student's information, we write two lines of code like this:

```
Student[150] = "Billy Gates"
Score[150] = 100
```

With these new definitions of student names and scores, the process of getting each name and score can be placed in a For loop:

```
For StudentNumber =1 to 300
  TextWindow.Write("Enter Student " + StudentNumber + " Name - ")
  Student[StudentNumber] = TextWindow.Read()
  TextWindow.Write("Enter Student " + StudentNumber + " Score - ")
  Score[StudentNumber] = TextWindow.Read()
EndFor
```

Study this code to convince yourself that it is the same as that long code we showed earlier. I think you agree this is much simpler (and easy to modify if there are more or fewer students).

Array variables can be used anywhere regular variables are used. They can be used on the left side of assignment statements or in expressions. To add up the first three test scores, you would write:

```
Sum = Score[1] + Score[2] + Score[3]
```

Or this For loop averages all 300 scores:

```
ScoreSum = 0
For StudentNumber = 1 to 300
  ScoreSum = ScoreSum + Score[StudentNumber]
EndFor
Average = ScoreSum / 300
```

To find an average of a group of numbers, you add up all the numbers then divide by the number of numbers you have. In this code, ScoreSum represents the sum of all the numbers. We set this to zero to start. Then, each time through the loop, we add the next score to that "running" sum. The loop adds up all 300 scores making use of the Score array. The first time through it adds in Score[1], then Score[2], then Score[3], and so on, until it finishes by adding in Score[300]. Once done, the Average is computed by dividing ScoreSum by 300.

Do you see how the For loop greatly simplifies the task of adding up 300 numbers? This is a nice shortcut method we can use when working with arrays. We will start to use arrays in our Small Basic programs. You will learn very quickly how nice they are when working with lots of variables.

"Shuffle" Method

Let's use our new knowledge of arrays and for loops to write a very useful subroutine. A common task in any computer program is to randomly sort a list of consecutive integer values. Why would you want to do this? Say you have four answers in a multiple choice quiz. Randomly sort the integers 1, 2, 3, and 4, so the answers are presented in random order. Or, you have a quiz with 30 questions. Randomly sort the questions for printing out as a worksheet. Or, the classic application is shuffling a deck of standard playing cards (there are 52 cards in such a deck). In that case, you can randomly sort the integers from 1 to 52 to "simulate" the shuffling process. Let's build a "shuffle" routine. We call it a shuffle routine, recognizing it can do more than shuffle a card deck. Our routine will sort any number of consecutive integers.

Usually when we need a computer version of something we can do without a computer, it is fairly easy to write down the steps taken and duplicate them in Small Basic code. We've done that with the programs built so far in this course. Other times, the computer version of a process is easy to do on a computer, but hard or tedious to do off the computer. When we shuffle a deck of cards, we separate the deck in two parts, then interleaf the cards as we fan each part. I don't know how you could write Small Basic code to do this. There is a way, however, to write Small Basic code to do a shuffle in a more tedious way (tedious to a human, easy for a computer).

We will perform what could be called a "one card shuffle." In a one card shuffle, you pull a single card (at random) out of the deck and lay it aside on a pile. Repeat this 52 times and the cards are shuffled. Try it! I think you see this idea is simple, but doing a one card shuffle with a real deck of cards would be awfully time-consuming. We'll use the idea of a one card shuffle here, with a slight twist. Rather than lay the selected card on a pile, we will swap it with the bottom card in the stack of cards remaining to be shuffled. This takes the selected card out of the deck and replaces it with the remaining bottom card. The result is the same as if we lay it aside.

Here's how the shuffle works with N numbers:

- Start with a list of N consecutive integers.
- Randomly pick one item from the list. Swap that item with the last item. You now have one fewer items in the list to be sorted (called the remaining list), or N is now N - 1.
- Randomly pick one item from the remaining list. Swap it with the item on the bottom of the remaining list. Again, your remaining list now has one fewer items.
- Repeatedly remove one item from the remaining list and swap it with the item on the bottom of the remaining list until you have run out of items. When done, the list will have been replaced with the original list in random order.

Confusing? Let's show a simple example with N = 5 (a very small deck of cards).

The starting list is (with 5 remaining items):

1	2	3	4	5

Remaining List

We want to pick one item, at random, from this list. Using the Small Basic random number generator, we would choose a random number from 1 to 5. Say it was 3. We take the third item in the list (the 3) and swap it with the last item in the list (the 5). We now have:

1 2 5 4 3

Remaining List

There are 4 items in the remaining list. Pick a random number from 1 to 4 - say it's 4. The fourth item in the remaining list is 4. Swap it with the last item in the remaining list. Wait a minute! The last item in the remaining list is the 4. In this case, we swap it with itself, or it stays put. If the random number was something other than 4, there really would have been a swap here. We now have:

1 2 5 4 3

Remaining List

There are 3 items in the remaining list. Pick a random number from 1 to 3 - say it's 1. The first item in the list is 1. Swap the 1 with the last item in the remaining list (the 5), giving us:

5 2 1 4 3

Remaining List

There are 2 items in the remaining list. Pick a random number from 1 to 2 - say it's 1. The first item in the list is 5. Swap the 5 with the last item in the remaining list (the 2), giving us the final result, the numbers 1 to 5 randomly sorted:

2 5 1 4 3

Pretty neat how this works, huh?

We want to describe the one card shuffle with Small Basic code. Most of the code is straightforward. The only question is how to do the swap involved in each step. This swap is easy on paper. How do we do a swap in Small Basic? Actually, this is a common Small Basic task and is relatively simple. At first thought, to swap variable A with variable B, you might write:

```
A = B
B = A
```

The problem with this code is that when you replace A with B in the first statement, you have destroyed the original value of A. The second statement just puts the newly assigned A value (B) back in B. Both A and B now have the original B value! Actually, swapping two variables is a three step process. First, put A in a temporary storage variable. Then, replace A by B. Then, replace B by the temporary variable (which holds the original A value). If T is the temporary variable, a swap of A and B is done using:

```
T = A
A = B
B = T
```

You use swaps like this in all kinds of Small Basic applications.

Now, we'll see the Small Basic code (a subroutine) that uses a one card shuffle to randomly sort N consecutive integer values. The subroutine is named **NIntegers** and has a single input value **NumberOfIntegers**, the number of integers to shuffle. When done the random list of integers is in the array **NumberList**. Other variables used in the subroutine are:

TempValue - temporary variable used for swapping
LoopCounter - loop counter variable
ItemPicked - variable giving item picked in remaining list
Remaining - loop variable giving number of items in remaining list

The code is:

```
Sub NIntegers
  'One card shuffle code
  'Initialize NumberList
  For LoopCounter = 1 to NumberOfIntegers
    NumberList[LoopCounter] = LoopCounter
  EndFor
  'Work through Remaining values
  'Start at NumberOfItems and swap one value
  'at each For loop step
  'After each step, Remaining is decreased by 1
  For Remaining = NumberOfIntegers to 2 Step -1
    'Pick item at random
    ItemPicked = Math.GetRandomNumber(Remaining)
    'Swap picked item with bottom item
    TempValue = NumberList[Remaining]
    NumberList[Remaining] = NumberList[ItemPicked]
    NumberList[ItemPicked] = TempValue
  EndFor
EndSub
```

Study this code and see how it implements the procedure followed in the simple five number example. It's not that hard to see. Understanding how such code works is a first step to becoming a good Small Basic programmer. Notice this bit of code uses both things we talked about in this class' Small Basic lesson: For loops and arrays.

Let's build a quick example using **Small Basic** to try all these new concepts and see how the shuffle routine works using 10 integers. Start Small Basic and add this code to the editor:

```
NumberOfIntegers = 10
NIntegers()
For I = 1 To 10
  TextWindow.WriteLine("Integer " + I + " is " + NumberList[i])
EndFor
```

This code computes an array **NumberList** of length 10 (**NumberOfIntegers** = 10). This array is filled with the random integers 1 to 10 by calling the **NIntegers** subroutine. The results are printed using 10 calls to **WriteLine** in the **For** loop.

Now, type in the **NIntegers** subroutine as shown earlier. Make sure this code goes after the main code above. The finished code looks like this:

```
NumberOfIntegers = 10
NIntegers()
For I = 1 To 10
  TextWindow.WriteLine("Integer " + I + " is " + NumberList[i])
EndFor

Sub NIntegers
  'One card shuffle code
  'Initialize NumberList
  For LoopCounter = 1 to NumberOfIntegers
    NumberList[LoopCounter] = LoopCounter
  EndFor
  'Work through Remaining values
  'Start at NumberOfItems and swap one value
  'at each For loop step
  'After each step, Remaining is decreased by 1
  For Remaining = NumberOfIntegers to 2 Step -1
    'Pick item at random
    ItemPicked = Math.GetRandomNumber(Remaining)
    'Swap picked item with bottom item
    TempValue = NumberList[Remaining]
    NumberList[Remaining] = NumberList[ItemPicked]
    NumberList[ItemPicked] = TempValue
```

```
    EndFor
EndSub
```

Once this code is in, run the program. Correct any errors that might occur. Double-check you have entered the NIntegers subroutine correctly. When I run this little example, I get (you will get different numbers – remember they're random!):

Notice how the array (**MyIntegers**) contains a random listing of the integers from 1 to 10, as desired. If I run it again, I get:

Obviously, the list is now different. For your reference, this program has been saved in the **Shuffle** folder in the course programs folder (**\BeginSB\BSB Code**).

Program – Card Wars

In this program, we create a simplified version of the kid's card game - War. You play against the computer. You each get half a deck of cards (26 cards). Each player turns over one card at a time. The one with the higher card wins the other player's card. The one with the most cards at the end wins. Obviously, the shuffle routine will come in handy here. We call this program Card Wars! This program is saved in the **CardWars** folder in the programs folder **(\BeginSB\BSB Code**).

Program Design

The game is conceptually simple. The steps to follow are:

1. Shuffle a deck of cards.
2. Computer gives itself a card and player a card.
3. Computer compares cards, the player with the higher card wins both cards.
4. Scores are computed and displayed.
5. Process continues until all cards have been dealt from the deck.

We can use our shuffle routine to shuffle the deck of cards (compute 52 random integers from 1 to 52). Describing the handed-out cards requires converting the integer card value to an actual card in the deck (value and suit). We will create a Small Basic method to do this. Comparing the cards is relatively easy (we'll add the capability to our card display method), as is updating and displaying the scores (we will use our old friend, the **WriteLine** method). No input is ever needed from the user (besides pressing a key on the keyboard to see the cards) – he/she merely watches the results go by.

Program Development

Before building the program, let's do a little "up front" work. In the **Program Design**, we see a need for a method that, given a card number (1 to 52), (1) determines and displays which card (suit, value) in a deck it represents, and (2) determines its corresponding **numerical** value to allow comparisons. We will create this method now.

Displaying a card consists of answering two questions: what is the card suit and what is the card value? The four suits are hearts, diamonds, clubs, and spades. The thirteen card values, from lowest to highest, are: 2, 3, 4, 5, 6, 7, 8, 9, 10, Jack (J), Queen (Q), King (K), Ace (A). We've seen in our shuffle routine that a card number will range from 1 to 52. How do we translate that card number to a card suit and value? (Notice the distinction between card **number** and card **value** - card number ranges from 1 to 52, card value can only range from 2 to Ace.) We need to develop some type of translation rule. This is done all the time in Small Basic. If the number you compute with or work with does not directly translate to information you need, you need to make up rules to do the translation. For example, the numbers 1 to 12 are used to represent the months of the year. But, these numbers tell us nothing about the names of the month. We need a rule to translate each number to a month name.

We know we need 13 of each card suit. Hence, an easy rule to decide suit is: cards numbered 1 - 13 are hearts, cards numbered 14 - 26 are diamonds, cards numbered 27 - 39 are clubs, and cards numbered 40 - 52 are spades. Suit is represented on the displayed card by the two picture boxes: picPlayer (your card) and picComputer (computer's card). For card values, lower numbers should represent lower cards. A rule that does this for each number in each card suit is:

Card Numbers

Hearts	Diamonds	Clubs	Spades	Card Value
1	14	27	40	2
2	15	28	41	3
3	16	29	42	4
4	17	30	43	5
5	18	31	44	6
6	19	32	45	7
7	20	33	46	8
8	21	34	47	9
9	22	35	48	10
10	23	36	49	J
11	24	37	50	Q
12	25	38	51	K
13	26	39	52	A

As examples, notice card 23 is a Jack of Diamonds. Card 31 is a 6 of Clubs. We now can describe cards. How do we compare them?

Card comparisons must be based on a numerical value, not displayed card value - it's difficult to check if K is greater than 7, though it can be done. So, one last rule is needed to relate card value to numerical value. It's a simple one - start with a 2 having a numerical value of 1 (lowest) and go up, with an Ace (A) having a numerical value of 13 (highest). This makes numerical card comparisons easy. Notice hearts card numbers already go from 1 to 13. If we subtract 13 from diamonds numbers, 26 from clubs numbers, and 39 from spades numbers, each of those card numbers will also range from 1 to 13. This gives a common basis for comparing cards. This all may seem complicated, but look at the Small Basic code and you'll see it really isn't.

Here is a Small Basic subroutine (**CardDisplay**) that takes the card number (**CardNumber**) as an input and returns its numeric value (**CardValue**) (1 to 13) to allow comparisons. The method also prints a description (value and suit) of the corresponding card, using the above table for translation .

```
Sub CardDisplay
  ' given CardNumber (1 - 52), prints description
  ' and returns numeric value CardValue
  Value[1] = "Two"
  Value[2] = "Three"
  Value[3] = "Four"
  Value[4] = "Five"
  Value[5] = "Six"
  Value[6] = "Seven"
  Value[7] = "Eight"
  Value[8] = "Nine"
  Value[9] = "Ten"
  Value[10] = "Jack"
  Value[11] = "Queen"
  Value[12] = "King"
  Value[13] = "Ace"
  'determine  card's suit,  numeric value CardValue
  If (CardNumber >= 1 And CardNumber <= 13) Then
    Suit = "Hearts"
    CardValue = CardNumber
  ElseIf (CardNumber >= 14 And CardNumber <= 26) Then
    Suit = "Diamonds"
    CardValue = CardNumber - 13
  ElseIf (CardNumber >= 27 And CardNumber <= 39) Then
    Suit = "Clubs"
    CardValue = CardNumber - 26
  Else
    Suit = "Spades"
    CardValue = CardNumber - 39
  EndIf
  ' print description
  TextWindow.WriteLine(Value[CardValue] + " of " + Suit)
EndSub
```

You should be able to see how this works. With this subroutine built, we can use it to create the complete Card Wars program.

Start **Small Basic**. Click the **New Program** button in the toolbar. A blank editor will appear. Immediately save the program as **CardWars** in a folder of your choice.

First, type the following header information and add a window title:

```
'
'  Card Wars
'  Beginning Small Basic
'

TextWindow.Title = "Card Wars"
```

We will use several variables. The current card number will be **CardIndex**, the two player scores are **ComputerScore** and **YourScore**. The values of the player cards are **ComputerCard** and Your Card. The shuffled 'deck' of cards is in the array **MyCards**. Start with necessary variable initializations:

```
CardIndex = 1
ComputerScore = 0
YourScore = 0
```

Next, shuffle the cards using the shuffle subroutine and setup the playing **While** loop (we keep playing as long as there are cards left):

```
'  shuffle the cards
NumberOfIntegers = 52
NIntegers()
MyCards = NumberList

' while loop starting game
While ((53 - cardIndex) > 0)
EndWhile
```

Now, in the While loop, start with the code that picks and displays the cards:

```
' display computer card, then your card
TextWindow.Write("My card:   ")
CardNumber = MyCards[CardIndex]
CardDisplay()
ComputerCard = CardValue
TextWindow.Write("Your card: ")
CardNumber = MyCards[CardIndex + 1]
CardDisplay()
YourCard = CardValue
```

In this code, we use the Write method, not **WriteLine**. This allows the card description to print on the same line as the "My card:" and "Your card:" headings.

Next, we check to see who wins (or if there is a tie) and compute the scores:

```
' see who won
If (YourCard > ComputerCard) Then
  TextWindow.WriteLine("You win!")
  YourScore = YourScore + 2
ElseIf (ComputerCard > YourCard) Then
  TextWindow.WriteLine("I win!")
  ComputerScore = ComputerScore + 2
Else
  TextWindow.WriteLine("It's a tie.")
  YourScore = YourScore + 1
  ComputerScore = ComputerScore + 1
EndIf
```

Next, we print the results:

```
  TextWindow.WriteLine("My Score:   " + ComputerScore)
  TextWindow.WriteLine("Your Score: " + YourScore)
  CardIndex = CardIndex + 2
  TextWindow.Write("There are " + (53 - cardIndex) + " cards
remaining.  Press any key.")
  TextWindow.Read()
  TextWindow.WriteLine("")
```

Note how we stop the code waiting for some user input to continue. This closes out the While loop. After the WhileEnd statement, a final game over message is printed::

```
TextWindow.WriteLine("Game over.")
```

After typing this code, you still need to add two subroutines: **DisplayCard** and the **NIntegers** shuffle subroutine. You can copy and paste NIntegers from the Shuffle program we built earlier in this class. And, if you want, you can copy and paste DisplayCard from these notes into the editor of Small Basic. That would save you lots of typing. But, go ahead and type the subroutines, if you'd like. In any case, make sure the two subroutines are there, after the main code.

For completeness, here is all the code from the Small Basic editor for the Card Wars program, including all methods (get ready, it's long!):

```
'
'  Card Wars
'  Beginning Small Basic
'
TextWindow.Title = "Card Wars"
CardIndexCardIndex == 1CardIndex = 1
ComputerScore = 0
YourScore = 0
'  shuffle the cards
NumberOfIntegers = 52
NIntegers()
```

```
MyCards = NumberList

' while loop starting game
While ((53 - cardIndex) > 0)
  ' display computer card, then your card
  TextWindow.Write("My card:   ")
  CardNumber = MyCards[CardIndex]
  CardDisplay()
  ComputerCard = CardValue
  TextWindow.Write("Your card: ")
  CardNumber = MyCards[CardIndex + 1]
  CardDisplay()
  YourCard = CardValue
  ' see who won
  If (YourCard > ComputerCard) Then
    TextWindow.WriteLine("You win!")
    YourScore = YourScore + 2
  ElseIf (ComputerCard > YourCard) Then
    TextWindow.WriteLine("I win!")
    ComputerScore = ComputerScore + 2
  Else
    TextWindow.WriteLine("It's a tie.")
    YourScore = YourScore + 1
    ComputerScore = ComputerScore + 1
  EndIf
  TextWindow.WriteLine("My Score:    " + ComputerScore)
  TextWindow.WriteLine("Your Score: " + YourScore)
  CardIndex = CardIndex + 2
  TextWindow.Write("There are " + (53 - cardIndex) + " cards
remaining.  Press any key.")
  TextWindow.Read()
  TextWindow.WriteLine("")
EndWhile
TextWindow.WriteLine("Game over.")


Sub CardDisplay
  ' given CardNumber (1 - 52), prints description
  ' and returns numeric value CardValue
  Value[1] = "Two"
  Value[2] = "Three"
  Value[3] = "Four"
  Value[4] = "Five"
  Value[5] = "Six"
  Value[6] = "Seven"
  Value[7] = "Eight"
```

```
  Value[8] = "Nine"
  Value[9] = "Ten"
  Value[10] = "Jack"
  Value[11] = "Queen"
  Value[12] = "King"
  Value[13] = "Ace"
  'determine  card's suit,  numeric value CardValue
  If (CardNumber >= 1 And CardNumber <= 13) Then
    Suit = "Hearts"
    CardValue = CardNumber
  ElseIf (CardNumber >= 14 And CardNumber <= 26) Then
    Suit = "Diamonds"
    CardValue = CardNumber - 13
  ElseIf (CardNumber >= 27 And CardNumber <= 39) Then
    Suit = "Clubs"
    CardValue = CardNumber - 26
  Else
    Suit = "Spades"
    CardValue = CardNumber - 39
  EndIf
  ' print description
  TextWindow.WriteLine(Value[CardValue] + " of " + Suit)
EndSub

Sub NIntegers
  'One card shuffle code
  'Initialize NumberList
  For LoopCounter = 1 to NumberOfIntegers
    NumberList[LoopCounter] = LoopCounter
  EndFor
  'Work through Remaining values
  'Start at NumberOfItems and swap one value
  'at each For loop step
  'After each step, Remaining is decreased by 1
  For Remaining = NumberOfIntegers to 2 Step -1
    'Pick item at random
    ItemPicked = Math.GetRandomNumber(Remaining)
    'Swap picked item with bottom item
    TempValue = NumberList[Remaining]
    NumberList[Remaining] = NumberList[ItemPicked]
    NumberList[ItemPicked] = TempValue
  EndFor
EndSub
```

Run the Program

Run the program. Eliminate any syntax, run-time or logic errors you may encounter. You may have to recheck your typing, especially in the method. You should see something like:

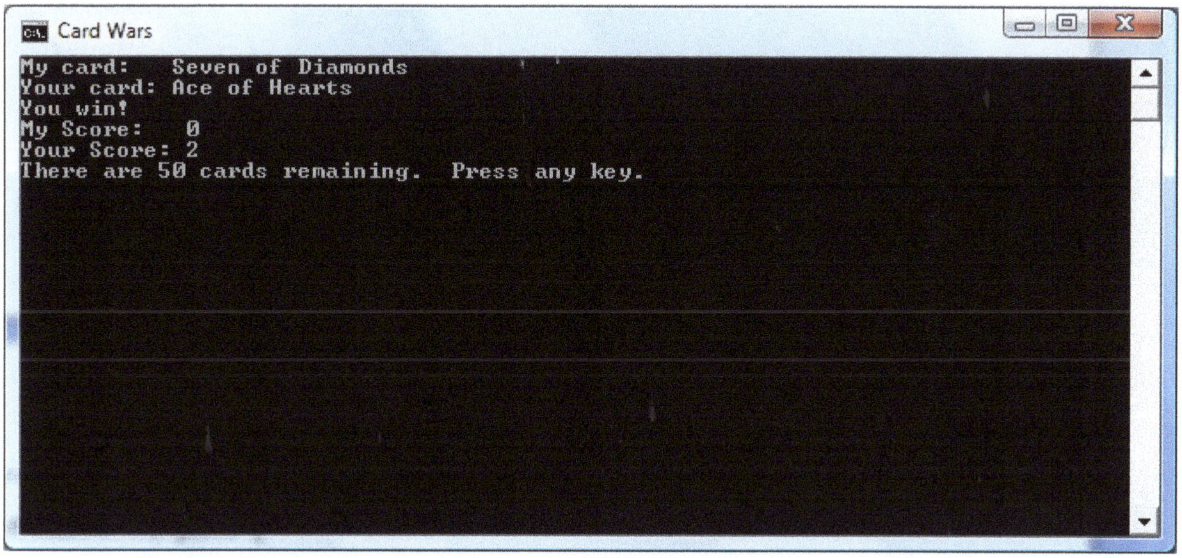

All you do at this point is press any key to see the next set of cards. You continue doing this until the card deck is empty (all 52 cards have been used). Make sure the program works correctly. Play through one game and check each comparison to make sure you get the correct result and score with each new card.

Here's the middle of my game:

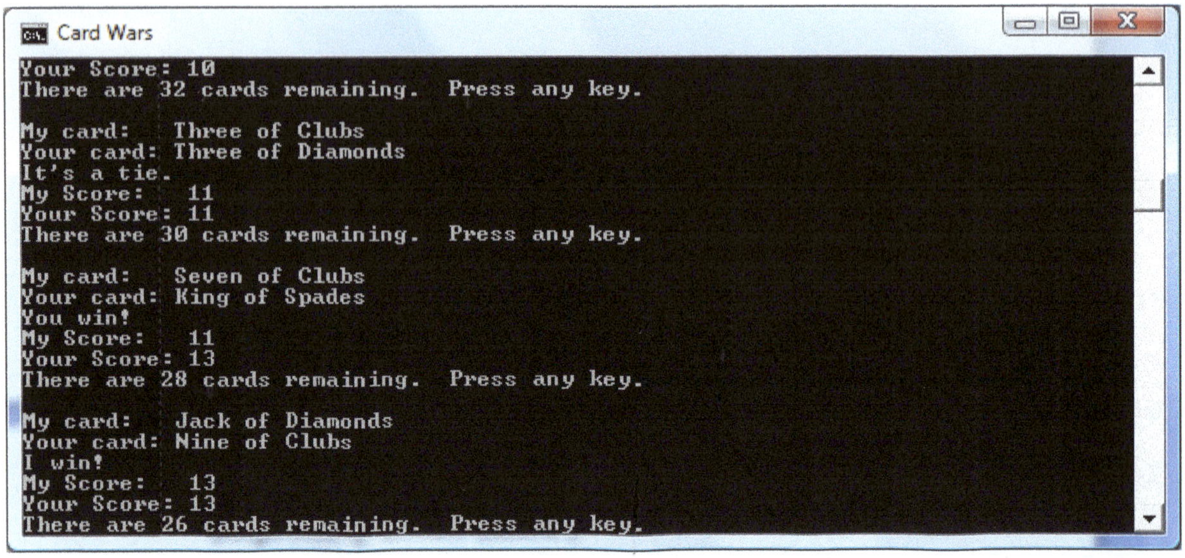

And here's the end:

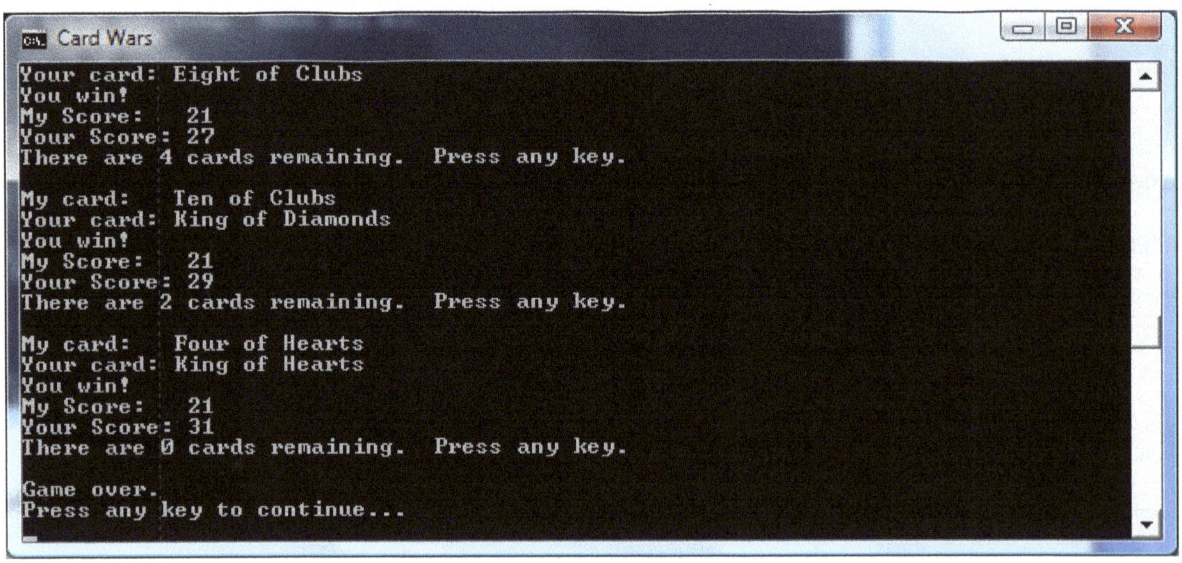

Go through the usual process of making sure the program works as it should. Once you're convinced everything is okay, have fun playing the game. Share your creation with friends. If you made any changes during the running process, make sure you save the program.

Other Things to Try

Possible changes to the Card Wars program are obvious, but not easy. One change would be to have more than two players. Set up three and four player versions. Perhaps add another loop to allow playing another game (without restarting the application).

In Card Wars, we stop the game after going through the deck one time. In the real card game of War, after the first round, the players pick up the cards they won, shuffle them, and play another round. Every time a player uses all the cards in their "hand," they again pick up their winnings pile, reshuffle and continue playing. This continues until one player has lost all of their cards. Another change to Card Wars would be to write code that plays the game with these rules. As we said, it's not easy. You would need to add code to keep track of which cards each player won, when they ran out of cards to play, how to reshuffle their remaining cards, and new logic to see when a game was over. Such code would use more arrays, more For loops, and more variables. If you want a programming challenge, go for it!

And, while you're tackling challenges, here's another. In the usual War game, when two cards have the same value - War is declared! This means each player takes three cards from their "hand" and lays them face down. Then another card is placed face up. The higher card at that time wins all 10 cards! If it's still a tie, there's another War. Try adding this logic to the game. You'll need to check if a player has enough cards to wage War. Another difficult task, but give it a try if you feel adventurous.

Summary

This class presented one of the more challenging programs yet. The code involved in shuffling cards and displaying cards, though straightforward, was quite involved. The use of arrays and For loops made the coding a bit easier. If you completely understood the Card Wars program, you are well on your way to being a good Small Basic programmer. Now, on to the next class, where we introduce an exciting programming area – graphics!

8

Small Basic Graphics, Mouse Methods

Review and Preview

You've seen and learned lots of Small Basic code by now. But, plain text window programs are a bit boring. In this class, we begin looking at a very fun part of Small Basic - adding graphics capabilities to our programs. We will also look at ways for Small Basic to recognize mouse inputs and have some fun with colors. You will build an electronic blackboard program.

Graphic User Interfaces (GUI)

All the Small Basic programs built in this course have been text applications. The computer asks some questions, you answer the questions. Because of the simplicity, using text applications is a good way to learn the Small Basic programming language. But, let's move on. Most programs in use feature what is called a **graphic user interface**. This is abbreviated **GUI** and pronounced "**gooey**." GUI applications are built with **windows** using **controls**, such as menus, toolbars, buttons, text boxes, selection boxes, scroll bars and other devices the user interacts with to operate the program. The primary interaction with these controls is via the computer mouse. If you've used a computer, you have used GUI applications. Examples include video games, spreadsheet programs, word processors, Internet browsers, the Windows operating system itself. The Small Basic environment is a GUI application. In each of these applications, you would be helpless without your mouse!

Running (and building) a GUI application is different than a text application. In a text application, everything runs sequentially – you are asked a series of questions, you provide a series of answers. In a GUI application, the computer sits and waits until the user does something – clicks on a menu item, chooses an option, types somewhere, moves a scroll bar, etc. We say the application is waiting for an **event** to occur. For this reason, GUI applications are called **event-driven**. When a particular event occurs, the application processes a series of statements (Small Basic statements in our applications) associated with that event. That series of statements is called an **event procedure**.

Here's how it works:

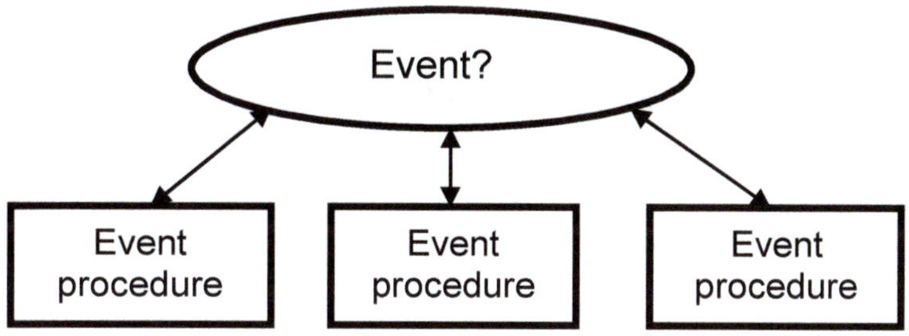

In this "model," the program waits (listens) for an **event** to occur. Once an event is detected, program control transfers to the corresponding **event procedure**. Once that procedure is executed, program control returns to the listener. In Small Basic, these procedures are subroutines. Each procedure is simply a set of Small Basic code with instructions on what to do if the particular event occurs. So, in GUI programming, we spend most of our time writing event procedures.

Let's look at some example of GUI applications and explain their use in the context of event-driven programming. Each of these examples should look very, very familiar. First, how about a **Savings Calculator** program:

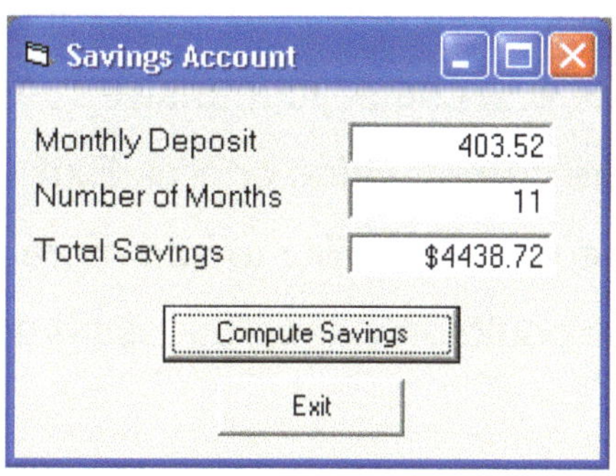

As I said, these examples will look familiar. This is a GUI version of the savings calculator program built in Class 4. This application uses controls called labels to display information and controls called text boxes for input. The user types in information in the boxes and, when done, clicks the button **Compute Savings** to get the desired results. This program has a procedure to process when it "hears"

(listens for) the **click** event on this button. That procedure will do the multiplication of the deposit amount and the number of months and display that result in the text box labeled **Total Savings**. The user can continue to try new values until clicking the **Exit** button (causing an exit event procedure to be executed). You should see some big advantages to GUI applications – easy to use, obvious to use, and they're really not too hard to develop.

How about a GUI **Guess the Number** game (from Class 5):

Here the computer tells you about the number it is thinking about. You enter your guess by adjusting the displayed value with the scroll bar control (causing a **scroll** event). You click the **Check Guess** button to invoke the corresponding event procedure where there is code to check your answer. At any time, you can click **Show Answer** to display the correct value or click **Exit** to stop the program. Notice GUI applications give you the ability to add more options. In the text version of this program, you could only keep guessing until you got the right answer.

Next, here's the GUI **Lemonade Stand** from Class 6:

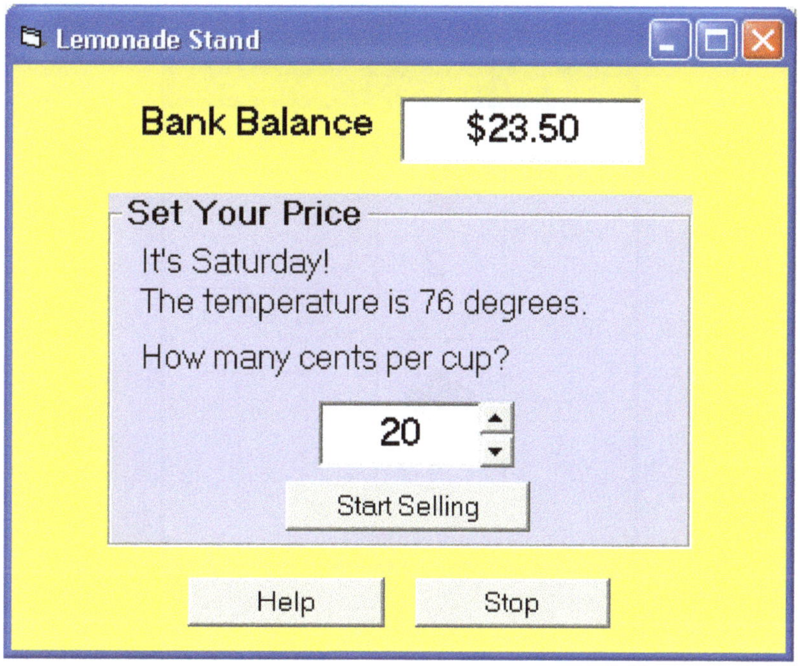

Your bank balance is displayed. You set the selling price (using a scroll bar) and click **Start Selling**. In this button's click event procedure is the code to compute the cups sold and present your sales results. Notice too, you can stop the application (**Stop** button) or even receive some clues (**Help** button). Again, GUI applications are very flexible.

Well, you must have known it was coming – the GUI **Card Wars** game from Class 7:

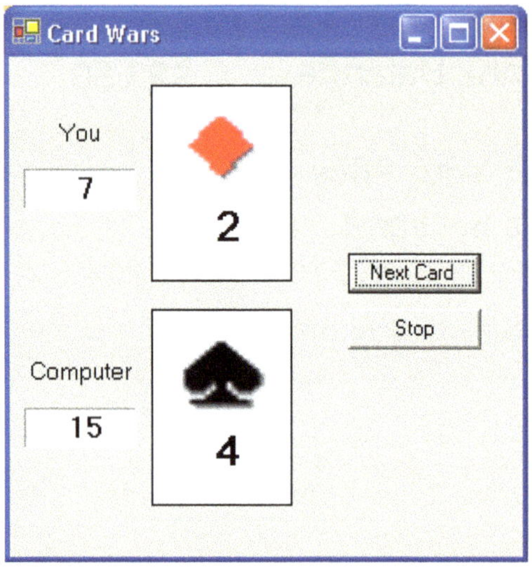

At this point in the game, you can see your score and the computer's score. And, notice rather than see a text description of the cards, a visual picture is shown! Another big advantage of GUI applications – they can show pictures! Clicking **Next Card** will process the code in the procedure to hand out two more cards, see who wins and adjust and display the scores.

You should be convinced by now that GUI applications are the way to go. They offer flexibility, ease of use, familiarity (every user has used a GUI application before), and they're nice to look at. In the rest of this course, we will build GUI (graphical) applications. They won't be as elaborate as the examples just seen. We won't use any controls – Small Basic does not provide controls. The Microsoft **Visual Basic** product does allow building of GUI applications with controls. BIBLEBYTE BOOKS (our company) produces more advanced courses that work with the Visual Basic language. If you want to learn more about GUI programs, these courses would be good to take after finishing **Beginning Small Basic**. In the remainder of this class, we will gain the skills needed to build a little drawing program. Again, there's a lot to learn and we'll take it step-by-step.

Small Basic Graphics

In this class, we will be looking at Small Basic to do one primary graphics task – drawing with the mouse. There are many steps with many new terms, but I know you are up to the task.

Graphics Window

The basic component of a graphics (GUI) application is the **graphics window**. It is a window with a title bar, a border and an area to build the application. It is the graphic counterpart to the text window we have been using. To display the graphics window, use the **Show** method:

```
GraphicsWindow.Show()
```

Try this and you will see (we've resized the window a bit):

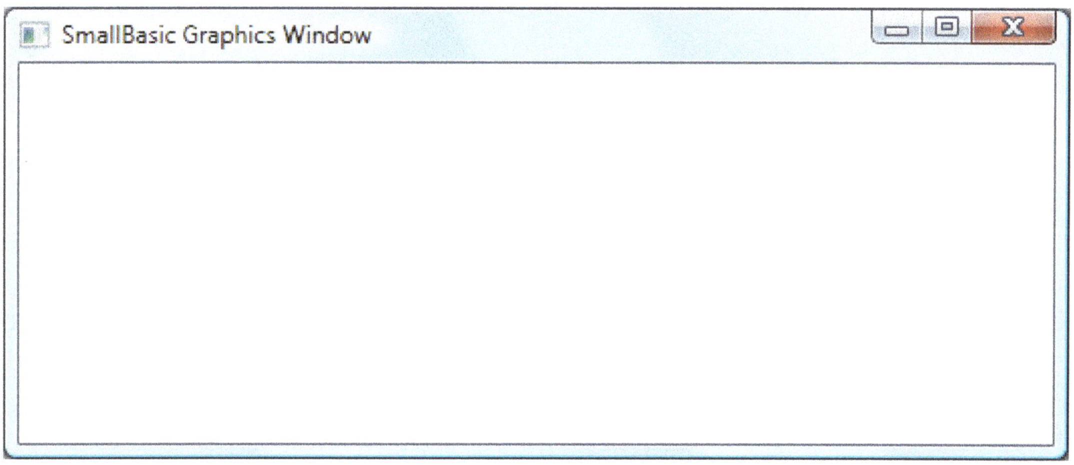

The graphics window has several **properties** we can change. The **Title** property sets the information in the title bar, the **Width** property sets the width of the window, while **Height** sets the height. Try this code:

```
GraphicsWindow.Show()
GraphicsWindow.Title ="Graphics Testing"
GraphicsWindow.Width = 400
GraphicsWindow.Height = 300
```

And you should see this smaller window:

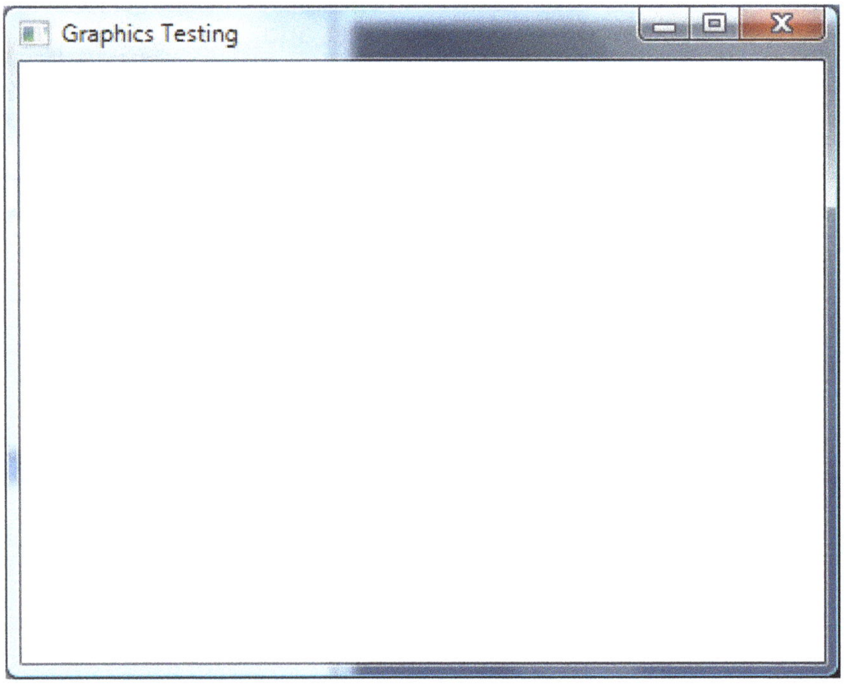

Not too hard, huh? We will use this window for drawing – save the code for now. Our drawing will require colors and objects called pens, so let's take a look at those concepts. Doesn't it make sense we need pens to do some drawing?

Colors

Colors play a big part in Small Basic graphics applications. Lines, rectangles, ovals can all be drawn and filled in various colors. The background color of the graphics window can be set to a particular color using the **BackgroundColor** property. These colors must be defined in Small Basic code. How do we do this? Small Basic has hundreds of colors we can use all referred to by specific names. The colors are listed in Appendix I to these notes. Some examples are:

Darker colors:

Black	DarkGray
Blue	Gray
Red	

Lighter colors:

White	Green
Cyan	Orange
LightGray	Yellow
Magenta	Pink

There are far more elaborate colors like **BlanchedAlmond**, **Linen**, **NavajoWhite, PeachPuff** and **SpringGreen**. As an example, to set the background color of the graphics window to yellow, use:

```
GraphicsWindow.BackgroundColor = "Yellow"
```

If you want, try this with the Graphics Test window we just built.

You can also define variables that take on color values. Say we want to define a variable named **MyRed** to represent the color red. Simply define your color in code using:

```
MyRed = "Red"
```

From this point on, you can use **MyRed** anywhere the red color is desired.

Pen Object

As mentioned, many of the graphics methods (including the method to draw lines) require a **Pen** object. This virtual pen is just like the pen you use to write and draw. You can choose color and width. Lines of code that accomplish this task are:

```
GraphicsWindow.PenColor = Color
GraphicsWindow.PenWidth = Width
```

where **Color** is the color your pen will draw in and **Width** is the integer width (a value of 1 by default) of the line (in pixels) drawn. This pen will draw a solid line.

We're almost ready to draw lines – be patient! Just one more concept and we're on our way.

Graphics Coordinates

We use Small Basic to draw using **graphics methods**. In this class, we will learn to draw lines and rectangles. Before looking at these methods, let's look at how we specify the points used to draw and connect lines. All graphics methods use a default **coordinate system**. This means we have a specific way to refer to individual points in the graphics window. The coordinate system used is:

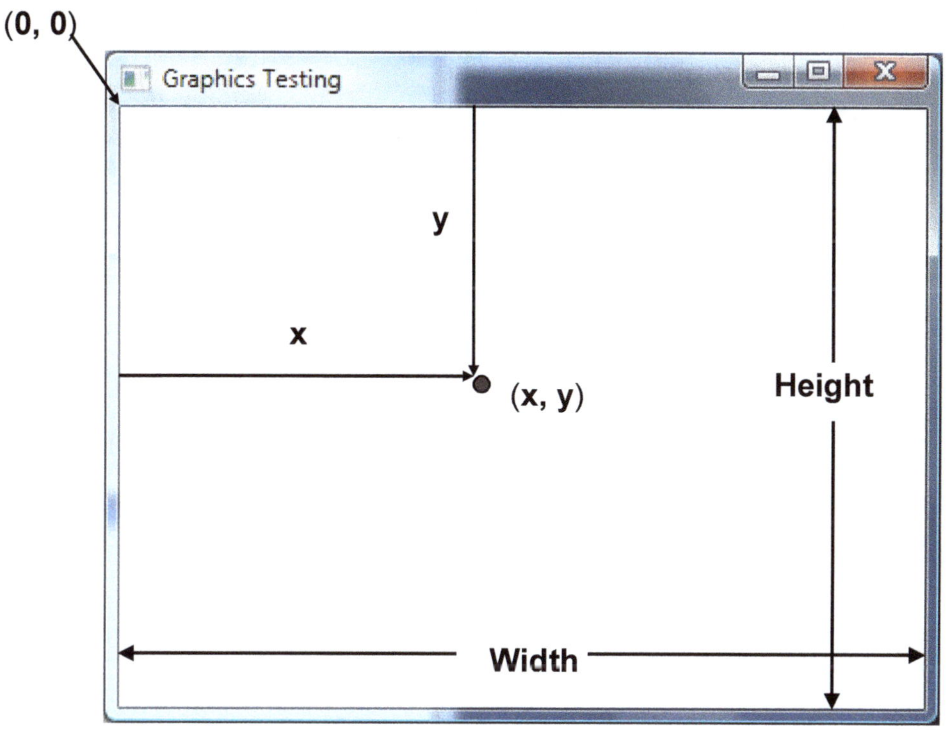

Recall the window is **Width** pixels wide and **Height** pixels high. We use two values (coordinates) to identify a single point in the window. The **x** (horizontal) coordinate increases from left to right, starting at **0**. The **y** (vertical) coordinate increases from top to bottom, also starting at **0**. Points in the region are referred to by the two coordinates enclosed in parentheses, or **(x, y)**. All values shown are in units of **pixels**. A pixel is a single dot in the graphics window. At long last, we're ready to draw some lines.

DrawLine Method

To do graphics (drawing) in Small Basic, we use the built-in **graphics methods**. In this class, we will look at graphics methods that can draw colored lines, rectangles and filled rectangles. As you progress in your programming skills, you are encouraged to study the many other graphics methods that can draw triangles, ellipses, polygons and virtually any shape, in any color. All graphics methods are applied to the **GraphicsWindow** object. Hence, to apply a graphics method named **GraphicsMethod**, use:

```
GraphicsWindow.GraphicsMethod(Arguments)
```

where **Arguments** are any needed arguments, or inputs needed by the graphics method.

The Small Basic **DrawLine** method is used to connect two points with a straight-line segment. If we wish to connect the point (**x1**, **y1**) with (**x2**, **y2**), the statement is:

```
GraphicsWindow.DrawLine(x1, y1, x2, y2)
```

The line will draw in the current pen **Color** and **Width**. To set these values, use (these lines go before the corresponding DrawLine method):

```
GraphicsWindow.PenColor = Color
GraphicsWindow.PenWidth = Width
```

To draw a blue line in our **Graphics Test** example we built earlier, add the three shaded lines to the code:

```
GraphicsWindow.Show()
GraphicsWindow.Title ="Graphics Testing"
GraphicsWindow.Width = 400
GraphicsWindow.Height = 300
GraphicsWindow.PenColor = "Blue"
GraphicsWindow.PenWidth = 1
GraphicsWindowGraphicsWindow.DrawLine(20, 50, 380, 280)
```

Run it in Small Basic. You should see:

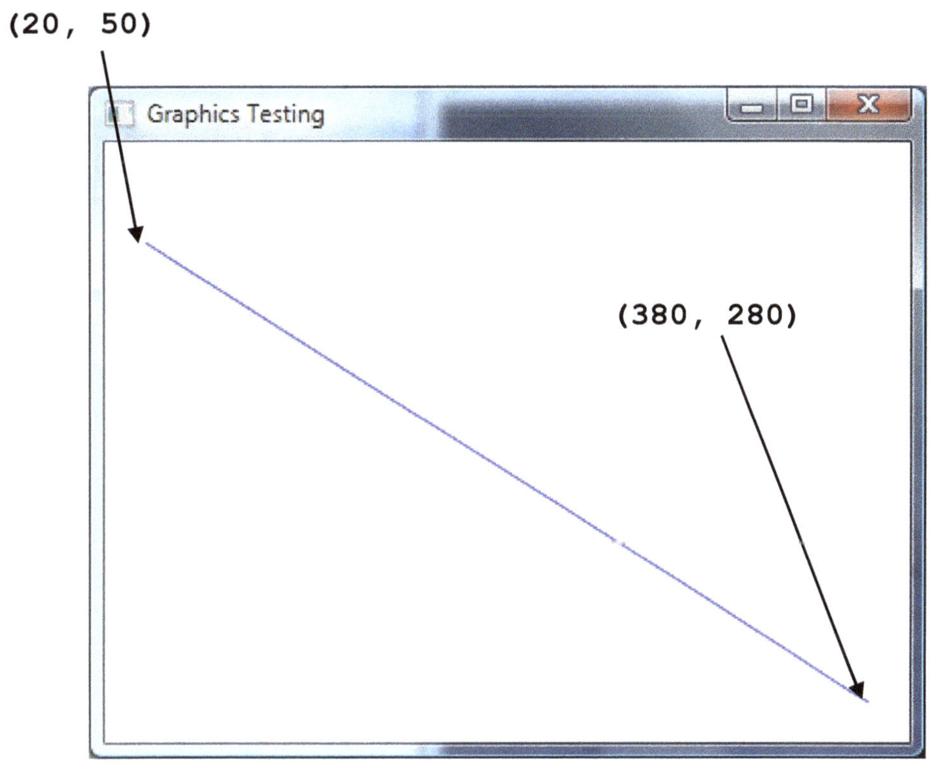

To connect the last point (**380, 280**) to another point (**200, 40**), add this line:

```
GraphicsWindow.DrawLine(380, 280, 200, 40)
```

This produces:

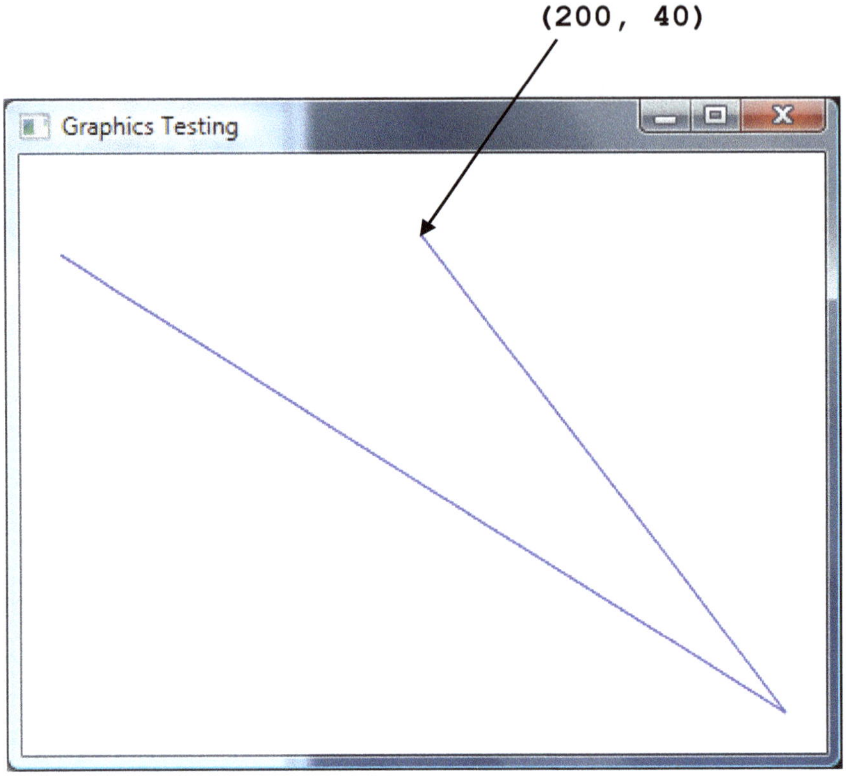

To continue the line (changing the pen color to red and width 5) to point (30, 290), add these lines:

```
GraphicsWindow.PenColor = "Red"
GraphicsWindow.PenWidth = 5
GraphicsWindow.DrawLine(200, 40, 30, 290)
```

You will see:

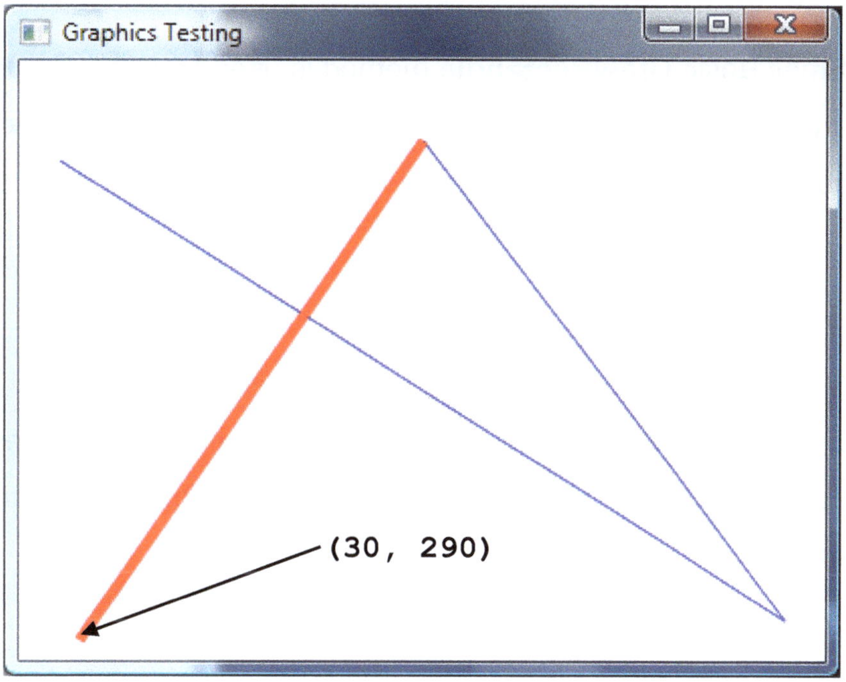

Add more line segments, using other points, colors and pen widths if you like. Note that for every line segment you draw, you need a separate **DrawLine** statement. To connect one line segment with another, you need to save the last point drawn to in the first segment (use two variables, one for x and one for y). This saved point will become the starting point for the next line segment. You can choose to change the color at any time you wish. Using many line segments, with many different colors, you can draw virtually anything you want! We'll do that with the Blackboard program in this class. As mentioned, there are many other graphics methods. Let's look at two more (dealing with rectangles) we will use in the Blackboard program.

DrawRectangle Method

The Small Basic **DrawRectangle** method is used to draw a rectangle. To draw a rectangle, we specify the upper left hand corner's coordinate (**x**, **y**) and the **width** and **height** of the rectangle. To draw such a rectangle in the graphics window:

```
GraphicsWindow.DrawRectangle(x, y, width, height)
```

The rectangle will draw with the current pen. To draw a blue rectangle (pen width 2) with the upper left corner at (20, 50), width 150 and height 100 in our **Graphics Test**, use this code:

```
GraphicsWindow.Show()
GraphicsWindow.Title ="Graphics Testing"
GraphicsWindow.Width = 400
GraphicsWindow.Height = 300
GraphicsWindow.PenColor = "Blue"
GraphicsWindow.PenWidth = 2
GraphicsWindow.DrawRectangle(20, 50, 150, 100)
```

This produces:

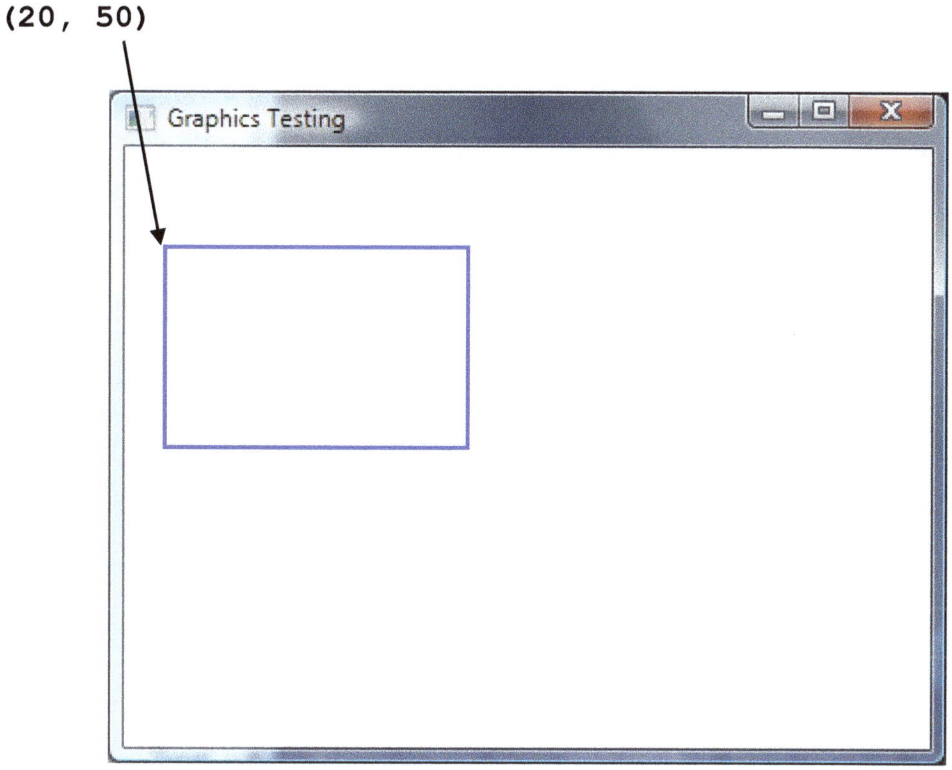

And, to draw a red rectangle of the same size with upper left corner at (140, 130), add these two lines:

```
GraphicsWindow.PenColor = "Red"
GraphicsWindow.DrawRectangle(140, 130, 150, 100)
```

This yields:

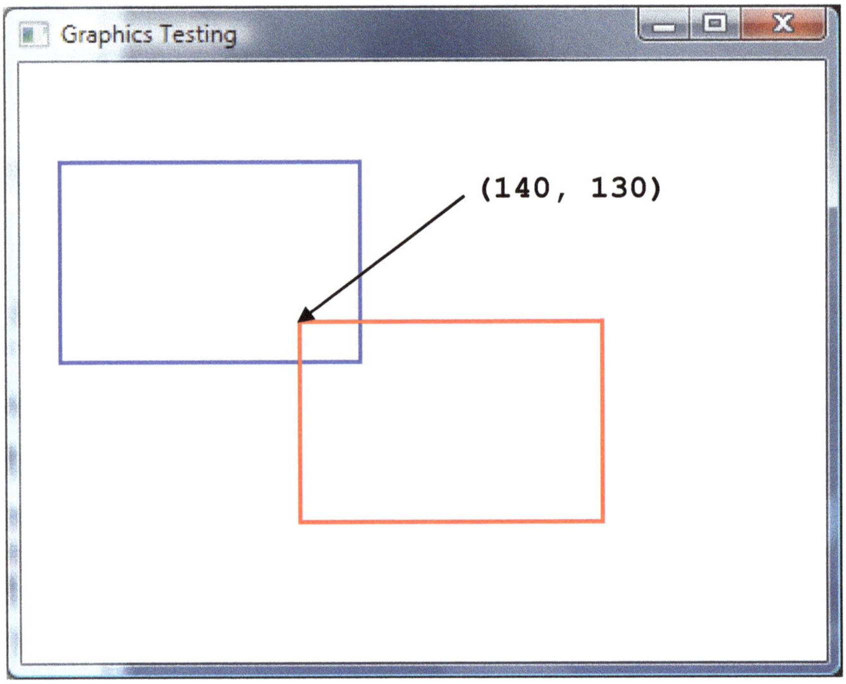

Try more rectangles if you like. Let's see how to fill the rectangles with color. To do this we need to look at the **Brush** object.

Brush Object

A **Brush** object is like a "wide" pen. It is used to fill areas with a color. It has a single property (**Color**). To set the brush color, use:

```
GraphicsWindow.BrushColor = Color
```

A brush is 'solid' – filling areas completely with the specified color.

FillRectangle Method

The Small Basic **FillRectangle** method is used to fill a rectangle with color. To fill a rectangle, we specify the upper left hand corner's coordinate (**x**, **y**) and the **width** and **height** of the rectangle. To draw such a rectangle in the graphics window, the statement is:

```
GraphicsWindow.FillRectangle(x, y, width,height)
```

The rectangle will draw and fill in the current brush object color. To set that color, use:

```
GraphicsWindow.BrushColor = Color
```

To draw and fill a blue rectangle with the upper left corner at (20, 50), width 150 and height 100 in our **Graphics Test**, use this code:

```
GraphicsWindow.Show()
GraphicsWindow.Title ="Graphics Testing"
GraphicsWindow.Width = 400
GraphicsWindow.Height = 300
GraphicsWindow.BrushColor = "Blue"
GraphicsWindow.FillRectangle(20, 50, 150, 100)
```

This produces in the window:

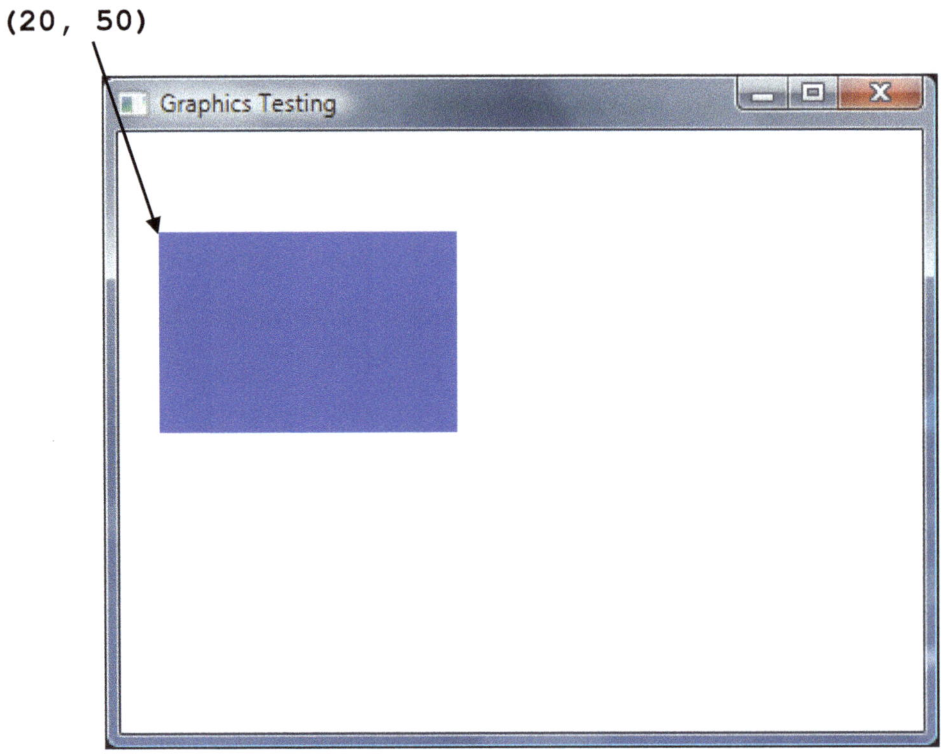

And, to draw a red filled rectangle of the same size with upper left corner at (140, 130), add these two lines of code:

```
GraphicsWindow.BrushColor = "Red"
GraphicsWindow.FillRectangle(140, 130, 150, 100)
```

This yields:

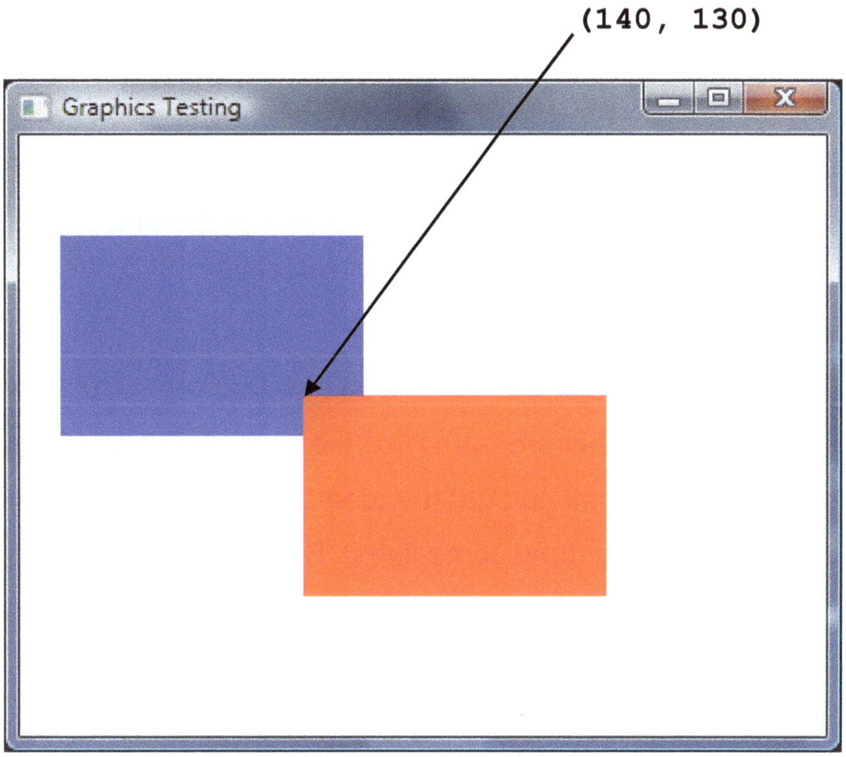

Try more rectangles if you like.

Clear Method

There is one last graphics method to introduce. After all of your hard work drawing in a graphics window, there are times you will want to erase or clear the window. This is done with the **Clear** method:

```
GraphicsWindow.Clear()
```

This statement will clear a graphics window and fill it with the window's specified **BackgroundColor**. Notice if you add this statement to the end of our test example, you will have a blank window. Try it if you like.

Keep playing around with the Graphics Test program. Try drawing more lines and rectangles. Save this program (use the name **GraphicsTest**)– we'll continue working with it. I think you get the idea of drawing. Just pick some points, pick some colors, and draw some lines. But, it's pretty boring to just specify points and see lines being drawn. It would be nice to have some user interaction, where points could be drawn using the mouse. And, that's just what we are going to do. We will use our newly gained knowledge about graphics methods to build a Small Basic drawing program. To do this, though, we need to know how to use the mouse in a program. We do that next.

Small Basic - The Sixth Lesson

In the beginning of this class, we introduced the concept of **events** where the computer responds to something a user does. When an event occurs, program control is transferred to an **event procedure** (Small Basic **subroutine**) where the event code is written. In the Small Basic lesson for this class, we examine how to recognize **mouse events** (clicking mouse buttons, moving the mouse) to help us build a drawing program using a graphics window. The mouse is a primary interface for doing graphics in Small Basic or any GUI application. We are interested in two mouse events: **MouseDown** and **MouseMove**. .

MouseDown Event

The **MouseDown** event is triggered whenever a mouse button is pressed while the mouse cursor is over the graphics window. If the subroutine to be executed in case of such an event is **MouseDownEvent**, we add this event to our program using:

```
GraphicsWindow.MouseDown = MouseDownEvent
```

Note that setting the **MouseDown** subroutine name (**MouseDownEvent**) is similar to setting a property for the **GraphicsWindow** object.

The corresponding subroutine is added to the program in the usual manner and has the form:

```
Sub MouseDownEvent
  ' Small Basic code for MouseDown event
EndSub
```

Every time the user clicks the mouse, a MouseDown event occurs and the subroutine (MouseDownEvent) is called automatically. In drawing applications, the **MouseDown** event is used to initialize a drawing process. The point clicked is used to start drawing a line.

Example

Let's try the **MouseDown** event with the example we've been using. Open that program (**GraphicsTest**) in Small Basic and delete any lines using drawing methods (so we just have a blank window when the program runs). Add this code to test the **MouseDown** event:

```
GraphicsWindow.MouseDown = MouseDownEvent

Sub MouseDownEvent
  GraphicsWindow.BackgroundColor = GraphicsWindow.GetRandomColor()
EndSub
```

With this code, each time the mouse is clicked the graphics window will change background color (a the newly introduced method, **GetRandomColor**, which does just that – sets a color randomly).

The finished code looks like this:

```
GraphicsWindow.Show()
GraphicsWindow.Title ="Graphics Testing"
GraphicsWindow.Width = 400
GraphicsWindow.Height = 300
GraphicsWindow.MouseDown = MouseDownEvent

Sub MouseDownEvent
  GraphicsWindow.BackgroundColor = GraphicsWindow.GetRandomColor()
EndSub
```

Run the program. Each time you click the window, the background color will change. Here's one of my clicks:

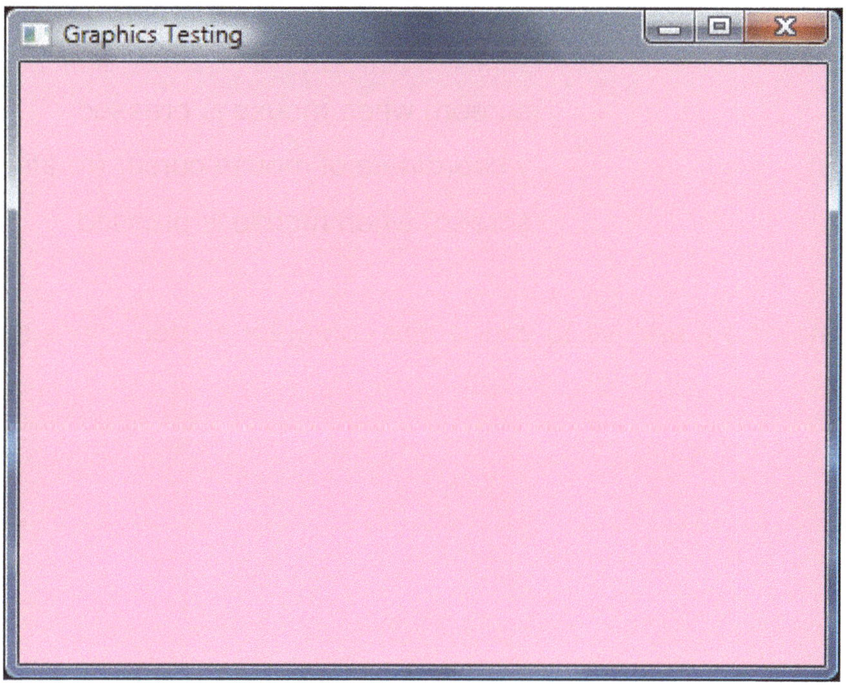

You should see it's pretty easy to implement the MouseDown event.

Mouse Properties

When we click the mouse, there is information available to us via **properties** of the Small Basic **Mouse** class. We can determine which button was clicked by examining two properties which return logical values that can be checked in If structures or While loops:

`Mouse.IsLeftButtonDown`	Returns a true value if left button is pressed.
`Mouse.IsRightButtonDown`	Returns a true value if right button is pressed.

The coordinates of the mouse cursor when a button is pressed are given by:

`Mouse.MouseX`	x coordinate of mouse cursor (relative to entire screen) when mouse is pressed
`Mouse.MouseY`	y coordinate of mouse cursor (relative to entire screen) when mouse is pressed

These coordinates are relative to your entire computer screen – let's see what that means.

Here is a graphics window displayed on your monitor showing **Mouse.MouseX** and **Mouse.MouseY**:

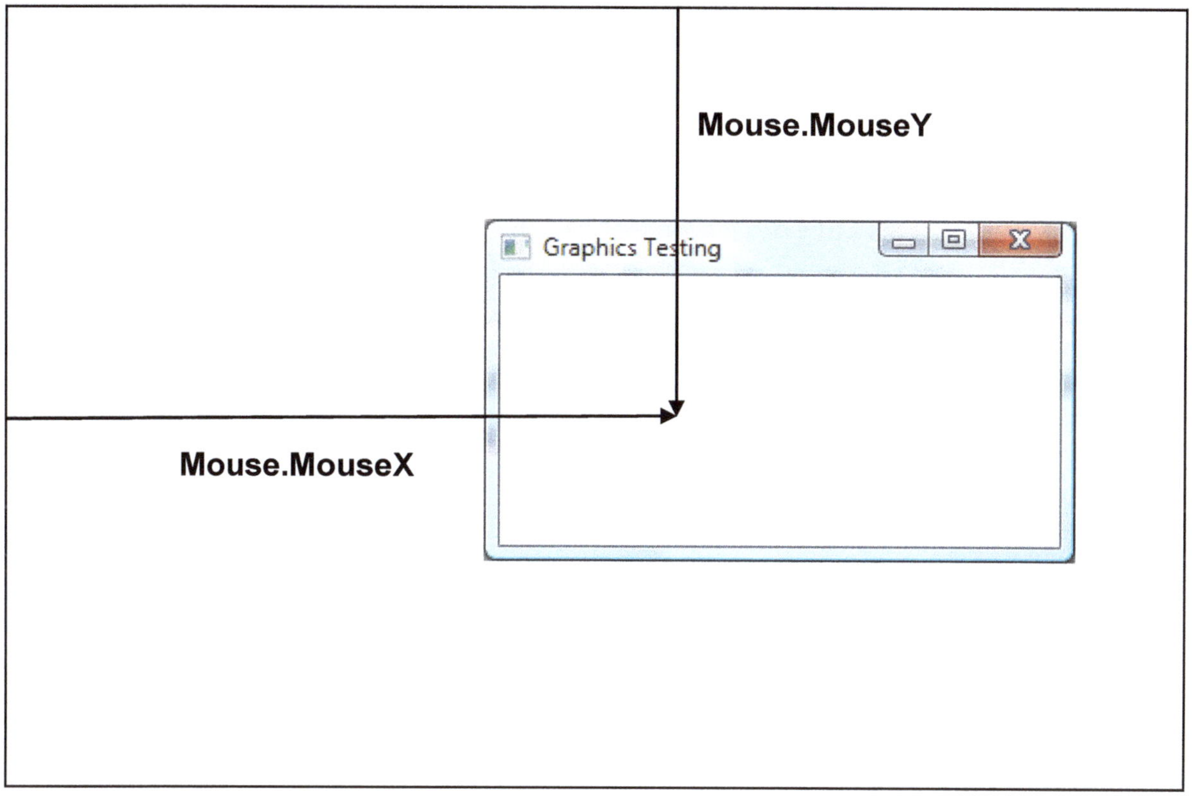

With these coordinates, you would get different results if you move the graphics window on your screen. We want to use our previously defined graphics coordinate system, where the upper left corner of the graphics window is (0, 0). Such coordinates are given by two **GraphicsWindow** properties:

`GraphicsWindow.MouseX`	x coordinate of mouse cursor in graphics window when mouse is pressed
`GraphicsWindow.MouseY`	y coordinate of mouse cursor in graphics window when mouse is pressed

Example

Add the shaded lines to the **MouseDownEvent** subroutine:

```
Sub MouseDownEvent
  GraphicsWindow.BackgroundColor = GraphicsWindow.GetRandomColor()
  If (Mouse.IsLeftButtonDown) Then
    TextWindow.WriteLine("You clicked the left mouse button")
  Else
    TextWindow.WriteLine("You clicked the right mouse button")
  EndIf
  TextWindow.WriteLine("At x = " + GraphicsWindow.MouseX + ", y =
" + GraphicsWindow.Mousey)
EndSub
```

With these lines, we can see which button was clicked and where the mouse was positioned when it was clicked. Run the program. Click the graphics window and a text window will appear telling you which button was clicked and the click coordinate. Move the graphics window and text window (resize it if you like) so you can see both windows.

Here's what I got when I clicked the left mouse button:

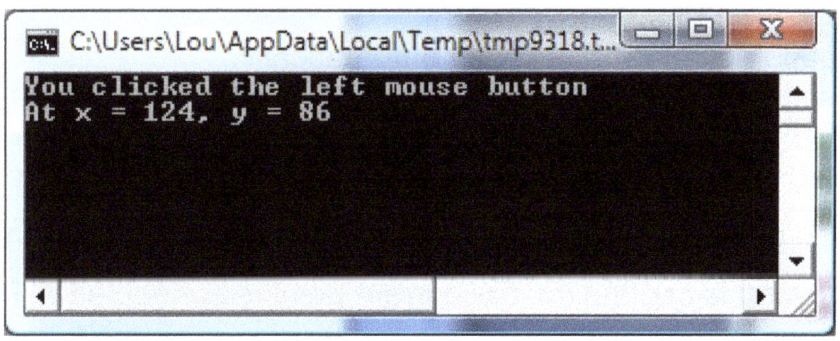

Click various spots in the window and see how the coordinates change. Try both mouse buttons. Notice you cannot detect mouse clicks in the title bar area. Play with this example until you are comfortable with how the MouseDown event works and what the coordinates mean. Stop and save the program.

MouseMove Event

The **MouseMove** event is continuously triggered whenever the mouse is being moved. If the subroutine to be executed in case of such an event is **MouseMoveEvent**, we add this event to our program using:

```
GraphicsWindow.MouseMove = MouseMoveEvent
```

The corresponding subroutine is added to the program in the usual manner and has the form:

```
Sub MouseMoveEvent
  ' Small Basic code for MouseMove event
EndSub
```

Whenever a user moves the mouse, a MouseMove event occurs and the subroutine (MouseMoveEvent) is called automatically.

In drawing processes, the **MouseMove** event is used to detect the continuation of a previously started line (you also make sure a button is being pressed). If drawing is continuing, the current point is connected to the previous point using the **DrawLine** method.

Example

Modify the graphics example, adding the shaded code:

```
GraphicsWindow.Show()
GraphicsWindow.Title ="Graphics Testing"
GraphicsWindow.Width = 400
GraphicsWindow.Height = 300
GraphicsWindow.MouseDown = MouseDownEvent
GraphicsWindow.MouseMove = MouseMoveEvent

Sub MouseDownEvent
  GraphicsWindow.BackgroundColor = GraphicsWindow.GetRandomColor()
  If (Mouse.IsLeftButtonDown) Then
    TextWindow.WriteLine("You clicked the left mouse button")
  Else
    TextWindow.WriteLine("You clicked the right mouse button")
  EndIf
  TextWindow.WriteLine("At x = " + GraphicsWindow.MouseX + ", y =
" + GraphicsWindow.Mousey)
EndSub

Sub MouseMoveEvent
  TextWindow.WriteLine("Moved to x = " + GraphicsWindow.MouseX +
", y = " + GraphicsWindow.Mousey)
EndSub
```

We establish a **MouseMove** event and in the corresponding subroutine (**MouseMoveEvent**), we use a **WriteLine** statement to specify the x and y coordinate the mouse has been moved to. This last version of the **GraphicsTest** is saved in the course programs folder (**\BeginSB\BSB Code**).

Run the program. Move the cursor into the graphics window and a text window will appear showing you the changing cursor location. Click the graphics window and notice the clicked point is displayed. Move the mouse around the window. Notice the coordinates (x, y) continuously change as the mouse is moving. Here's the text window from one of my runs:

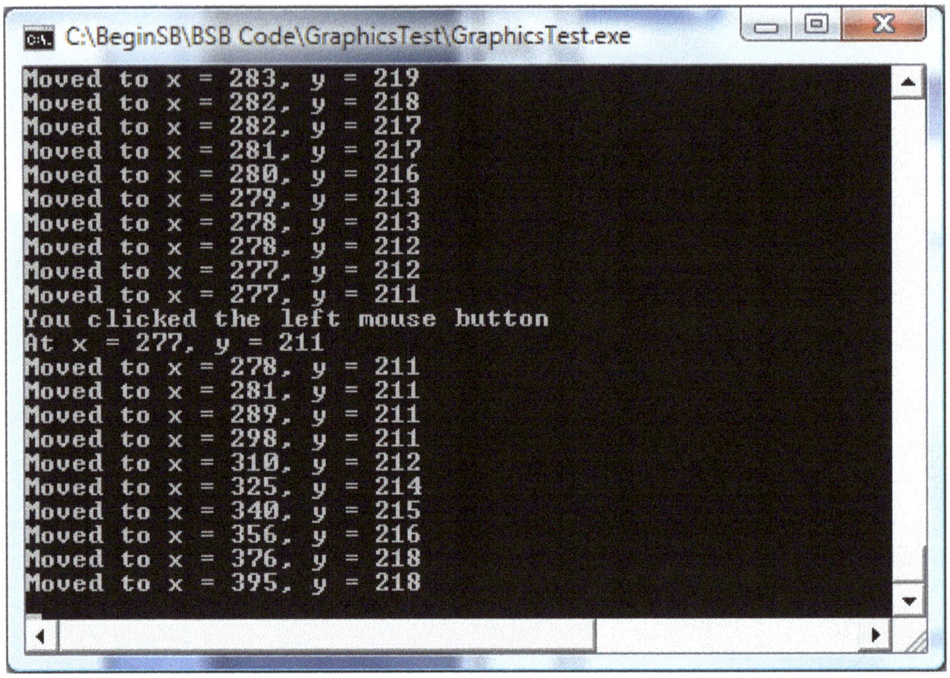

Program – Blackboard Fun

Have you ever drawn on a blackboard with colored chalk? You'll be doing that with the "electronic" blackboard you build in this program. This program is saved in the **Blackboard** folder in the course programs folder (**\BeginSB\BSB Code**).

Program Design

This is a simple program in concept. Using the mouse, you draw colored lines on a computer blackboard. A graphics window will represent the blackboard. We will use rectangles drawn along the edge of the window to choose "chalk" color. Mouse events will control the drawing and color selection process. The basic program steps are very simple:

1. Establish graphics window, add event procedures and setup color choice rectangles.
2. Listen for mouse down, when one is detected, either change the color or initialize drawing process.
3. Listen for mouse moving. If mouse is moving (with button press), continue drawing line in current color.

We will write code that takes care of all the initialization steps and write code for each (MouseDown, MouseMove) event procedures.

Program Development

To help visualize what's going to be in this program, let's look ahead at how we want to layout the window. We will create a window that is 600 pixels wide and 450 pixels high. On the right-edge of the window, we will draw 9 small filled rectangles. These rectangles will be used to select drawing color. The coordinates used for all this are:

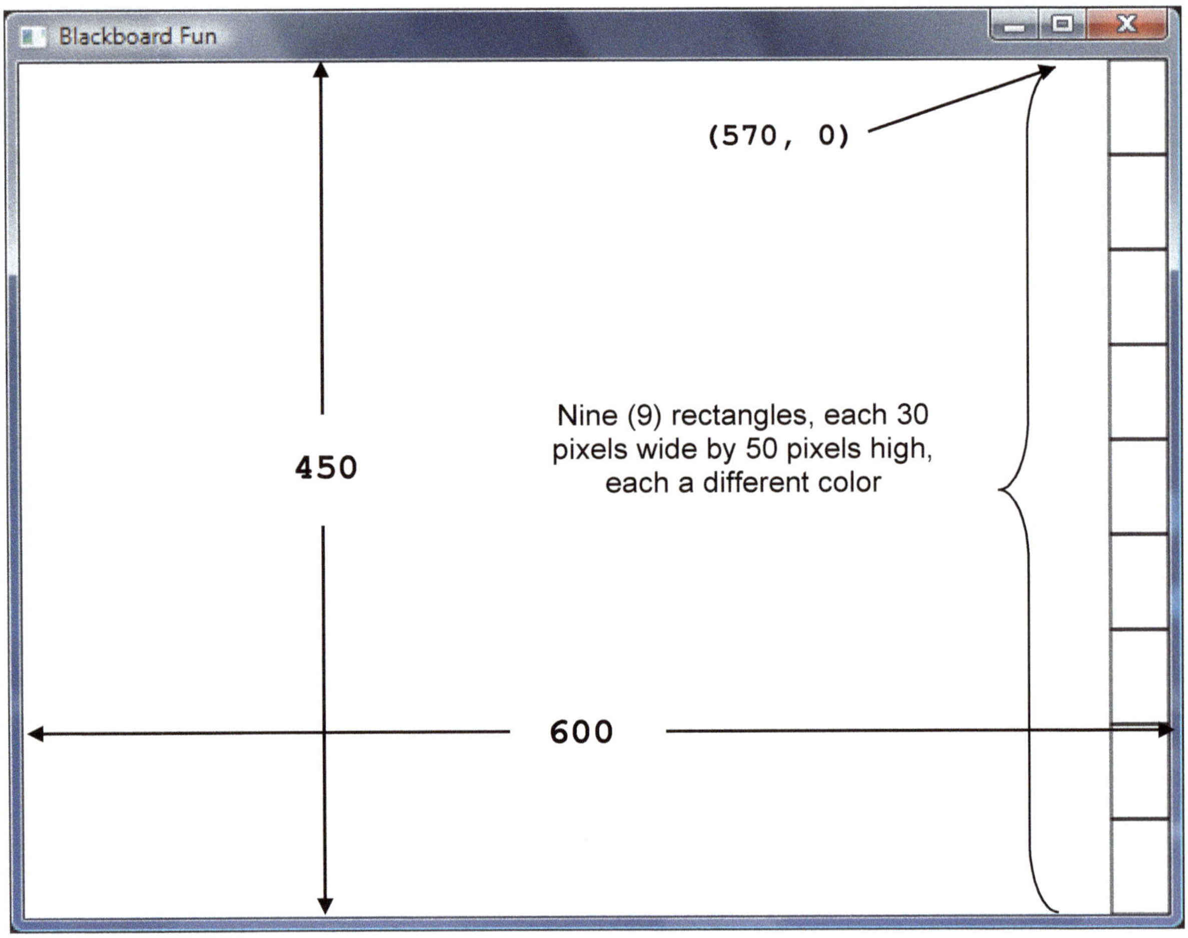

This program will work like any paint type program you may have used. Click on a color in one of the eight rectangles to choose a color to draw with. Then, move to the blackboard area, left-click to start the drawing process. Drag the mouse to draw lines. Release the mouse button to stop drawing. It's that easy. Clicking in the black rectangle under the eight color selection rectangles will clear the blackboard and, as usual, clicking the **X** in the upper right corner of the graphics window will stop the program. Every step, but initializing things and stopping the program, is handled by the mouse events.

Start **Small Basic**. Click the **New Program** button in the toolbar. A blank editor will appear. Immediately save the program as **Blackboard** in a folder of your choice.

First, type the following header information, add a window title and establish a graphics window:

```
'
'  Blackboard Fun
'  Beginning Small Basic
'
GraphicsWindow.Title = "Blackboard Fun"
GraphicsWindow.Show()
GraphicsWindow.Width = 600
GraphicsWindow.Height = 450
GraphicsWindow.BackgroundColor = "Black"
```

Save the program.

Run the program to make sure the graphics window appears (it should be black, like a blackboard!):

In long, detailed programs like this, it is good practice to occasionally stop and try your program even if it's not complete. This gives you some confidence things are working okay and you can move on.

As a variable, **DrawingColor** will hold the current drawing color. And, we need two variables (**PreviousX** and **PreviousY**) that save the last point drawn in a line (we will always connect the "current" point to the "last" point).

We need to establish some initial values. First, draw the nine rectangles we will use for color selection. Add these lines:

```
' setup color choice rectangles
GraphicsWindow.BrushColor = "White"
GraphicsWindow.FillRectangle(570, 0, 30, 50)
GraphicsWindow.BrushColor = "LightGray"
GraphicsWindow.FillRectangle(570, 50, 30, 50)
GraphicsWindow.BrushColor = "RoyalBlue"
GraphicsWindow.FillRectangle(570, 100, 30, 50)
GraphicsWindow.BrushColor = "Cyan"
GraphicsWindow.FillRectangle(570, 150, 30, 50)
GraphicsWindow.BrushColor = "Green"
GraphicsWindow.FillRectangle(570, 200, 30, 50)
GraphicsWindow.BrushColor = "Magenta"
GraphicsWindow.FillRectangle(570, 250, 30, 50)
GraphicsWindow.BrushColor = "Yellow"
GraphicsWindow.FillRectangle(570, 300, 30, 50)
GraphicsWindow.BrushColor = "Red"
GraphicsWindow.FillRectangle(570, 350, 30, 50)
GraphicsWindow.BrushColor = "Black"
GraphicsWindow.FillRectangle(570, 400, 30, 50)
```

You should see that this code just draws and fills eight rectangles along the side of the window. The eight colors were selected to look good on a black background. A last step is to initialize the DrawingColor:

```
' initialize drawing color
DrawingColor = "White"
GraphicsWindow.PenColor = DrawingColor
GraphicsWindow.PenWidth = 1
```

You'll see that this is pretty cool in how it works. Save and run the program to test it out. The color choice rectangles should appear:

Now, we are ready to code the drawing process. There are two events we look for:

- Mouse button press (**MouseDown**) – picks color or starts drawing (if left mouse button)
- Mouse moving (**MouseMove**) - continues drawing (if left mouse button is pressed)

Each of these is a separate mouse event. Add these lines to establish subroutines for these events:

```
' setup event subroutines
GraphicsWindow.MouseDown = MouseDownEvent
GraphicsWindow.MouseMove = MouseMoveEvent

Sub MouseDownEvent
EndSub

Sub MouseMoveEvent
EndSub
```

The **MouseDown** event is executed when a mouse button is clicked. We will only look for **left** button clicks. When that happens, we check the x coordinate (GraphicsWindow.MouseX) to see if it exceeds 570 (the boundary of the color selection rectangles). If so, we determine which rectangle has been clicked (by checking the value of GraphicsWindow.MouseY) and change the **DrawingColor** variable. If the lowest rectangle (the black area) is selected, the graphics window is cleared. If the x coordinate is less than 570, we are starting to draw a line. In this case, we initialize the “last point” variables, **PreviousX** and **PreviousY**.

The event procedure is (it's kind of long):

```
Sub MouseDownEvent
  '  drawing begins or color is changed with left button click
  If (Mouse.IsLeftButtonDown) Then
    If (GraphicsWindow.MouseX > 570) Then
      ' new color
      If (GraphicsWindow.MouseY > 400) Then
        ' clear drawing area
        GraphicsWindow.BrushColor = "Black"
        GraphicsWindow.FillRectangle(0, 0, 570, 450)
      ElseIf (GraphicsWindow.MouseY > 350) Then
        DrawingColor = "Red"
      ElseIf (GraphicsWindow.MouseY > 300) Then
        DrawingColor = "Yellow"
      ElseIf (GraphicsWindow.MouseY > 250) Then
        DrawingColor = "Magenta"
      ElseIf (GraphicsWindow.MouseY > 200) Then
        DrawingColor = "Green"
      ElseIf (GraphicsWindow.MouseY > 150) Then
        DrawingColor = "Cyan"
      ElseIf (GraphicsWindow.MouseY > 100) Then
        DrawingColor = "RoyalBlue"
      ElseIf (GraphicsWindow.MouseY > 50) Then
        DrawingColor = "LightGray"
      Else
        DrawingColor = "White"
      EndIf
    else
    '  drawing begins, save point
      PreviousX = GraphicsWindow.MouseX
      PreviousY = GraphicsWindow.MouseY
    EndIf
  EndIf
EndSub
```

You might wonder why we don't use the **Clear** method to erase the window. Doing this would clear the entire window including the color selection windows. In this code, we use the **FillRectangle** method to 'black out' everything but those rectangles. Save and run to make sure the code is correct. You can't draw yet but you can eliminate any errors.

The **MouseMove** event is executed when the mouse is being moved over the graphics window. In this event, (if the left button is still down) we connect the last point (**PreviousX, PreviousY**) to the current point (**GraphicsWindow.MouseX, GraphicsWindow.MouseY**) using the **DrawLine** method. Once done drawing, the "last point" becomes the "current point." This event subroutine is:

```
Sub MouseMoveEvent
  If (Mouse.IsLeftButtonDown) Then
    '  drawing continues
    GraphicsWindow.PenColor = DrawingColor
    GraphicsWindow.DrawLine(PreviousX, PreviousY,
GraphicsWindow.MouseX, GraphicsWindow.MouseY)
    PreviousX = GraphicsWindow.MouseX
    PreviousY = GraphicsWindow.MouseY
  EndIf
EndSub
```

That's all the code. Make sure both mouse event procedures are typed correctly in the proper location. Save the program by clicking the **Save** button in the Small Basic toolbar.

Here is the complete Blackboard Fun Small Basic code listing (from the editor) – it's your biggest program yet:

```
'
'  Blackboard Fun
'  Beginning Small Basic
'
GraphicsWindow.Title = "Blackboard Fun"
GraphicsWindow.Show()
GraphicsWindow.Width = 600
GraphicsWindow.Height = 450
GraphicsWindow.BackgroundColor = "Black"
' setup color choice rectangles
GraphicsWindow.BrushColor = "White"
GraphicsWindow.FillRectangle(570, 0, 30, 50)
GraphicsWindow.BrushColor = "LightGray"
GraphicsWindow.FillRectangle(570, 50, 30, 50)
GraphicsWindow.BrushColor = "RoyalBlue"
GraphicsWindow.FillRectangle(570, 100, 30, 50)
GraphicsWindow.BrushColor = "Cyan"
GraphicsWindow.FillRectangle(570, 150, 30, 50)
GraphicsWindow.BrushColor = "Green"
GraphicsWindow.FillRectangle(570, 200, 30, 50)
GraphicsWindow.BrushColor = "Magenta"
GraphicsWindow.FillRectangle(570, 250, 30, 50)
GraphicsWindow.BrushColor = "Yellow"
GraphicsWindow.FillRectangle(570, 300, 30, 50)
GraphicsWindow.BrushColor = "Red"
GraphicsWindow.FillRectangle(570, 350, 30, 50)
GraphicsWindow.BrushColor = "Black"
GraphicsWindow.FillRectangle(570, 400, 30, 50)
' initialize drawing color
DrawingColor = "White"
GraphicsWindow.PenColor = DrawingColor
GraphicsWindow.PenWidth = 1

' setup event subroutines
GraphicsWindow.MouseDown = MouseDownEvent
GraphicsWindow.MouseMove = MouseMoveEvent

Sub MouseDownEvent
  '  drawing begins or color is changed with left button click
  If (Mouse.IsLeftButtonDown) Then
    If (GraphicsWindow.MouseX > 570) Then
```

```
      ' new color
      If (GraphicsWindow.MouseY > 400) Then
        ' clear drawing area
        GraphicsWindow.BrushColor = "Black"
        GraphicsWindow.FillRectangle(0, 0, 570, 450)
      ElseIf (GraphicsWindow.MouseY > 350) Then
        DrawingColor = "Red"
      ElseIf (GraphicsWindow.MouseY > 300) Then
        DrawingColor = "Yellow"
      ElseIf (GraphicsWindow.MouseY > 250) Then
        DrawingColor = "Magenta"
      ElseIf (GraphicsWindow.MouseY > 200) Then
        DrawingColor = "Green"
      ElseIf (GraphicsWindow.MouseY > 150) Then
        DrawingColor = "Cyan"
      ElseIf (GraphicsWindow.MouseY > 100) Then
        DrawingColor = "RoyalBlue"
      ElseIf (GraphicsWindow.MouseY > 50) Then
        DrawingColor = "LightGray"
      Else
        DrawingColor = "White"
      EndIf
    else
    '  drawing begins, save point
      PreviousX = GraphicsWindow.MouseX
      PreviousY = GraphicsWindow.MouseY
    EndIf
  EndIf
EndSub

Sub MouseMoveEvent
  If (Mouse.IsLeftButtonDown) Then
    '  drawing continues
    GraphicsWindow.PenColor = DrawingColor
    GraphicsWindow.DrawLine(PreviousX, PreviousY,
GraphicsWindow.MouseX, GraphicsWindow.MouseY)
    PreviousX = GraphicsWindow.MouseX
    PreviousY = GraphicsWindow.MouseY
  EndIf
EndSub
```

Run the Program

Run the program. By building and testing in stages, any errors seen now (if any) should be minimal. The finished running product should look like this:

Choose a color by clicking one of the eight displayed rectangles. Draw a line in the window. Try other colors. Draw something.

Here's my attempt at art:

I've had students draw perfect pictures of Fred Flintstone and Homer Simpson using this program. Make sure each color works. Make sure the clear function (click below the last colored rectangle) works. As always, thoroughly test your program. Save it if you had to make any changes while running it.

Do you see how simple the drawing part of this program is? Most of the code is used just to set and select colors. The actual drawing portion of the code (MouseDown, MouseMove events) is only a few lines of Small Basic! This shows two things: (1) those drawing programs you use are really not that hard to build and (2) there is a lot of power in the Small Basic graphics methods.

Other Things to Try

The Blackboard Fun program offers lots of opportunity for improvement with added options. Add the ability to change the background color of the blackboard. Determine and build logic that allows drawing different colored lines depending on whether you press the left or right mouse button. For this, I'd suggest creating a left pen and a right pen. You will also need some way for the user to choose colors for each pen. Then, apply the appropriate pen in the various mouse events depending on what button is pressed.

As written, you can draw lines in the color selection area. Correct this problem. Notice, too, if you click a color and move the mouse before releasing the mouse button, unintended lines are drawn. See if you can correct this problem.

Have a adjustable pen width. Here's a little picture I drew with a pen 20 pixels wide:

Here's another possibility to try. Delete (or 'comment out') these lines in the **MouseMove** event:

```
PreviousX = GraphicsWindow.MouseX
PreviousY = GraphicsWindow.MouseY
```

By doing this, the first point clicked (in the Mousedown event) is always the last point and all line drawing originates from this original point. Now, run the program again. Notice the "fanning" effect. Pretty, huh?

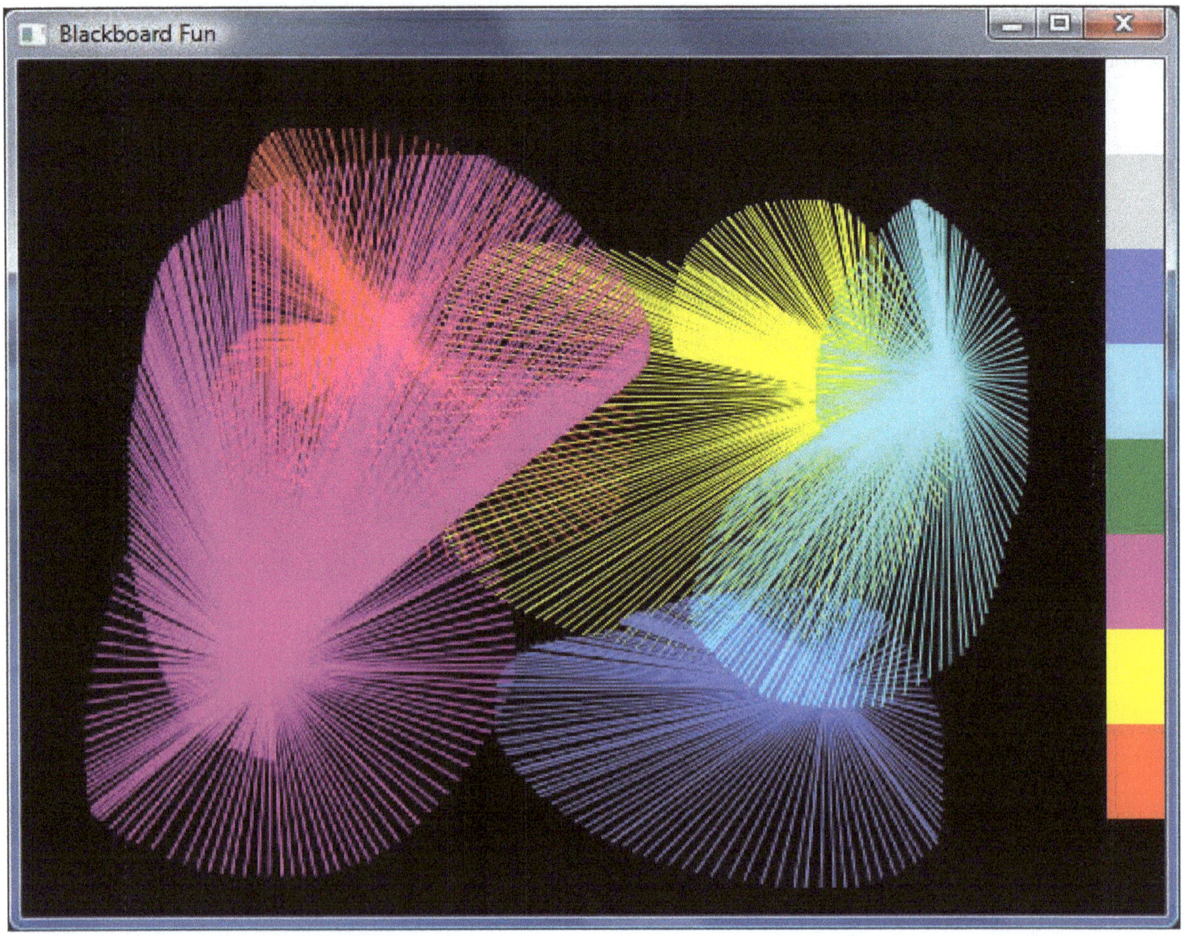

Play around and see what other effects (change colors randomly, draw little filled rectangles). Have fun!

Summary

You've now had your first experience with graphics programming in Small Basic using the DrawLine, DrawRectangle and FillRectangle methods. You learned about two important events to help in drawing: MouseDown and MouseMove. And, you learned about colors. In the next class, we'll continue looking at using graphics in programs. And, we'll look at some ways to design simple computer games.

9

Timers, Animation, Keyboard Methods

Review and Preview

By now, you should have some confidence in your abilities as a Small Basic programmer. In this class, we'll look at another item that's a lot of fun - the Timer object. It's a key object for adding animation (motion) to graphics in programs using the Shapes object. We study some animation techniques. We will also examine how to recognize user inputs from the keyboard via keyboard events. You'll build another program - your first video game! And, we'll see how you can share your programs with others over the Internet.

Timer Object

In the Class 8, we saw that event procedures (subroutines) were executed in a GUI application when the user caused some event to happen (usually with the mouse). The Small Basic **Timer object** has an interesting feature. It can generate events (called **Tick** events) without any input from the user. Timer objects work in your program's background, generating events at time intervals you specify. This event generation feature comes in handy for graphics animation where screen displays need to be updated at regular intervals.

Using a timer object is fairly simple:

- Assign the timer's **Tick** event to an event procedure (subroutine) that contains code to be executed with each event.
- Decide how often you want to generate Tick events; this is the timer's **Interval** property. The interval is measured in milliseconds. There are 1000 milliseconds in one second.

These steps are straightforward. Here is code to assign the **Tick** event to a subroutine named **TimerTickEvent** and set the **Interval** property to 1000 milliseconds.

```
Timer.Tick = TimerTickEvent
Timer.Interval = 1000
```

The **TimerTickEvent** would be in a subroutine of the form:

```
Sub TimerTickEvent
  ' code to execute with each Tick event
EndSub
```

There are two timer object methods we need to monitor status. To start a timer and begin event processing, use:

```
Timer.Resume()
```

To stop the timer and stop event processing, use:

```
Timer.Pause()
```

Note: By default, the timer is "turned on" meaning event processing will immediately begin when starting a program with a timer object.

Examples

A few examples should clarify how the timer object works. It's very simple and very powerful. To review, here's what happens. When a timer is running, every **Interval** milliseconds, Small Basic will generate an event and execute the corresponding **Tick** event subroutine. No user interaction is needed.

The Interval property is important. This property is set to the number of milliseconds between timer events. A millisecond is 1/1000th of a second, or there are 1,000 milliseconds in a second. If you want to generate N events per second, set the delay to 1000 / N. For example, if you want a timer event to occur 4 times per second, use a delay of 250. About the lowest practical value for delay is 50 and values that differ by 5, 10, or even 20 are likely to produce similar results. It all depends on your particular computer. Now, let's try some examples.

Start Small Basic, start a new program and save it as **Timer**. Add this code:

```
GraphicsWindow.Show()
GraphicsWindow.Width = 400
GraphicsWindow.Height = 300
GraphicsWindow.Title = "Timer Example"
Timer.Tick = TimerTickEvent
Timer.Interval = 1000

Sub TimerTickEvent
  Sound.PlayBellRing()
EndSub
```

In this listing, the first four lines of the code should be familiar and understood by you – it just creates and sizes a graphics window.

The remaining code states the **TimerTickEvent** will be the subroutine holding code for the timer's **Tick** event and that the timer's **Interval** is 1000 milliseconds (1 second). The TimerTickEvent subroutine has a single line of code:

```
Sub TimerTickEvent
  Sound.PlayBellRing()
EndSub
```

This line makes your computer play a bell ringing sound, or is that obvious? The code uses the Small Basic **Sound** object which has some built-in sounds.

Save and run the program. A blank graphics window will appear. Recall the timer is on by default, so your computer will play a bell sound every second (the Tick event is generated every 1000 milliseconds, the Interval value) until you stop the program. Notice it does this no matter what else is going on. It requires no input (once the timer is on) from you, the user. Stop the program when you get tired of the ringing.

Let's modify the program so you can control starting and stopping of the ringing. When the user clicks the graphics window, we want the timer (and associated ringing) to start. When it is clicked again, we want it to stop. Add the shaded lines to the 'main' code in the program:

```
GraphicsWindow.Show()
GraphicsWindow.Width = 400
GraphicsWindow.Height = 300
GraphicsWindow.Title = "Timer Example"
Timer.Tick = TimerTickEvent
Timer.Interval = 1000
Timer.Pause()
TimerOn = "false"
GraphicsWindow.MouseDown = MouseDownEvent
```

Here, we make sure the timer object is initially off (paused). We establish a variable **TimerOn** to keep track of timer status (initially set to "false"). And we point the **MouseDown** event to the **MouseDownEvent** subroutine, where we will turn the timer on and off.

Add the **MouseDownEvent** subroutine:

```
Sub MouseDownEvent
  If (TimerOn = "true") Then
    TimerOn = "false"
    Timer.Pause()
  Else
    TimerOn = "true"
    Timer.Resume()
  EndIf
EndSub
```

This code is executed whenever the graphics window is clicked by the mouse. What does this code do? If the timer is on (TimerOn is "true"), it stops (Pause method) the timer and vice versa. We say this code "toggles" the timer.

Save and run the program. A blank graphics window will appear. There should be no ringing since the timer is off. Click the window. The timer will start and your computer will play a bell sound every second (the Tick event is generated every 1000 milliseconds, the Interval value) until you click the window again. Once again, stop the program when you get tired of the ringing.

Add the shaded line to the timer's **TimerTickEvent** subroutine, so it reads:

```
Sub TimerTickEvent
  Sound.PlayBellRing()
  GraphicsWindow.BackgroundColor = GraphicsWindow.GetRandomColor()
EndSub
```

Can you see that this code changes the graphics window background color using random values? Run the program. Click the window. Now, every second, the computer rings and the window changes color. Stop the timer. Stop the program.

Let's use the timer to do some flashier stuff. Change the timer **Interval** property to **50**. Replace the **TimerTickEvent** subroutine with this code:

```
Sub TimerTickEvent
  GraphicsWindow.PenColor = GraphicsWindow.GetRandomColor()
  GraphicsWindow.DrawEllipse(Delta, Delta, 400 - 2 * Delta, 300 -
2 * Delta)
  Delta = Delta + 1
  If (Delta > 150) Then
    Delta = 0
    GraphicsWindow.Clear()
  EndIf
EndSub
```

You should recognize most of what's here. We've speeded up the timer object. In the event subroutine, a random color is selected and used to draw an ellipse. This (**DrawEllipse**) is a graphics method we haven't seen before. You should be able to understand it and you'll see it gives a really neat effect in this example.

The **DrawEllipse** method has the form:

```
GraphicsWindow.DrawEllipse(x, y, width, height)
```

This statement draws an ellipse, with a width **width** and height **height**, in the graphics window starting at the point (**x**, **y**). A picture shows the result:

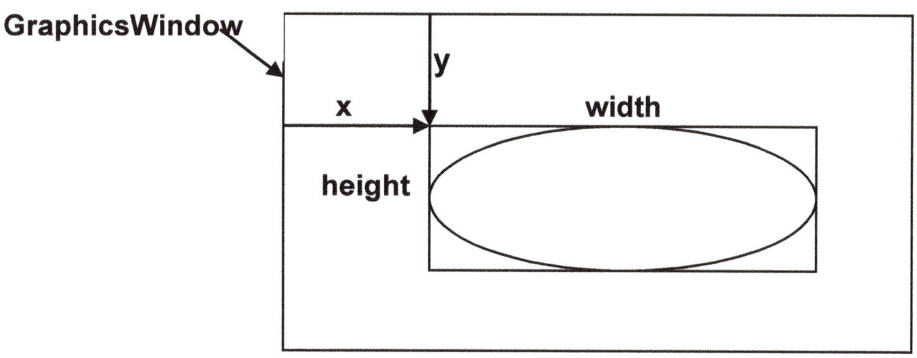

In your work with Small Basic, you will often see code you don't recognize. Use the usual reference facilities, such as the on-line help offered by Small Basic, other programmers, text books or the old reliable Microsoft website in these cases. Try it with **DrawEllipse**. Also look at **FillEllipse** – it has an identical form as DrawOval, the difference being an oval filled with the current brush color will be drawn.

Back to the code, you should see the **DrawEllipse** method draws the first ellipse around the border of the window (**x = 0** initially). The surrounding rectangle moves "in" an amount **Delta** (in each direction) with each "tick" of the timer, resulting in a smaller rectangle (the width and height are decreased by both **2 * Delta**). Once Delta (incremented by one in each step) exceeds half of the window height (150 in this case), it is reset to 0, the window is cleared and the process starts all over. Run the program. Click the window. Are you hypnotized? Here's one of my runs:

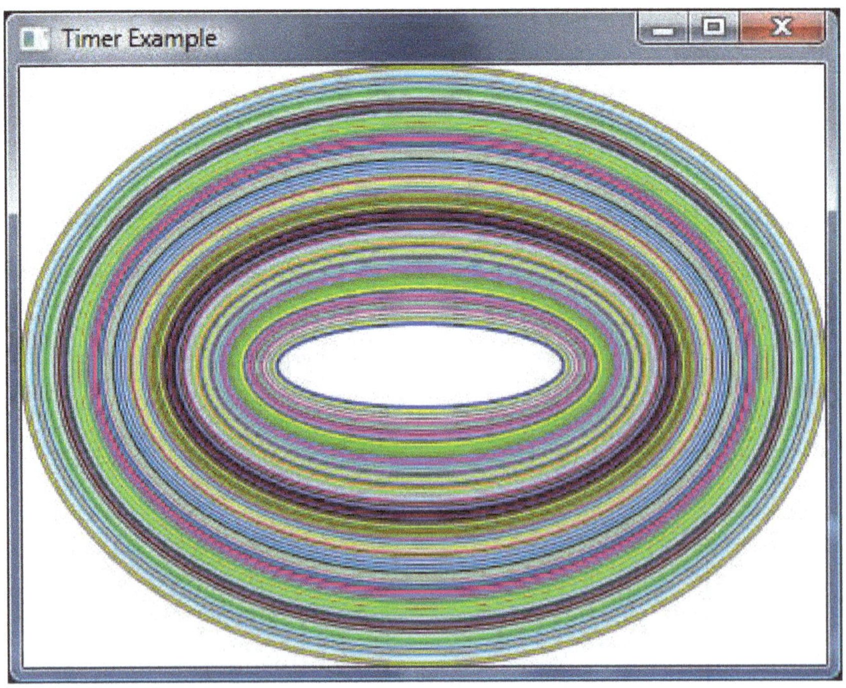

Can you think of other things you could draw using other graphics methods? Look at **DrawRectangle** for example. Try your ideas.

In this last example, the periodic (every 0.050 seconds) changing of the display in the graphics object, imparted by the timer object, gives the appearance of motion – the ovals seem to be moving inward. This is the basic concept behind a very powerful graphics technique - **animation**. In animation, we have a sequence of pictures, each a little different from the previous one. With the ellipse example, in each picture, we add a new ellipse. By displaying this sequence over time, we can trick the viewer into thinking things are moving. It all has to do with how fast the human eye and brain can process information. That's how cartoons work - 24 different pictures are displayed every second - it makes things look like they are moving, or animated. Obviously, the timer object is a key element to animation, as well as for other Small Basic timing tasks. In the Small Basic lesson for this class, we will look at how to do simple animations and some other things.

For your reference, this last version of the program is saved in the **Timer** folder in the course programs folder (**\BeginSB\BSB Code**).

Small Basic - The Final Lesson

In this last Small Basic lesson, we look at how to add text to a graphics application, study some simple animation techniques using shapes, look at math needed with animations, and learn how to detect keyboard events.

DrawText Method

We would like some capability to add text information to a window. We'll use this in the program we build at the end of this class. You will find it useful for adding labeling information to graphics applications. The method that does such a task is the **DrawText** graphics method – yes, text is "drawn" to the window. The **DrawText** method is:

```
GraphicsWindow.DrawText(x, y, text)
```

In this statement, **text** represents the string to print in the window and the point (**x, y**) is where the string will be located. The string will draw in the graphics window using the current brush color using the default font. Note this method uses the brush color, not the pen color – text is truly drawn like other graphics objects.

Let's try a quick example. Start Small Basic, start a new program. Use this code:

```
GraphicsWindow.Show()
Graphicswindow.Width = 400
GraphicsWindow.Height = 300
GraphicsWindow.DrawText(40, 100, "Isn't Beginning Small Basic
fun?")
```

This code simply creates a graphics window and displays the text information "Isn't Beginning Small Basic fun?" Run the program. You should see:

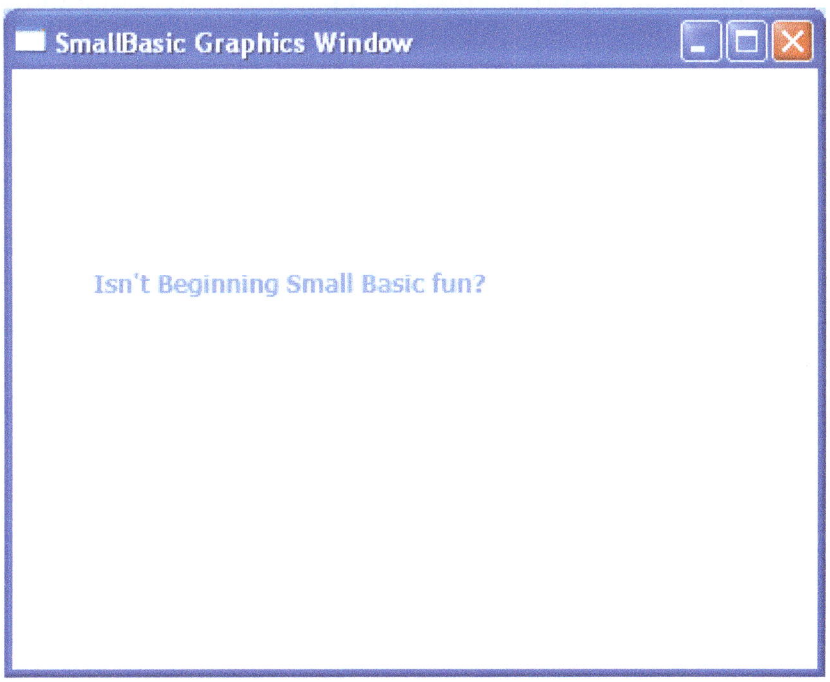

By setting the (x, y) point, you can left or right justify the text, or center it horizontally and/or vertically by knowing the window dimensions. It is possible to change the font (type, size, style) using Small Basic code, but that is beyond our discussion in this class. Perhaps, you can do some research on your own to figure out how to do this. It involves something called a **Font** object – what else?

Animation

In an earlier example (the one with the hypnotic ellipses), we saw that by using a timer to periodically change the display in a window, a sense of motion, or animation, is obtained. We will use that idea here to do a specific kind of animation - moving objects around. This is the basis for nearly every video game ever made. The objects we move will be rectangular regions like rectangles and ellipses. As you advance in your Small Basic programming, you will find that all graphics objects (including pictures) are rectangular, so the information here will apply when you learn how to add pictures to a program. The objects we move are Small Basic **Shapes** objects.

A **Shapes** object is a rectangular region we can add, move and remove within the graphics window. Such an object makes animation (moving objects) very simple. For now, we will use two types of **Shapes** objects – a rectangle and an ellipse. To create a rectangular shape (**MyRectangle**) that is **RectW** pixels wide and **RectH** pixels high, use the **AddRectangle** method:

```
MyRectangle = Shapes.AddRectangle(RectW, RectH)
```

This will create a 'bordered' rectangle. The current pen color establishes the rectangle's border color, while the current brush color establishes the fill color. By default, it will be put in the upper left corner of the graphics window.

Start Small Basic and type these lines of code in the editor:

```
GraphicsWindow.Show()
GraphicsWindow.PenColor = "Blue"
GraphicsWindow.BrushColor = "Red"
MyRectangle = Shapes.AddRectangle(100, 50)
```

Run the program to see the resulting rectangle (100 pixels wide, 50 pixels high, blue border, red fill) in the upper left corner of the window:

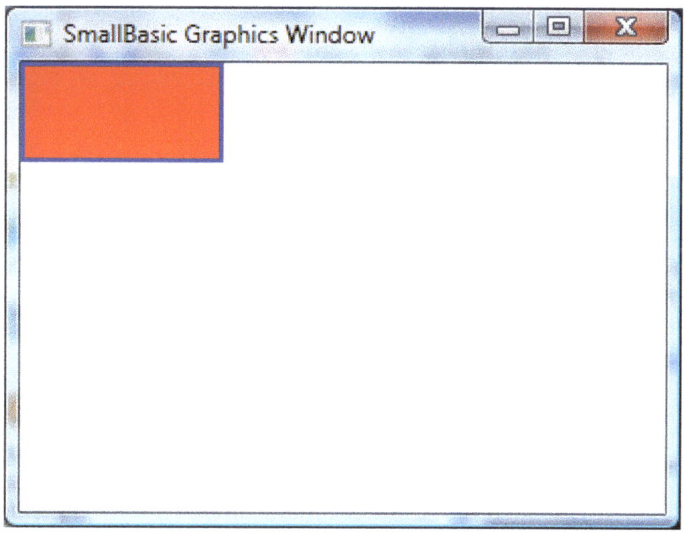

Analogously, to create an elliptical shape (**MyEllipse**) that is **EllW** pixels wide and **EllH** pixels high, use the **AddEllipse** method:

```
MyEllipse = Shapes.AddEllipse(EllW, EllH)
```

This will create a 'bordered' ellipse. The current pen color establishes the ellipse border color, while the current brush color establishes the fill color. By default, it will be put in the upper left corner of the graphics window.

Replace the code in the Small Basic editor with this code:

```
GraphicsWindow.Show()
GraphicsWindow.PenColor = "Red"
GraphicsWindow.BrushColor = "Yellow"
MyEllipse = Shapes.AddRectangle(50, 100)
```

When run this, you will see an ellipse 50 pixels wide by 100 pixels high with a red border and yellow fill:

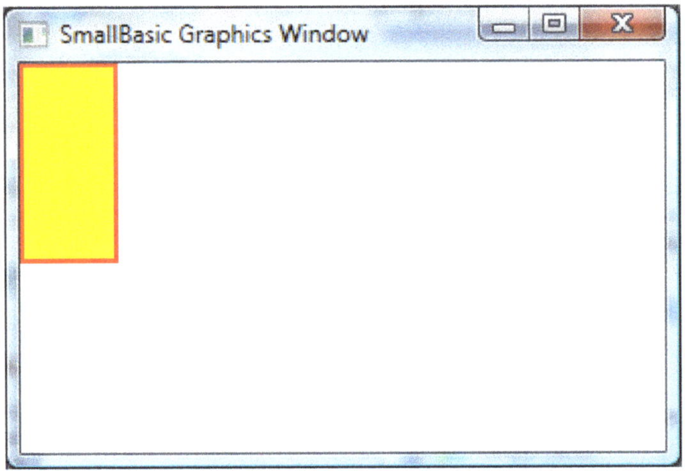

Moving shape objects in a graphics window is easy to do. It is a simple two step process: use some rule to determine a new position, then redraw it in this new position using the Shapes object **Move** method. If you have a shape object named **MyShape** and you want to move it to (**NewX**, **NewY**), the code is:

```
Shapes.Move(MyShape, NewX, NewY)
```

This code will 'erase' **MyShape** at its current position, then 'redraw' it at the newly specified position. Successive transfers (or moves) gives the impression of motion, or animation. Modify the ellipse example by adding the one line of code using the **Move** method:

```
Shapes.Move(MyEllipse, 100, 50)
```

Rerun and you will see the ellipse has disappeared from the upper left corner](0, 0)] of the window and moved to the new position at (100, 50).

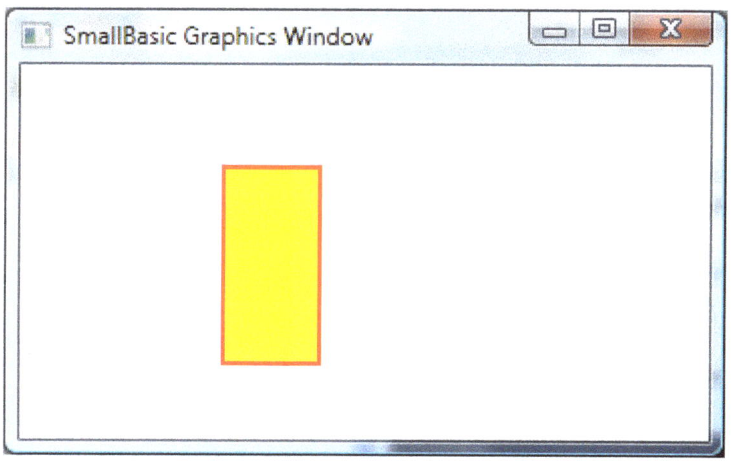

Where do we put the statements implementing this erase-then-draw process? Each object to be moved must have an associated timer object. The "drawing" statement is placed in the timer object's Tick event. Whenever a timer event is triggered, a new shape position is computed and the corresponding graphics method to move the shape is executed. This periodic movement is animation. Let's look at an example to see how simple animation with shapes really is.

Example

Return to Small Basic and start a new program. Name it **Animate**. We resize the graphics window to make it taller than it is wide. We add a timer object (100 millisecond **Interval**) and an empty **Tick** event subroutine (**TimerTickEvent**). We make sure the timer is off initially (using **TimerOn** to monitor status). We also add a **MouseDown** event subroutine (**MouseDownEvent**) to toggle the timer. You can copy much of this code from the **Timer** example we tried earlier. The code is:

```
GraphicsWindow.Show()
GraphicsWindow.Width = 200
GraphicsWindow.Height = 400
GraphicsWindow.Title = "Animation"
Timer.Tick = TimerTickEvent
Timer.Interval = 100
Timer.Pause()
TimerOn = "false"
GraphicsWindow.MouseDown = MouseDownEvent

Sub TimerTickEvent
EndSub

Sub MouseDownEvent
  If (TimerOn = "true") Then
    TimerOn = "false"
    Timer.Pause()
  Else
    TimerOn = "true"
    Timer.Resume()
  EndIf
EndSub
```

We will use this example a lot.

Save and run to make sure things look okay – the graphics window should appear as:

Now, let's add the code to try some animation.

We will see if we can make a ball (represented by an ellipse) drop down the window. Add this code to the 'main' code region to define a shape object (**Ball**):

```
BallX = 75
BallY = 0
BallW = 50
BallH = 50
BallDir = 1
GraphicsWindow.PenColor = "Black"
GraphicsWindow.BrushColor = "Red"
Ball = Shapes.AddEllipse(BallW, BallH)
Shapes.Move(Ball, BallX, BallY)
```

The ball is 50 pixels wide (**BallW**) and 50 pixels high (**BallH**) (which technically makes it a circle, not an ellipse) and is colored red, with a black border. We use a variable (**BallY**) to keep track of the vertical position. We initially move the ball to horizontally center it (using **BallX** = 75) at the top of the window. Now, use this code in the timer's **TimerTickEvent** subroutine to move the ball:

```
Sub TimerTickEvent
  BallY = BallY + 10
  Shapes.Move(Ball, BallX, BallY)
EndSub
```

In this routine, the vertical position of the ball (**BallY**) is increased by 10 pixels each time the event is executed (every 0.1 seconds). The ball is moving down. It should take 40 executions of this routine, or about 4 seconds, for the ball to reach the bottom of the window. Let's try it.

Run the example program. Click the window to start the timer. Watch the ball drop. Here's what it should look like:

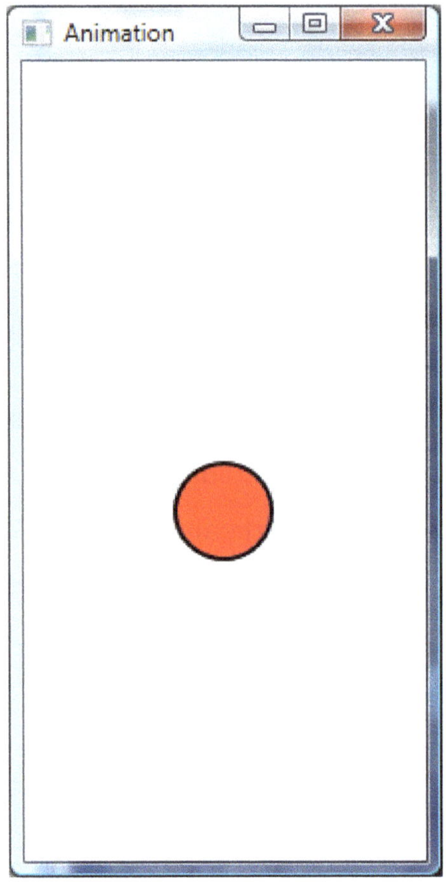

Pretty easy, wasn't it? How long does it take the ball to reach the bottom? What happens when it reaches the bottom? It just keeps on going down through the window and out through the bottom of your computer monitor to who knows where! We need to be able to detect this disappearance and do something about it. We'll look at two ways to handle this. First, we'll make the ball reappear at the top of the window, or scroll. Then, we'll make it bounce. Stop the program. Save it too. We'll be using it again.

Object Disappearance

When shape objects are moving in a window, we need to know when they move out of the window across a border. Such information is often needed in video type games. We just saw this need with the falling ball example. When an **object disappearance** happens, we can either ignore that object or perhaps make it "scroll" around to other side of the window. How do we decide if an object has disappeared? It's basically a case of comparing various positions and dimensions.

We need to detect whether an object has completely moved across one of four window borders (top, bottom, left, right). Each of these detections can be developed using this diagram of a rectangular object within a graphics window (**GraphicsWindow**):

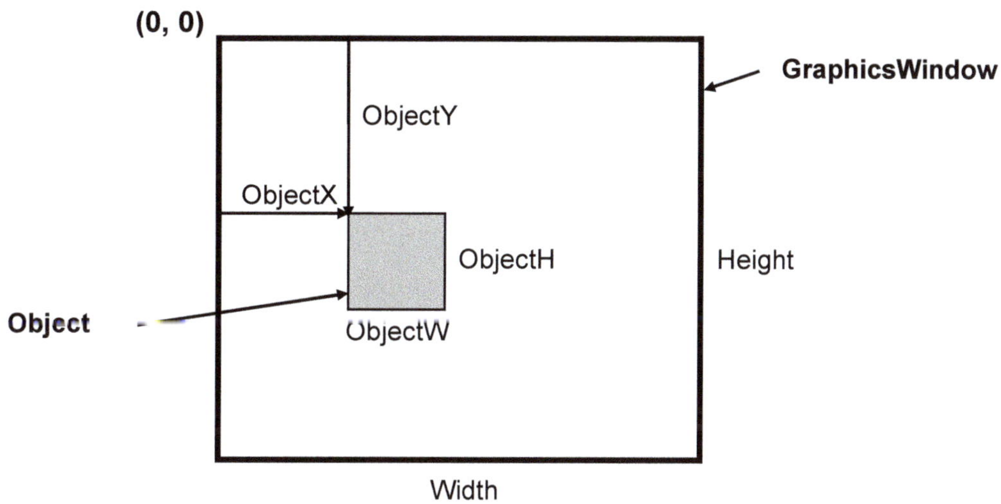

Notice the object is located at (**ObjectX**, **ObjectY**) and is **ObjectW** pixels wide and **ObjectH** pixels high.

The graphics window is **Width** pixels wide and **Height** pixels high. You usually know these values from the statement that originally created the window. To obtain these values in code, you can use (this makes your code more general):

```
Width = GraphicsWindow.Width
Height = GraphicsWindow.Height
```

If the object is moving down, it completely crosses the window bottom border when its top (**ObjectY**) is lower than the bottom border. The bottom of the window is **GraphicsWindow.Height**. Small Basic code for a bottom border disappearance is:

```
If (ObjectY > GraphicsWindow.Height) Then
  'Small Basic code for bottom border disappearance
EndIf
```

If the object is moving up, the window top border is completely crossed when the bottom of the object (**ObjectY + ObjectH**) becomes less than 0. In Small Basic, this is detected with:

```
If ((ObjectY + ObjectH) < 0) Then
  'Small Basic code for top border disappearance
EndIf
```

If the object is moving to the left, the window left border is completely crossed when object right side (**ObjectX + ObjectW)** becomes less than 0. In Small Basic, this is detected with:

```
If ((ObjectX + ObjectW) < 0) Then
  'Small Basic code for left border disappearance
EndIf
```

If the object is moving to the right, it completely crosses the window right border when its left side (**ObjectX**) passes the border. The right side of the window is **GraphicsWindow.Width**. Small Basic code for a right border disappearance is:

```
If (ObjectX > GraphicsWindow.Width) Then
  'Small Basic code for right border disappearance
EndIf
```

Let's add disappearance detection to our "falling ball" example. Return to that program. Say, instead of having the ball disappear when it reaches the bottom, we have it magically reappear at the top of the window - the object is scrolling. Modify the **TimerTickEvent** subroutine to this (new lines are shaded):

```
Sub TimerTickEvent
  BallY = BallY + 10
  If (BallY > GraphicsWindow.Height) Then
    BallY = -BallH
  EndIf
  Shapes.Move(Ball, BallX, BallY)
EndSub
```

We added the bottom border disappearance logic. When the ball disappears, we reset its BallY value so it is repositioned just off the top of the window. Run the program. Watch the ball scroll. Pretty easy, wasn't it? Stop and save the program.

Border Crossing

What if, in the falling ball example, instead of scrolling, we want the ball to bounce back up when it reaches the bottom border? This is another common animation task - detecting the initiation of **border crossings**. Such crossings are used to change the direction of moving objects, that is, make them bounce. How do we detect border crossings?

The same diagram used for image disappearances can be used here. Checking to see if an image has crossed a window border is like checking for object disappearance, except the object has not moved quite as far. For top and bottom checks, the object movement is less by an amount equal to its height (ObjectH). For left and right checks, the movement is less by an amount equal to its width (ObjectW). Look back at that diagram and you should see these code segments accomplish the respective border crossing directions:

```
If (ObjectY < 0) Then
  'Small Basic code for top border crossing
EndIf

If ((ObjectY + ObjectH) > GraphicsWindow.Height) Then
  'Small Basic code for bottom border crossing
EndIf

If (ObjectX < 0) Then
  'Small Basic code for left border crossing
EndIf

If ((ObjectX + ObjectW) > GraphicsWindow.Width) Then
  'Small Basic code for right border crossing
EndIf
```

Let's modify the falling ball example to have it bounce when it reaches the bottom of the window. Define a new variable **BallDir.** BallDir is used to indicate which way the object (ball) is moving. When BallDir is 1, the ball is moving down (BallY is increasing). When BallDir is -1, the ball is moving up (BallY is decreasing). Initialize the variable to 1 in the main code:

```
BallDir = 1
```

Change the **TimerTickEvent** subroutine to this (again, changed and/or new lines are shaded):

```
Sub TimerTickEvent
  BallY = BallY + BallDir * 10
  If ((BallY + BallH) > GraphicsWindow.Height) Then
    BallY = GraphicsWindow.Height - BallH
    BallDir = -1
  EndIf
  Shapes.Move(Ball, BallX, BallY)
EndSub
```

We modified the calculation of BallY to account for the BallDir variable. Notice how it is used to impart the proper direction to the ball motion (down when BallDir is 1, up when BallDir is –1). We have also added the If structure for a bottom border crossing. Notice when a crossing is detected, the ball is repositioned (by resetting BallY) at the bottom of the window (**GraphicsWindow.Height - BallH**) and BallDir is set to -1 (direction is changed so the ball will start moving up). Run the program. Now when the ball reaches the bottom of the window, it reverses direction and heads back up. We've made the ball bounce! But, once it reaches the top, it's gone again!

Add top border crossing detection, so the timer **TimerTickEvent** subroutine is now (changes are shaded):

```
Sub TimerTickEvent
  BallY = BallY + BallDir * 10
  If ((BallY + BallH) > GraphicsWindow.Height) Then
    BallY = GraphicsWindow.Height - BallH
    BallDir = -1
    Sound.PlayBellRing()
  ElseIf (BallY < 0) Then
    BallY = 0
    BallDir = 1
    Sound.PlayBellRing()
  EndIf
  Shapes.Move(Ball, BallX, BallY)
EndSub
```

In the top crossing code (the ElseIf portion), we reset BallY to 0 (the top of the window) and change BallDir to 1. We've also added a couple of "bell ring" statements so there is some audible feedback when either bounce occurs. Run the program again. Your ball will now bounce up and down, ringing with each bounce, until you stop it. Stop and save the program.

The code we've developed here for checking and resetting object positions is a common task in Small Basic. As you develop your programming skills, you should make sure you are comfortable with what all these locations and dimensions mean and how they interact. As an example, can you see why a horizontal position of 75 centers the ball in the window? The equation used was:

```
BallX = 0.5 * (GraphicsWindow.Width - BallW)
```

Plug in the window width of 200 and ball width of 50 and the calculation gives you the resulting 75.

You've now seen how to do lots of things with animations. You can make objects move, make them disappear and reappear, and make them bounce. Do you have some ideas of simple video games you would like to build? You still need two more skills – object erasure and collision detection - which are discussed next.

Object Erasure

The **Shapes** method **Move** erases a shape in its previous location before moving it to a new location. This erasure is automatic. What if you need to do this in a program – that is, you need to remove a shape from the graphics window? Perhaps in a video game, your spaceship shoots down an alien ship and you need to erase that ship. The **Shapes** method that does this is **Remove**. If we want to completely erase a previously defined shape object (**MyShape**) from the graphics window, use:

```
Shapes.Remove(MyShape)
```

This does not delete the shape object from the program. It is still available for animation use. Subsequent Move methods can be used to place the shape back in the window.

Collision Detection

Another requirement in animation is to determine if two objects have collided. This is needed in games to see if a ball hits a paddle, if an alien rocket hits its target, or if a cute little character grabs some reward. Each object is described by a rectangular area, so the **collision detection** problem is to see if two rectangles collide, or overlap. This check is done using each object's position and dimensions.

Here are two objects (**Object1** and **Object2**) in a window:

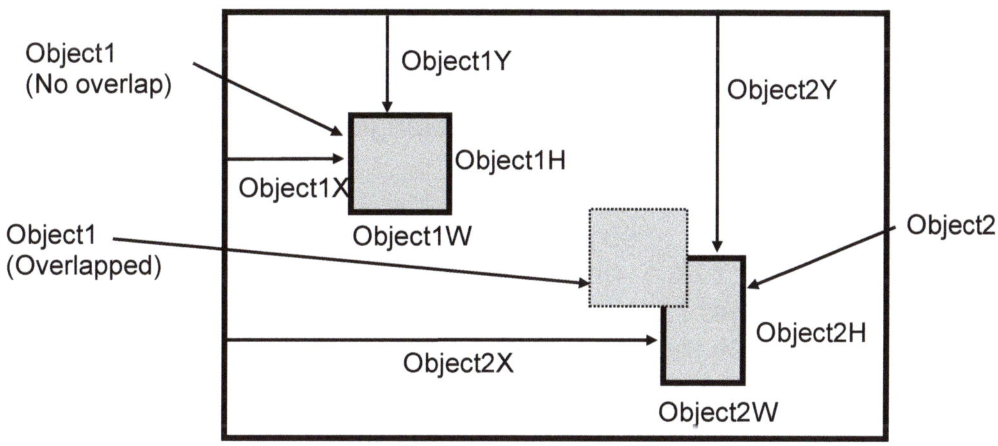

Object1 is positioned at (**Object1X**, **Object1Y**), is **Object1W** wide and **Object1H** high. Similarly, **Object2** is positioned at (**Object2X**, **Object2Y**), is **Object2W** wide and **Object2H** high.

Looking at this diagram, you should see there are four requirements for the two rectangles to overlap:

1. The right side of Object1 (**Object1X + Object1H**) must be "farther right" than the left side of Object2 (**Object2X**)
2. The left side of Object1 (**Object1X**) must be "farther left" than the right side of Object2 (**Object2X + Object2W**)
3. The bottom of Object1 (**Object1Y + Object1H**) must be "farther down" than the top of Object2 (**Object2Y**)
4. The top of Object1 (**Object1Y**) must be "farther up" than the bottom of Object2 (**Object2Y + Object2H**)

All four of these requirements must be met for a collision.

The Small Basic code to check if these rectangles overlap is:

```
If ((Object1X + Object1W) > Object2X) Then
  If (Object1X < (Object2X + Object2W)) Then
    If ((Object1Y + Object1H) > Object2Y) Then
      If (Object1Y < (Object2Y + Object2H)) Then
        ' Small Basic code for overlap, or collision
      EndIf
    EndIf
  EndIf
EndIf
```

This code checks the four conditions for overlap using four "nested" If structures. The Small Basic code for a collision is executed only if all four conditions are found to be true.

Let's try some collision detection with the bouncing ball example. We will draw a small paddle (a rectangle) near the bottom of the window and see if the ball collides with the paddle. Add these variables to establish the paddle object (**Paddle**) (I placed these lines at the end of my main code):

```
PaddleX = 100
PaddleY = 380
PaddleW= 20
PaddleH = 20
GraphicsWindow.PenColor = "Black"
GraphicsWindow.BrushColor = "Blue"
Paddle = Shapes.AddRectangle(PaddleW, PaddleH)
Shapes.Move(Paddle, PaddleX, PaddleY)
```

Modify the timer **TimerTickEvent** subroutine code to (added code is shaded):

```
Sub TimerTickEvent
  BallY = BallY + BallDir * 10
  Collision = "false"
  If ((BallX + BallW) > PaddleX) Then
    If (BallX < (PaddleX + PaddleW)) Then
      If ((BallY + BallH) > PaddleY) Then
        If (BallY < (PaddleY + PaddleH)) Then
          Collision = "true"
        EndIf
      EndIf
    EndIf
  EndIf
  If (Collision = "true") Then
    BallY = PaddleY - BallH
    BallDir = -1
    Sound.PlayBellRing()
  ElseIf (BallY < 0) Then
    BallY = 0
    BallDir = 1
    Sound.PlayBellRing()
  EndIf
  Shapes.Move(Ball, BallX, BallY)
EndSub
```

We use a variable **Collision** to indicate an overlap (true for overlap, false for no overlap). The overlap code (using the paddle object variables PaddleX, PaddleY, PaddleW, PaddleH) precedes the Move method. If a collision is detected, the object (ball) is repositioned so it just touches the top of the rectangle, its direction is reversed and a ring is played. The code for bouncing off the top of the window is unchanged.

Run the program. You should see:

Notice the ball now bounces off the paddle. Stop the program. Move the paddle out of the way (set PaddleX to 0) so the ball won't collide with it. The ball should just drop off the screen. See how close the ball can pass by the paddle without colliding to make sure the overlap routine works properly. Stop and save the program.

Now that you know how to detect collisions, you're well on your way to knowing how to build a simple video game. Next, we'll learn how to detect keyboard events from the user. One possible use for these events, among many, is to allow a user to move the little paddle to "hit" the dropping ball. The collision technique we just learned will come in handy for such a task.

Keyboard Methods

In Class 8, we looked at ways for a user to interact with a Small Basic program using the mouse for input. We studied two mouse events and associated methods: **MouseDown** and **MouseMove**. Another input device available for use is the computer keyboard. Here we look at **keyboard events** which give our programs the ability to detect user input from the keyboard. Just one keyboard event is studied: the **KeyDown** event.

KeyDown Event

The **KeyDown** event has the ability to detect the pressing of a key on the computer keyboard. Among others, it can detect:

- Letter and number keys
- Numeric keypad keys (it can distinguish these numbers from those on the top row of the keyboard)
- Cursor control keys

The **KeyDown** event is triggered whenever a key is pressed. If the subroutine to be executed in case of such an event is **KeyDownEvent**, we add this event to our program using:

```
GraphicsWindow.KeyDown = KeyDownEvent
```

The corresponding subroutine is added to the program in the usual manner and has the form:

```
Sub KeyDownEvent
  ' Small Basic code for KeyDown event
EndSub
```

To determine which key was pressed, use the **LastKey** method of the graphics window:

```
KeyPressed = GraphicsWindow.LastKey
```

KeyPressed returns a string representation of the pressed key. Here are returned values for some of the keys on a standard keyboard.

Letter and Number Keys

Key	Value	Key	Value	Key	Value	Key	Value
A	"A"	J	"J"	S	"S"	1	"D1"
B	"B"	K	"K"	T	"T"	2	"D2"
C	"C"	L	"L"	U	"U"	3	"D3"
D	"D"	M	"M"	V	"V"	4	"D4"
E	"E"	N	"N"	W	"W"	5	"D5"
F	"F"	O	"O"	X	"X"	6	"D6"
G	"G"	P	"P"	Y	"Y"	7	"D7"
H	"H"	Q	"Q"	Z	"Z"	8	"D8"
I	"I"	R	"R"	0	"D0"	9	"D9"

Numeric Keypad Keys

Key	Value	Key	Value
0	"NumPad0"	8	"NumPad8"
1	"NumPad1"	9	"NumPad9"
2	"NumPad2"	/	"Divide"
3	"NumPad3"	*	"Multiply"
4	"NumPad4"	-	"Subtract"
5	"NumPad5"	+	"Add"
6	"NumPad6"	Enter	"Return"
7	"NumPad7"	.	"Decimal"

Cursor Control Keys

Key	Value	Key	Value
Left arrow	"Left"	Delete	"Delete"
Right arrow	"Right"	Home	"Home"
Up arrow	"Up"	End	"End"
Down arrow	"Down"	Page Up	"PageUp"
Insert	"Insert"	Page Down	"Next"

Using the **KeyDown** event is not easy. There is a lot of work involved in interpreting the information provided in the KeyDown event and **LastKey** method. For example, the KeyDown event cannot distinguish between an upper and lower case letter and many symbols (!, @, #, …) cannot be easily recognized (it is possible to make such distinctions but beyond the scope of this tutorial). You usually use an If structure to determine which key was pressed. For example, to see if the letter Q is pressed, we would write code like this:

```
If (GraphicsWindow.LastKey = "Q") Then
  ' code to execute if Q is pressed
EndIf
```

Notice you must enclose the desired key value in quotes since it is a string value. Let's see how to use KeyDown to recognize some keys.

Start Small Basic and start a new program. Add this code:

```
GraphicsWindow.KeyDown = KeyDownEvent

Sub KeyDownEvent
  TextWindow.WriteLine("You pressed " + GraphicsWindow.LastKey)
EndSubEndSub
```

Here we assign the **KeyDown** event to the **KeyDownEvent** subroutine. In this subroutine, we have a single line that writes out the pressed key value (using the **LastKey** method) in the text window.

Run this little program. An empty graphics window will appear. Press a key – a text window will appear with a message indicating which key you pressed. Move the graphics and text windows so you can see them both. At this point, click in the graphics window to make it the active window and able to accept further key presses. Type a letter. The letter's corresponding **LastKey** value (without quotes) is shown. Press the same letter while holding down the <Shift> key. The same value will appear – there is no distinction between upper and lower case. Press each of the four arrow keys to see their different values. Type numbers using the top row of the keyboard and the numeric keypad. Notice the keypad numbers have different key code values than the "keyboard numbers." This lets us distinguish the keypad from the keyboard. Try various keys on the keyboard to see which keys have a key code (all of them). Notice it works with function keys, cursor control keys, letters, numbers, everything! Stop the program.

Now, let's modify the animation example we've been working on to use the left and right cursor control keys to move the little rectangle. Open your saved copy of the animation program (**Animate**). Add this line of code (in the main code area) to set up the **KeyDown** event:

```
GraphicsWindow.KeyDown = KeyDownEvent
```

Add the **KeyDownEvent** subroutine:

```
Sub KeyDownEvent
  '  compute new location of paddle
  If (GraphicsWindow.LastKey = "Left") Then
    PaddleX = PaddleX -1
  ElseIf (GraphicsWindow.LastKey = "Right") Then
    PaddleX = PaddleX + 1
  EndIf
  ' move paddle
  Shapes.Move(Paddle, PaddleX, PaddleY)
EndSub
```

In this code, if either the left or right cursor key is pressed, the paddle's x coordinate is updated. The paddle is moved. Save and run the program. Notice how the cursor control keys move the rectangle. We have that "paddle" we've been looking for. This last version is saved in the **Animate** folder in the course program folder (**\BeginSB\BSB Code**).

Program –Balloons

In this class program, we will build a little video game. Colorful balloons are dropping from the sky. You maneuver a popping device under them to make them pop and get a point. You try to pop as many balloons as you can in one minute. This program is saved in the **Balloons** folder in the programs folder (**\BeginSB\BSB Code**).

Program Design

All of the game action will go on in a graphics window. There will be five possible balloons, all ellipse shape objects. An arrow (a triangle shape object) will be the "popping arrow." This arrow will be moved using cursor keys on the keyboard. Clicking the graphics window will control starting and stopping the game. The current score (number of balloons popped) will be displayed in the window. The steps of the program we will follow:

1. Initialize score and balloon locations.
2. When graphics window is clicked, start the timer dropping the balloons.
3. Monitor KeyDown event for arrow movement.
4. Monitor timer's Tick event for collisions and misses – update score.

When writing the code, we will look at each of these steps in more detail.

Program Development

The Balloons game is simple, in concept. To play, click the window. The five balloons will drop down the window, each at a different speed. Use the left and right arrow keys to move the arrow. If the arrow is under a balloon when a collision occurs, the balloon pops and you get a point. Balloons reappear at the top after popping or after reaching the bottom of the screen without being popped. You pop as many balloons as you can in 60 seconds. At that point, the game ends.

There are a few events to write code for: clicking the window to start and checking for arrow key presses. And, we will also need a timer (and its Tick event) to control the balloon animation, updating the window 10 times a second (Interval will be 100). There is a substantial amount of Small Basic code to write here, even though you will see there is a lot of repetition. We suggest writing the event subroutines in stages. Write one subroutine or a part of a subroutine. Save and run the program. Make sure the code you wrote works. Add more code. Run the program again. Make sure the added code works. Continue adding code until complete. Building a program this way minimizes the potential for error and makes the debugging process much easier. Let’s go.

Start Small Basic and start a new program. Save it as **Balloons**. Add this initial code:

```
'
'  Balloons
'  Beginning Small Basic
'
GraphicsWindow.Show()
GraphicsWindow.Title = "Balloons"
GraphicsWindow.Width = 400
GraphicsWindow.Height = 400
' start message
GraphicsWindow.BrushColor = "Black"
GraphicsWindow.DrawText(100, 200 "Click Window To Start")
```

This just sets up the graphics window and prints a starting message. Save and run the program to insure you have a good starting point. Note the window is 400 x 400 pixels in size. This lets us space five balloons (50 pixels wide) across the window (with 10 pixels between each balloon). We also leave some room on the right side of the window to print the score.

Here's what I see when I run this little program:

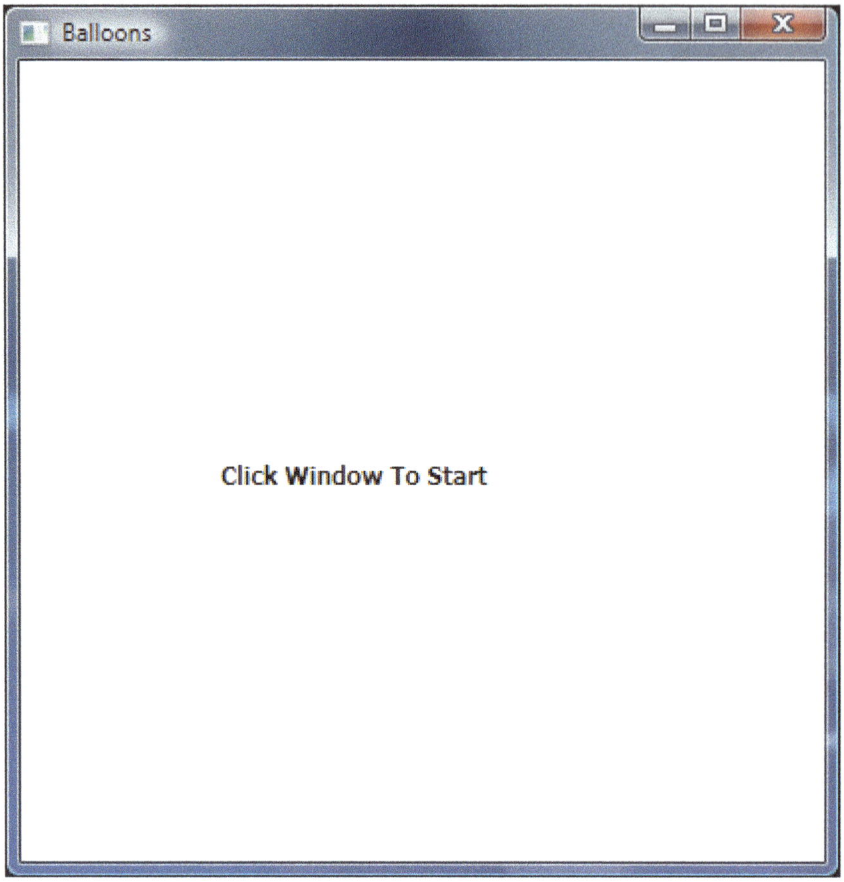

Clicking the window with the mouse will initialize the game, setting up the balloons and popping arrow. The **MouseDown** method does the work. Add this line after the code printing the message:

```
GraphicsWindow.MouseDown = MouseDownEvent
```

And add the empty subroutine:

```
Sub MouseDownEvent
EndSub
```

The balloons will be represented by an array of shape objects (**Balloon**). Each balloon will be a different color and occupy a square region, 50 pixels (**BalloonSize**) wide by 50 pixels high. We will also use arrays to keep track of each balloon's location (**BalloonX**, **BalloonY**) and dropping speed (**BalloonSpeed**). The arrow will be a shape object (**Arrow**). Its width (**ArrowSize**) will be half the width of a balloon and its position will be given by **ArrowX**. When the program first starts, we need to follow these steps:

- Create each balloon object and initialize the positions
- Create the arrow object and initialize its position
- Initialize the score

Let's add code to the editor to perform each of these steps. First, set up the balloon objects with this code in the **MouseDownEvent** subroutine:

```
Sub MouseDownEvent
  GraphicsWindow.Clear()
  Score = 0
  UpdateScore()
  BalloonSize = 50
  GraphicsWindow.PenColor = "Black"
  GraphicsWindow.BrushColor = "Red"
  Balloon[1] = Shapes.AddEllipse(BalloonSize, BalloonSize)
  GraphicsWindow.BrushColor = "Blue"
  Balloon[2] = Shapes.AddEllipse(BalloonSize, BalloonSize)
  GraphicsWindow.BrushColor = "Green"
  Balloon[3] = Shapes.AddEllipse(BalloonSize, BalloonSize)
  GraphicsWindow.BrushColor = "Magenta"
  Balloon[4] = Shapes.AddEllipse(BalloonSize, BalloonSize)
  GraphicsWindow.BrushColor = "Cyan"
  Balloon[5] = Shapes.AddEllipse(BalloonSize, BalloonSize)
  ' put 10 pixels between each balloon
  For i = 1 To 5
    BalloonX[i] = 10 + (i - 1) * (BalloonSize + 10)
    BalloonY[i] = 0
    BalloonSpeed[i] = Math.GetRandomNumber(4) + 2
    Shapes.Move(Balloon[i], BalloonX[i], BalloonY[i])
  EndFor
EndSub
```

First, it clears the message screen, initializes the score (**Score**) and calls a yet unwritten subroutine (**UpdateScore**) to display this score. Next, it sets up the balloons. A little about how we determined balloon speeds. The array **BalloonSpeed** holds the five speeds, representing the number of pixels a balloon will drop with each update of the viewing window. We want each balloon to drop at a different rate. In code, each speed is computed using:

```
Math.GetRandomNumber(4) + 2
```

Or, it will be a random value between 3 and 6. A new speed will be computed each time a balloon starts its trip down the window. How do we know this will be a good speed, providing reasonable dropping rates? We didn't before the program began. This expression was arrived at by 'trial and error.' We built the game and tried different speeds until we found values that worked. You do this a lot in developing games. You may not know values for some numbers before you start. So, you go ahead and build the game and try all kinds of values until you find ones that work. Then, you build these numbers into your code.

As mentioned, for this code to work, we need one additional subroutine. The subroutine (**UpdateScore**) to update the score is:

```
Sub UpdateScore
  ' draw the score
  GraphicsWindow.BrushColor = GraphicsWindow.BackgroundColor
  GraphicsWindow.FillRectangle(340, 80, 400, 120)
  GraphicsWindow.BrushColor = "Black"
  GraphicsWindow.DrawText(320, 60, "Your Score:")
  GraphicsWindow.DrawText(350, 90, Score)
EndSub
```

Here, we clear any previous score, then redraw it in the graphics window. Add this subroutine.

Save and run the program. Click the window and this is what you should see:

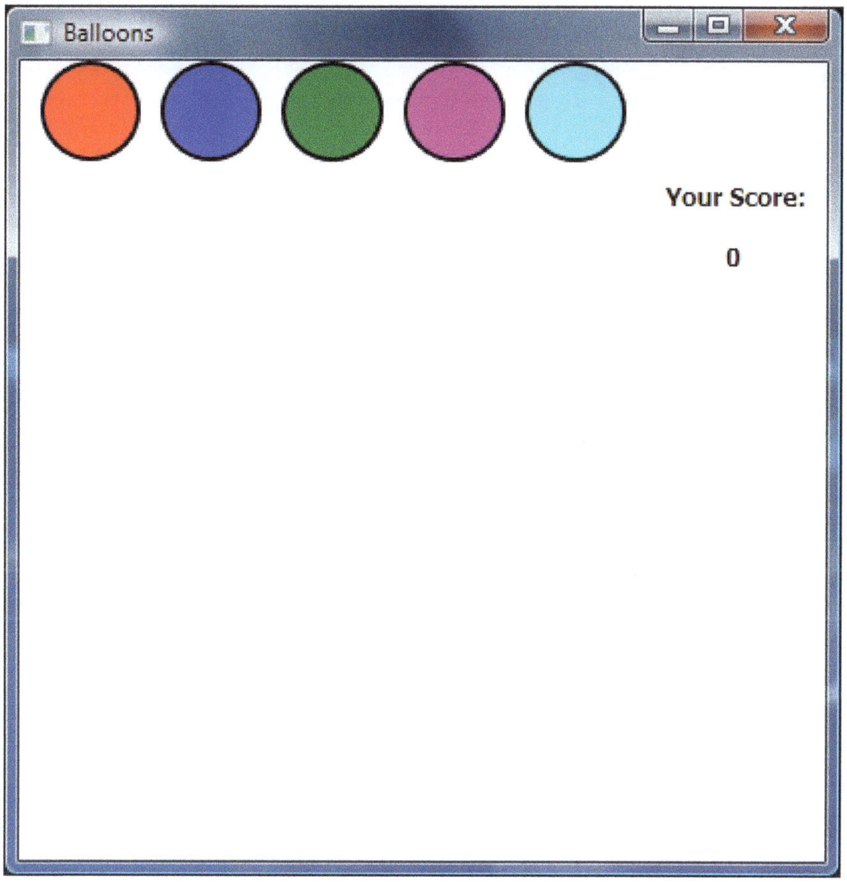

The five created balloon objects are at the top of the graphics window. The initial score is show to the right.

Let's add the arrow. Add this code (after the code setting up the balloons in the MouseDownEvent subroutine) to create and position the arrow object:

```
ArrowSize = BalloonSize / 2
ArrowX = 150
ArrowY = 370
GraphicsWindow.PenColor = "Black"
GraphicsWindow.BrushColor = "Yellow"
Arrow = Shapes.AddTriangle(0, 20, ArrowSize / 2, 0, ArrowSize,
20)
Shapes.Move(Arrow, ArrowX, ArrowY)
```

The **AddTriangle** method draws a triangle connecting the three points given. You should see that this code draws a black outlined, yellow filled triangle connecting these points:

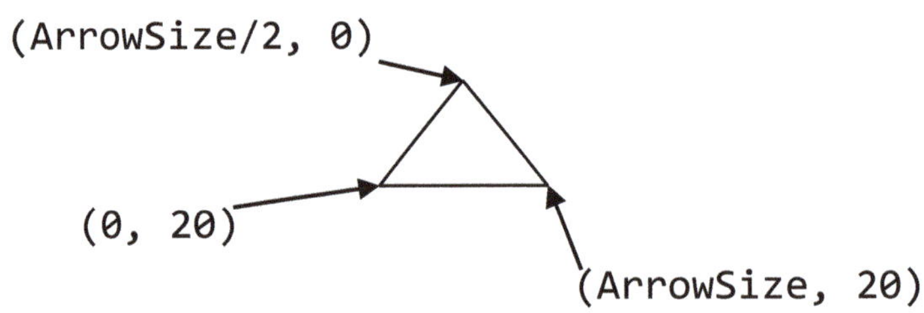

It is initially placed near the bottom approximately centered horizontally in the window.

Run to make sure you have no errors. Click and now you should see the score, the balloons and the popping arrow:

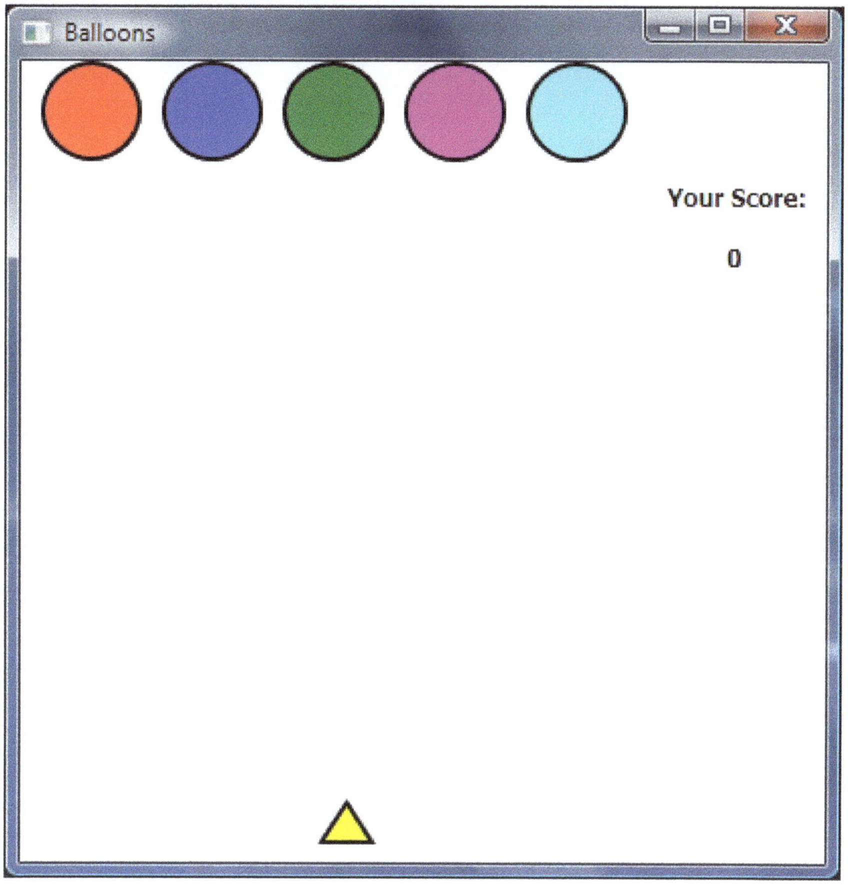

To move the arrow, we need a **KeyDown** event subroutine Pick a key that will move the arrow to the left and a key that will move it to the right. I chose **F** for **left** movement and **J** for **right** movement. Why? The keys are in the middle of the keyboard, with F to the left of J, and are easy to reach with a natural typing position. You could pick others. The arrow keys are one possibility. I hardly ever use these because they are always at some odd location on a keyboard and just not "naturally" reached. Also, the arrow keys are often used (in more elaborate GUI programs) to move among controls in the window and this can get confusing.

In the main code region, add this line to establish the subroutine (**KeyDownEvent**):

```
GraphicsWindow.KeyDown = KeyDownEvent
```

And the subroutine is:

```
Sub KeyDownEvent
  ' Check for F key (left) and J key (right) and compute arrow
position
  If (GraphicsWindow.LastKey = "F") Then
    ArrowX = ArrowX - 5
  ElseIf (GraphicsWindow.LastKey = "J") Then
    ArrowX = ArrowX + 5
  EndIf
  ' Position arrow
  Shapes.Move(Arrow, ArrowX, ArrowY)
EndSub
```

Notice if the F key is pressed, the arrow is moved to the left by 5 pixels. The arrow is moved right by 5 pixels if the J key is pressed. Again, the 5 pixels value was found by 'trial and error' - it seems to provide smooth motion. After typing in this subroutine, save the program, then run it. Click the window to start things. Make sure the arrow moves as expected. It should start near the middle of the window. Notice there is no code that keeps the arrow from moving out of the window - you could add it if you like. You would need to detect a left or right border crossing. Stop the program.

Let's add capability to use a timer object to control the balloon's dropping. Add these lines to assign the subroutine **TimerTickEvent** to the **Tick** event and establish the **Interval** property:

```
Timer.Tick = TimerTickEvent
Timer.Interval = 100
Timer.Pause()
```

Notice we also make sure the timer is initially paused. Add these two lines at the end of the **MouseDownEvent** subroutine to turn on the timer and initialize a variable **TickCount**:

```
  Timer.Resume()
  TickCount = 0
```

TickCount is used to determine when to stop the game. It counts how many time's the timer's Tick event occurs. Once it reaches a particular value, we stop the game. We choose to let a game last for 60 seconds. Since the Tick event Interval is 100 or 0.1 seconds, we will stop the game once **TickCount** reaches **600**.

Now, what goes on in the timer event subroutine (**TimerTickEvent**)? Let's do the easy part first – stopping the game after 60 seconds. Recall we will use the **TickCount** variable to stop the game – once **TickCount** exceeds 600, we stop the game and setup for another game, if desired. The code that does this is:

```
Sub TimerTickEvent
  ' increment TickCount
  TickCount = TickCount + 1
  If (TickCount > 600) Then
    ' game over
    Timer.Pause()
    GraphicsWindow.Clear()
    GraphicsWindow.BrushColor = "Black"
    GraphicsWindow.DrawText(50, 200, "Game is over. Final score is
" + Score + " points.")
    GraphicsWindow.DrawText(50, 250, "Click window to play
again.")
  EndIf
EndSub
```

Save the program and run it. Play with the arrow again. After about 60 seconds, you should see the 'Game Over' notice pop up in the window. If this happens, the game stopping code is working. If it doesn't happen, you need to fix something.

Now, to the heart of the Balloons game. We haven't seen any dropping balloons yet. Here's where we do that, and more. Additional code in the **TimerTickEvent** subroutine handles the animation sequence. It drops the balloons down the screen, checks for popping, and checks for balloons reaching the bottom of the window. It gets new balloons started. There's a lot going on. The procedure steps are identical for each balloon. They are:

- Move the balloon.
- Check to see if balloon has popped. If so, sound a noise, make the balloon disappear, increment score and make balloon reappear at the top with a new speed.
- Check to see if balloon has reached the bottom without being popped. If so, start a new balloon with a new speed.

The steps are easy to write, just a little harder to code. Moving a balloon simply involves using the shape object **Move** method to position it at its new location (determined by the **BalloonY** value). To check if the balloon has reached the bottom, we use the border crossing logic discussed earlier. The trickiest step is checking if a balloon has popped. One way to check for a balloon pop is to check to see if the balloon rectangle overlaps the arrow rectangle using the collision detection logic developed earlier. This would work, but a balloon would pop if the arrow barely touched the balloon. In our code, we modify the collision logic such that we will not consider a balloon to be popped unless the entire width of the arrow is within the width of the balloon.

Here's the modified **TimerTickEvent** subroutine implementing these steps. The new code is shaded and placed before the code used to check if the game should stop. The balloons are handled individually within the structure of a For loop:

```
Sub TimerTickEvent
  For i = 1 To 5
    ' move balloon
    BalloonY[i] = BalloonY[i] + BalloonSpeed[i]
    ' check if balloon has popped
    If ((BalloonY[i] + BalloonSize) > ArrowY) Then
      If (BalloonX[i] < ArrowX) Then
        If ((BalloonX[i] + BalloonSize) > (ArrowX + ArrowSize))
Then
          ' Balloon has popped
          ' Increase score - move back to top
          Sound.PlayChime()
          Score = Score + 1
          UpdateScore()
          BalloonY[i] = - BalloonSize
          BalloonSpeed[i] = Math.GetRandomNumber(4) + 2
        EndIf
      EndIf
    EndIf
    ' check for moving off bottom
    If ((BalloonY[i] + BalloonSize) > GraphicsWindow.Height) Then
      ' Balloon reaches bottom without popping
      ' Move back to top with new speed
      BalloonY[i] = -BalloonSize
      BalloonSpeed[i] = Math.GetRandomNumber(4) + 2
    EndIf
    ' redraw balloon at new location, redraw arrow too
    Shapes.Move(Balloon[i], BalloonX[i], BalloonY[i])
  EndFor
  ' increment TickCount
  TickCount = TickCount + 1
  If (TickCount > 600) Then
    ' game over
    Timer.Pause()
    GraphicsWindow.Clear()
    GraphicsWindow.BrushColor = "Black"
    GraphicsWindow.DrawText(50, 200, "Game is over. Final score is
" + Score + " points.")
```

```
    GraphicsWindow.DrawText(50, 250, "Click window to play
again.")
  EndIf
EndSub
```

Do you see how all the steps are implemented? We added a sounding chime statement for some audio feedback when a balloon pops.

The code is complete. Make sure you have saved the files. The **Balloons** listing from the Small Basic editor is:

```
'
'  Balloons
'  Beginning Small Basic
'
GraphicsWindow.Show()
GraphicsWindow.Title = "Balloons"
GraphicsWindow.Width = 400
GraphicsWindow.Height = 400
' start message
GraphicsWindow.BrushColor = "Black"
GraphicsWindow.DrawText(100, 200 "Click Window To Start")
GraphicsWindow.MouseDown = MouseDownEvent
GraphicsWindow.KeyDown = KeyDownEvent
Timer.Tick = TimerTickEvent
Timer.Interval = 100
Timer.Pause()


Sub MouseDownEvent
  GraphicsWindow.Clear()
  Score = 0
  UpdateScore()
  BalloonSize = 50
  GraphicsWindow.PenColor = "Black"
  GraphicsWindow.BrushColor = "Red"
  Balloon[1] = Shapes.AddEllipse(BalloonSize, BalloonSize)
  GraphicsWindow.BrushColor = "Blue"
  Balloon[2] = Shapes.AddEllipse(BalloonSize, BalloonSize)
  GraphicsWindow.BrushColor = "Green"
  Balloon[3] = Shapes.AddEllipse(BalloonSize, BalloonSize)
  GraphicsWindow.BrushColor = "Magenta"
```

```
  Balloon[4] = Shapes.AddEllipse(BalloonSize, BalloonSize)
  GraphicsWindow.BrushColor = "Cyan"
  Balloon[5] = Shapes.AddEllipse(BalloonSize, BalloonSize)
  ' put 10 pixels between each balloon
  For i = 1 To 5
    BalloonX[i] = 10 + (i - 1) * (BalloonSize + 10)
    BalloonY[i] = 0
    BalloonSpeed[i] = Math.GetRandomNumber(4) + 2
    Shapes.Move(Balloon[i], BalloonX[i], BalloonY[i])
  EndFor
  ArrowSize = BalloonSize / 2
  ArrowX = 150
  ArrowY = 370
  GraphicsWindow.PenColor = "Black"
  GraphicsWindow.BrushColor = "Yellow"
  Arrow = Shapes.AddTriangle(0, 20, ArrowSize / 2, 0, ArrowSize,
20)
  Shapes.Move(Arrow, ArrowX, ArrowY)
  Timer.Resume()
  TickCount = 0
EndSub

Sub UpdateScore
  ' draw the score
  GraphicsWindow.BrushColor = GraphicsWindow.BackgroundColor
  GraphicsWindow.FillRectangle(340, 80, 400, 120)
  GraphicsWindow.BrushColor = "Black"
  GraphicsWindow.DrawText(320, 60, "Your Score:")
  GraphicsWindow.DrawText(350, 90, Score)
EndSub

Sub KeyDownEvent
  ' Check for F key (left) and J key (right) and compute arrow
position
  If (GraphicsWindow.LastKey = "F") Then
    ArrowX = ArrowX - 5
  ElseIf (GraphicsWindow.LastKey = "J") Then
    ArrowX = ArrowX + 5
  EndIf
  ' Position arrow
  Shapes.Move(Arrow, ArrowX, ArrowY)
EndSub

Sub TimerTickEvent
  For i = 1 To 5
    ' move balloon
```

```
    BalloonY[i] = BalloonY[i] + BalloonSpeed[i]
    ' check if balloon has popped
    If ((BalloonY[i] + BalloonSize) > ArrowY) Then
      If (BalloonX[i] < ArrowX) Then
        If ((BalloonX[i] + BalloonSize) > (ArrowX + ArrowSize))
Then
          ' Balloon has popped
          ' Increase score - move back to top
          Sound.PlayChime()
          Score = Score + 1
          UpdateScore()
          BalloonY[i] = - BalloonSize
          BalloonSpeed[i] = Math.GetRandomNumber(4) + 2
        EndIf
      EndIf
    EndIf
    ' check for moving off bottom
    If ((BalloonY[i] + BalloonSize) > GraphicsWindow.Height) Then
      ' Balloon reaches bottom without popping
      ' Move back to top with new speed
      BalloonY[i] = -BalloonSize
      BalloonSpeed[i] = Math.GetRandomNumber(4) + 2
    EndIf
    ' redraw balloon at new location, redraw arrow too
    Shapes.Move(Balloon[i], BalloonX[i], BalloonY[i])
  EndFor
  ' increment TickCount
  TickCount = TickCount + 1
  If (TickCount > 600) Then
    ' game over
    Timer.Pause()
    GraphicsWindow.Clear()
    GraphicsWindow.BrushColor = "Black"
    GraphicsWindow.DrawText(50, 200, "Game is over. Final score is
" + Score + " points.")
    GraphicsWindow.DrawText(50, 250, "Click window to play
again.")
  EndIf
EndSub
```

I know this is lots of code, but by building in stages, using subroutines, the work has not been too difficult, I hope.

Run the Program

Run the program. Click the window to get the balloons dropping. Make sure it works. Make sure each balloon falls. Make sure when a balloon reaches the bottom, a new one is initialized. Make sure you can pop each balloon. And, following a pop, make sure a new balloon appears. Make sure the score changes by one with each pop. Here's my finished version:

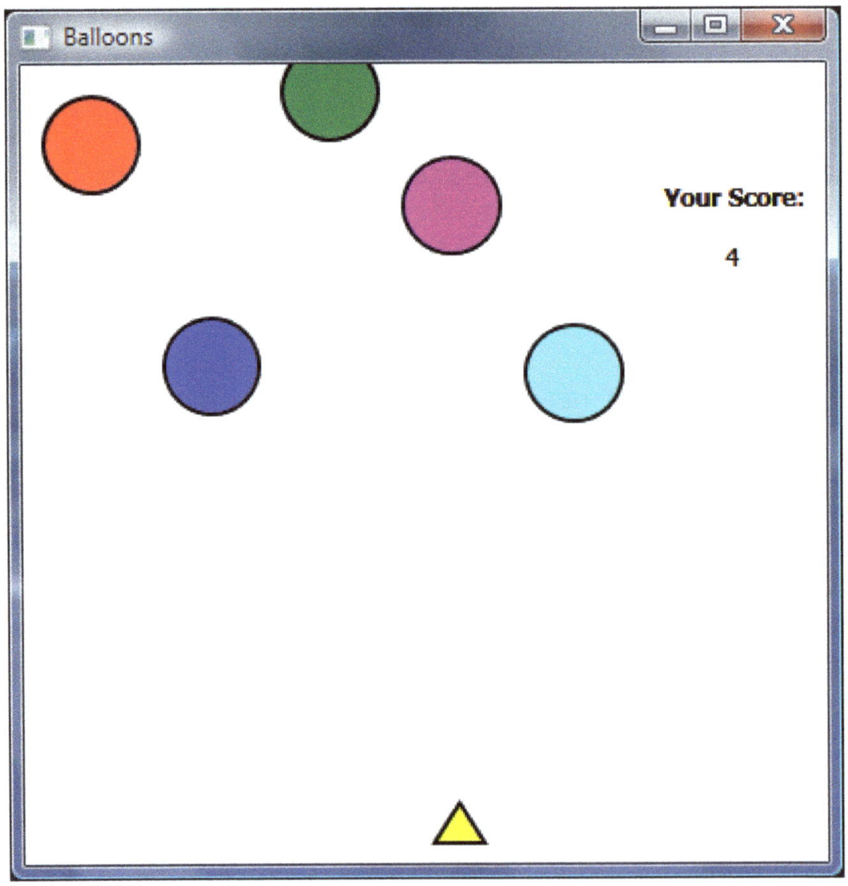

And here's my final screen:

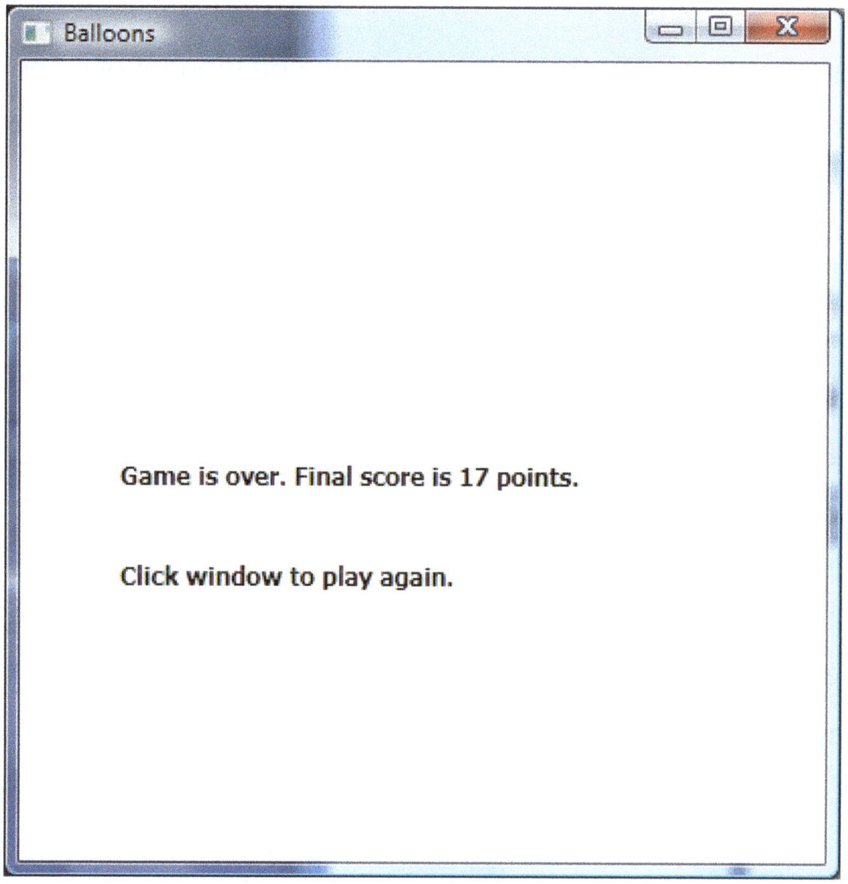

By building and testing the program in stages, you should now have a thoroughly tested, running version of Balloons. So relax and have fun playing it. Show your friends and family your great creation. If you do find any bugs and need to make any changes, make sure you resave your program.

Other Things to Try

I'm sure as you played the Balloons game, you thought of some changes you could make. Go ahead - give it a try! Here are some ideas we have.

When a balloon pops, it just disappears from the screen. Can you think of a more dramatic way to show popping? Maybe flash the window background color. Give the balloons a random color each time a new one appears.

Add selectable difficulty levels to the game. This could be used to make the game easy for little kids and very hard for experts. What can you do to adjust the game difficulty? One thing you could do is adjust the size of the popping arrow. To pop a balloon, the entire arrow width must fit within the width of a balloon. Hence, a smaller (narrower) arrow would make it easier to pop balloons before they reach the bottom of the window. A larger (wider) arrow makes popping harder. The balloon dropping speed also affects game difficulty. Slowly dropping balloons are easy to pop - fast ones are not. Play with the game to see what speeds would work for different difficulty levels.

Make it possible to play longer games and, as the game goes on, make the game more difficult using some of the ideas above (smaller arrow, faster balloons). You've seen this in other games you may have played - games usually get harder as time goes on.

Players like to know how much time they have left in a game. Add this capability to your game. Use **DrawText** to print this on the window. The TickCount variable can be used to compute this value. You should be comfortable making such a change to your program.

Another thing players like to know is the highest score on a game. Add this capability. Define a new variable to keep track of the highest score. After each game is played, compare the current score with the highest score to see if a new high has been reached. Decide how to display the highest score. One problem, though. When you stop the program, the highest score value will be lost. A new high needs to be established each time you run the program. As you become a more advanced Small Basic programmer, you'll learn ways to save the highest score.

Sharing a Small Basic Program

I bet you're ready to show your friends and colleagues some of the programs you have built using Small Basic. Just give them a copy of your code, ask them to install Small Basic and learn how to open and run a program. Then, have them open your program and run it. I think you'll agree this might be asking a lot of your friends, colleagues, and, ultimately, your user base. We need to know how to run a program **without** Small Basic.

To run a program without Small Basic, you need to create an **executable** version of the program. So, how is an executable created? A little secret is that Small Basic builds an executable version of a program every time we run the program! This executable file is in the same folder you save your program in. Open the folder for any program you have built and you'll see a file with your program name of type **Program**. For example, using Windows Explorer to open the program folder for the **Balloons** program we just built:

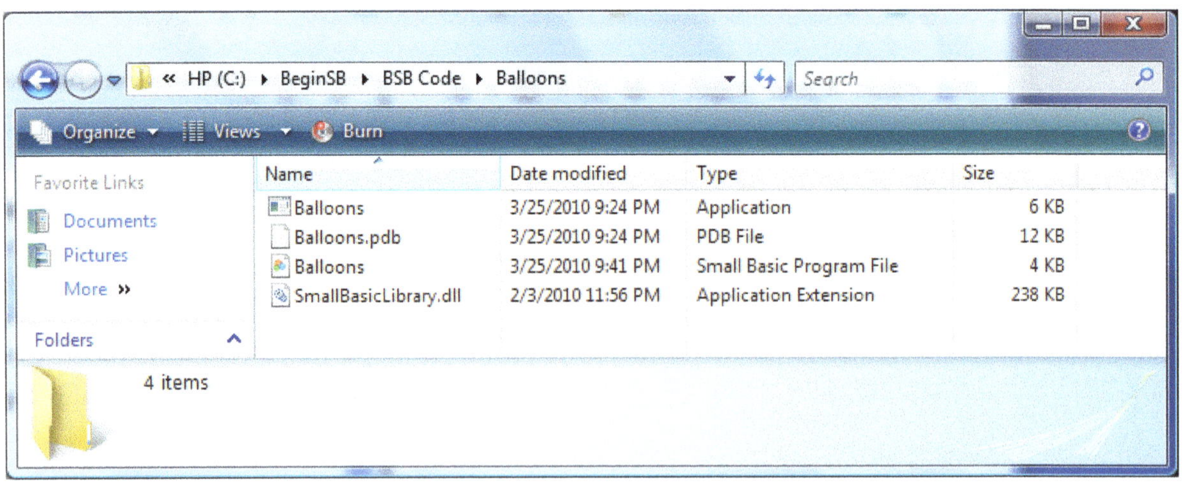

The file named **Balloons** of type **Application** (size 6 KB) is the executable version of the program. If I make sure Small Basic is not running and double-click this file, the following appears:

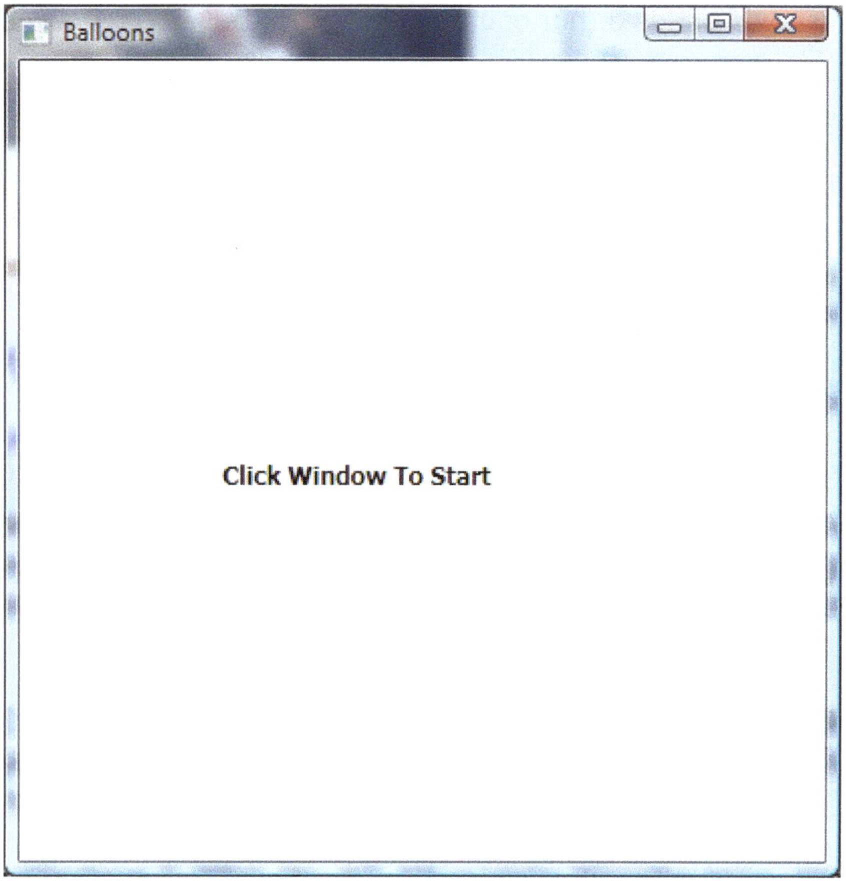

Voila! The Balloons program is running outside of the Small Basic development environment! Go ahead and play the game if you like.

So distributing a Small Basic program is as simple as giving your user a copy of the executable file (and the **SmallBasic.dll** file in your program folder - this has some support code), having them place the files in a folder on their computer and double-clicking the executable file to run it? Maybe. This worked on my computer (and will work on yours) because I have a very important set of files known as the **.NET Framework** installed (they are installed when Small Basic is installed). Every Small Basic program needs the .NET Framework to be installed on the hosting computer.

The next question is: how do you know if your user has the .NET Framework installed on his or her computer? And, if they don't, how can you get it installed? These are difficult questions. So, in addition to our program's executable file, we also need to give a potential user the Microsoft .NET Framework files and inform them how to install and register these files on their computer. Things are getting complicated. Let's look at an easier and very flashy solution – letting users access and run your programs over the Internet!

Start Small Basic and take a look at the toolbar. There are two buttons there we haven't talked about yet. Between the buttons to open and save files and the ones for editing are buttons marked **Import** and **Publish**:

These are remarkable buttons. Clicking **Import** will take you to a Microsoft website where you can import and open a program stored on the Internet by you or other users. **Publish** allows you to store your programs on the Internet for others to use.

Make sure your computer is connected to the Internet. Go ahead and click **Import**. You should see:

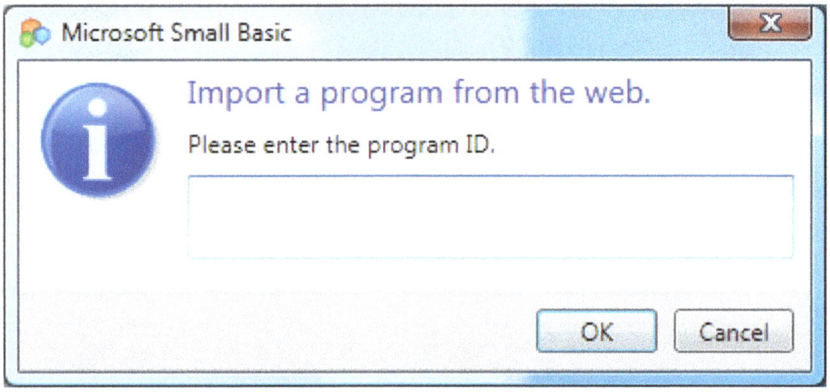

To import a program, you require a **Program ID**. How do you get such an ID? It is assigned when you **Publish** a program, so let's try that. Click the **Cancel** button for now.

Open one of your Small Basic programs. I'll be using the **Balloons** program we just built. Make sure the program runs and is free of errors. Click **Publish**. You will see a message something like this:

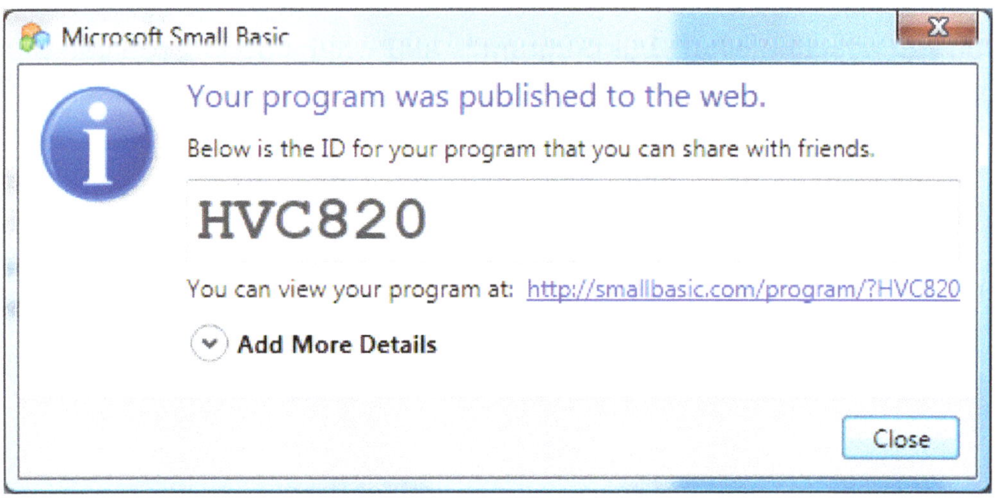

Your program is assigned a Program **ID** (remember we need this to import a program). Click **Add More Details**:

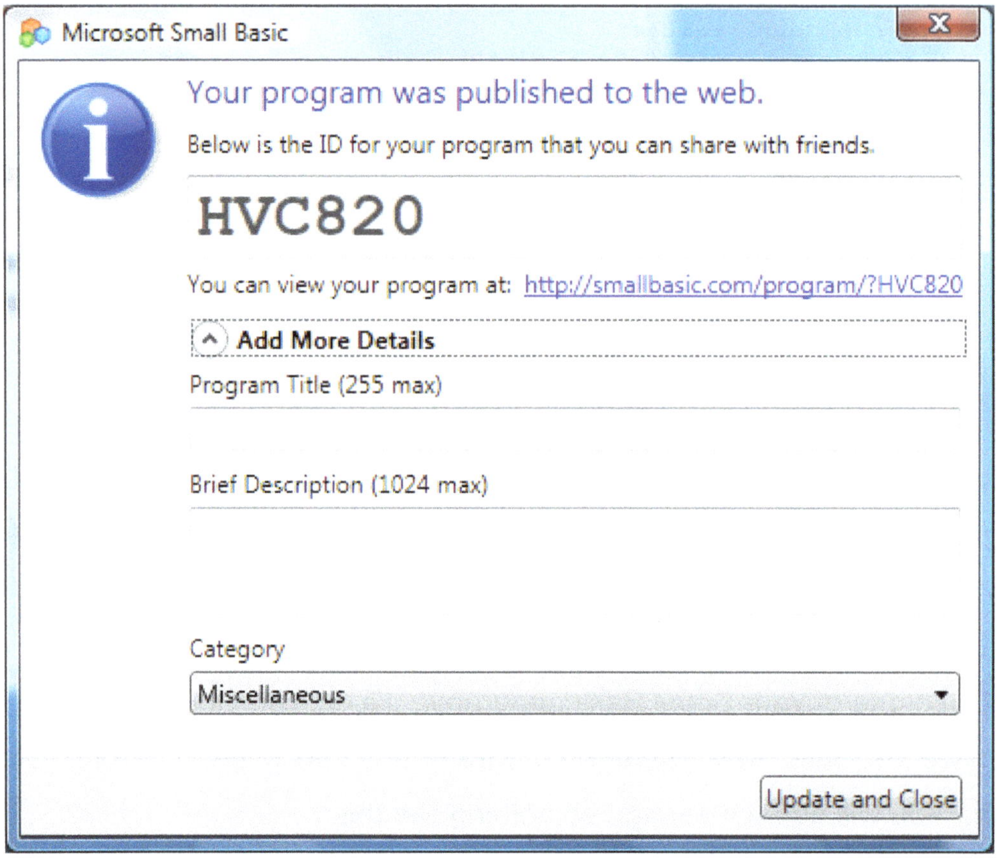

Here, you can describe what your program is and what it does. You can provide a category. This will help users find your program

Also listed in this window is this very interesting piece of information:

```
You can view your program at:
http://smallbasic.com/program/?HVC820
```

If you click this link (or give the link to others and let them click it), "magic" occurs.

When I click it, I am taken to this website hosted by Microsoft:

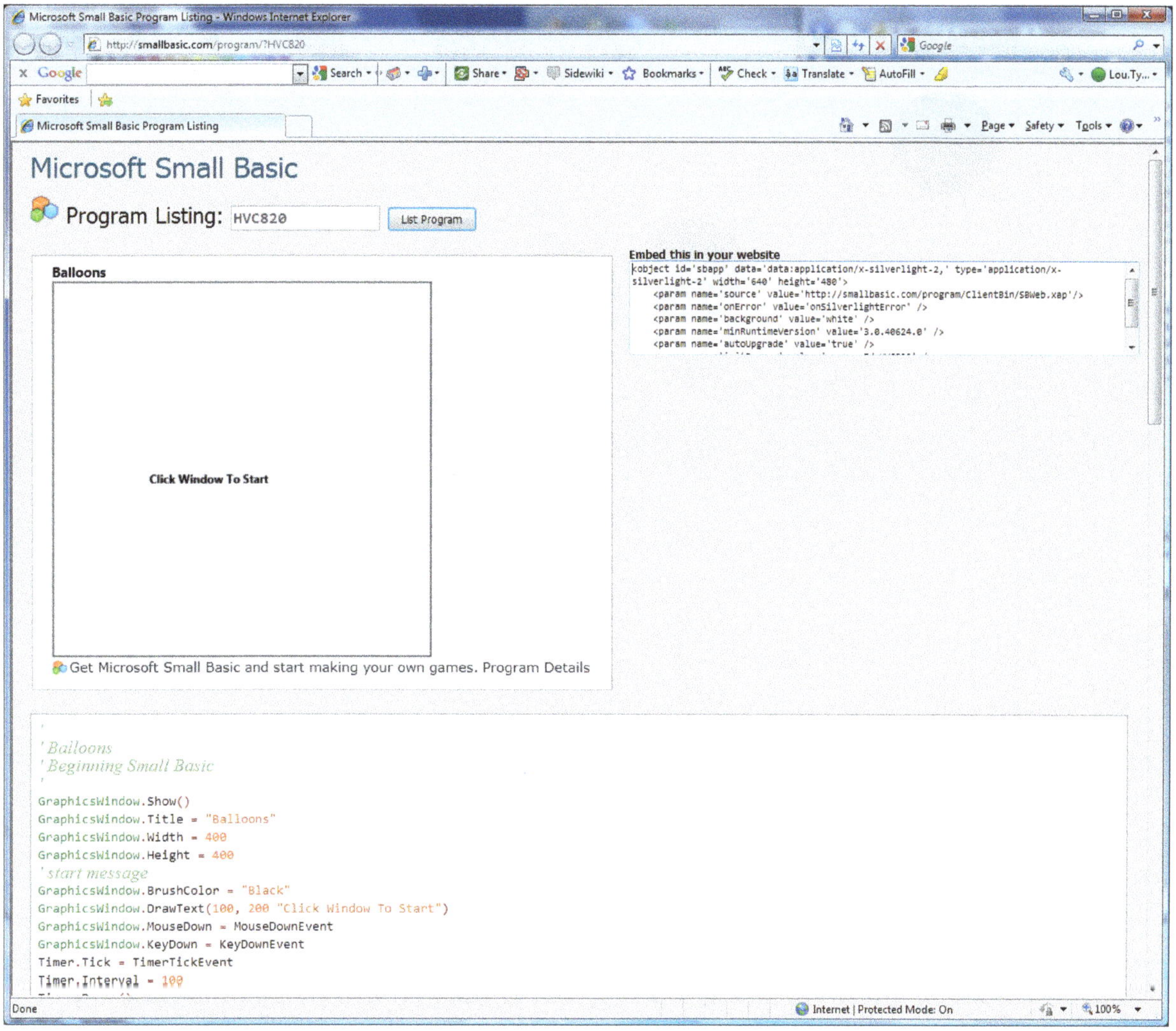

The running **Balloons** program is shown, along with a code listing.

If I click the **Balloons** program window, I can play the game on-line!

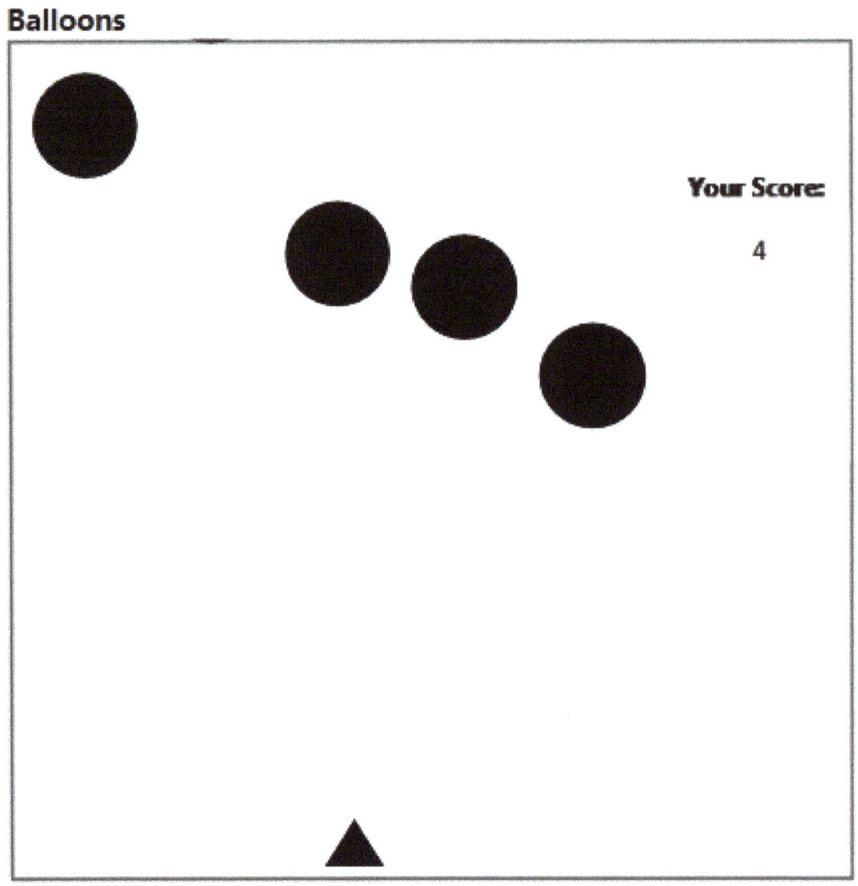

Looks like there might be a "color" bug in the current program, but it is running. I think you'll agree this pretty neat. To share your programs with other users, **Publish** them, then give them the program link given to you. If they click the link, they can run the program. Well, almost. To use this feature, a user's computer must have a Microsoft product called **Silverlight** installed on their computer. It can be downloaded from this website:

http://www.silverlight.net/

If a user attempts to access your Small Basic program via a provided link and they do not have the required Silverlight product, they will be taken through the installation steps.

Return to the website with your running program. In the upper right corner is a box marked **Embed this in your website**. In this box is some code that allows you to put your running application on your own website, if you have one. The steps to do this are beyond this discussion, but I wanted you to know such a step was possible.

Before leaving, lets return to the **Import** button in Small Basic. Click it again and enter the program ID for your program (I used **HVC820**):

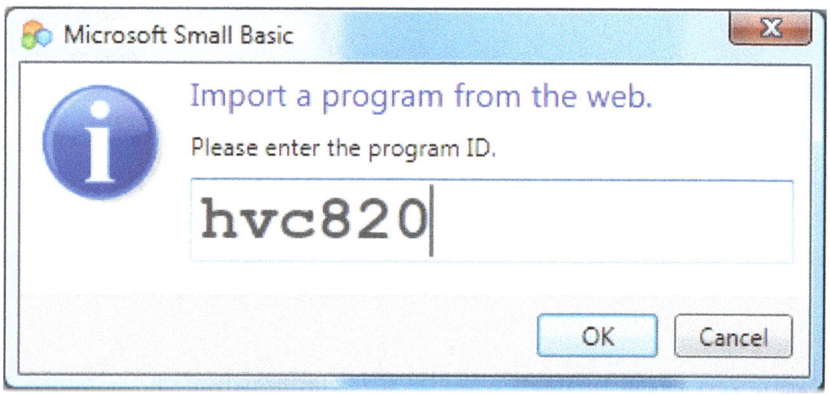

Click **OK**. The imported code will appear in your editor:

hvc820 - Imported *

```
'
' Balloons
' Beginning Small Basic
'
GraphicsWindow.Show()
GraphicsWindow.Title = "Balloons"
GraphicsWindow.Width = 400
GraphicsWindow.Height = 400
'start message
GraphicsWindow.BrushColor = "Black"
GraphicsWindow.DrawText(100, 200 "Click Window To Start")
GraphicsWindow.MouseDown = MouseDownEvent
GraphicsWindow.KeyDown = KeyDownEvent
Timer.Tick = TimerTickEvent
Timer.Interval = 100
Timer.Pause()


Sub MouseDownEvent
  GraphicsWindow.Clear()
  Score = 0
```

So, you have access to any code published to the Microsoft Small Basic library. I'm guessing this library will be growing very quickly.

Summary

In this class, we found that the timer object is a key element in computer animation. By periodically changing the display in a window, the sensation of motion was obtained. We studied "animation math" - how to detect if an object disappeared from a window, how to detect if an object crosses the border of a window, and how to detect if two objects (rectangles) collide. We learned how to detect keyboard events. You built your first video game. And, you learned how to share your work with others and look at programs others have written using Small Basic.

10

Noah's Ark Project

Preview

In Genesis 6:9 – 9:17, Noah was commanded by God to take two of every kind of animal into the ark. In this chapter, we build a game where turtles race to get on Noah's Ark. You pick two turtles (out of ten maximum) and see if your turtles are the winners. The purpose of this Bible story is to remember that God has promised never to flood the earth again. God displays a beautiful rainbow in the sky to remind us of His promises to us.

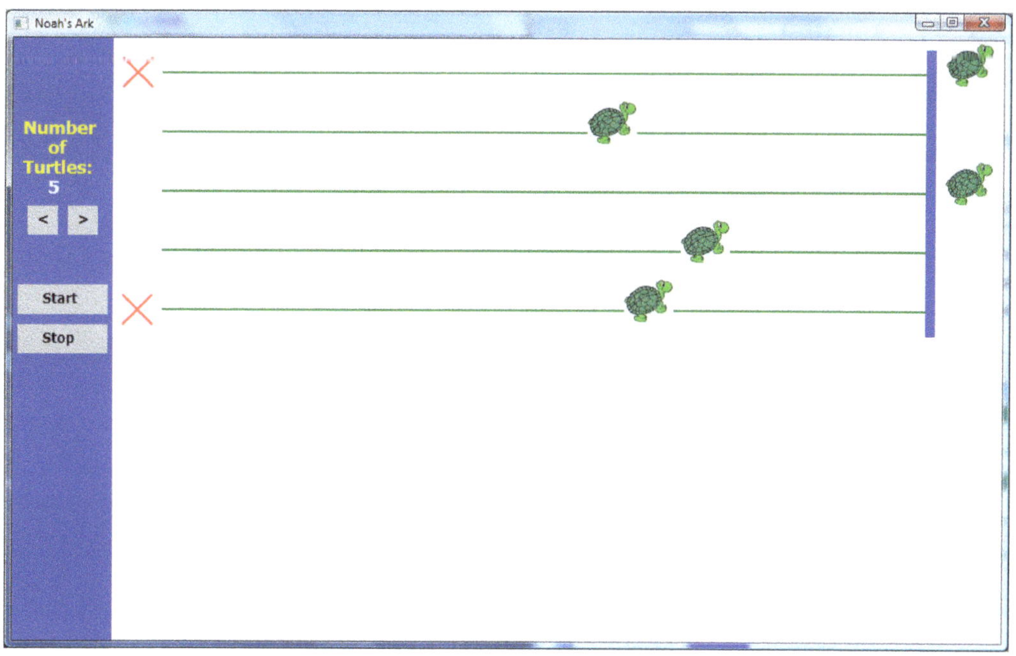

Noah's Ark Program Preview

In this chapter, we will build the **Noah's Ark** game. It's a simple game. Up to 10 turtles line up to race to the ark. You select two turtles you want to win the race. Clicking a '**Start'** button gets the race going. The turtles then move across the screen toward the finish line.

The finished program is saved as **Noah** in the **BeginSB\BSB Codes\Noahs Ark** folder. Start Small Basic and open the finished program. Run the program (click the **Run** toolbar button or press <**F5**>). The game will appear in its 'initial' state. A game description and program instructions are given. At this point, you can click the **Start** button to start the game, click arrow buttons to change the number of turtles racing or click **Stop** to stop the program.

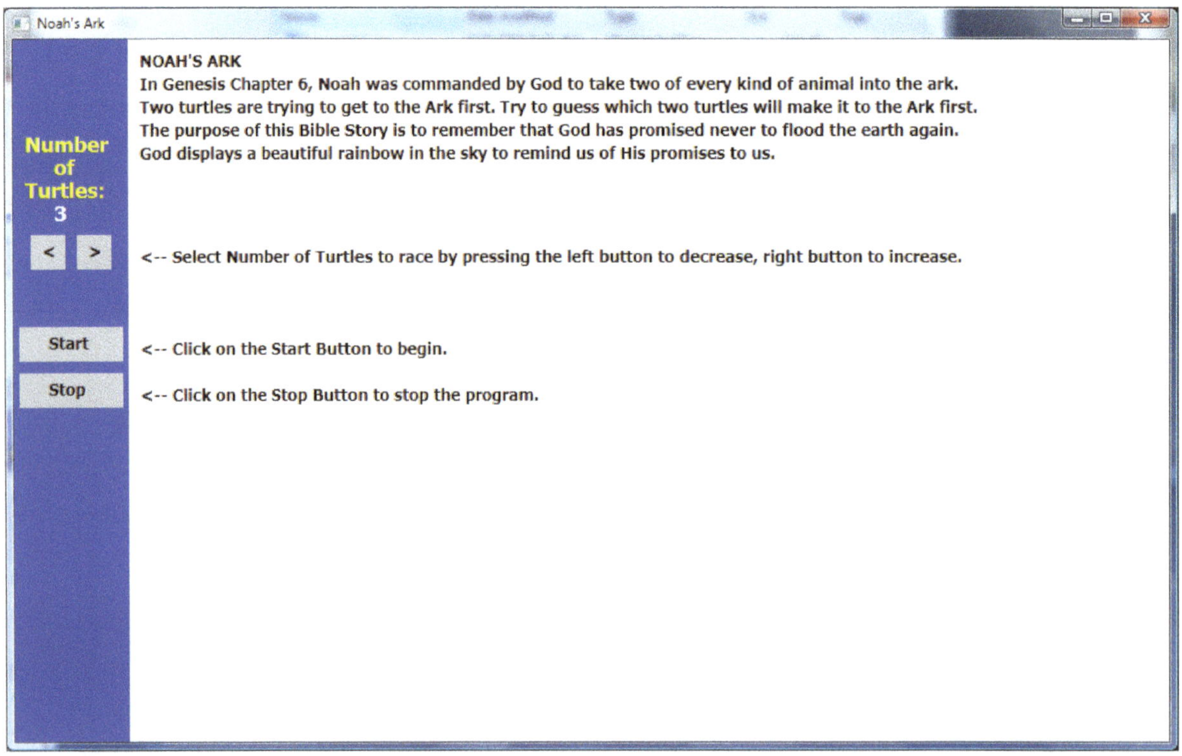

Change the number of turtles if you want (I picked five) by clicking the little arrows under **Number of Turtles**. Click the **Start** button to start playing. The program instructions disappear. Five turtles are poised, ready to race. This is the game's 'stopped' state:

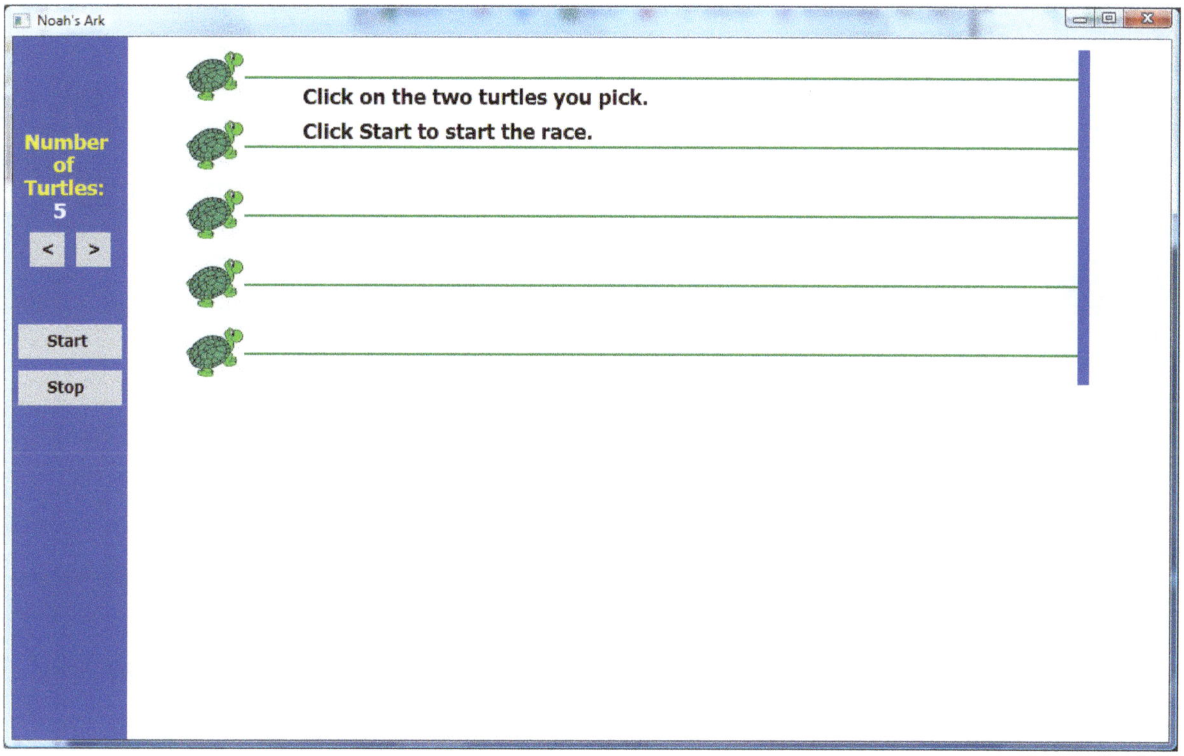

In this state, you pick two turtles you want to win the race. To do this, simple click on your selected turtle with the mouse – a red X will appear next to the selected turtle. Once two turtles are selected, you can start the race by clicking **Start**. If you select two turtles and want to change your mind, click on a selected turtle and the red X will disappear allowing you to pick another.

Choose two turtles. I picked the top one and the bottom one:

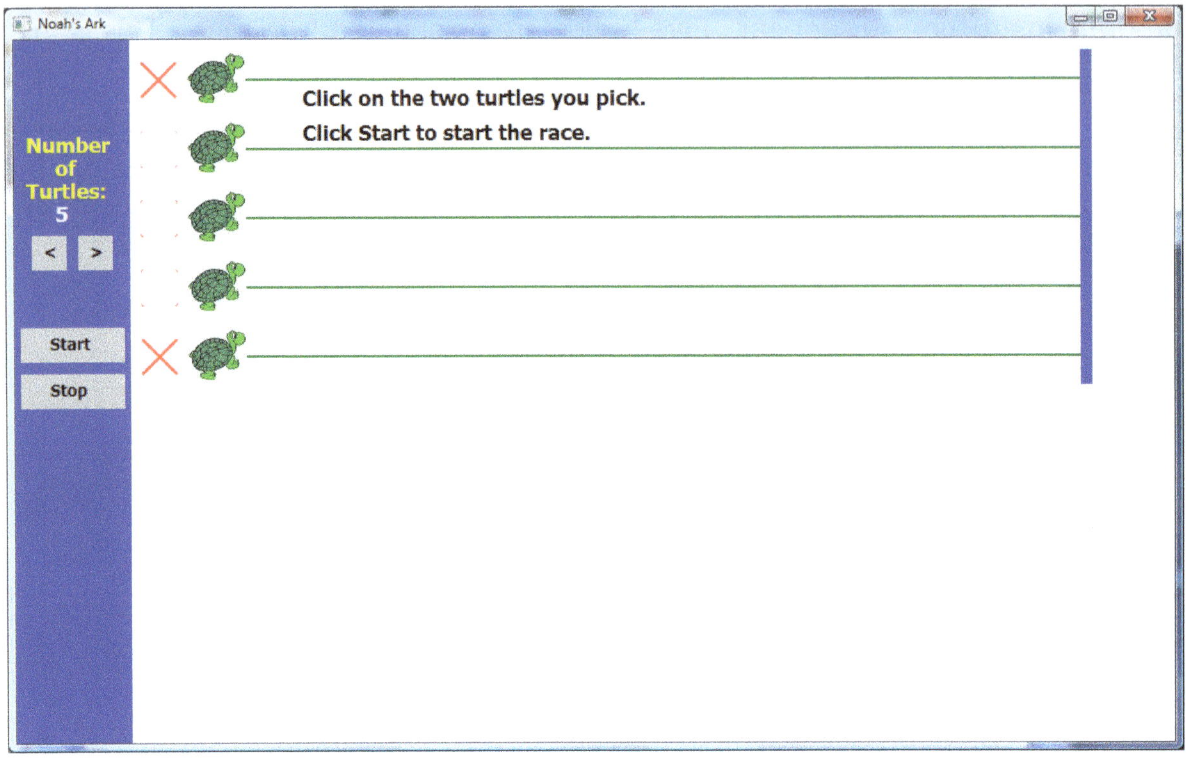

I then click **Start**. A bell sound is heard. The race is on. The program is in 'moving' state. The turtles move across the screen until two cross the finish line.

Here's the results:

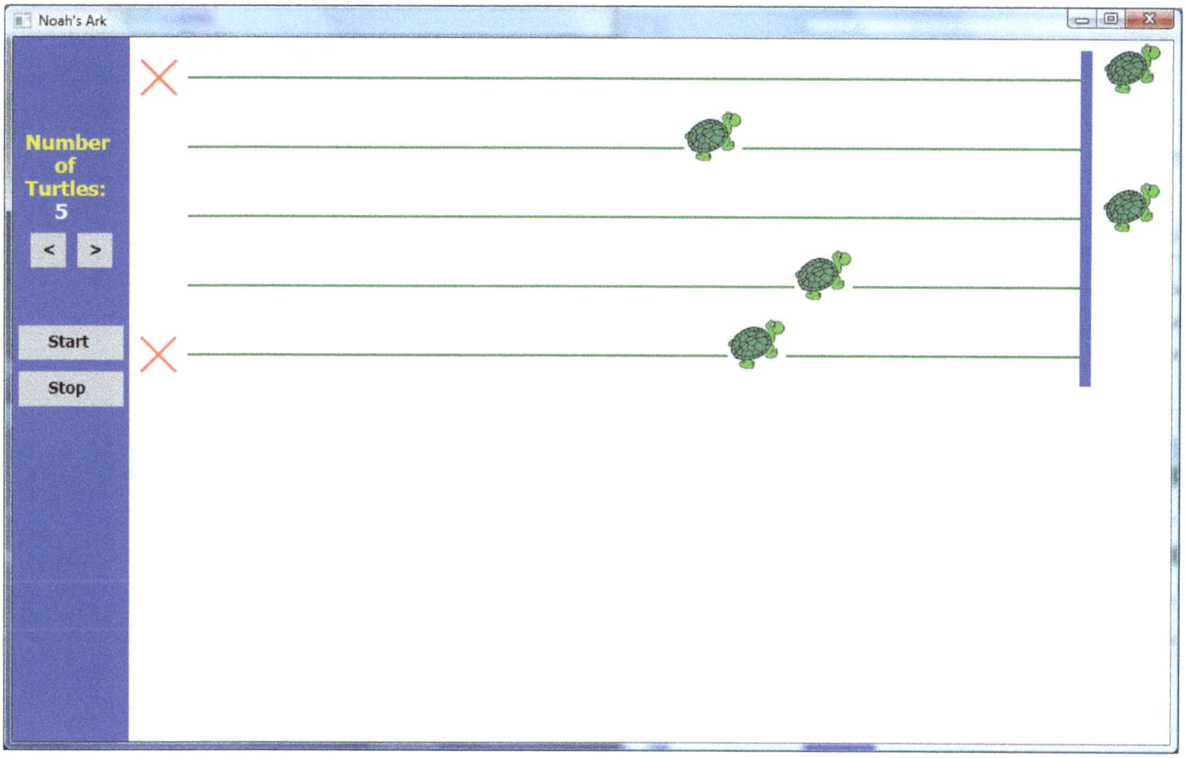

One of my turtles won! At this point, if you want, you can change the number of turtles. You can also click **Start** to race again or click **Stop** to stop the program. Continue playing the game to understand its operation.

You will now build this program in stages. As you build Small Basic programs, we always recommend taking a slow, step-by-step process. It minimizes programming errors and helps build your confidence as things come together in a complete program. We address **window design**. And, we address **code design**. We discuss how to use the 'buttons', how to display the racing turtles, and how to move the turtles.

Noah's Ark Window Design

Here is a sketch for the window layout of the **Noah's Ark** game:

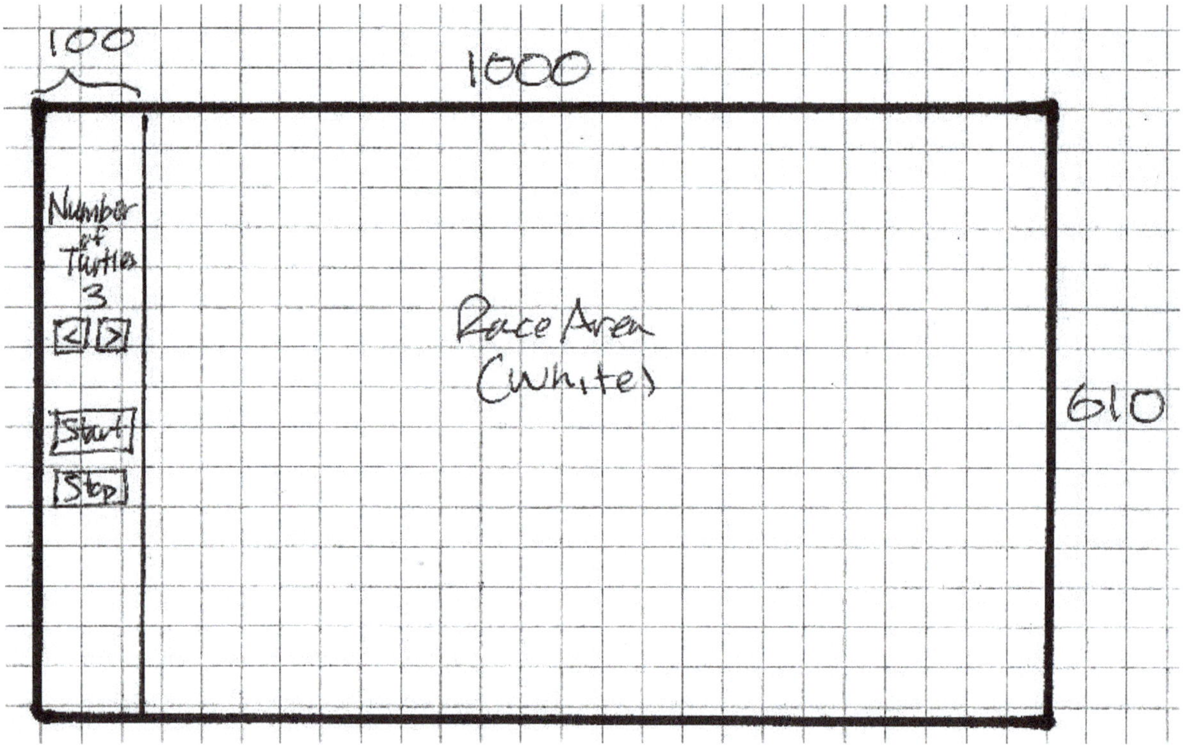

The graphics window is 1000 pixels wide and 610 pixels high. The blue background area on the left (100 pixels wide) is used to control game play. The white area on the right (900 pixels wide) displays game instructions when the program first begins and shows the turtle races. In the area on the left are gray rectangles used to represent clickable buttons. Four 'buttons' will be used: two to change the number of turtles, one to start the game, and one to stop the program.

We now begin writing code for the **Noah's Ark** game. We will write the code in several steps. As a first step, we will write the code that draws the window, then starts the game and establishes its 'initial' state. Then, we look at how to go to 'stopped' state following clicking of the **Start** button from initial state. Lastly, we write code to race the turtles once **Start** is clicked again. During the code development process, recognize you may modify a particular procedure several times before arriving at the finished product.

Start a new program in Small Basic. Once started, we suggest you immediately save the program with a name you choose. This sets up the folder and file structure needed for your program.

Code Design – Initial State (Instructions)

Any time we start a program, there are certain initializations that must take place. Let's look at the initializations needed in the **Noah's Ark** game. When the program first begins, we want to display the game instructions and the control buttons. We also initialize the number of turtles (**NumberOfTurtles**) and the game status (**GameStatus**). We set up the game screen and display the instructions first.

Add this code to your empty code window:

```
' Noah's Ark
' Small Basic Version

' Intro screen
NumberOfTurtles = 3
GameStatus = "Initial"
GraphicsWindow.Show()
GraphicsWindow.Title = "Noah's Ark"
GraphicsWindow.BackgroundColor = "White"
GraphicsWindow.Width = 1000
GraphicsWindow.Height = 610
GraphicsWindow.BrushColor = "Black"
GraphicsWindow.FontSize = 14
GraphicsWindow.DrawText(110, 10, "NOAH'S ARK")
GraphicsWindow.DrawText(110, 30, "In Genesis Chapter 6, Noah was
commanded by God to take two of every kind of animal into the
ark.")
GraphicsWindow.DrawText(110, 50, "Two turtles are trying to get to
the Ark first. Try to guess which two turtles will make it to the
Ark first.")
GraphicsWindow.DrawText(110, 70, "The purpose of this Bible Story
is to remember that God has promised never to flood the earth
again.")
GraphicsWindow.DrawText(110, 90, "God displays a beautiful rainbow
in the sky to remind us of His promises to us.")
GraphicsWindow.DrawText(110, 180, "<-- Select Number of Turtles to
race by pressing the left button to decrease, right button to
increase.")
```

```
GraphicsWindow.DrawText(110, 260, "<-- Click on the Start Button to begin.")
GraphicsWindow.DrawText(110, 300, "<-- Click on the Stop Button to stop the program.")
GraphicsWindow.BrushColor = "Blue"
GraphicsWindow.FillRectangle(0, 0, 100, GraphicsWindow.Height)
```

As mentioned, we set **NumberOfTurtles** to **3** and the **GameStatus** to "**Initial**". Next, after setting up the **GraphicsWindow**, using a series of **DrawText** statements, we write out the game instructions. **Save** and **Run** the program to see:

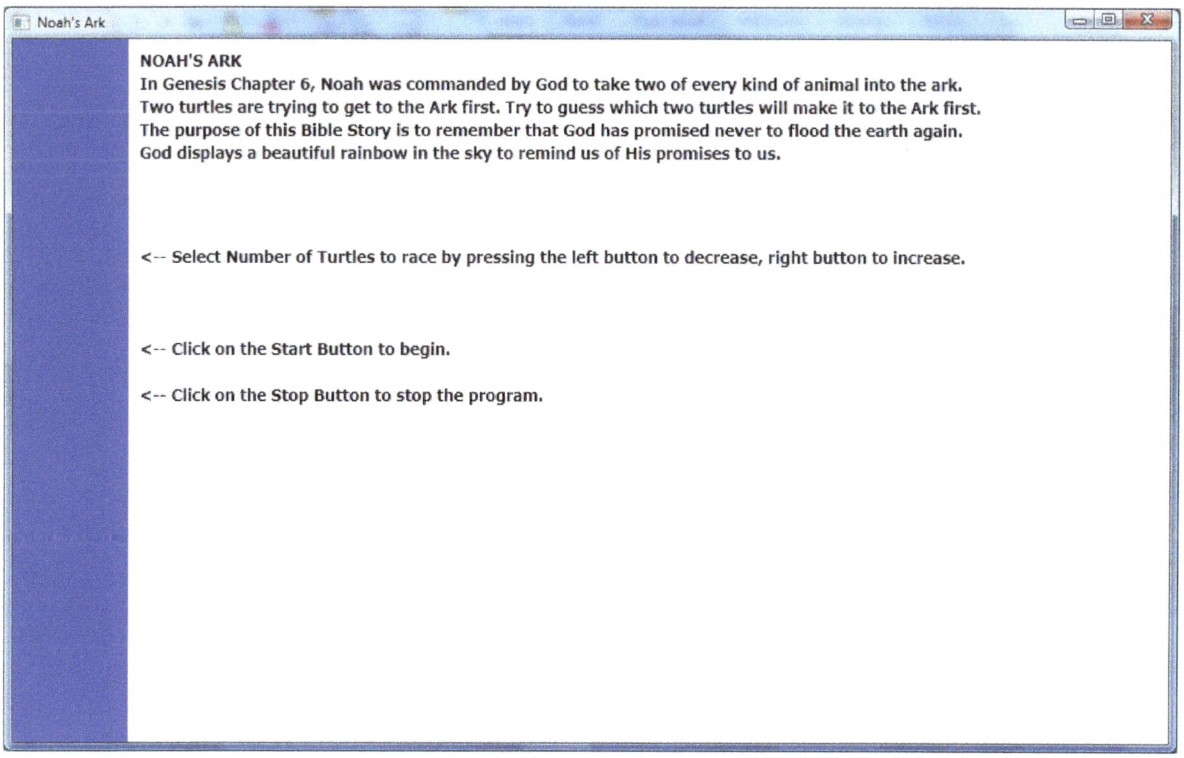

You may wonder how we came up with all the position numbers in the **DrawText** statements. They were set by trial and error. You do this a lot in Small Basic. Try some values and see how they look. Make corrections until things appear as you desire.

Code Design – Initial State (Titling and Buttons)

The other element we need when the program begins are the 'buttons' used to control the game. Each button is a gray rectangular area that can be clicked with the mouse. We will detect these clicks using the **GraphicsWindow MouseDown** event. For now, let's just draw the buttons (and titling information for the number of turtles).

Add this code to your program:

```
GraphicsWindow.BrushColor = "Yellow"
GraphicsWindow.FontSize = 18
GraphicsWindow.DrawText(10, 80, "Number")
GraphicsWindow.DrawText(35, 100, "of")
GraphicsWindow.DrawText(10, 120, "Turtles:")
GraphicsWindow.BrushColor = "White"
GraphicsWindow.FontSize = 18
GraphicsWindow.DrawText(35, 140, NumberOfTurtles)
GraphicsWindow.BrushColor = "LightGray"
GraphicsWindow.FillRectangle(15, 170, 30, 30)
GraphicsWindow.FillRectangle(55, 170, 30, 30)
GraphicsWindow.FillRectangle(5, 250, 90, 30)
GraphicsWindow.FillRectangle(5, 290, 90, 30)
GraphicsWindow.BrushColor = "Black"
GraphicsWindow.FontSize = 14
GraphicsWindow.DrawText(25, 175, "<")
GraphicsWindow.DrawText(65, 175, ">")
GraphicsWindow.DrawText(30, 255, "Start")
GraphicsWindow.DrawText(30, 295, "Stop")
```

Each button is a gray rectangle with black text. There are two buttons (**<** and **>**) used to change the number of turtles. There are two buttons (**Start** and **Stop**) used to control the game. Like the game instructions, the size and position for each of these elements were arrived at by trial and error. You can change any values you want. Just make sure to note where each button is located – you will need this information when writing the code to detect mouse clicks.

Save and **Run** the program to see the finished initial game screen:

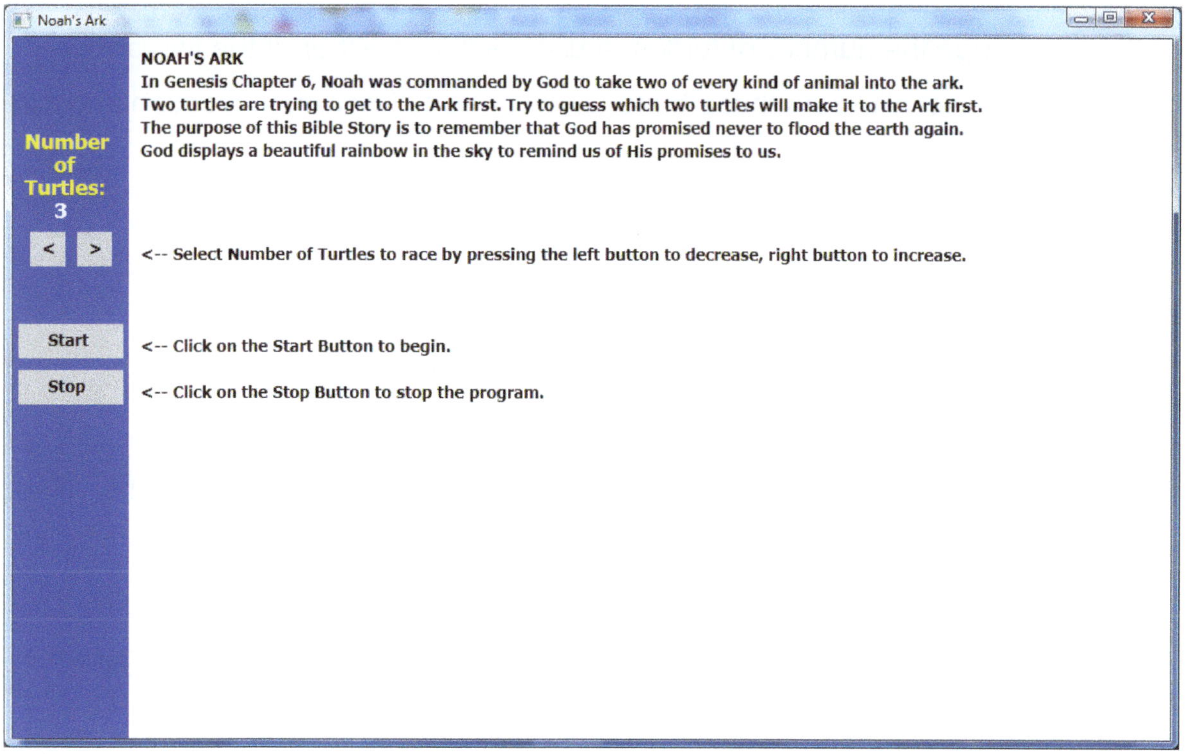

Notice the added buttons and the heading information for the **Number of Turtles**.

Code Design – Select Number of Turtles

To change the number of turtles, a user clicks on either of the two arrow buttons. To detect clicks on these buttons, we need to know their location and size in the window. Looking back at the code, you can see:

button; located at (15, 170), width 30, height 30

button; located at (55, 170), width 30, height 30

We write code to see if a user clicks within the region defined by the buttons. If so, we take the necessary action of changing the number of turtles.

We need to detect mouse clicks, so add this line of code to your program:

```
GraphicsWindow.MouseDown = MouseDownEvent
```

With this line, each time a mouse button is pressed (a **MouseDown** event) the subroutine **MouseDownEvent** is called. All remaining code will be placed in this subroutine. Let's do the code for changing the number of turtles.

Add this subroutine at the end of your program:

```
Sub MouseDownEvent
  X = GraphicsWindow.MouseX
  Y = GraphicsWindow.MouseY
  If (GameStatus = "Initial") Then
    If (Y > 175 And Y < 205) Then
      If (X > 15 And X < 45) Then
        ' decrease number of turtles
        NumberOfTurtles = NumberOfTurtles - 1
        If (NumberOfTurtles < 3) Then
          NumberOfTurtles = 3
        EndIf
      ElseIf (X > 55 And X < 85) Then
        'increase number of turtles
        NumberOfTurtles = NumberOfTurtles + 1
        If (NumberOfTurtles > 10) Then
          NumberOfTurtles = 10
        EndIf
      EndIf
      GraphicsWindow.BrushColor = "Blue"
      GraphicsWindow.FillRectangle(0, 140, 100, 20)
      GraphicsWindow.BrushColor = "White"
      GraphicsWindow.FontSize = 18
      GraphicsWindow.DrawText(35, 140, NumberOfTurtles)
    EndIf
  EndIf
EndSub
```

The code is straightforward. The number of turtles can only be changed when the game is in "**Initial**" state. We look to see if the clicked coordinate (**X, Y**) is within the regions of the two arrow buttons. If the **<** button is clicked, we decrease the number of turtles by one (minimum of 3). If the **>** button is clicked, we increase the number of turtles (maximum of 10). The new value for the number of turtles is then displayed (after first clearing the area with the previous value).

Save and **Run** the program. Make sure the arrow buttons work – make sure the number of turtles is always between 3 and 10. Here's my run where I changed the number of turtles to five:

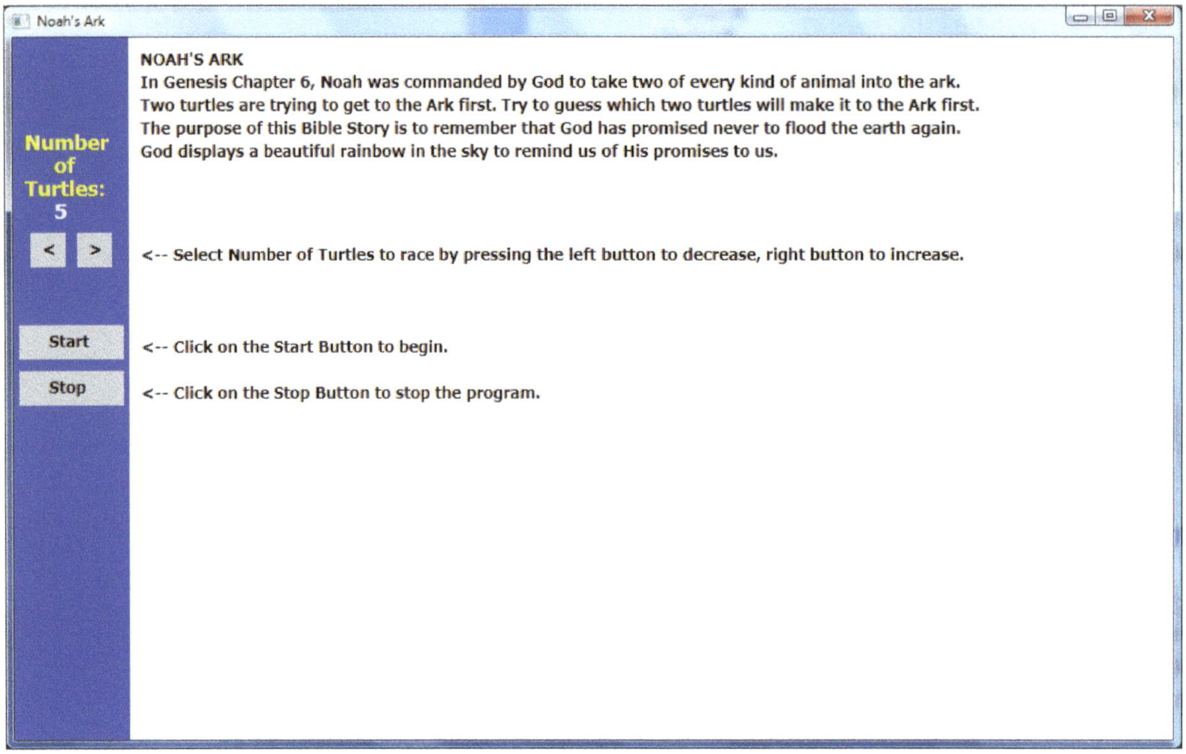

Code Design – Initial to Stopped State

Once the number of turtles is finalized, the next step is to click the **Start** button to allow selection of the turtles you want to win. Hence, we need code to move from the "**Initial**" state to "**Stopped**" state. Like the arrow buttons, to detect clicks on the **Start** button, we need to know its location and size in the window. From the code, we see:

button; located at (5, 250), width 90, height 30

When the **Start** button is clicked in "**Initial**" state, we need to take the following steps:

- Change **GameStatus** to "**Stopped**"
- Clear game screen
- Draw the turtles and "lane lines" for each
- Draw the finish line
- Display instructions for the user

To draw the turtles, we divide the race region into 10 equal size areas (set up for the maximum number of turtles). We then just move down the screen adding each turtle.

A Small Basic **Shape** object is used to represent the turtle. The graphic file **turtle.jpg** is used for this object:

The turtle is 50 pixels wide and 45 pixels high. Make sure you have copied this file to your program folder.

Now, add the shaded code to the **MouseDownEvent** subroutine:

```
Sub MouseDownEvent
  X = GraphicsWindow.MouseX
  Y = GraphicsWindow.MouseY
  If (GameStatus = "Initial") Then
    If (Y > 175 And Y < 205) Then
      If (X > 15 And X < 45) Then
        ' decrease number of turtles
        NumberOfTurtles = NumberOfTurtles - 1
        If (NumberOfTurtles < 3) Then
          NumberOfTurtles = 3
        EndIf
      ElseIf (X > 55 And X < 85) Then
        'increase number of turtles
        NumberOfTurtles = NumberOfTurtles + 1
        If (NumberOfTurtles > 10) Then
          NumberOfTurtles = 10
        EndIf
      EndIf
      GraphicsWindow.BrushColor = "Blue"
      GraphicsWindow.FillRectangle(0, 140, 100, 20)
      GraphicsWindow.BrushColor = "White"
      GraphicsWindow.FontSize = 18
      GraphicsWindow.DrawText(35, 140, NumberOfTurtles)
    ElseIf (Y > 250 And Y < 280) Then
      If (X > 5 And X < 95) Then
        'clicked start
        GameStatus = "Stopped"
        GraphicsWindow.BrushColor = "White"
```

```
        GraphicsWindow.FillRectangle(100, 0, GraphicsWindow.Width
- 100, GraphicsWindow.Height)
        'draw turtles
        TurtleImage = ImageList.LoadImage(Program.Directory +
"\turtle.jpg")
        For i = 1 To NumberOfTurtles
          Shapes.Remove(Turtle[i])
          Turtle[i] = Shapes.AddImage(TurtleImage)
          Shapes.Move(Turtle[i], 150, (i - 1) * 60 +10)
          GraphicsWindow.PenColor = "Green"
          GraphicsWindow.DrawLine(150, (i - 1) * 60 + 35, 920, (i
- 1) * 60 + 35)
        EndFor
        ' draw finish line
        GraphicsWindow.BrushColor = "Blue"
        GraphicsWindow.FillRectangle(920, 10, 10, NumberOfTurtles
* 60 -10)
        GraphicsWindow.BrushColor = "Black"
        GraphicsWindow.FontSize = 18
        GraphicsWindow.DrawText(250, 40, "Click on the two turtles
you pick.")
        GraphicsWindow.DrawText(250, 70, "Click Start to start the
race.")
        TurtlesSelected = 0
        For i = 1 to NumberOfTurtles
          TurtlePicked[i] = 0
        EndFor
      EndIf
    EndIf
  EndIf
EndSub
```

You should be able to identify each step in this new code. Notice in particular how we load, create and display the **Turtle** array. Two new variables are introduced. **TurtlesSelected** (the number of turtles picked by the user) is initialized at zero. The array **TurtlePicked** is used to keep track of which turtles are selected by the user.

Save and **Run** the program. Choose a number of turtles (I picked 5). Click **Start** and you should see:

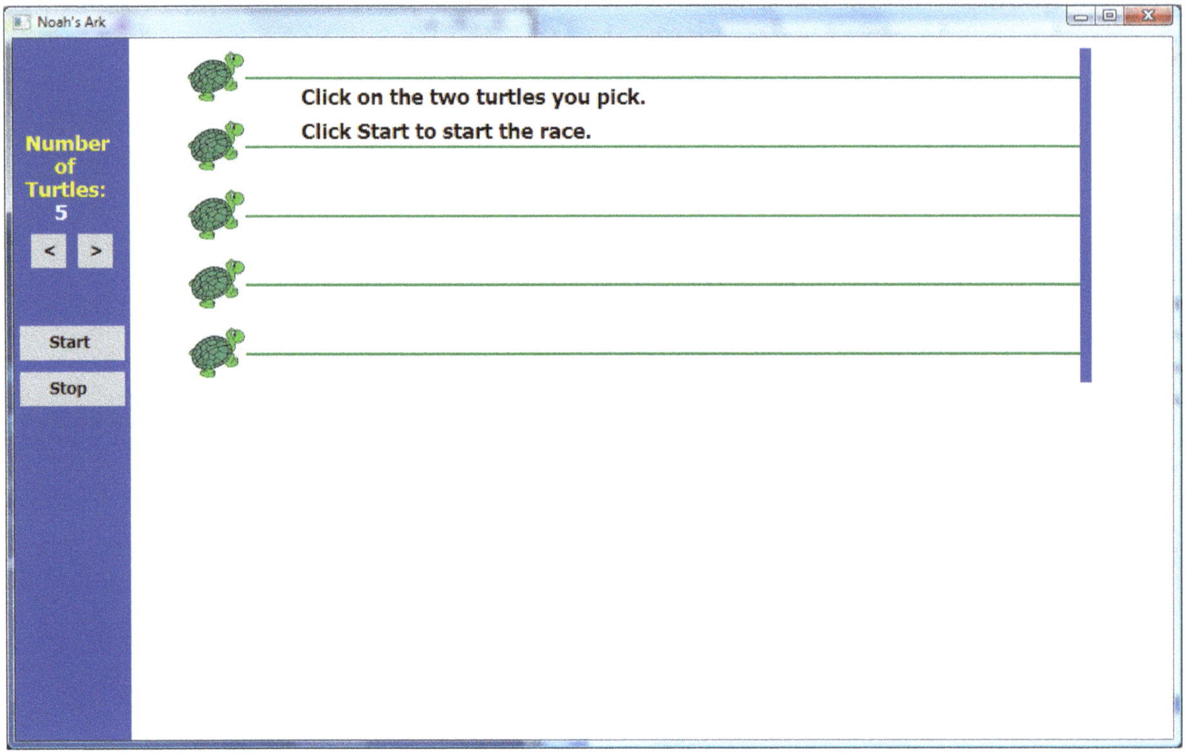

The next step is to select two turtles you want in the race. We do that selection code soon. But first, let's take care of one last thing you can do while in "**Initial**" state – stop the program.

Code Design – Stop the Program

One last thing you can do while the game is in "**Initial**" state is to click on the **Stop** button. This will stop the game. The location and size of this button are (from code):

button; located at (5, 290), width 90, height 30

The code here is simple. Add the few shaded lines in the **MouseDownEvent** subroutine:

```
Sub MouseDownEvent
  X = GraphicsWindow.MouseX
  Y = GraphicsWindow.MouseY
  If (GameStatus = "Initial") Then
    If (Y > 175 And Y < 205) Then
      If (X > 15 And X < 45) Then
        ' decrease number of turtles
        NumberOfTurtles = NumberOfTurtles - 1
        If (NumberOfTurtles < 3) Then
          NumberOfTurtles = 3
        EndIf
      ElseIf (X > 55 And X < 85) Then
        'increase number of turtles
        NumberOfTurtles = NumberOfTurtles + 1
        If (NumberOfTurtles > 10) Then
          NumberOfTurtles = 10
        EndIf
      EndIf
      GraphicsWindow.BrushColor = "Blue"
      GraphicsWindow.FillRectangle(0, 140, 100, 20)
      GraphicsWindow.BrushColor = "White"
      GraphicsWindow.FontSize = 18
      GraphicsWindow.DrawText(35, 140, NumberOfTurtles)
    ElseIf (Y > 250 And Y < 280) Then
      If (X > 5 And X < 95) Then
        'clicked start
        GameStatus = "Stopped"
```

```
        GraphicsWindow.BrushColor = "White"
        GraphicsWindow.FillRectangle(100, 0, GraphicsWindow.Width
- 100, GraphicsWindow.Height)
        'draw turtles
        TurtleImage = ImageList.LoadImage(Program.Directory +
"\turtle.jpg")
        For i = 1 To NumberOfTurtles
          Shapes.Remove(Turtle[i])
          Turtle[i] = Shapes.AddImage(TurtleImage)
          Shapes.Move(Turtle[i], 150, (i - 1) * 60 +10)
          GraphicsWindow.PenColor = "Green"
          GraphicsWindow.DrawLine(150, (i - 1) * 60 + 35, 920, (i
- 1) * 60 + 35)
        EndFor
        ' draw finish line
        GraphicsWindow.BrushColor = "Blue"
        GraphicsWindow.FillRectangle(920, 10, 10, NumberOfTurtles
* 60 -10)
        GraphicsWindow.BrushColor = "Black"
        GraphicsWindow.FontSize = 18
        GraphicsWindow.DrawText(250, 40, "Click on the two turtles
you pick.")
        GraphicsWindow.DrawText(250, 70, "Click Start to start the
race.")
        TurtlesSelected = 0
        For i = 1 to NumberOfTurtles
          TurtlePicked[i] = 0
        EndFor
      EndIf
    ElseIf (Y > 290 And Y < 320) Then
      If (X > 5 And X < 95) Then
        'clicked stop
        Program.End()
      EndIf
    EndIf
  EndIf
EndSub
```

As desired, if the **Stop** button is clicked, the program ends.

Save and **Run** the program. Make sure the **Stop** button works.

Code Design – Selecting Turtles

Once the game is in "**Stopped**" state, the user picks the two turtles they want in the **Noah's Ark** race. Like the buttons, to detect clicks on a turtle, we need to know their location and size. From the code placing the turtles on the screen, you should see that for turtle i (where i goes from 1 to **NumberOfTurtles**):

 located at (150, (i - 1) * 60 +10), width 50, height 45

The array **TurtlePicked** is used to tell us which turtles have been selected. A red **X** will appear next to a selected turtle. Once two turtles are selected (**TurtlesSelected = 2**), you can start the race by clicking **Start**. If you select two turtles and want to change your mind, click on a selected turtle and the red **X** will disappear allowing you to pick another.

When a turtle i is clicked, the following steps are taken:

- If turtle has been selected selected previously, decrement **TurtlesSelected**, set **TurtlePicked[i]** to **0**. Remove red **X** next to turtle.
- If turtle has not been selected and **TurtlesSelected** is less than 2, increment **TurtlesSelected**, set **TurtlePicked[i]** to **1**. Draw red **X** next to turtle.

We do the steps in this order to make sure we don't click on a turtle that has already been selected.

The shaded code in the **MouseDownEvent** subroutine implements these steps:

```
Sub MouseDownEvent
  X = GraphicsWindow.MouseX
  Y = GraphicsWindow.MouseY
  If (GameStatus = "Initial") Then
      .
      .
  ElseIf (GameStatus = "Stopped") Then
    If (X > 150 And X < 200 And Y > 10 And Y < NumberOfTurtles *
60 + 10) Then
      ' want to pick two and only two turtles
      'which turtle clicked
      TurtleClicked = Math.Floor((Y - 10) / 60) + 1
      'if clicked before, remove from list
      If (TurtlePicked[TurtleClicked] = 1) Then
        TurtlesSelected = TurtlesSelected - 1
        TurtlePicked[TurtleClicked] = 0
        GraphicsWindow.BrushColor = "White"
        GraphicsWindow.FillRectangle(110, (TurtleClicked - 1) * 60
+ 20, 30, 30)
      ElseIf (TurtlesSelected < 2) Then
        'add to list if two have not been selected yet
        TurtlesSelected = TurtlesSelected + 1
        TurtlePicked[TurtleClicked] = 1
        GraphicsWindow.PenColor = "Red"
        GraphicsWindow.DrawLine(110, (TurtleClicked - 1) * 60 +
20, 140, (TurtleClicked - 1) * 60 + 50)
        GraphicsWindow.DrawLine(110, (TurtleClicked - 1) * 60 +
50, 140, (TurtleClicked - 1) * 60 + 20)
      EndIf
    EndIf
  EndIf
EndSub
```

To save room, we have not shown the code for mouse clicks when the program is in "**Initial**" state – that code is complete. You should see how the clicks on the turtles are handled.

Save and **Run** the program. Choose a number of turtles (I picked 5). Click **Start**. Then, select two turtles for your race. I picked the first and last turtle:

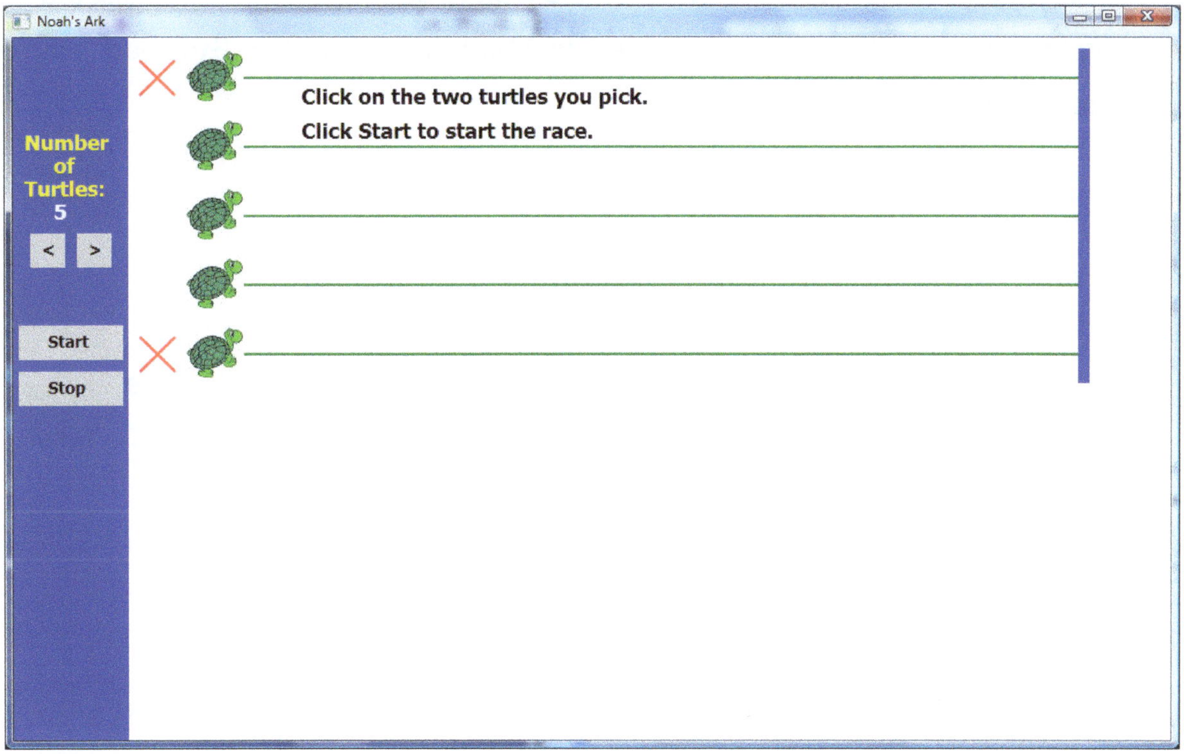

Make sure you can 'unselect' a turtle. Now, let's race!

Code Design - Stopped to Moving State

Once turtles are selected, we click the **Start** button to get the race started, moving to "**Moving**" state. So, when the **Start** button is clicked in "**Stopped**" state, we take these steps:

- Play a ringing bell sound.
- Change **GameStatus** to "**Moving**".
- Clear instructions.
- For each turtle, pick a random final position <u>before</u> the finish line.
- Pick two winners at random. Assign these final positions <u>after</u> the finish line.
- Move the turtles to their final positions.
- Change **GameStatus** to "**Initial**" to allow another race.

What we do is pick two of the displayed turtles to be winners. These turtles finish across the line – all others finish before the line.

To move the turtles, we use the **Shapes Animate** method. This ia a new concept. If we have a shape named **myShape** we want it to move if from its current position to position (**X, Y**) in **T** milliseconds, we use:

```
Shapes.Animate(myShape, X, Y, T)
```

This method provides a smooth animation from start to finish. With the turtles, we move each from its starting position to final position in 5000 milliseconds (5 seconds). You can change the time if you want.

The code that implements these steps in the **MouseDownEvent** subroutine is shaded:

```
Sub MouseDownEvent
  X = GraphicsWindow.MouseX
  Y = GraphicsWindow.MouseY
  If (GameStatus = "Initial") Then
      .
      .
  ElseIf (GameStatus = "Stopped") Then
    If (X > 150 And X < 200 And Y > 10 And Y < NumberOfTurtles *
60 + 10) Then
      ' want to pick two and only two turtles
      'which turtle clicked
      TurtleClicked = Math.Floor((Y - 10) / 60) + 1
      'if clicked before, remove from list
      If (TurtlePicked[TurtleClicked] = 1) Then
        TurtlesSelected = TurtlesSelected - 1
        TurtlePicked[TurtleClicked] = 0
        GraphicsWindow.BrushColor = "White"
        GraphicsWindow.FillRectangle(110, (TurtleClicked - 1) * 60
+ 20, 30, 30)
      ElseIf (TurtlesSelected < 2) Then
        'add to list if two have not been selected yet
        TurtlesSelected = TurtlesSelected + 1
        TurtlePicked[TurtleClicked] = 1
        GraphicsWindow.PenColor = "Red"
        GraphicsWindow.DrawLine(110, (TurtleClicked - 1) * 60 +
20, 140, (TurtleClicked - 1) * 60 + 50)
        GraphicsWindow.DrawLine(110, (TurtleClicked - 1) * 60 +
50, 140, (TurtleClicked - 1) * 60 + 20)
      EndIf
    ElseIf ((Y > 250 And Y < 280) And TurtlesSelected = 2) Then
      If (X > 5 And X < 95) Then
        'clicked start after picking two turtles
        Sound.PlayBellRing()
        GameStatus = "Moving"
        GraphicsWindow.BrushColor = "White"
        GraphicsWindow.FillRectangle(250, 40, 300, 50)
        'get final positions
        For i = 1 To NumberOfTurtles
          FinalPosition[i] = 500 + Math.GetRandomNumber(360)
        EndFor
        ' pick two winners
```

```
        Winner[1] = Math.GetRandomNumber(NumberOfTurtles)
        NextWinner:
        Winner[2] = Math.GetRandomNumber(NumberOfTurtles)
        If (Winner[1] = Winner[2]) Then
          Goto NextWinner
        EndIf
        FinalPosition[Winner[1]] = 940
        FinalPosition[Winner[2]] = 940
        For i = 1 To NumberOfTurtles
          Shapes.Animate(Turtle[i], FinalPosition[i], (i - 1) * 60
+ 1, 5000)
        EndFor
        GameStatus = "Initial"
      EndIf
    EndIf
  EndIf
EndSub
```

Again, we do not show the code associated with “**Initial**” mode. Notice how the final positions are determined. Once the turtles are moved, you can play again by choosing a new number of turtles (if you want) and click **Start**. Or, you can click **Stop** to end the program.

One last time, **Save** and **Run** the program. Choose a number of turtles (again, I picked 5). Click **Start**, choose two turtles (I chose the top and bottom ones). Click **Start** – a bell is heard and the turtles start the race. Here's the middle of my race:

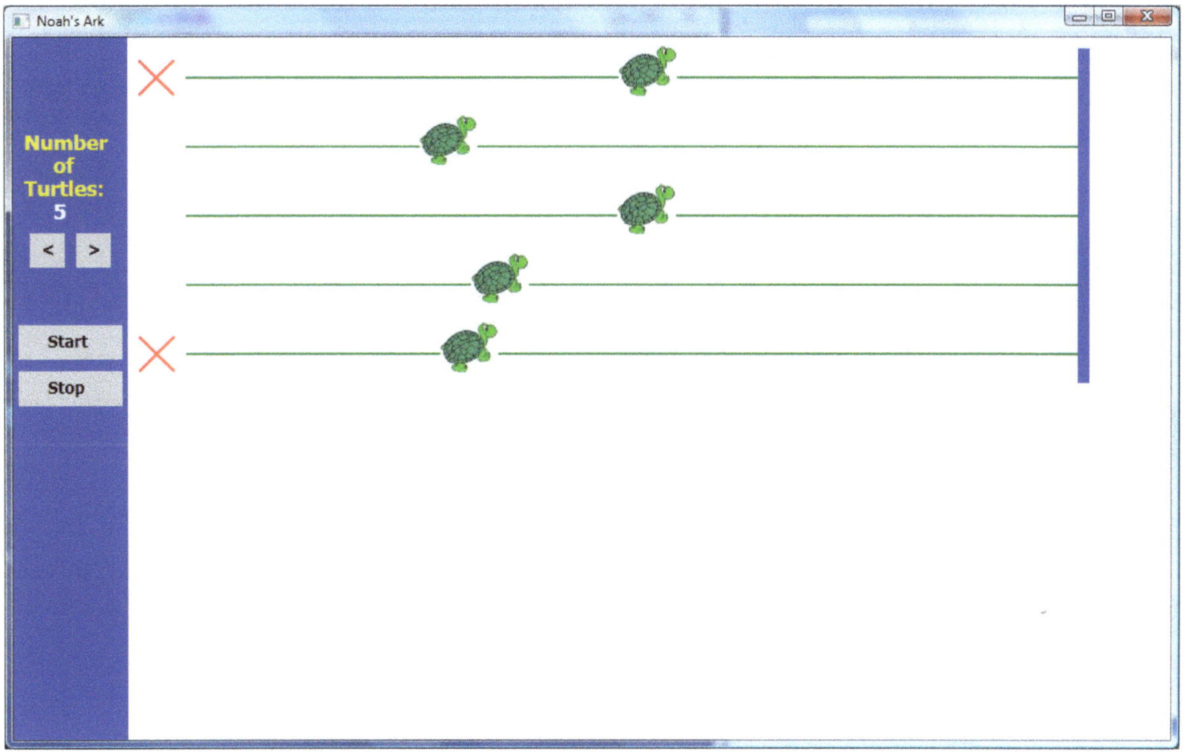

And the finish:

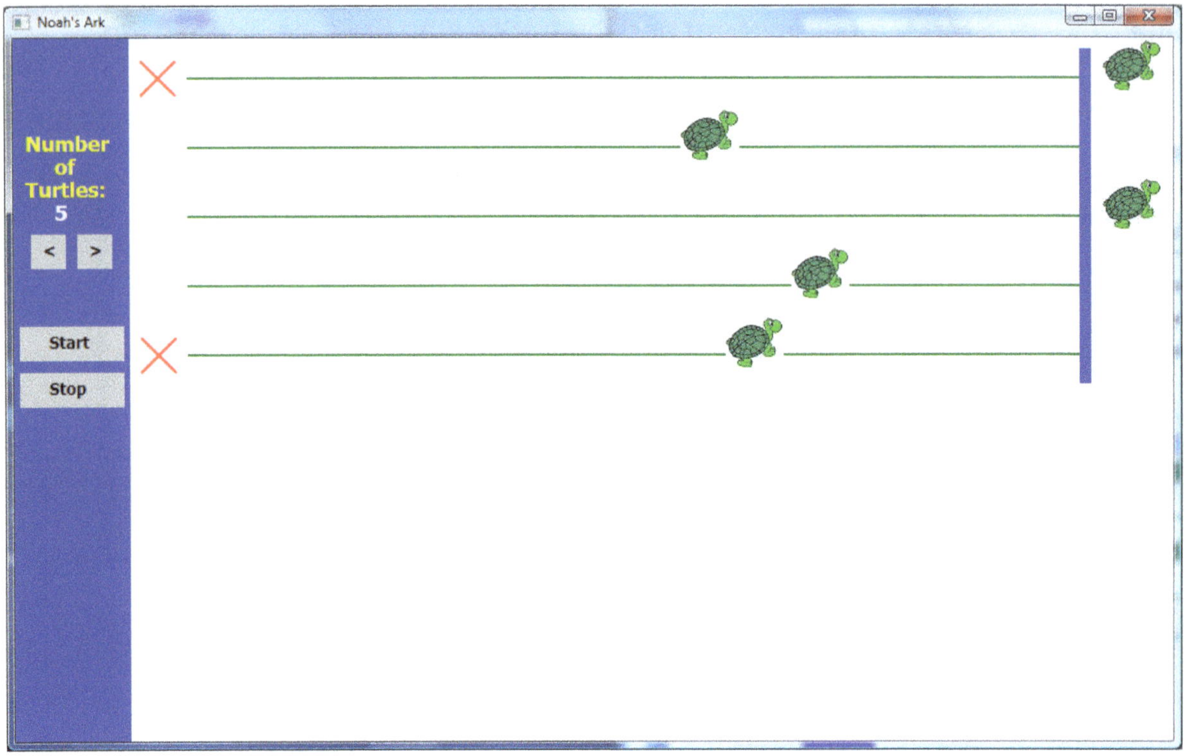

Our work is done. Enjoy the game!

Noah's Ark Program Listing

Here is the complete listing of the **Noah's Ark** Small Basic program:

```
' Noah's Ark
' Small Basic Version

' Intro screen
NumberOfTurtles = 3
GameStatus = "Initial"
GraphicsWindow.Show()
GraphicsWindow.Title = "Noah's Ark"
GraphicsWindow.BackgroundColor = "White"
GraphicsWindow.Width = 1000
GraphicsWindow.Height = 610
GraphicsWindow.BrushColor = "Black"
GraphicsWindow.FontSize = 14
GraphicsWindow.DrawText(110, 10, "NOAH'S ARK")
GraphicsWindow.DrawText(110, 30, "In Genesis Chapter 6, Noah was
commanded by God to take two of every kind of animal into the
ark.")
GraphicsWindow.DrawText(110, 50, "Two turtles are trying to get to
the Ark first. Try to guess which two turtles will make it to the
Ark first.")
GraphicsWindow.DrawText(110, 70, "The purpose of this Bible Story
is to remember that God has promised never to flood the earth
again.")
GraphicsWindow.DrawText(110, 90, "God displays a beautiful rainbow
in the sky to remind us of His promises to us.")
GraphicsWindow.DrawText(110, 180, "<-- Select Number of Turtles to
race by pressing the left button to decrease, right button to
increase.")
GraphicsWindow.DrawText(110, 260, "<-- Click on the Start Button
to begin.")
GraphicsWindow.DrawText(110, 300, "<-- Click on the Stop Button to
stop the program.")
GraphicsWindow.BrushColor = "Blue"
GraphicsWindow.FillRectangle(0, 0, 100, GraphicsWindow.Height)
GraphicsWindow.BrushColor = "Yellow"
GraphicsWindow.FontSize = 18
GraphicsWindow.DrawText(10, 80, "Number")
GraphicsWindow.DrawText(35, 100, "of")
GraphicsWindow.DrawText(10, 120, "Turtles:")
```

```
GraphicsWindow.BrushColor = "White"
GraphicsWindow.FontSize = 18
GraphicsWindow.DrawText(35, 140, NumberOfTurtles)
GraphicsWindow.BrushColor = "LightGray"
GraphicsWindow.FillRectangle(15, 170, 30, 30)
GraphicsWindow.FillRectangle(55, 170, 30, 30)
GraphicsWindow.FillRectangle(5, 250, 90, 30)
GraphicsWindow.FillRectangle(5, 290, 90, 30)
GraphicsWindow.BrushColor = "Black"
GraphicsWindow.FontSize = 14
GraphicsWindow.DrawText(25, 175, "<")
GraphicsWindow.DrawText(65, 175, ">")
GraphicsWindow.DrawText(30, 255, "Start")
GraphicsWindow.DrawText(30, 295, "Stop")
GraphicsWindow.MouseDown = MouseDownEvent

Sub MouseDownEvent
  X = GraphicsWindow.MouseX
  Y = GraphicsWindow.MouseY
  If (GameStatus = "Initial") Then
    If (Y > 175 And Y < 205) Then
      If (X > 15 And X < 45) Then
        ' decrease number of turtles
        NumberOfTurtles = NumberOfTurtles - 1
        If (NumberOfTurtles < 3) Then
          NumberOfTurtles = 3
        EndIf
      ElseIf (X > 55 And X < 85) Then
        'increase number of turtles
        NumberOfTurtles = NumberOfTurtles + 1
        If (NumberOfTurtles > 10) Then
          NumberOfTurtles = 10
        EndIf
      EndIf
      GraphicsWindow.BrushColor = "Blue"
      GraphicsWindow.FillRectangle(0, 140, 100, 20)
      GraphicsWindow.BrushColor = "White"
      GraphicsWindow.FontSize = 18
      GraphicsWindow.DrawText(35, 140, NumberOfTurtles)
    ElseIf (Y > 250 And Y < 280) Then
      If (X > 5 And X < 95) Then
        'clicked start
        GameStatus = "Stopped"
        GraphicsWindow.BrushColor = "White"
        GraphicsWindow.FillRectangle(100, 0, GraphicsWindow.Width
 - 100, GraphicsWindow.Height)
```

```
        'draw turtles
        TurtleImage = ImageList.LoadImage(Program.Directory +
"\turtle.jpg")
        For i = 1 To NumberOfTurtles
          Shapes.Remove(Turtle[i])
          Turtle[i] = Shapes.AddImage(TurtleImage)
          Shapes.Move(Turtle[i], 150, (i - 1) * 60 +10)
          GraphicsWindow.PenColor = "Green"
          GraphicsWindow.DrawLine(150, (i - 1) * 60 + 35, 920, (i
- 1) * 60 + 35)
        EndFor
        ' draw finish line
        GraphicsWindow.BrushColor = "Blue"
        GraphicsWindow.FillRectangle(920, 10, 10, NumberOfTurtles
* 60 -10)
        GraphicsWindow.BrushColor = "Black"
        GraphicsWindow.FontSize = 18
        GraphicsWindow.DrawText(250, 40, "Click on the two turtles
you pick.")
        GraphicsWindow.DrawText(250, 70, "Click Start to start the
race.")
        TurtlesSelected = 0
        For i = 1 to NumberOfTurtles
          TurtlePicked[i] = 0
        EndFor
      EndIf
    ElseIf (Y > 290 And Y < 320) Then
      If (X > 5 And X < 95) Then
        'clicked stop
        Program.End()
      EndIf
    EndIf
  ElseIf (GameStatus = "Stopped") Then
    If (X > 150 And X < 200 And Y > 10 And Y < NumberOfTurtles *
60 + 10) Then
      ' want to pick two and only two turtles
      'which turtle clicked
      TurtleClicked = Math.Floor((Y - 10) / 60) + 1
      'if clicked before, remove from list
      If (TurtlePicked[TurtleClicked] = 1) Then
        TurtlesSelected = TurtlesSelected - 1
        TurtlePicked[TurtleClicked] = 0
        GraphicsWindow.BrushColor = "White"
        GraphicsWindow.FillRectangle(110, (TurtleClicked - 1) * 60
+ 20, 30, 30)
      ElseIf (TurtlesSelected < 2) Then
```

```
        'add to list if two have not been selected yet
        TurtlesSelected = TurtlesSelected + 1
        TurtlePicked[TurtleClicked] = 1
        GraphicsWindow.PenColor = "Red"
        GraphicsWindow.DrawLine(110, (TurtleClicked - 1) * 60 +
20, 140, (TurtleClicked - 1) * 60 + 50)
        GraphicsWindow.DrawLine(110, (TurtleClicked - 1) * 60 +
50, 140, (TurtleClicked - 1) * 60 + 20)
      EndIf
    ElseIf ((Y > 250 And Y < 280) And TurtlesSelected = 2) Then
      If (X > 5 And X < 95) Then
        'clicked start after picking two turtles
        Sound.PlayBellRing()
        GameStatus = "Moving"
        GraphicsWindow.BrushColor = "White"
        GraphicsWindow.FillRectangle(250, 40, 300, 50)
        'get final positions
        For i = 1 To NumberOfTurtles
          FinalPosition[i] = 500 + Math.GetRandomNumber(360)
        EndFor
        ' pick two winners
        Winner[1] = Math.GetRandomNumber(NumberOfTurtles)
        NextWinner:
        Winner[2] = Math.GetRandomNumber(NumberOfTurtles)
        If (Winner[1] = Winner[2]) Then
          Goto NextWinner
        EndIf
        FinalPosition[Winner[1]] = 940
        FinalPosition[Winner[2]] = 940
        For i = 1 To NumberOfTurtles
          Shapes.Animate(Turtle[i], FinalPosition[i], (i - 1) * 60
+ 1, 5000)
        EndFor
        GameStatus = "Initial"
      EndIf
    EndIf
  EndIf
EndSub
```

Noah's Ark Program Review

The **Noah's Ark** program is now complete. **Save** and **Run** the program and make sure it works as promised. Check that all options work correctly.

If there are errors in your implementation, go back over the steps of window and code design. Go over the developed code – make sure you understand how different parts of the program were coded. As mentioned in the beginning of this chapter, the completed program is saved as **Noah** in the **BeginSB\BSB Codes\Noahs Ark** folder.

11

Daniel and the Lions Project

Preview

In Daniel, King Darius is tricked into putting Daniel into the lion's den. Daniel prays for God's protection and god sends His Angel to shut the lion's mouth. In this chapter, you build a computer game based on this story. Daniel is surrounded by lion's in a grid. As he moves, they move closer to him. He shoots prayers at the lions to dispatch them.

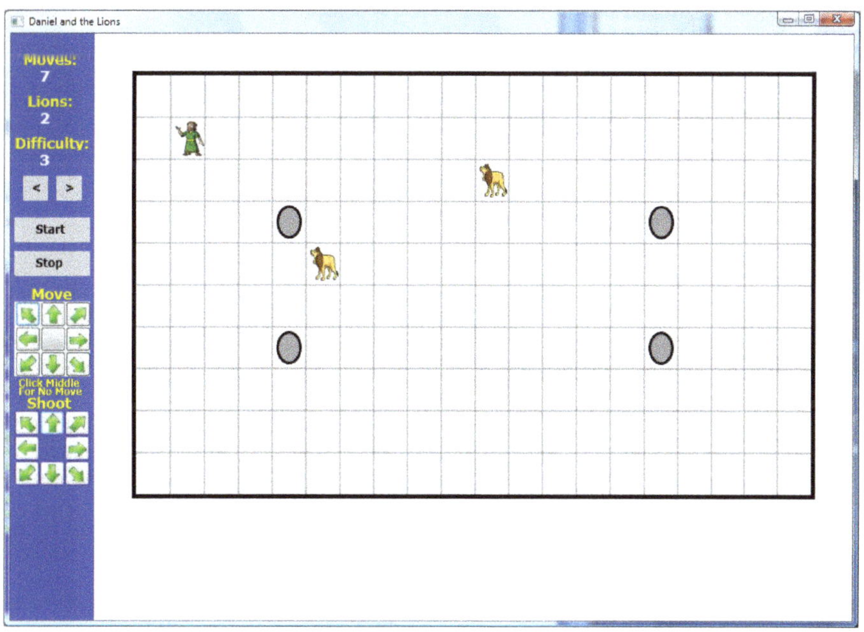

Daniel and the Lions Program Preview

In this chapter, we will build the **Daniel and the Lions** game. Daniel is placed in a grid with a number of lions (and four rocks). The idea is for Daniel to dispatch (eliminate) each lion by shooting a prayer at it. The game is over when Daniel has dispatched all the lions or the moving lions reach Daniel first.

The finished program is saved as **Daniel** in the **BeginSB\BSB Codes\Daniel** folder. Start Small Basic and open the finished program. Run the program (click the **Run** toolbar button or press <**F5**>). The game will appear in its 'initial' state. A game description and program instructions are given. At this point, you can click the **Start** button to start the game, click arrow buttons to change the game **Difficulty** or click **Stop** to stop the program.

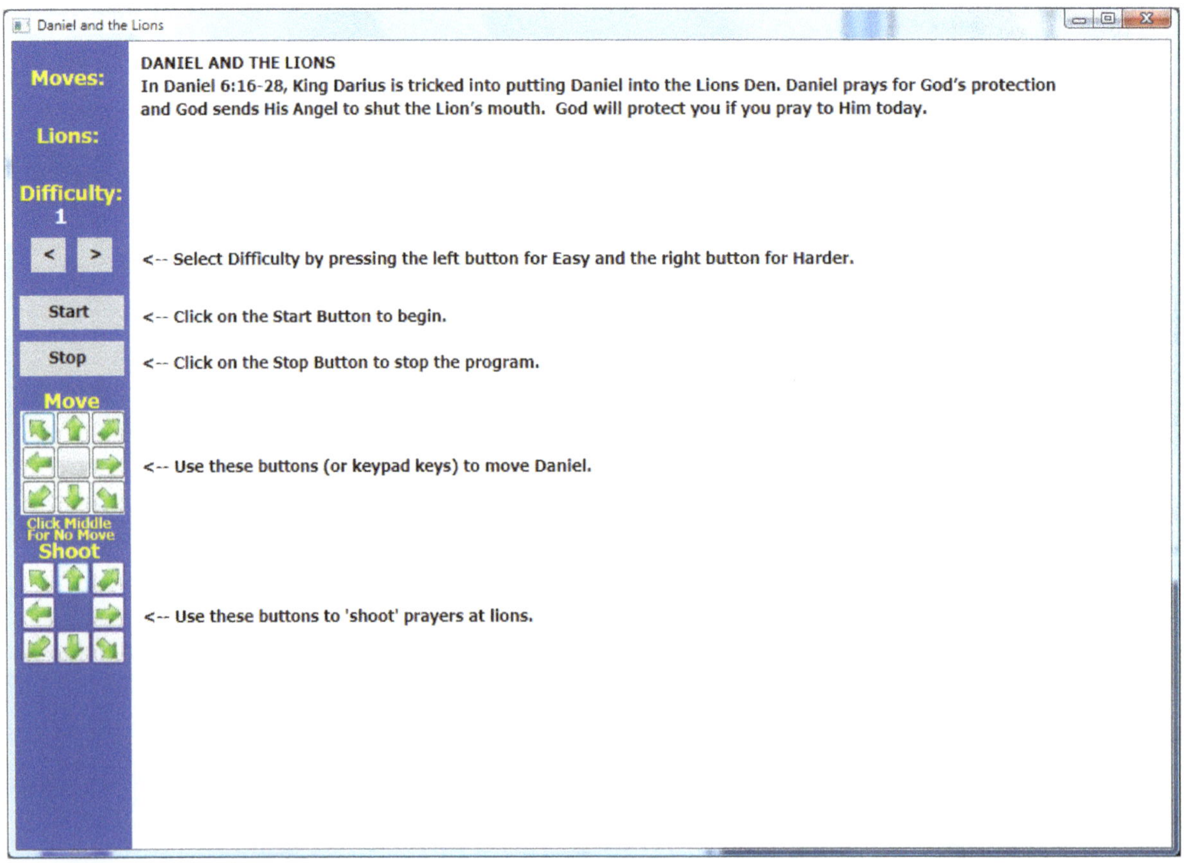

Change the **Difficulty** if you want. The higher the difficulty, the more lions that Daniel must dispatch. I set the value to **3** by clicking the little arrows under **Difficulty**. Click the **Start** button to start playing. The program instructions disappear. Five turtles are poised, ready to race. This is the game's '**DanielMove'** state:

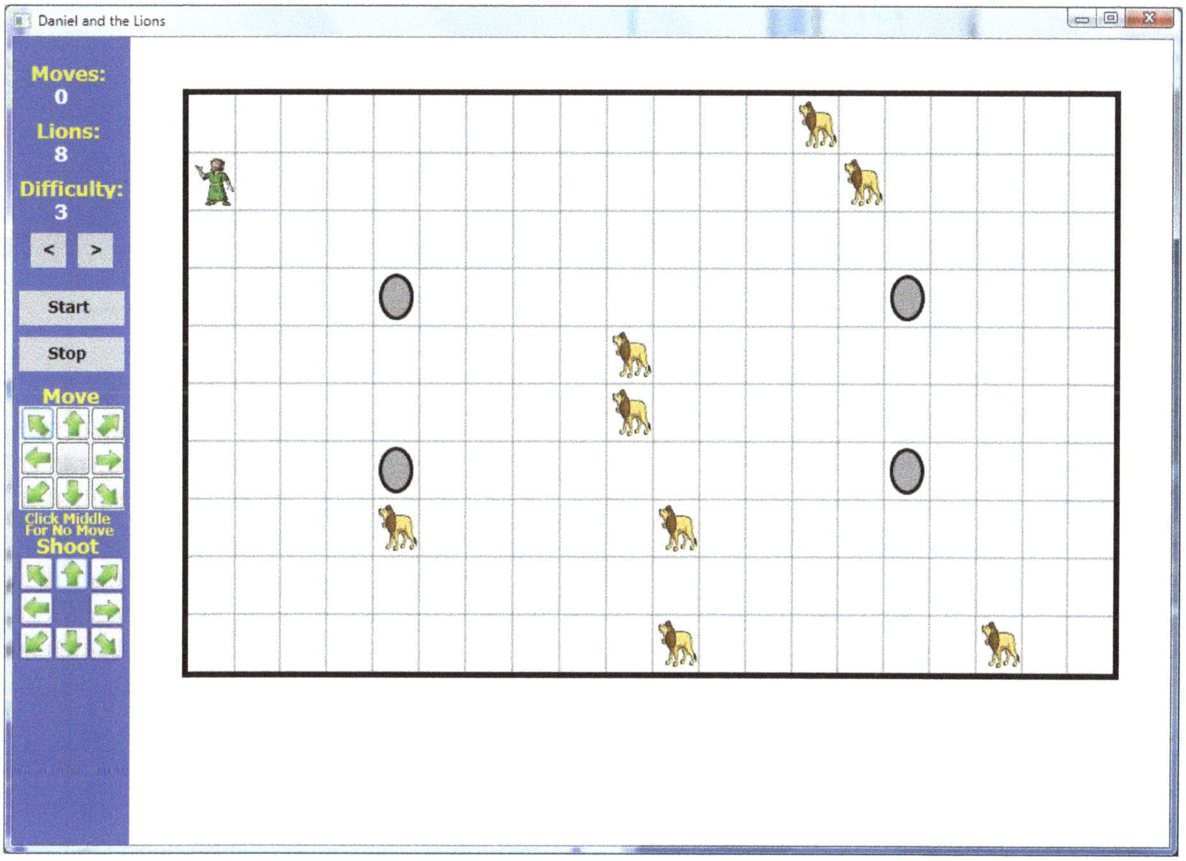

You can see Daniel in the upper left corner of the grid. A number of lions are in the grid along with four rocks (gray ovals). In the upper left corner you are shown how many **Moves** you have taken and how many **Lions** remain. You have two choices. You can move Daniel by clicking one of the arrows under **Move** (or alternately use corresponding key on the numeric keypad). Or, you can shoot a prayer at a lion by clicking one of the green arrows under **Shoot**.

If you move Daniel, he will move one square in the chosen direction (or click the middle to have him remain where he is). Following his move, all the lions will move closer to Daniel, so be careful. Note lions cannot move through the rocks. If you shoot a prayer, it will travel in the selected direction. If it intercepts a lion, that lion is dispatched (taken out of the grid). A prayer will not move through a rock. The goal of the game is to dispatch all the lions before one reaches Daniel.

In our example, notice a lion far to the right of Daniel. Click the right **Shoot** arrow and that lion is gone:

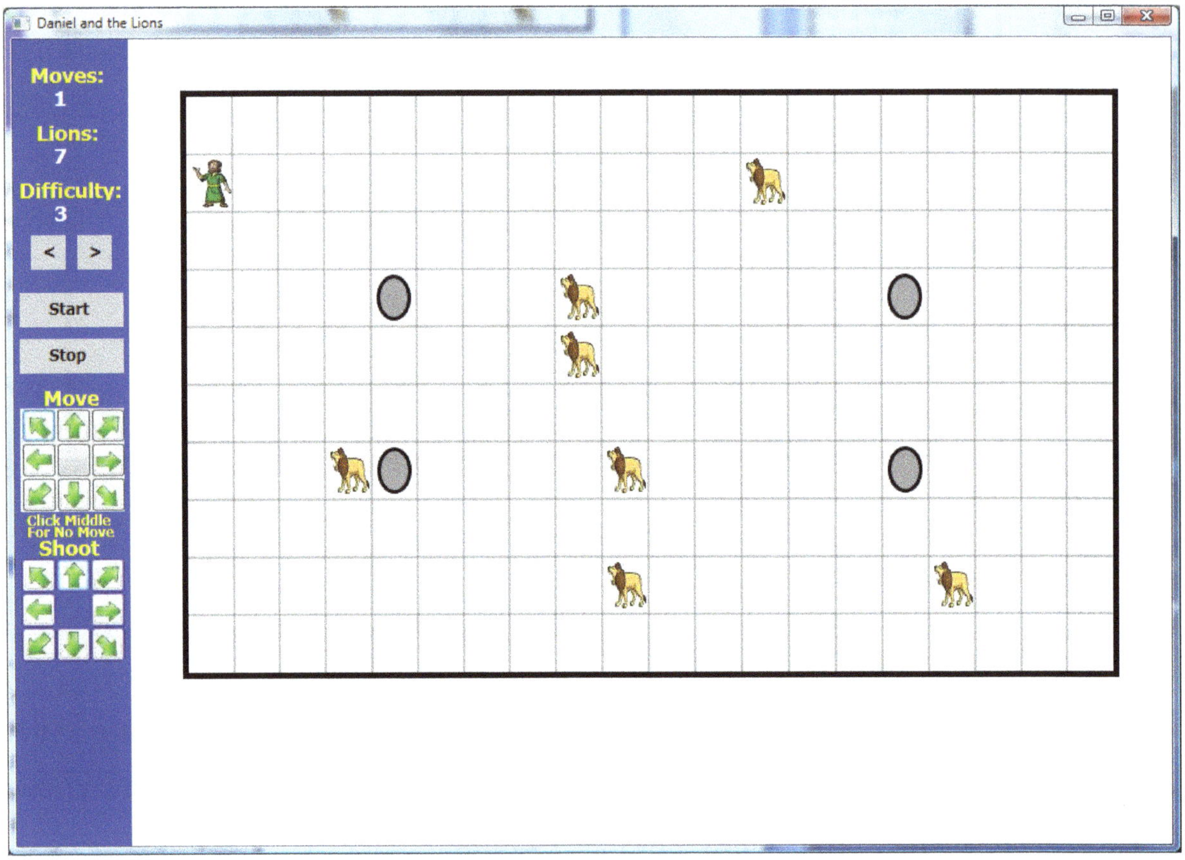

Also notice the remaining lions have moved toward Daniel. There's another to his right. Click the right **Shoot** arrow again.

Another lion is dispatched, but they continue to close in on Daniel:

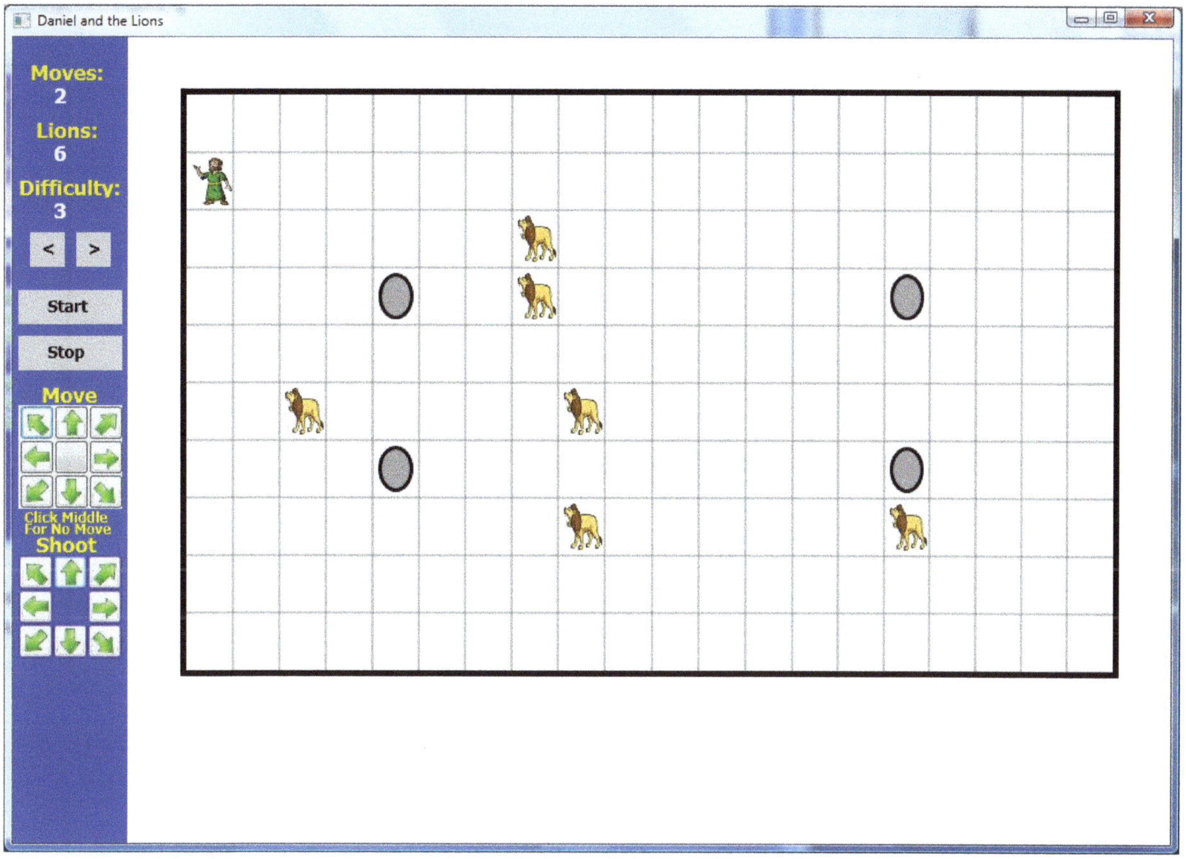

At this point, no lions are in the direct path of a 'prayer shot' so we can only move Daniel.

I moved him to the right (and the lions moved too):

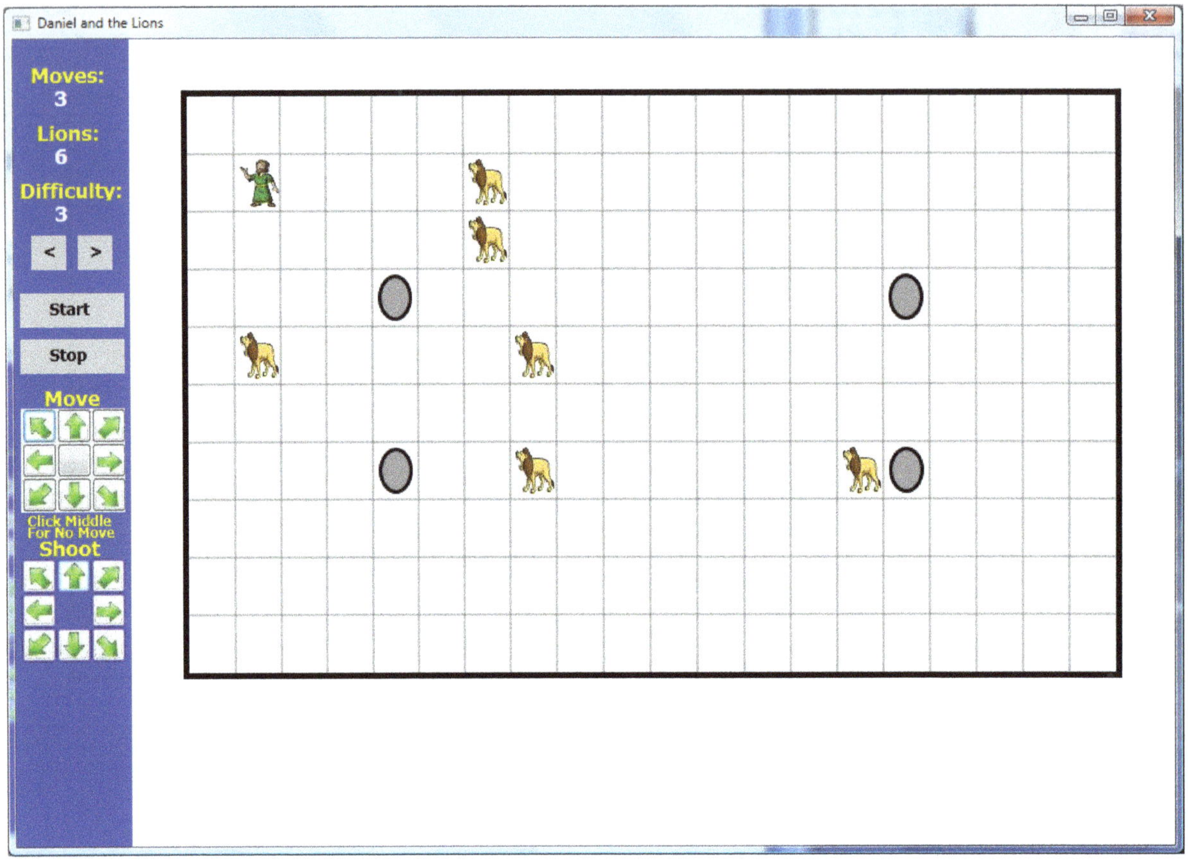

I can either shoot to the right or down.

A shot down, then three to the right led me to this state:

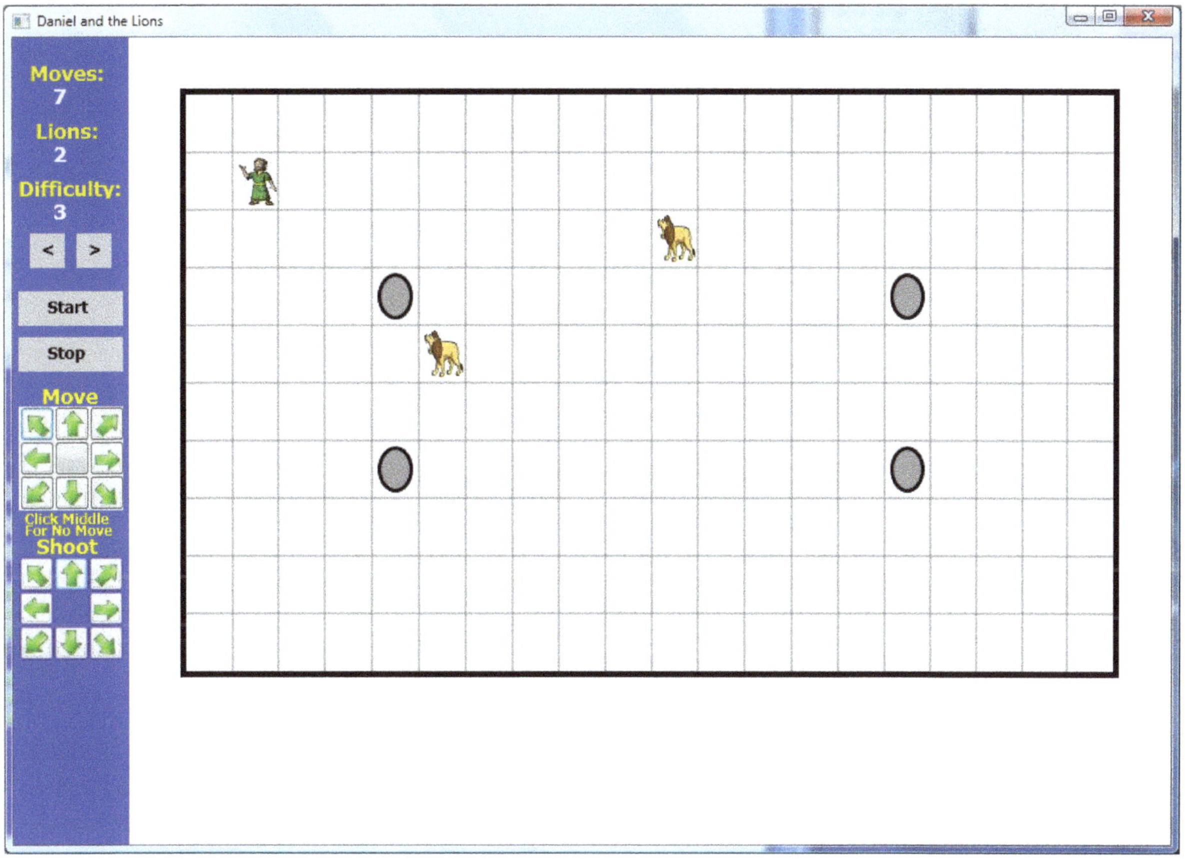

You should see how the game is played. When a lion is in shot range, take a shot. If a lion gets stuck behind a rock, you need to move Daniel until the lion moves in range. I continued this game and dispatched all 8 lions in 13 moves. At this point, I got this message:

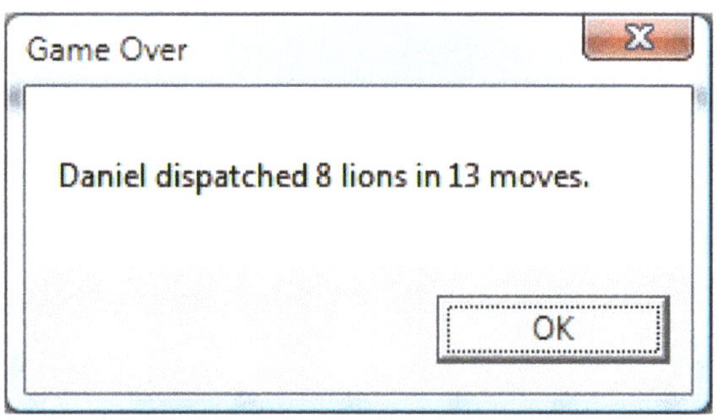

If you aren't successful in dispatching all the lions, you will see this message:

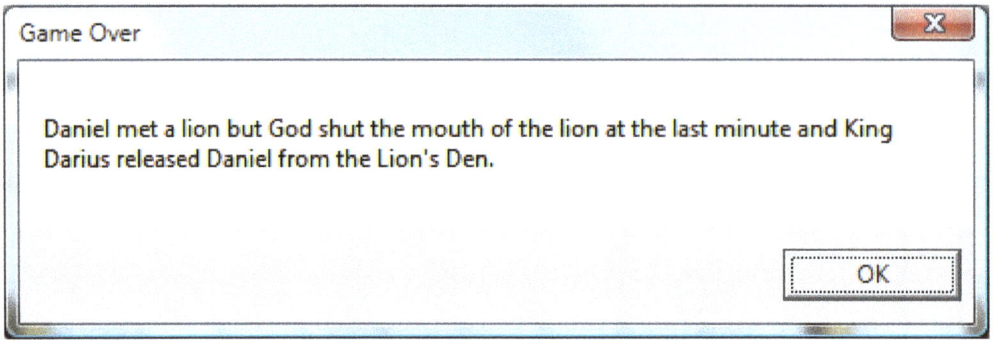

When a game is over, you can change the **Difficulty**. You can also click **Start** to play again or click **Stop** to stop the program. Continue playing the game to understand its operation.

You will now build this program in stages. As you build Small Basic programs, we always recommend taking a slow, step-by-step process. It minimizes programming errors and helps build your confidence as things come together in a complete program. We address **window design**. And, we address **code design**. We discuss how to use the 'buttons', how to draw the grid, how to display Daniel, the lions and the rocks, and how to move Daniel and the lions.

Daniel and the Lions Window Design

Here is a sketch for the window layout of the **Daniel and the Lions** game:

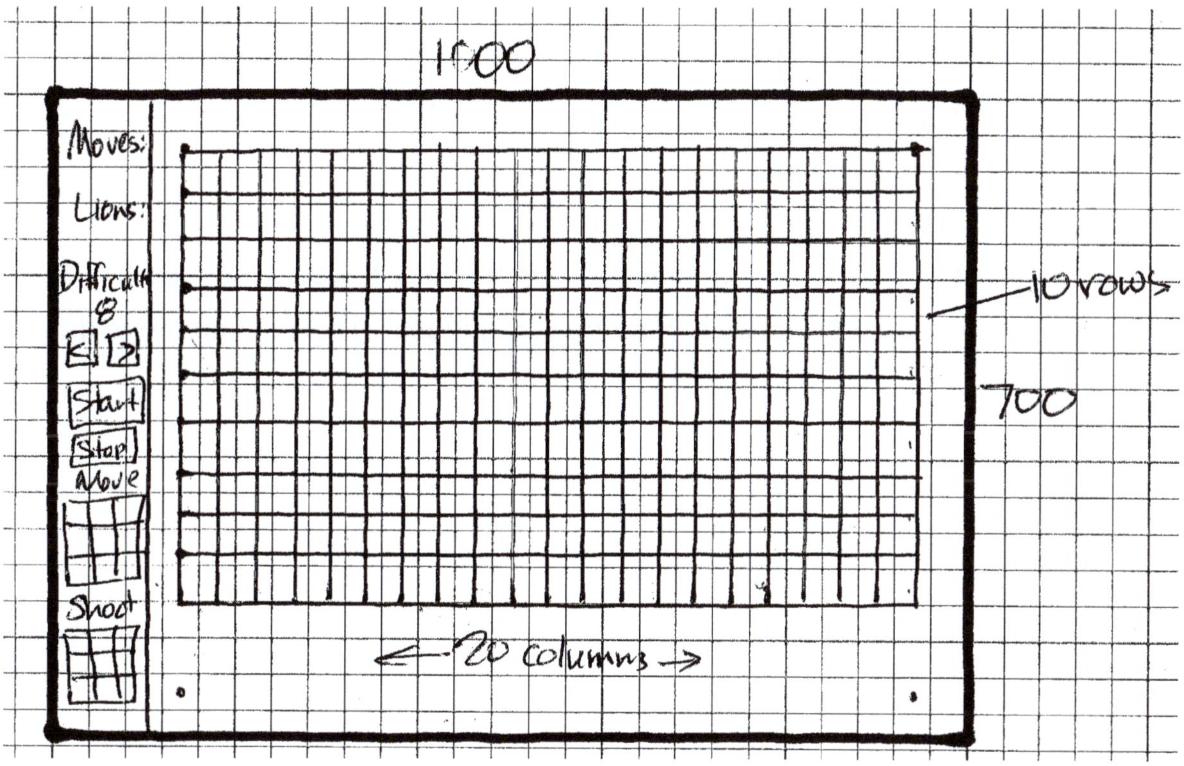

The graphics window is 1000 pixels wide and 700 pixels high. The blue background area on the left (100 pixels wide) is used to control game play. The white area on the right (900 pixels wide) displays game instructions when the program first begins and shows the grid with Daniel and the lions. In the area on the left indicators of the number of moves taken (**Moves**), the number of lions remaining (**Lions**), and the game difficulty (**Difficulty**). Under these are gray rectangles used to represent clickable game control buttons. Four 'buttons' are used: two to change the difficulty, one to start the game, and one to stop the program. Under the game control buttons are two sets of directional buttons (represented by graphics files). The first set of nine buttons are used to move Daniel. The last set of eight buttons are used to fire prayers at the lions.

We now begin writing code for the **Daniel and the Lions** game. We will write the code in several steps. As a first step, we will write the code that draws the window and establishes its 'initial' state. Then, we look at how to go to the state allowing Daniel to move following clicking of the **Start** button. We then write code to move Daniel (using mouse clicks or keyboard presses), move the lions toward Daniel and shoot prayers at the lions. During the code development process, recognize you may modify a particular procedure several times before arriving at the finished product.

Start a new program in Small Basic. Once started, we suggest you immediately save the program with a name you choose. This sets up the folder and file structure needed for your program.

Code Design – Initial State (Instructions)

Any time we start a program, there are certain initializations that must take place. Let's look at the initializations needed in the **Daniel and the Lions** game. When the program first begins, we want to display the game instructions, any needed titling and the control buttons. We also initialize the difficulty (**Difficulty**) and the game status (**GameStatus**). We set up the game screen and display the instructions first.

Add this code to your empty code window:

```
' Daniel and the Lions
' Small Basic Version

' Intro screen
IntroScreen:
Difficulty = 1
GameStatus = "Initial"
GraphicsWindow.Show()
GraphicsWindow.Title = "Daniel and the Lions"
GraphicsWindow.BackgroundColor = "White"
GraphicsWindow.Width = 1000
GraphicsWindow.Height = 700
GraphicsWindow.BrushColor = "Black"
GraphicsWindow.FontSize = 14
GraphicsWindow.DrawText(110, 10, "DANIEL AND THE LIONS")
GraphicsWindow.DrawText(110, 30, "In Daniel 6:16-28, King Darius
is tricked into putting Daniel into the Lions Den. Daniel prays
for God’s protection")
GraphicsWindow.DrawText(110, 50, "and God sends His Angel to shut
the Lion’s mouth.  God will protect you if you pray to Him
today.")
GraphicsWindow.DrawText(110, 180, "<-- Select Difficulty by
pressing the left button for Easy and the right button for
Harder.")
GraphicsWindow.DrawText(110, 230, "<-- Click on the Start Button
to begin.")
GraphicsWindow.DrawText(110, 270, "<-- Click on the Stop Button to
stop the program.")
```

```
GraphicsWindow.DrawText(110, 360, "<-- Use these buttons (or
keypad keys) to move Daniel.")
GraphicsWindow.DrawText(110, 490, "<-- Use these buttons to
'shoot' prayers at lions.")
GraphicsWindow.BrushColor = "Blue"
GraphicsWindow.FillRectangle(0, 0, 100, GraphicsWindow.Height)
```

As mentioned, we set **Difficulty** to **1** and the **GameStatus** to "**Initial**". Next, after setting up the **GraphicsWindow**, using a series of **DrawText** statements, we write out the game instructions. **Save** and **Run** the program to see:

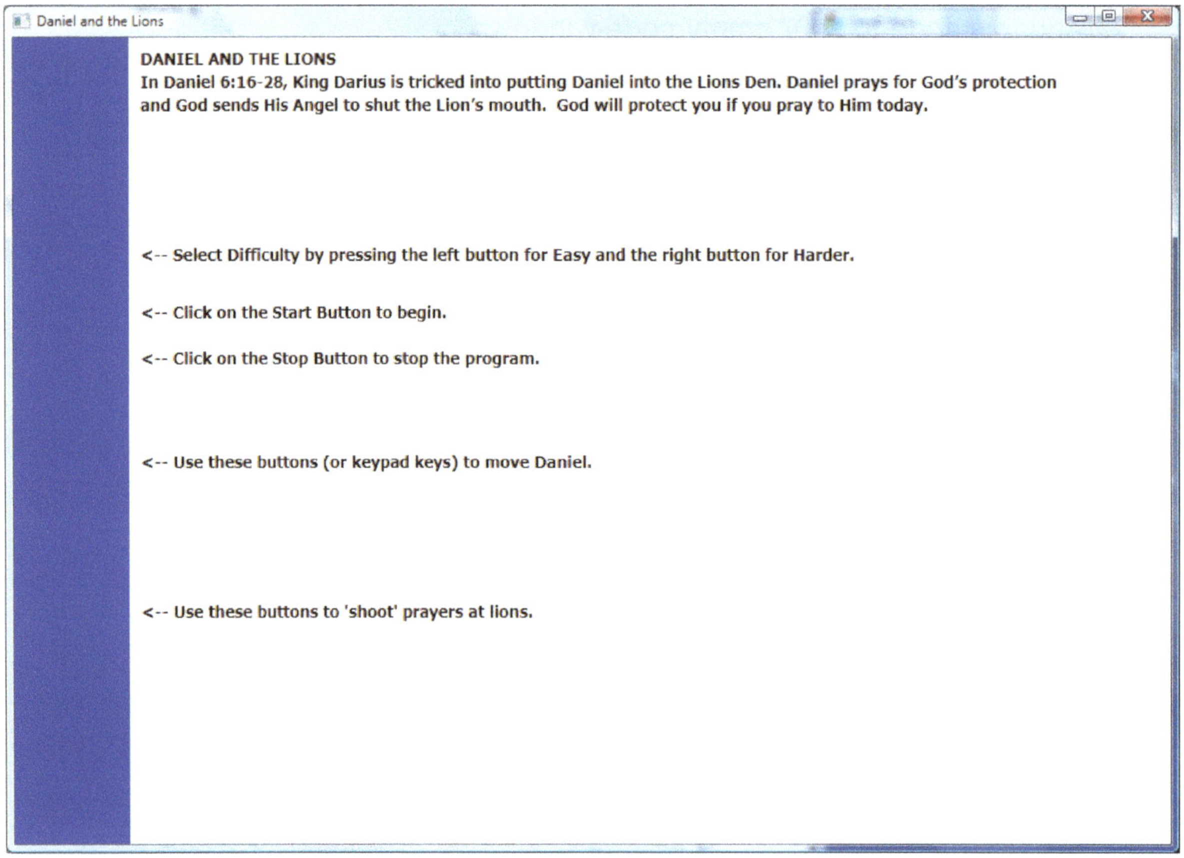

You may wonder how we came up with all the position numbers in the **DrawText** statements. They were set by trial and error. You do this a lot in Small Basic. Try some values and see how they look. Make corrections until things appear as you desire.

Code Design – Initial State (Titling and Buttons)

The other elements we need when the program begins are the titling information (number of moves, number of lions, difficulty) and the 'buttons' used to control the game. The first four buttons are each a gray rectangular area that can be clicked with the mouse. The buttons to move Daniel and shoot prayers are Small Basic **Shapes** objects that can also be clicked. They are represented by the two graphics files:

MoveButtons.jpg

ShootButtons.jpg

Copy both of these graphics files to your program folder. We will detect button clicks using the **GraphicsWindow MouseDown** event. For now, let's just draw the buttons and titling information.

Add this code to your program:

```
GraphicsWindow.BrushColor = "Yellow"
GraphicsWindow.FontSize = 18
GraphicsWindow.DrawText(15, 20, "Moves:")
GraphicsWindow.DrawText(20, 70, "Lions:")
GraphicsWindow.DrawText(5, 120, "Difficulty:")
GraphicsWindow.DrawText(25, 300, "Move")
GraphicsWindow.DrawText(20, 430, "Shoot")
GraphicsWindow.FontSize = 12
GraphicsWindow.DrawText(10, 410, "Click Middle")
GraphicsWindow.DrawText(10, 420, "For No Move")
GraphicsWindow.BrushColor = "White"
GraphicsWindow.FontSize = 18
GraphicsWindow.DrawText(35, 140, Difficulty)
GraphicsWindow.BrushColor = "LightGray"
```

```
GraphicsWindow.FillRectangle(15, 170, 30, 30)
GraphicsWindow.FillRectangle(55, 170, 30, 30)
GraphicsWindow.FillRectangle(5, 220, 90, 30)
GraphicsWindow.FillRectangle(5, 260, 90, 30)
GraphicsWindow.BrushColor = "Black"
GraphicsWindow.FontSize = 14
GraphicsWindow.DrawText(25, 175, "<")
GraphicsWindow.DrawText(65, 175, ">")
GraphicsWindow.DrawText(30, 225, "Start")
GraphicsWindow.DrawText(30, 265, "Stop")
MoveImage = ImageList.LoadImage(Program.Directory +
"\MoveButtons.jpg")
MoveButtons = Shapes.AddImage(MoveImage)
Shapes.Move(MoveButtons, 5, 320)
ShootImage  = ImageList.LoadImage(Program.Directory +
"\ShootButtons.jpg")
ShootButtons = Shapes.AddImage(ShootImage)
Shapes.Move(ShootButtons, 5, 450)
```

Most of the titling information is near the top. Each game control button (those that change the difficulty and start and stop the program) is a gray rectangle with black text. There are two buttons (< and >) used to change the difficulty. There are two buttons (**Start** and **Stop**) used to control the game. The two shapes objects (**MoveButtons**, **ShootButtons**) are used to move Daniel and shoot prayers. Like the game instructions, the size and position for each of these elements were arrived at by trial and error. You can change any values you want. Just make sure to note where each button is located – you will need this information when writing the code to detect mouse clicks.

Save and **Run** the program to see the finished initial game screen:

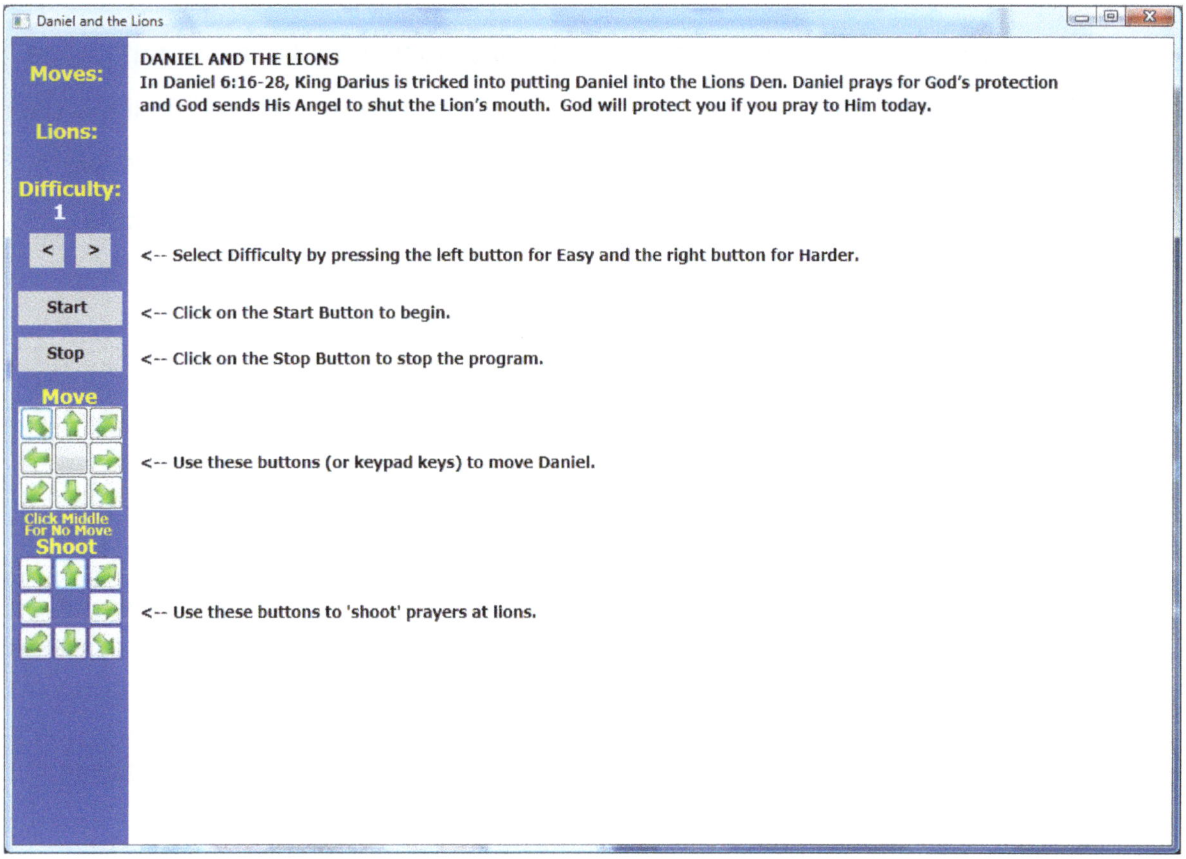

Notice the added buttons and the heading information for the **Moves, Lions, Difficulty, Move** and **Shoot**. Values for **Moves** and **Lions** will be displayed when the game is played.

Code Design – Select Difficulty

The **Difficulty** variable is used to determine how many lions are put on the game grid (the higher the difficulty, the more lions). To change the difficulty, a user clicks on either of the two arrow buttons. To detect clicks on these buttons, we need to know their location and size in the window. Looking back at the code, you can see:

button; located at (15, 170), width 30, height 30

button; located at (55, 170), width 30, height 30

We write code to see if a user clicks within the region defined by the buttons. If so, we take the necessary action of changing the difficulty.

We need to detect mouse clicks, so add this line of code to your program:

```
GraphicsWindow.MouseDown = MouseDownEvent
```

With this line, each time a mouse button is pressed (a **MouseDown** event) the subroutine **MouseDownEvent** is called. Most of the remaining code will be placed in this subroutine. Let's do the code for changing the difficulty.

Add this subroutine at the end of your program:

```
Sub MouseDownEvent
  X = GraphicsWindow.MouseX
  Y = GraphicsWindow.MouseY
  If (GameStatus = "Initial") Then
    If (Y > 175 And Y < 205) Then
      If (X > 15 And X < 45) Then
        ' decrease difficulty
        Difficulty = Difficulty - 1
        If (Difficulty < 1) Then
          Difficulty = 1
        EndIf
      ElseIf (X > 55 And X < 85) Then
        'increase difficulty
        Difficulty = Difficulty + 1
        If (Difficulty > 10) Then
          Difficulty = 10
        EndIf
      EndIf
      GraphicsWindow.BrushColor = "Blue"
      GraphicsWindow.FillRectangle(0, 140, 100, 20)
      GraphicsWindow.BrushColor = "White"
      GraphicsWindow.FontSize = 18
      GraphicsWindow.DrawText(35, 140, Difficulty)
    EndIf
  EndIf
EndSub
```

The code is straightforward. The difficulty can only be changed when the game is in "**Initial**" state. We look to see if the clicked coordinate (**X, Y**) is within the regions of the two arrow buttons. If the **<** button is clicked, we decrease the difficulty by one (minimum of 1). If the **>** button is clicked, we increase the difficulty (maximum of 10). The new value for the difficulty is then displayed (after first clearing the area with the previous value).

Save and **Run** the program. Make sure the arrow buttons work – make sure the difficulty is always between 1 and 10. Here's my run where I changed the difficulty to three:

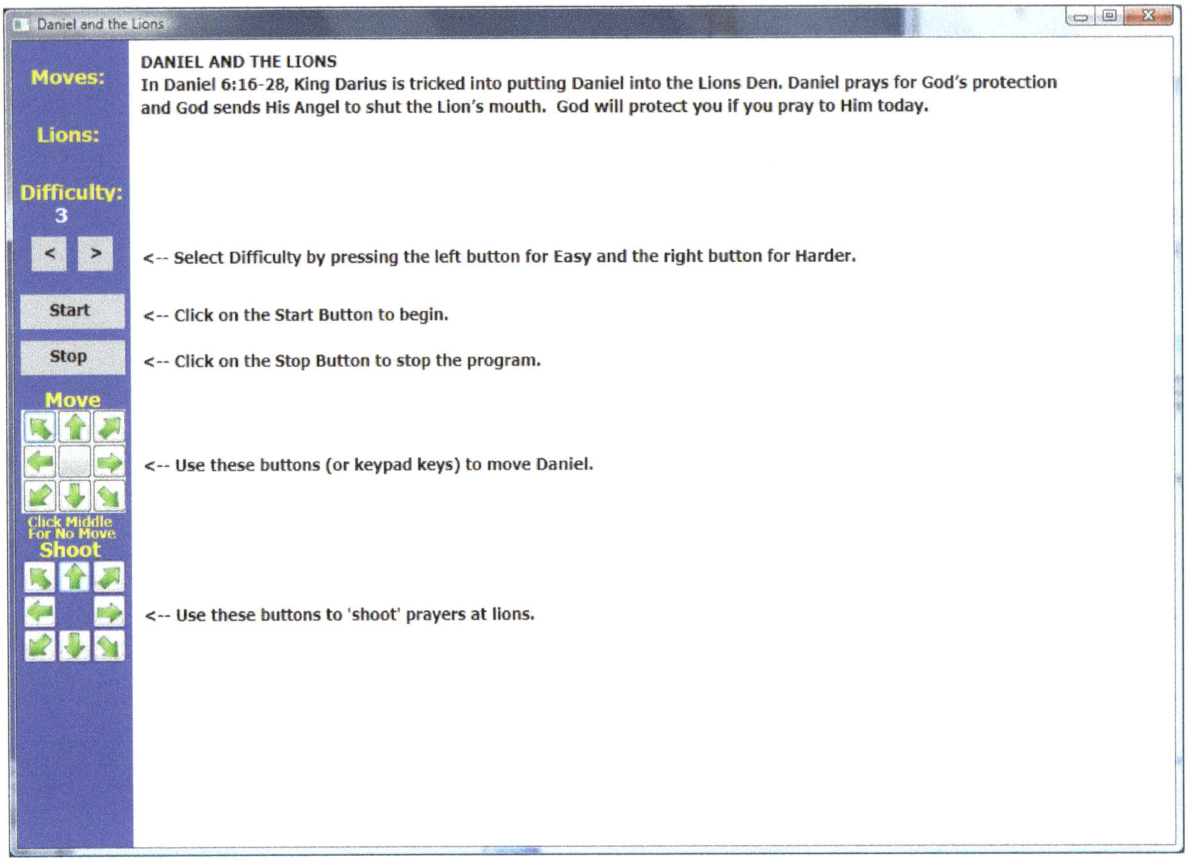

Code Design – Draw Grid

Once the difficulty is set, the next step is to click the **Start** button to allow the game to begin. Hence, we need code to move from the "**Initial**" state to what we'll call "**DanielMove**" state. Like the arrow buttons, to detect clicks on the **Start** button, we need to know its location and size in the window. From the code, we see:

button; located at (5, 220), width 90, height 30

When the **Start** button is clicked in "**Initial**" state, we need to take the following steps:

- Change **GameStatus** to "**DanielMove**"
- Initialize variables
- Clear game screen
- Draw game grid with rocks
- Randomly place Daniel on the grid
- Randomly place lions on the grid

There is a lot to do here, so we will take it in steps. First, we'll initialize variables and draw the grid.

Three variables are used in game control. **GameOver** is a Boolean variable that tells us if the game has ended – it is initialized at "**false**". **Moves** (initialized at zero) tells us how many times Daniel has moved. Lastly, **NumberLions** tells us how many lions are placed in the grid (initialized to **Difficulty + 5**). The game grid has 10 rows and 20 columns (each grid space 40 pixels wide by 50 pixels high).

Add the shaded code to the **MouseDownEvent** subroutine:

```
Sub MouseDownEvent
  X = GraphicsWindow.MouseX
  Y = GraphicsWindow.MouseY
  If (GameStatus = "Initial") Then
    If (Y > 175 And Y < 205) Then
      If (X > 15 And X < 45) Then
        ' decrease difficulty
        Difficulty = Difficulty - 1
        If (Difficulty < 1) Then
          Difficulty = 1
        EndIf
      ElseIf (X > 55 And X < 85) Then
        'increase difficulty
        Difficulty = Difficulty + 1
        If (Difficulty > 10) Then
          Difficulty = 10
        EndIf
      EndIf
      GraphicsWindow.BrushColor = "Blue"
      GraphicsWindow.FillRectangle(0, 140, 100, 20)
      GraphicsWindow.BrushColor = "White"
      GraphicsWindow.FontSize = 18
      GraphicsWindow.DrawText(35, 140, Difficulty)
    ElseIf (Y > 220 And Y < 250) Then
      If (X > 5 And X < 95) Then
        'clicked start
        GameStatus = "DanielMove"
        GameOver = "false"
        GraphicsWindow.BrushColor = "White"
        GraphicsWindow.FillRectangle(100, 0, GraphicsWindow.Width
- 100, GraphicsWindow.Height)
        Moves = 0
        NumberLions = Difficulty + 5
        LionsLeft = NumberLions
        DisplayMovesLions()
        '  draw grid structure
        GraphicsWindow.BrushColor = "Black"
        GraphicsWindow.FillRectangle(145, 45, 810, 510)
        GraphicsWindow.BrushColor = "White"
        GraphicsWindow.FillRectangle(150, 50, 800, 500)
        GraphicsWindow.PenWidth = 1
        GraphicsWindow.PenColor = "Gray"
        For i = 1 to 9
```

```
      GraphicsWindow.DrawLine(150, (i + 1) * 50, 950, (i + 1)
* 50)
    EndFor
    For i = 1 to 19
      GraphicsWindow.DrawLine(150 + i * 40, 50, 150 + i * 40,
550)
    EndFor
   EndIf
  EndIf
 EndIf
EndSub
```

You should be able to identify each step in this new code. We clear the area and set variables. The grid structure is established as a white rectangle with a black border. Horizontal lines are drawn every 50 pixels and vertical lines are drawn every 40 pixels. Notice this line of code:

```
DisplayMovesLions()
```

This line calls a subroutine that updates the displayed value for **Moves** and **LionsLeft** (the number of lions remaining to be found). Add this subroutine at the end of your program:

```
Sub DisplayMovesLions
  GraphicsWindow.FontSize = 18
  GraphicsWindow.BrushColor = "Blue"
  GraphicsWindow.FillRectangle(0, 40, 100, 20)
  GraphicsWindow.FillRectangle(0, 90, 100, 20)
  GraphicsWindow.BrushColor = "White"
  GraphicsWindow.DrawText(35, 40, Moves)
  GraphicsWindow.DrawText(35, 90, LionsLeft)
EndSub
```

Here, we clear out previous vaues for **Moves** and **LionsLeft** and draw the new values (using **DrawText**).

Save and **Run** the program. Choose a difficulty (I picked 3). Click **Start** and you should see:

Notice the displayed values for **Moves** and **Lions**. Notice the nice grid structure.

Code Design – Position Rocks

Four rocks are placed in the grid. Daniel can hide behind these rocks if needed for protection from the lions. Elliptical **Shapes** objects are used for each of the rocks.

Recall the grid has 10 rows and 20 columns. We use a two-dimensional array **A** to keep track of what is in each location within the grid. The first index in the array is the **row**, the second is the **column**, so the value at:

```
A[Row][Column]
```

tells us what is in that location. We use this system:

`A[Row][Column] = 0`	Nothing is there
`A[Row][Column] = 1`	Rock is there
`A[Row][Column] = 2`	Lion is there
`A[Row][Column] = 3`	Daniel is there

The rocks are in fixed locations: Row 4, Column 5 and Column 16 and Row 7, Column 5 and Column 16.

Add the shaded code to the **MouseDownEvent** subroutine to initialize the **A** array to all zeroes, then position the four rocks on the grid:

```
Sub MouseDownEvent
  X = GraphicsWindow.MouseX
  Y = GraphicsWindow.MouseY
  If (GameStatus = "Initial") Then
    If (Y > 175 And Y < 205) Then
      If (X > 15 And X < 45) Then
        ' decrease difficulty
        Difficulty = Difficulty - 1
        If (Difficulty < 1) Then
          Difficulty = 1
        EndIf
      ElseIf (X > 55 And X < 85) Then
        'increase difficulty
        Difficulty = Difficulty + 1
        If (Difficulty > 10) Then
          Difficulty = 10
        EndIf
      EndIf
      GraphicsWindow.BrushColor = "Blue"
      GraphicsWindow.FillRectangle(0, 140, 100, 20)
      GraphicsWindow.BrushColor = "White"
      GraphicsWindow.FontSize = 18
      GraphicsWindow.DrawText(35, 140, Difficulty)
    ElseIf (Y > 220 And Y < 250) Then
      If (X > 5 And X < 95) Then
        'clicked start
        GameStatus = "DanielMove"
        GameOver = "false"
        GraphicsWindow.BrushColor = "White"
        GraphicsWindow.FillRectangle(100, 0, GraphicsWindow.Width
- 100, GraphicsWindow.Height)
        Moves = 0
        NumberLions = Difficulty + 5
        LionsLeft = NumberLions
        DisplayMovesLions()
        '  draw grid structure
        GraphicsWindow.BrushColor = "Black"
        GraphicsWindow.FillRectangle(145, 45, 810, 510)
        GraphicsWindow.BrushColor = "White"
        GraphicsWindow.FillRectangle(150, 50, 800, 500)
        GraphicsWindow.PenWidth = 1
```

```
        GraphicsWindow.PenColor = "Gray"
        For i = 1 to 9
          GraphicsWindow.DrawLine(150, (i + 1) * 50, 950, (i + 1)
* 50)
        EndFor
        For i = 1 to 19
          GraphicsWindow.DrawLine(150 + i * 40, 50, 150 + i * 40,
550)
        EndFor
        For i = 1 to 10
          For j = 1 to 20
            A[i][j] = 0
          EndFor
        EndFor
        '  Place rocks
        ' A array (0- nothing, 1-rock, 2-lion, 3-Daniel)
        A[4][5] = 1
        A[4][16] = 1
        A[7][5] = 1
        A[7][16] = 1
        GraphicsWindow.PenWidth = 3
        GraphicsWindow.PenColor = "Black"
        GraphicsWindow.BrushColor = "DarkGray"
        Rock[1] = Shapes.AddEllipse(30, 40)
        Rock[2] = Shapes.AddEllipse(30, 40)
        Rock[3] = Shapes.AddEllipse(30, 40)
        Rock[4] = Shapes.AddEllipse(30, 40)
        Shapes.Move(Rock[1], 315, 205)
        Shapes.Move(Rock[2], 755, 205)
        Shapes.Move(Rock[3], 315, 355)
        Shapes.Move(Rock[4], 755, 355)
      EndIf
    EndIf
  EndIf
EndSub
```

The (x, y) coordinates used in the **Move** methods were found by knowing where the grid lines are located (by looking at the code that draws these lines). For example, the first rock is at row 4, column 5. The top left corner at that position is (**310**, **200**).

Save and **Run** the program. Click **Start**. The rocks will appear:

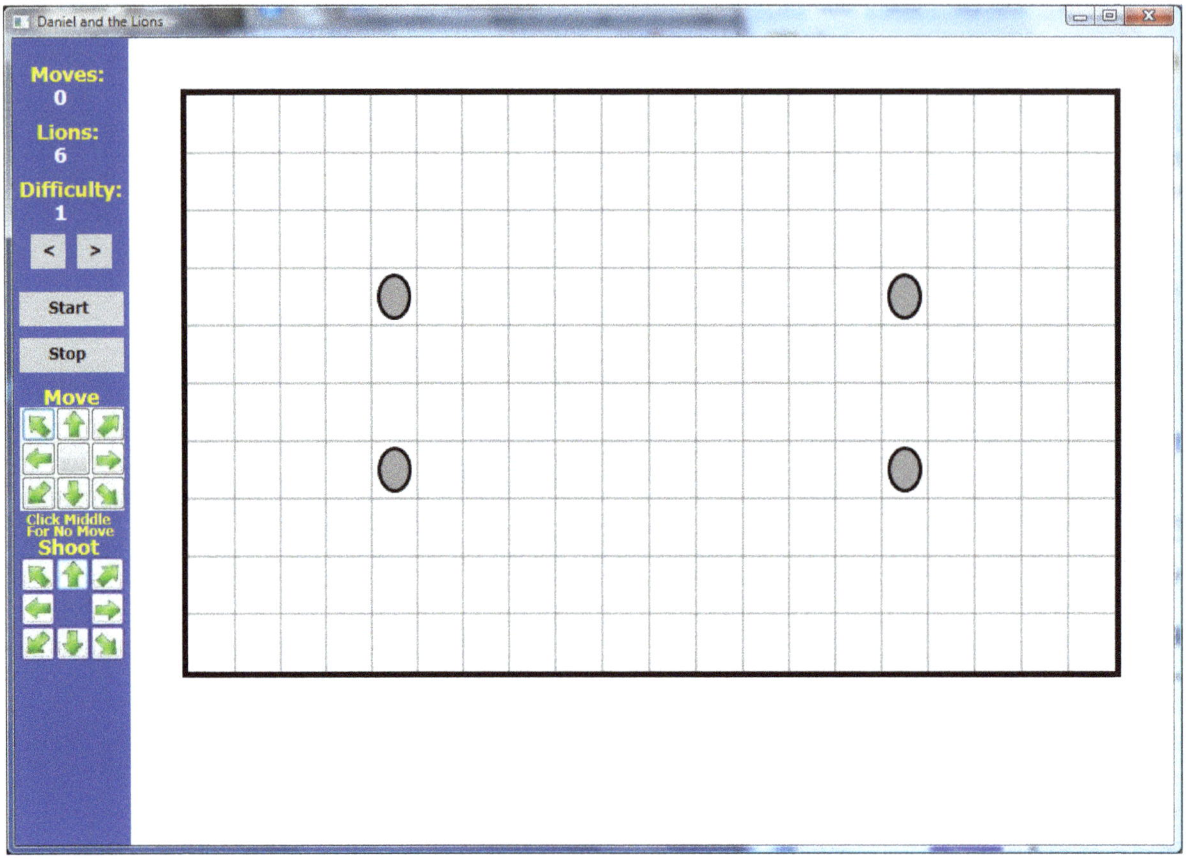

Code Design – Position Daniel and Lions

The last initialization step is to randomly place Daniel and the lions (**NumberLions**) onto the grid. **Shapes** objects are used for Daniel and lions and are represented by the two graphics files:

Daniel.jpg

Lion.jpg

Copy both of these graphics files to your program folder.

The code to position Daniel and the lions in the grid is similar. We randomly pick a row and column. If nothing is already at that position, put it there. The variables **DanielRow** and **DanielColumn** tell us where Daniel is. The arrays **LionRow** and **LionColumn** tell us where each lion is. Positioning coordinates (x, y) are determined like we did for rock placement.

Add the shaded code to the **MouseDownEvent** subroutine:

```
Sub MouseDownEvent
  X = GraphicsWindow.MouseX
  Y = GraphicsWindow.MouseY
  If (GameStatus = "Initial") Then
    If (Y > 175 And Y < 205) Then
      If (X > 15 And X < 45) Then
        ' decrease difficulty
        Difficulty = Difficulty - 1
        If (Difficulty < 1) Then
          Difficulty = 1
        EndIf
      ElseIf (X > 55 And X < 85) Then
        'increase difficulty
        Difficulty = Difficulty + 1
        If (Difficulty > 10) Then
          Difficulty = 10
        EndIf
      EndIf
      GraphicsWindow.BrushColor = "Blue"
      GraphicsWindow.FillRectangle(0, 140, 100, 20)
      GraphicsWindow.BrushColor = "White"
      GraphicsWindow.FontSize = 18
      GraphicsWindow.DrawText(35, 140, Difficulty)
    ElseIf (Y > 220 And Y < 250) Then
      If (X > 5 And X < 95) Then
        'clicked start
        GameStatus = "DanielMove"
        GameOver = "false"
        GraphicsWindow.BrushColor = "White"
        GraphicsWindow.FillRectangle(100, 0, GraphicsWindow.Width
- 100, GraphicsWindow.Height)
        Moves = 0
        NumberLions = Difficulty + 5
        LionsLeft = NumberLions
        DisplayMovesLions()
        '  draw grid structure
        GraphicsWindow.BrushColor = "Black"
        GraphicsWindow.FillRectangle(145, 45, 810, 510)
        GraphicsWindow.BrushColor = "White"
        GraphicsWindow.FillRectangle(150, 50, 800, 500)
        GraphicsWindow.PenWidth = 1
        GraphicsWindow.PenColor = "Gray"
        For i = 1 to 9
```

```
      GraphicsWindow.DrawLine(150, (i + 1) * 50, 950, (i + 1)
* 50)
    EndFor
    For i = 1 to 19
      GraphicsWindow.DrawLine(150 + i * 40, 50, 150 + i * 40,
550)
    EndFor
        For i = 1 to 10
      For j = 1 to 20
        A[i][j] = 0
      EndFor
    EndFor
    '  Place rocks
    ' A array (0- nothing, 1-rock, 2-lion, 3-Daniel)
    A[4][5] = 1
    A[4][16] = 1
    A[7][5] = 1
    A[7][16] = 1
    GraphicsWindow.PenWidth = 3
    GraphicsWindow.PenColor = "Black"
    GraphicsWindow.BrushColor = "DarkGray"
    Rock[1] = Shapes.AddEllipse(30, 40)
    Rock[2] = Shapes.AddEllipse(30, 40)
    Rock[3] = Shapes.AddEllipse(30, 40)
    Rock[4] = Shapes.AddEllipse(30, 40)
    Shapes.Move(Rock[1], 315, 205)
    Shapes.Move(Rock[2], 755, 205)
    Shapes.Move(Rock[3], 315, 355)
    Shapes.Move(Rock[4], 755, 355)
    'Place Daniel
    DanielImage = ImageList.LoadImage(Program.Directory +
"\Daniel.jpg")
    Daniel = Shapes.AddImage(DanielImage)
    PlaceDaniel:
    Row = Math.GetRandomNumber(10)
    Column = Math.GetRandomNumber(20)
    If (A[Row][Column] = 0) Then
      A[Row][Column] = 3
      DanielRow = Row
      DanielColumn = Column
      Shapes.Move(Daniel, DanielColumn * 40 + 115, DanielRow *
50 +5)
    Else
      Goto PlaceDaniel
    EndIf
    'Place Lions
```

```
        LionImage = ImageList.LoadImage(Program.Directory +
"\Lion.jpg")
        For i = 1 To NumberLions
          Lion[i] = Shapes.AddImage(LionImage)
          PlaceLion:
          Row = Math.GetRandomNumber(10)
          Column = Math.GetRandomNumber(20)
          If (A[Row][Column] = 0) Then
            A[Row][Column] = 2
            LionRow[i] = Row
            LionColumn[i] = Column
            Shapes.Move(Lion[i], LionColumn[i] * 40 + 115,
LionRow[i] * 50 +5)
          Else
            Goto PlaceLion
          EndIf
        Endfor
       EndIf
    EndIf
  EndIf
EndSub
```

Save and **Run** the program. Set the **Difficulty** (I used 3). Click **Start**. The complete initialized game grid is now seen:

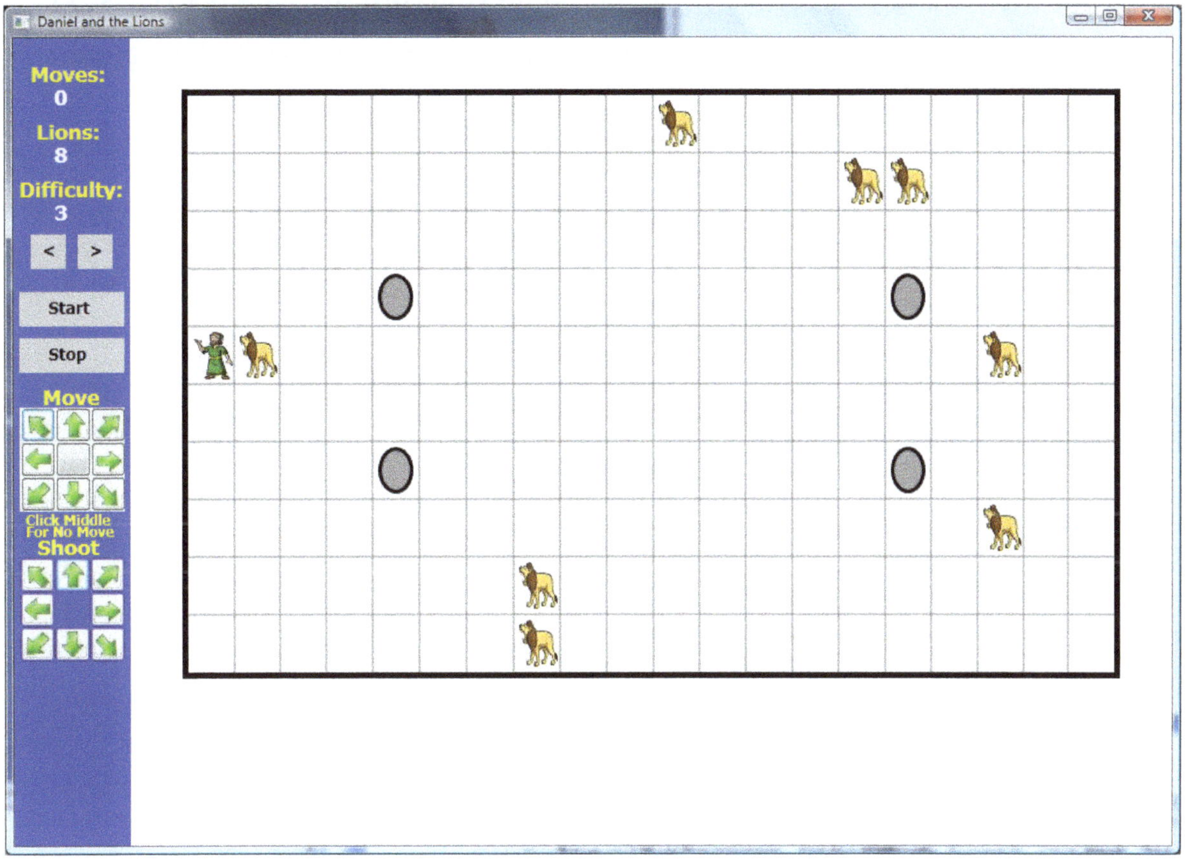

Since **Difficulty** is 3, there are 8 lions. The next step is to either move Daniel or shoot a prayer at a lion. We write code to do these steps soon. But first, let's take care of one last thing you can do while in "**Initial**" state – stop the program.

Code Design – Stop the Program

One last thing you can do while the game is in "**Initial**" state is to click on the **Stop** button. This will stop the program. The location and size of this button are (from code):

button; located at (5, 260), width 90, height 30

The code here is simple. Add the few shaded lines in the **MouseDownEvent** subroutine:

```
Sub MouseDownEvent
  X = GraphicsWindow.MouseX
  Y = GraphicsWindow.MouseY
  If (GameStatus = "Initial") Then
    If (Y > 175 And Y < 205) Then
      If (X > 15 And X < 45) Then
        ' decrease difficulty
        Difficulty = Difficulty - 1
        If (Difficulty < 1) Then
          Difficulty = 1
        EndIf
      ElseIf (X > 55 And X < 85) Then
        'increase difficulty
        Difficulty = Difficulty + 1
        If (Difficulty > 10) Then
          Difficulty = 10
        EndIf
      EndIf
      GraphicsWindow.BrushColor = "Blue"
      GraphicsWindow.FillRectangle(0, 140, 100, 20)
      GraphicsWindow.BrushColor = "White"
      GraphicsWindow.FontSize = 18
      GraphicsWindow.DrawText(35, 140, Difficulty)
    ElseIf (Y > 220 And Y < 250) Then
      If (X > 5 And X < 95) Then
        'clicked start
        GameStatus = "DanielMove"
```

```
      GameOver = "false"
      GraphicsWindow.BrushColor = "White"
      GraphicsWindow.FillRectangle(100, 0, GraphicsWindow.Width
- 100, GraphicsWindow.Height)
      Moves = 0
      NumberLions = Difficulty + 5
      LionsLeft = NumberLions
      DisplayMovesLions()
      '  draw grid structure
      GraphicsWindow.BrushColor = "Black"
      GraphicsWindow.FillRectangle(145, 45, 810, 510)
      GraphicsWindow.BrushColor = "White"
      GraphicsWindow.FillRectangle(150, 50, 800, 500)
      GraphicsWindow.PenWidth = 1
      GraphicsWindow.PenColor = "Gray"
      For i = 1 to 9
        GraphicsWindow.DrawLine(150, (i + 1) * 50, 950, (i + 1)
* 50)
      EndFor
      For i = 1 to 19
        GraphicsWindow.DrawLine(150 + i * 40, 50, 150 + i * 40,
550)
      EndFor
      For i = 1 to 10
        For j = 1 to 20
          A[i][j] = 0
        EndFor
      EndFor
      '  Place rocks
      ' A array (0- nothing, 1-rock, 2-Lion, 3-Daniel)
      A[4][5] = 1
      A[4][16] = 1
      A[7][5] = 1
      A[7][16] = 1
      GraphicsWindow.PenWidth = 3
      GraphicsWindow.PenColor = "Black"
      GraphicsWindow.BrushColor = "DarkGray"
      Rock[1] = Shapes.AddEllipse(30, 40)
      Rock[2] = Shapes.AddEllipse(30, 40)
      Rock[3] = Shapes.AddEllipse(30, 40)
      Rock[4] = Shapes.AddEllipse(30, 40)
      Shapes.Move(Rock[1], 315, 205)
      Shapes.Move(Rock[2], 755, 205)
      Shapes.Move(Rock[3], 315, 355)
      Shapes.Move(Rock[4], 755, 355)
      'Place Daniel
```

```
        DanielImage = ImageList.LoadImage(Program.Directory +
"\Daniel.jpg")
        Daniel = Shapes.AddImage(DanielImage)
        PlaceDaniel:
        Row = Math.GetRandomNumber(10)
        Column = Math.GetRandomNumber(20)
        If (A[Row][Column] = 0) Then
          A[Row][Column] = 3
          DanielRow = Row
          DanielColumn = Column
          Shapes.Move(Daniel, DanielColumn * 40 + 115, DanielRow *
50 +5)
        Else
          Goto PlaceDaniel
        EndIf
        'Place lions
        LionImage = ImageList.LoadImage(Program.Directory +
"\Lion.jpg")
        For i = 1 To NumberLions
          Lion[i] = Shapes.AddImage(LionImage)
          PlaceLion:
          Row = Math.GetRandomNumber(10)
          Column = Math.GetRandomNumber(20)
          If (A[Row][Column] = 0) Then
            A[Row][Column] = 2
            LionRow[i] = Row
            LionColumn[i] = Column
            Shapes.Move(Lion[i], LionColumn[i] * 40 + 115,
LionRow[i] * 50 +5)
          Else
            Goto PlaceLion
          EndIf
        Endfor
      EndIf
    ElseIf (Y > 260 And Y < 290) Then
      If (X > 5 And X < 95) Then
        'clicked stop
        Program.End()
      EndIf
    EndIf
  EndIf
EndSub
```

As desired, if the **Stop** button is clicked, the program ends.

Save and **Run** the program. Make sure the **Stop** button works. This completes the code for moving from "**Initial**" game status to '**DanielMove**' status. Now, let's look at code to move Daniel around the grid.

Code Design – Moving Daniel

Once the game begins, you move Daniel around the grid so he can begin 'shooting' prayers at the lions. Daniel can be moved using two different methods. First, he can be moved by using the 'buttons' under the **Move** heading on the game screen (**MoveButtons.jpg**):

The code to place this image on the screen has already been added to the program. Clicking on any of the arrows will move Daniel one grid in the corresponding direction. Clicking the middle button will leave Daniel at his current position. The code to detect clicking on any of these buttons is placed in the **MouseDownEvent** subroutine.

Like detecting clicks on other 'buttons', we need to know the position of each of the nine buttons. From code, we see that the upper left corner of the nine 'move' buttons is at (5, 320). The **MoveButtons** graphic is 90 pixels wide by 90 pixels high, making each button 30 pixels by 30 pixels. We use these values to determine which button, if any, is clicked. Once a move is made, we need to check to see if it is a valid move. Invalid moves include moving off the top, bottom, left or right side of the grid, moving onto a rock or moving into a lion. If an invalid move is attempted, it is not allowed, and, if a move is into a lion, the game ends! Let's do the code.

Add the shaded code to the **MouseMoveEvent** subroutine:

```
Sub MouseDownEvent
  X = GraphicsWindow.MouseX
  Y = GraphicsWindow.MouseY
  If (GameStatus = "Initial") Then
      .
      .
  ElseIf (GameStatus = "DanielMove") Then
    'clicks on move buttons
    MoveMade = "false"
    If (X > 5 And X < 95) Then
      If (Y > 320 And Y < 410) Then
        DeltaRow = Math.Floor((Y - 320) / 30) - 1
        DeltaColumn = Math.Floor((X - 5) / 30) - 1
        CheckMove()
      EndIf
    EndIf
  EndIf
EndSub
```

For clarity, we have not shown the code for mouse clicks when the program is in "**Initial**" state – that code is complete.

In this code, we set **MoveMade** to "**false**" while we check the status of the move. Two values, **DeltaRow** and **DeltaColumn**, are determined from a mouse click. **DeltaRow** tells us how many rows to move Daniel – it will be either +1 (down one row), 0 (no row change), or -1 (up one row). Similarly, **DeltaColumn** tells us how many columns to move Daniel - it will be either +1 (right one column), 0 (no column change), or -1 (left one column). You should be able to see that clicking any button in the top row yields **DeltaRow** = - 1, any button in the middle row yields **DeltaRow** = 0 and any button in the bottom row yields **DeltaRow** = +1. Likewise, clicking any button in the left column gives **DeltaColumn** = - 1, any button in the middle column gives **DeltaColumn** = 0 and any button in the right column gives **DeltaColumn** = +1. Make sure you see how this code works.

Once **DeltaRow** and **DeltaColumn** are known, we call the subroutine **CheckMove** to see if this is a valid move. Add this subroutine to your program:

```
Sub CheckMove
  Moves = Moves + 1
  MoveMade = "true"
  'check if move is okay
  NewRow = DanielRow + DeltaRow
  NewColumn = DanielColumn + DeltaColumn
  MoveOkay = "true"
  If (NewRow < 1 Or NewRow > 10 Or NewColumn < 1 Or NewColumn >
20) Then
    ' off grid
    MoveOkay = "false"
  ElseIf (A[NewRow][NewColumn] = 1) Then
    'moving to rock
    MoveOkay = "false"
  ElseIf (A[NewRow][NewColumn] = 2) Then
    'moving to lion
    MoveOkay = "false"
    GameOver = "true"
    Shapes.Remove(Daniel)
  EndIf
  If (MoveOkay = "true") Then
    Shapes.Animate(Daniel, NewColumn * 40 + 115, NewRow * 50 +5,
200)
    A[DanielRow][DanielColumn] = 0
    DanielRow = NewRow
    DanielColumn = NewColumn
    A[DanielRow][DanielColumn] = 3
  EndIf
EndSub
```

We increment **Moves** and set new values for Daniel's row and column (**NewRow** and **NewColumn**). We then check the validity of the move. If Daniel moves off the grid, onto a rock, or into a lion, we set **MoveOkay** to "**false**". If Daniel moves into a lion, we set **GameOver** to "**true**" and remove Daniel from the grid. If we have a valid move, Daniel is moved (using the **Animate** method) to his new location from his old location.

Save and **Run** the program. Choose a difficulty (I picked 3). Click **Start**.

Here's what I see:

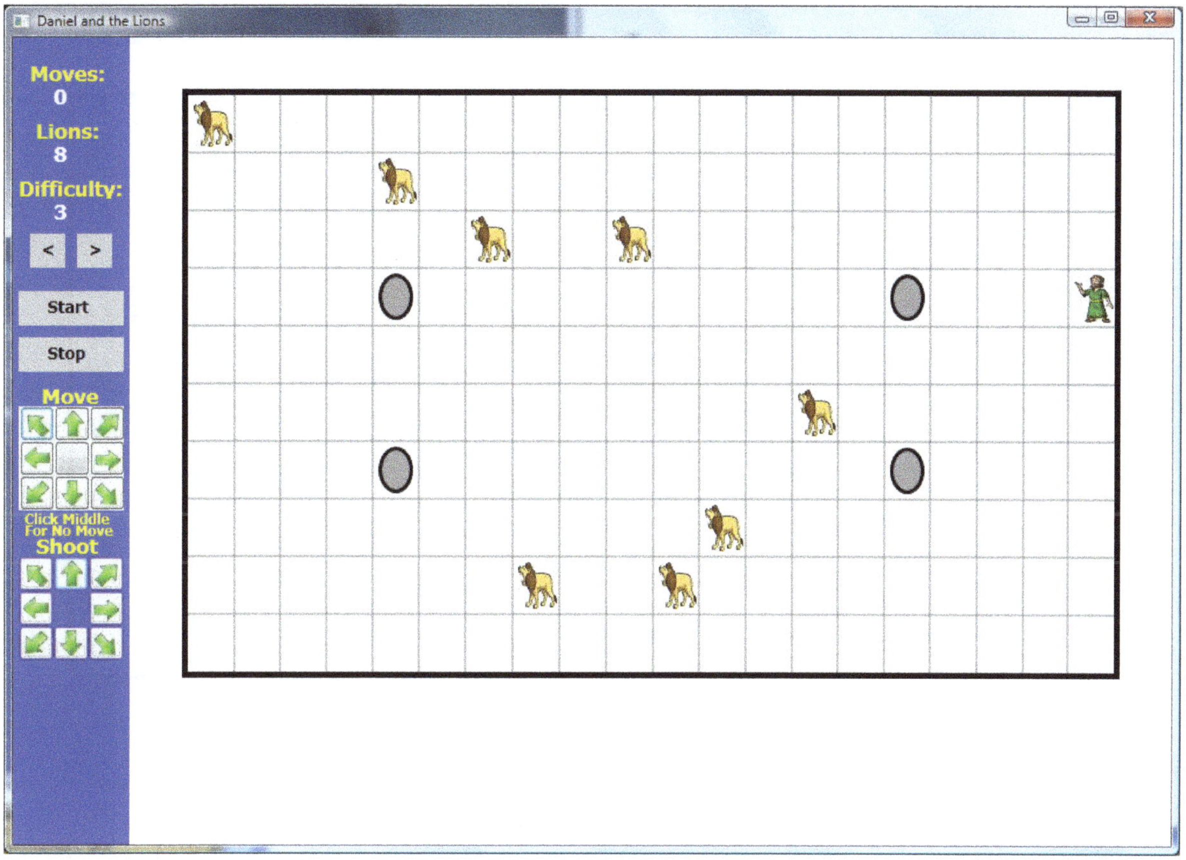

Daniel's at the far right (your Daniel will be at a different random location).

If I click the left move arrow, he moves one column to the left (**DeltaRow** = 0, **DeltaColumn** = -1):

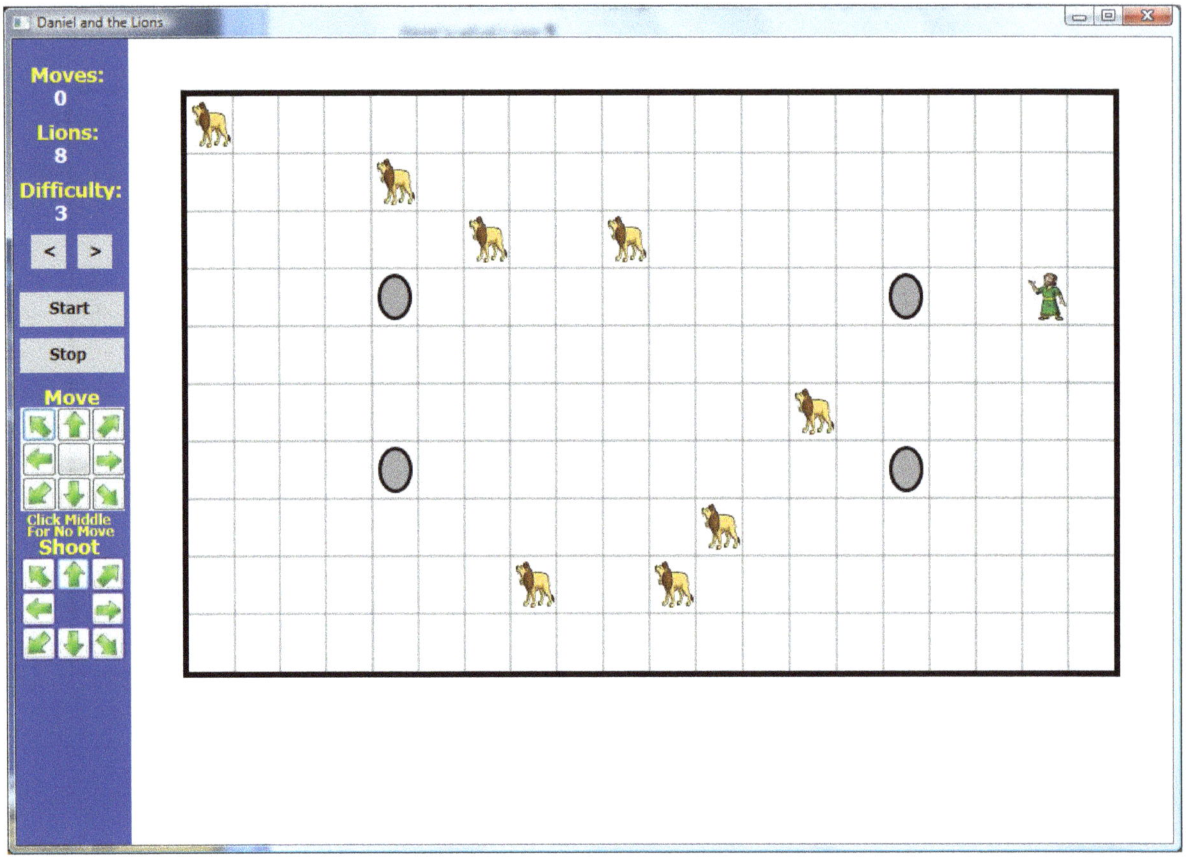

Try all the **Move** buttons to make sure they work properly. Try moving off the grid. Try moving onto a rock. Stay away from lions for now – we don't have logic to end a game yet.

When we started this section, we said there were two ways to move Daniel. Let's write code for the second method – using the numeric keypad on your keyboard. Here's a numeric keypad:

Notice the 9 number keys line up just like the **Move** buttons on the game screen. Many times, users prefer using the keyboard to the mouse. We'll add code so the 7, 8, and 9 keys work like the top row of the move buttons, the 4, 5, and 6 keys work like the middle row and the 1, 2, and 3 keys work like the bottom row.

We will be detecting keyboard presses, so add this single line of code in the main part of your program (before the subroutines start):

```
GraphicsWindow.KeyDown = KeyDownEvent
```

With this, any time a key is pressed, the **KeyDownEvent** subroutine is called. We want this subroutine to recognize clicking on any of the keypad keys while the game is in "**DanielMove**" status.

Add this subroutine to your program:

```
Sub KeyDownEvent
  If (GameStatus = "DanielMove") Then
    'Daniel options - move using keypad
    MoveMade = "false"
    K = GraphicsWindow.LastKey
    If (K = "NumPad7") Then
      DeltaRow = -1
      DeltaColumn = -1
      CheckMove()
    EndIf
    If (K = "NumPad8") Then
      DeltaRow = -1
      DeltaColumn = 0
      CheckMove()
    EndIf
    If (K = "NumPad9") Then
      DeltaRow = -1
      DeltaColumn = 1
      CheckMove()
    EndIf
    If (K = "NumPad4") Then
      DeltaRow = 0
      DeltaColumn = -1
      CheckMove()
    EndIf
    If (K = "NumPad5") Then
      DeltaRow = 0
      DeltaColumn = 0
      CheckMove()
    EndIf
    If (K = "NumPad6") Then
      DeltaRow = 0
      DeltaColumn = 1
      CheckMove()
    EndIf
    If (K = "NumPad1") Then
      DeltaRow = 1
      DeltaColumn = -1
      CheckMove()
    EndIf
    If (K = "NumPad2") Then
      DeltaRow = 1
      DeltaColumn = 0
```

```
      CheckMove()
    EndIf
    If (K = "NumPad3") Then
      DeltaRow = 1
      DeltaColumn = 1
      CheckMove()
    EndIf
  EndIf
EndSub
```

Here, based on whatever key is pressed, the correct values for **DeltaRow** and **DeltaColumn** are set and **CheckMove** is called.

Save and **Run** the program again. Click **Start**. Make sure you can move Daniel both by clicking the move buttons and using the numeric keypad (**NumLock** must be selected to use this option). Again, be careful not to move into a lion – there is no game ending logic. We'll fix that now.

Code Design – Moving Lions

Once Daniel makes a move, all the lions also make a move – closer to Daniel! If Daniel and a lion meet, the game ends. We put this basic logic in a subroutine named **UpdateGame**. This subroutine is called after making a move using either the mouse or the numeric keypad. So, first add the single shaded line in the **MouseDownEvent** subroutine:

```
Sub MouseDownEvent
  X = GraphicsWindow.MouseX
  Y = GraphicsWindow.MouseY
  If (GameStatus = "Initial") Then
      .
      .
  ElseIf (GameStatus = "DanielMove") Then
    'clicks on move buttons
    MoveMade = "false"
    If (X > 5 And X < 95) Then
      If (Y > 320 And Y < 410) Then
        DeltaRow = Math.Floor((Y - 320) / 30) - 1
        DeltaColumn = Math.Floor((X - 5) / 30) - 1
        CheckMove()
      EndIf
    EndIf
    UpdateGame()
  EndIf
EndSub
```

We add a similar line to the **KeyDownEvent** subroutine:

```
Sub KeyDownEvent
  If (GameStatus = "DanielMove") Then
    'Daniel options - move using keypad
    MoveMade = "false"
    K = GraphicsWindow.LastKey
    If (K = "NumPad7") Then
      DeltaRow = -1
      DeltaColumn = -1
      CheckMove()
```

```
    EndIf
    If (K = "NumPad8") Then
      DeltaRow = -1
      DeltaColumn = 0
      CheckMove()
    EndIf
    If (K = "NumPad9") Then
      DeltaRow = -1
      DeltaColumn = 1
      CheckMove()
    EndIf
    If (K = "NumPad4") Then
      DeltaRow = 0
      DeltaColumn = -1
      CheckMove()
    EndIf
    If (K = "NumPad5") Then
      DeltaRow = 0
      DeltaColumn = 0
      CheckMove()
    EndIf
    If (K = "NumPad6") Then
      DeltaRow = 0
      DeltaColumn = 1
      CheckMove()
    EndIf
    If (K = "NumPad1") Then
      DeltaRow = 1
      DeltaColumn = -1
      CheckMove()
    EndIf
    If (K = "NumPad2") Then
      DeltaRow = 1
      DeltaColumn = 0
      CheckMove()
    EndIf
    If (K = "NumPad3") Then
      DeltaRow = 1
      DeltaColumn = 1
      CheckMove()
    EndIf
    UpdateGame()
  EndIf
EndSub
```

Add the **UpdateGame** subroutine to your program:

```
Sub UpdateGame
  DisplayMovesLions()
  If (MoveMade = "true" And GameOver = "false") Then
    'move lions
    MoveLions()
  EndIf
  If (GameOver = "true") Then
    'game is over
    GameOverMessage()
  EndIf
EndSub
```

We update the number of moves (and number of lions) with a call to **DisplayMovesLions**. If a move has been made and **GameOver** is "**false**", we call a subroutine **MoveLions**. If **GameOver** is "**true**", we call a subroutine **GameOverMessage**. Let's add those subroutines.

For now, we'll program the game over logic. When the game ends, we change **GameStatus** to "**Initial**". If there are lions remaining (**LionsLeft > 0**), Daniel has met a lion. If no lions remain, Daniel has dispatched all the lions with prayers. This logic is reflected in this **GameOverMessage** subroutine:

```
Sub GameOverMessage
  GameStatus = "Initial"
  If (LionsLeft > 0) Then
    GraphicsWindow.ShowMessage("Daniel met a lion but God shut the
mouth of the lion at the last minute and King Darius released
Daniel from the Lion's Den.", "Game Over")
    For i = 1 To NumberLions
      Shapes.Remove(Lion[i])
    EndFor
  Else
    GraphicsWindow.ShowMessage("Daniel dispatched " + NumberLions
+ " lions in " + Moves + " moves.", "Game Over")
    Shapes.Remove(Daniel)
  EndIf
EndSub
```

To test this, we need to add an empty **MoveLions** subroutine:

```
Sub MoveLions
EndSub
```

Save and **Run** the program. Click **Start**. Move Daniel around until he meets a lion. You should see this message:

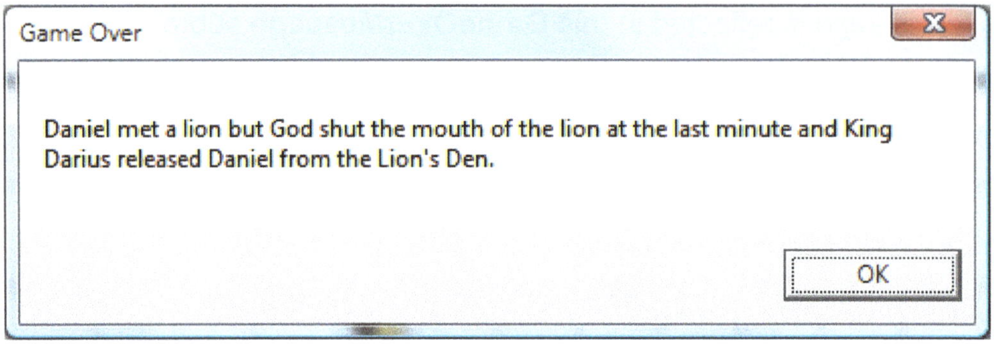

You will see a different message if Daniel dispatches all the lions. Before this can happen, though, we need code to move the lions, then code to shoot the prayers.

When the lions move, the game is switched to "**LionsMove**" status. The goal is move each lion one grid square closer to Daniel. So, for each lion remaining, the steps taken are:

- If Daniel is above lion, move lion up one grid square. If Daniel is below lion, move lion down one grid square. If Daniel and lion are in same row, do not move lion vertically.
- If Daniel is to left of lion, move lion left one grid square. If Daniel is to right of lion, move lion righ one grid square. If Daniel and lion are in same column, do not move lion horizontally.
- Lion cannot move off of grid.
- Lion cannot move into rock or another lion.
- If lion moves into Daniel, the game ends.
- Once move is complete, change **GameStatus** to "**DanielMove**"

The code that implements these steps is placed in the **MoveLions** subroutine:

```
Sub MoveLions
  GameStatus = "LionsMove"
  For i = 1 To NumberLions
    If (A[LionRow[i]][LionColumn[i]] = 2) Then
      If (LionRow[i] > DanielRow) Then
        DeltaRow = -1
      ElseIf (LionRow[i] < DanielRow) Then
        DeltaRow = 1
      Else
        DeltaRow = 0
      EndIf
      If (LionColumn[i] > DanielColumn) Then
        DeltaColumn = -1
      ElseIf (LionColumn[i] < DanielColumn) Then
        DeltaColumn = 1
      Else
        DeltaColumn = 0
      EndIf
      NewRow = LionRow[i] + DeltaRow
      NewColumn = LionColumn[i] + DeltaColumn
      MoveOkay = "true"
      If (NewRow < 1 Or NewRow > 10 Or NewColumn < 1 Or NewColumn
> 20) Then
        ' off grid
        MoveOkay = "false"
      ElseIf (A[NewRow][NewColumn] = 1) Then
        'moving to rock
        MoveOkay = "false"
      ElseIf (A[NewRow][NewColumn] = 2) Then
        'moving to another lion
        MoveOkay = "false"
      EndIf
      If (MoveOkay = "true") Then
        If (A[NewRow][NewColumn] = 3) Then
          'moving to Daniel
          GameOver = "true"
          Shapes.Remove(Daniel)
        EndIf
        Shapes.Animate(Lion[i], NewColumn * 40 + 115, NewRow * 50
+5, 500)
        A[LionRow[i]][LionColumn[i]] = 0
```

```
        LionRow[i] = NewRow
        LionColumn[i] = NewColumn
        A[LionRow[i]][LionColumn[i]] = 2
      EndIf
    EndIf
  EndFor
  GameStatus = "DanielMove"
EndSub
```

We cycle through all the lions (**NumberLions**) in a **For/Next** loop. If a lion is still on the grid, we determine values for **DeltaRow** and **DeltaColumn** (how much a lion moves) and the proposed new position (**NewRow** and **NewColumn**). If it is an acceptable move, the lion is moved using the **Animate** method. Notice if the lion moves into Daniel, **GameOver** is set to "**true**" and Daniel is removed from the grid. This will end the game.

Save and **Run** the program. Choose a **Difficulty** (I used 3). Click **Start**.

My game looks like this:

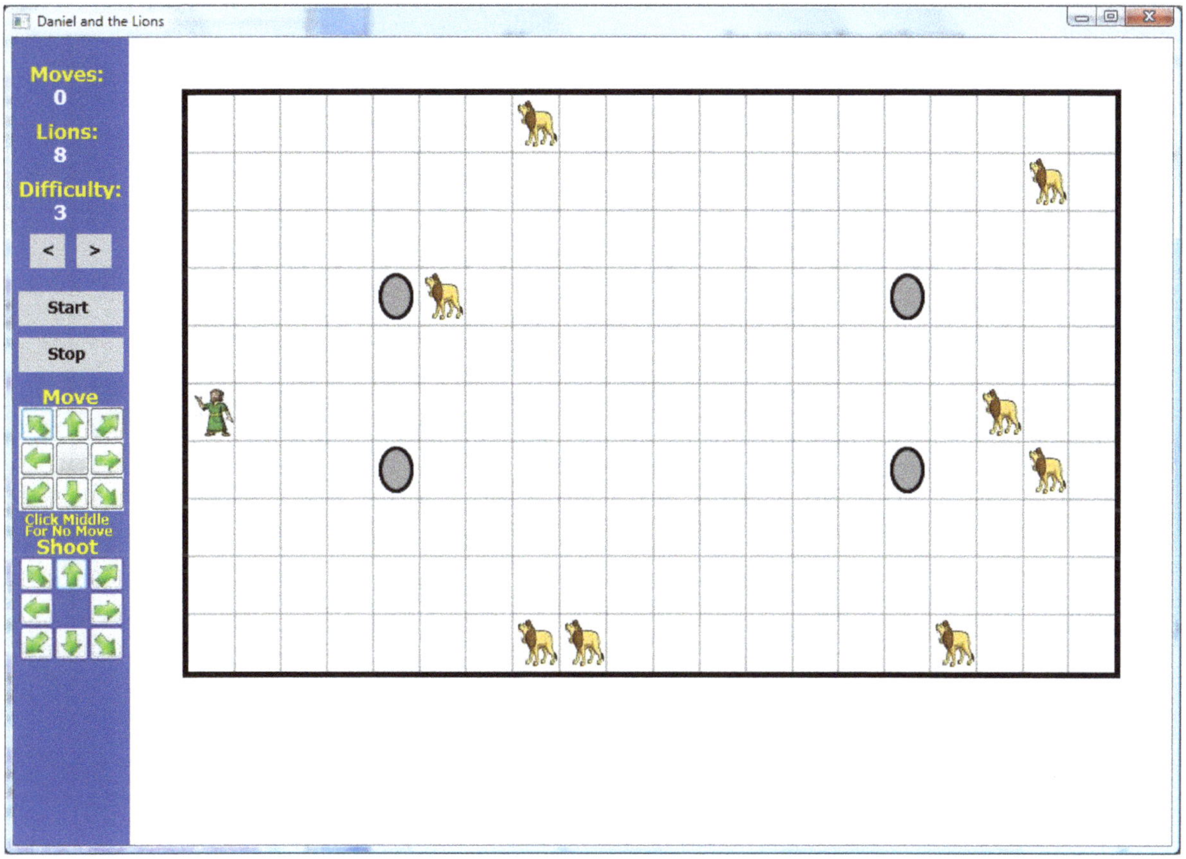

I move Daniel one square up.

Following my move, all the lions are closer:

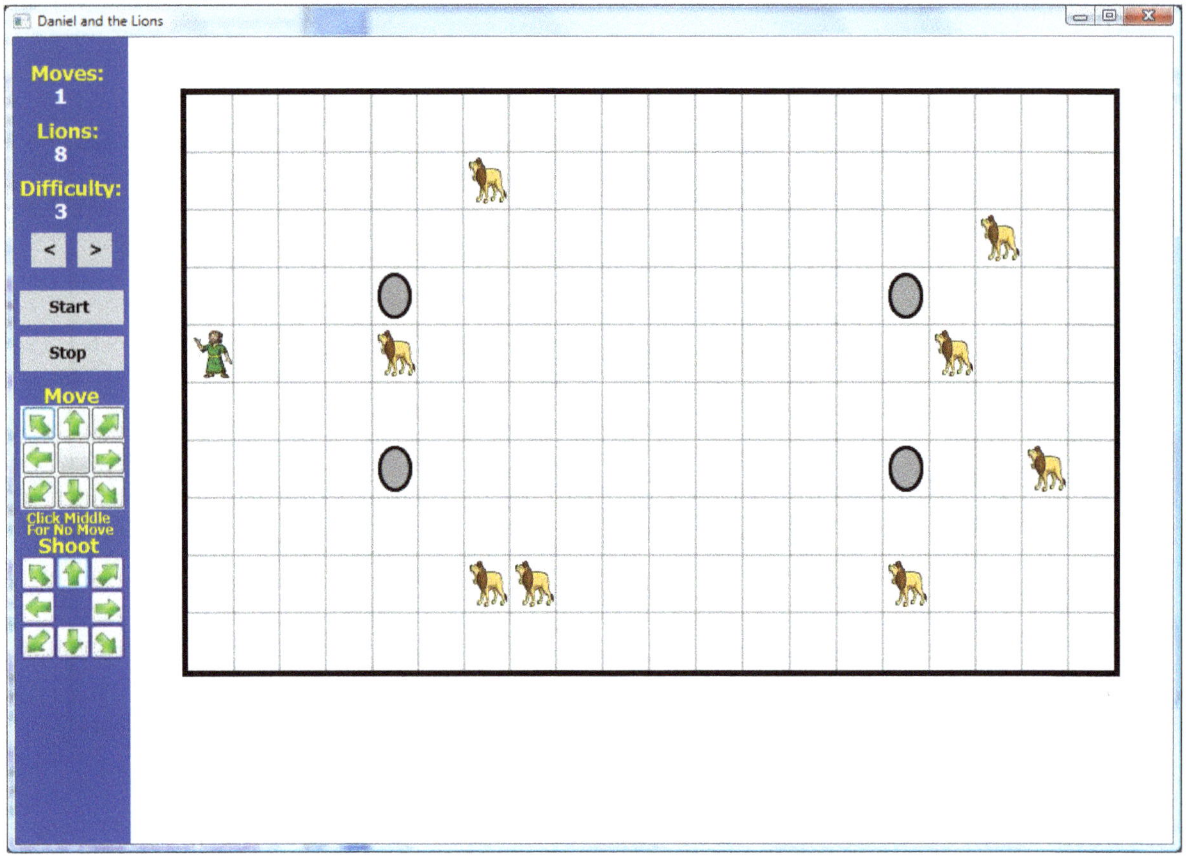

After three more moves up, the lions are right next to Daniel:

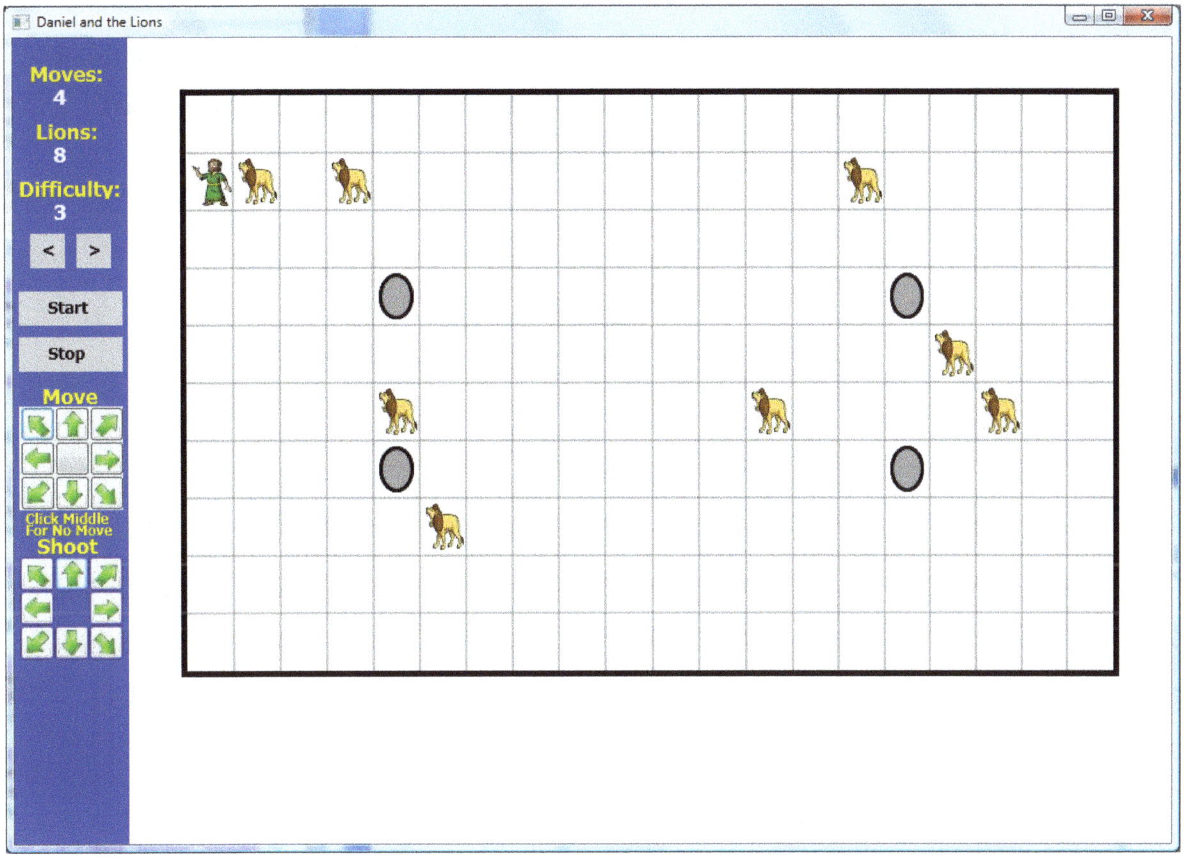

One more move and the ultimate happens:

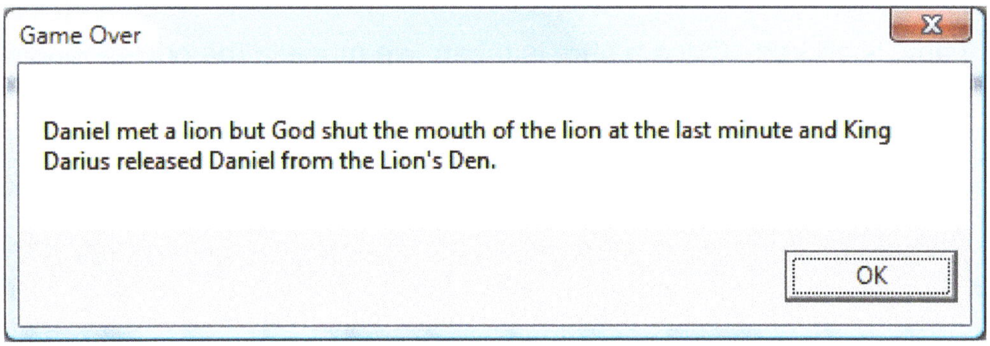

If Daniel could have shot some prayers, the lions wouldn't have gotten to him.

Let's add that logic now.

Code Design – Shooting Prayers

To keep the lions away, Daniel can 'shoot' prayers at the lions to remove them from the grid. Prayers are shot by using the 'buttons' under the **Shoot** heading on the game screen (**ShootButtons.jpg**):

The code to place this image on the screen has already been added to the program. Clicking on any of the arrows will shoot a prayer in the corresponding direction. If the prayer intercepts a lion, it is removed from the grid. The code to detect clicking on any of these buttons is placed in the **MouseDownEvent** subroutine.

To detect the clicks, we need to know the position of each of the eight buttons. From code, we see that the upper left corner of the 'shoot' buttons is at (5, 450). The **ShootButtons** graphic is 90 pixels wide by 90 pixels high, making each button 30 pixels by 30 pixels. We use these values to determine which button, if any, is clicked. Once a shot is taken, we move in the corresponding direction until we hit a rock, move off the grid or hit a lion. If a lion is hit, that lion is removed. Once all lions are removed, the game ends! Let's do the code.

Add the shaded code to the **MouseMoveEvent** subroutine:

```
Sub MouseDownEvent
  X = GraphicsWindow.MouseX
  Y = GraphicsWindow.MouseY
  If (GameStatus = "Initial") Then
     .
     .
  ElseIf (GameStatus = "DanielMove") Then
    'clicks on move buttons
    MoveMade = "false"
    If (X > 5 And X < 95) Then
      If (Y > 320 And Y < 410) Then
        DeltaRow = Math.Floor((Y - 320) / 30) - 1
        DeltaColumn = Math.Floor((X - 5) / 30) - 1
        CheckMove()
      EndIf
    EndIf
    'clicks on shoot buttons
    If (X > 5 And X < 95) Then
      If (Y > 450 And Y < 540) Then
        DeltaRow = Math.Floor((Y - 450) / 30) - 1
        DeltaColumn = Math.Floor((X - 5) / 30) - 1
        If (DeltaRow <> 0 Or DeltaColumn <> 0) Then
          Moves = Moves + 1
          MoveMade = "true"
        EndIf
        PrayerRow = DanielRow
        PrayerColumn = DanielColumn
        MoveAgain:
        'check if move is okay
        PrayerRow = PrayerRow + DeltaRow
        PrayerColumn = PrayerColumn + DeltaColumn
        MoveOkay = "true"
        If (PrayerRow < 1 Or PrayerRow > 10 Or PrayerColumn < 1 Or
PrayerColumn > 20 Or (DeltaRow = 0 And DeltaColumn = 0)) Then
          ' off grid or center button area clicked
          MoveOkay = "false"
        ElseIf (A[PrayerRow][PrayerColumn] = 1) Then
          'moving to rock
          MoveOkay = "false"
        EndIf
        If (A[PrayerRow][PrayerColumn] = 2) Then
          ' dispatched a lion - find that lion
          For i = 1 to NumberLions
```

```
          If (PrayerRow = LionRow[i] And PrayerColumn =
LionColumn[i]) Then
            Goto FoundHim
          EndIf
        EndFor
        FoundHim:
        MoveOkay = "false"
        A[PrayerRow][PrayerColumn] = 0
        LionRow[i] = 0
        LionColumn[i] = 0
        Shapes.Remove(Lion[i])
        Sound.PlayChime()
        LionsLeft = LionsLeft - 1
        If (LionsLeft = 0) Then
          GameOver = "true"
        EndIf
      EndIf
      If (MoveOkay = "true") Then
        Goto MoveAgain
      Endif
    EndIf
  EndIf
  UpdateGame()
 EndIf
EndSub
```

Again, for clarity, we have not shown the code for mouse clicks when the program is in "**Initial**" state. Though long, the code is fairly easy to follow. We determine the **DeltaRow** and **DeltaColumn** values corresponding to the clicked button. We then initialize **PrayerRow** and **PrayerColumn** to Daniel's position (where the prayer starts). From that point on, we change **PrayerRow** and **PrayerColumn** (by **DeltaRow** and **DeltaColumn**) until the prayer moves off the grid, hits a rock or hits a lion. If a lion is hit, we determine which lion, play a chime sound and remove it from the grid. Make sure you understand how all this works.

Save and **Run** the program again. The game is nearly complete. Choose a difficulty (I use 3) and click **Start**. Here's my screen:

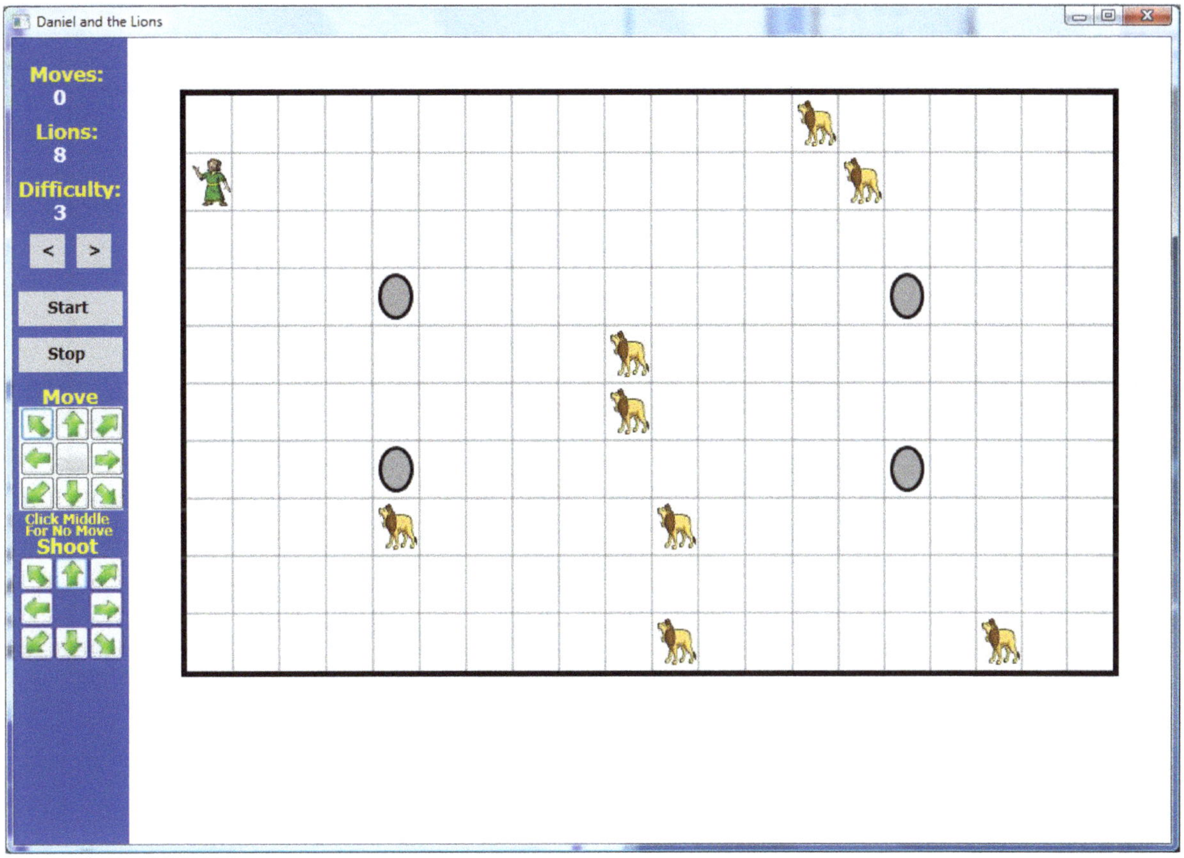

There are 8 lions to eliminate.

Notice a lion far to the right of Daniel in the same row. Click the right **Shoot** arrow and that lion is gone:

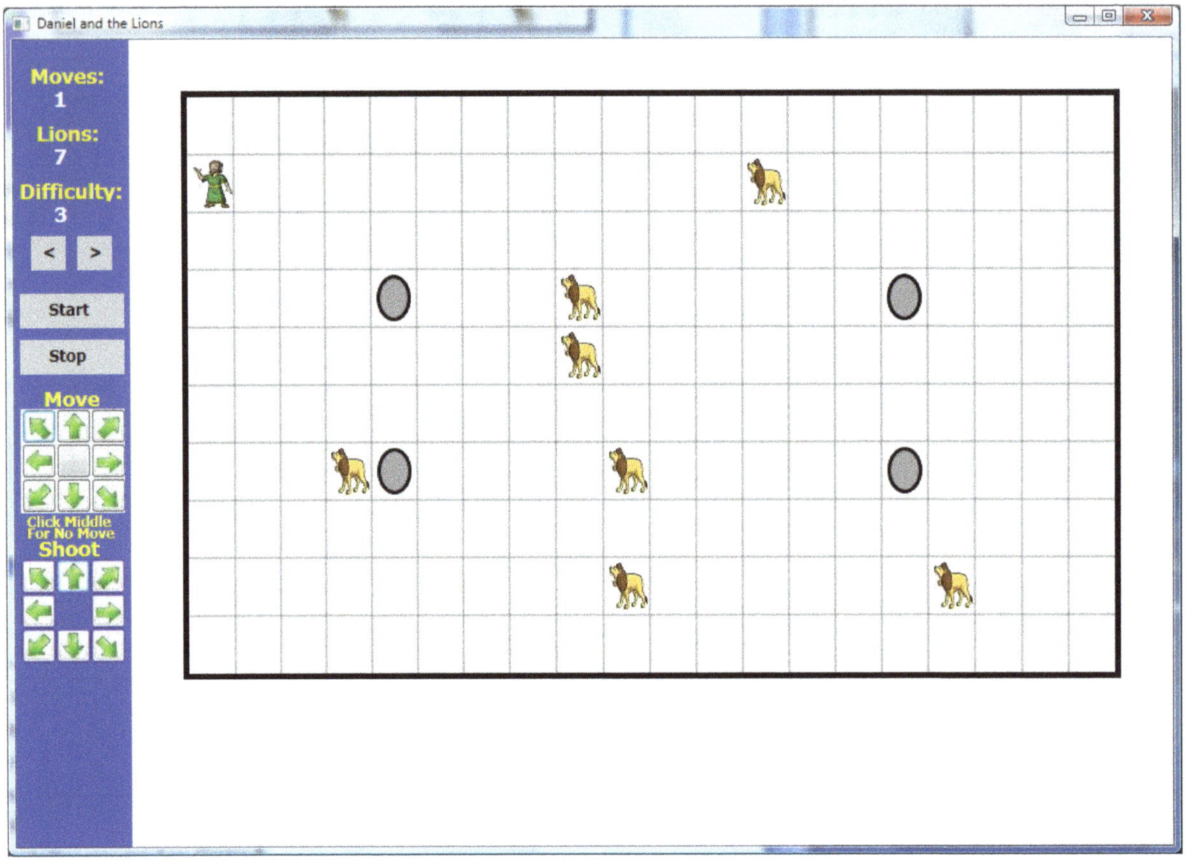

Also notice the remaining lions have moved toward Daniel. There's another to his right. Click the right **Shoot** arrow again.

Another lion is dispatched, but they continue to close in on Daniel:

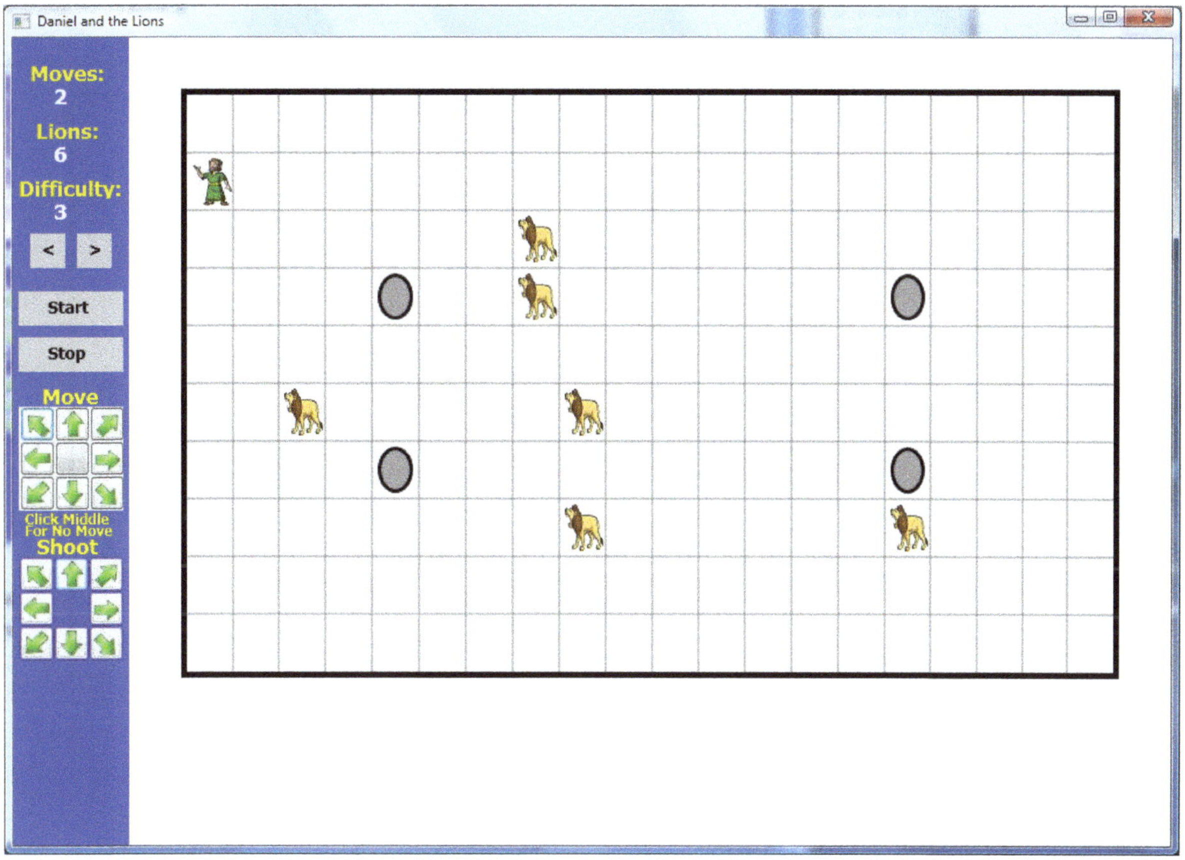

At this point, no lions are in the direct path of a 'prayer shot' so we can only move Daniel.

I moved him to the right (and the lions moved too):

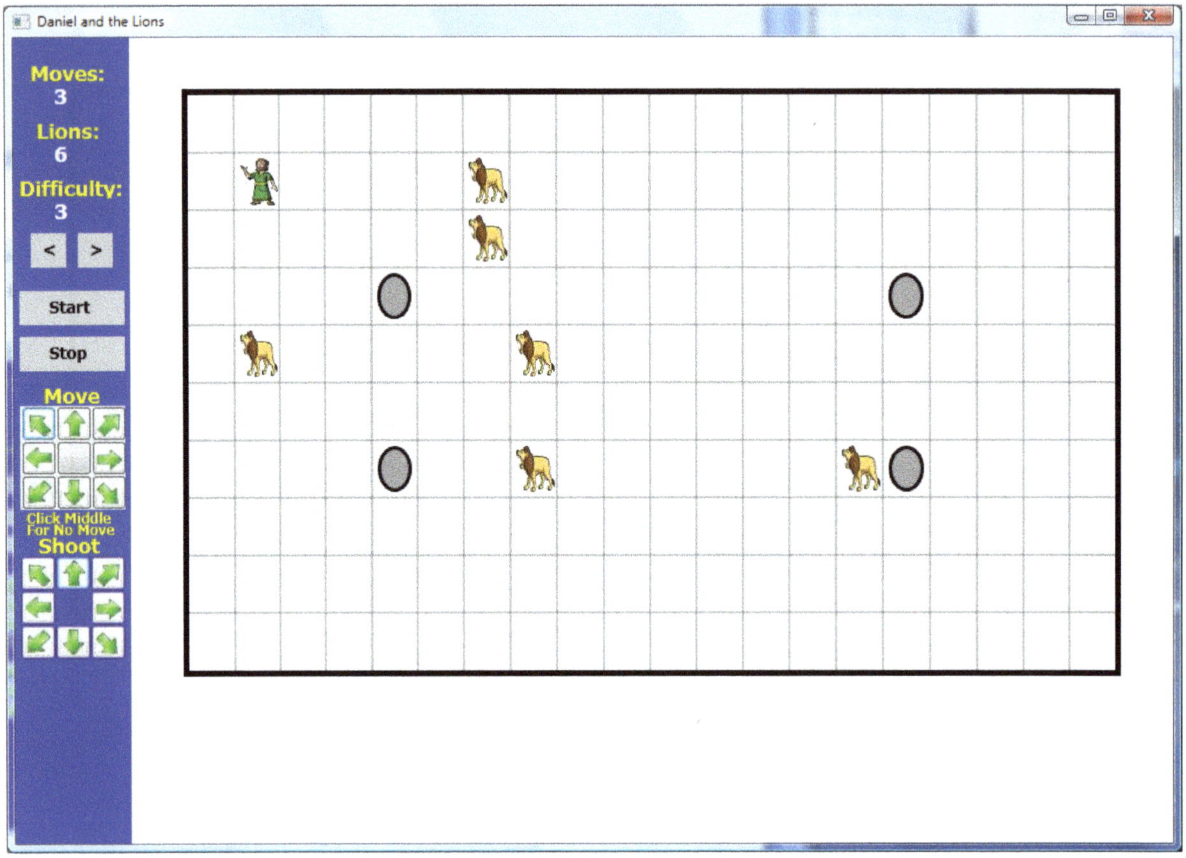

I can either shoot to the right or down.

A shot down, then three shots to the right led me to this state:

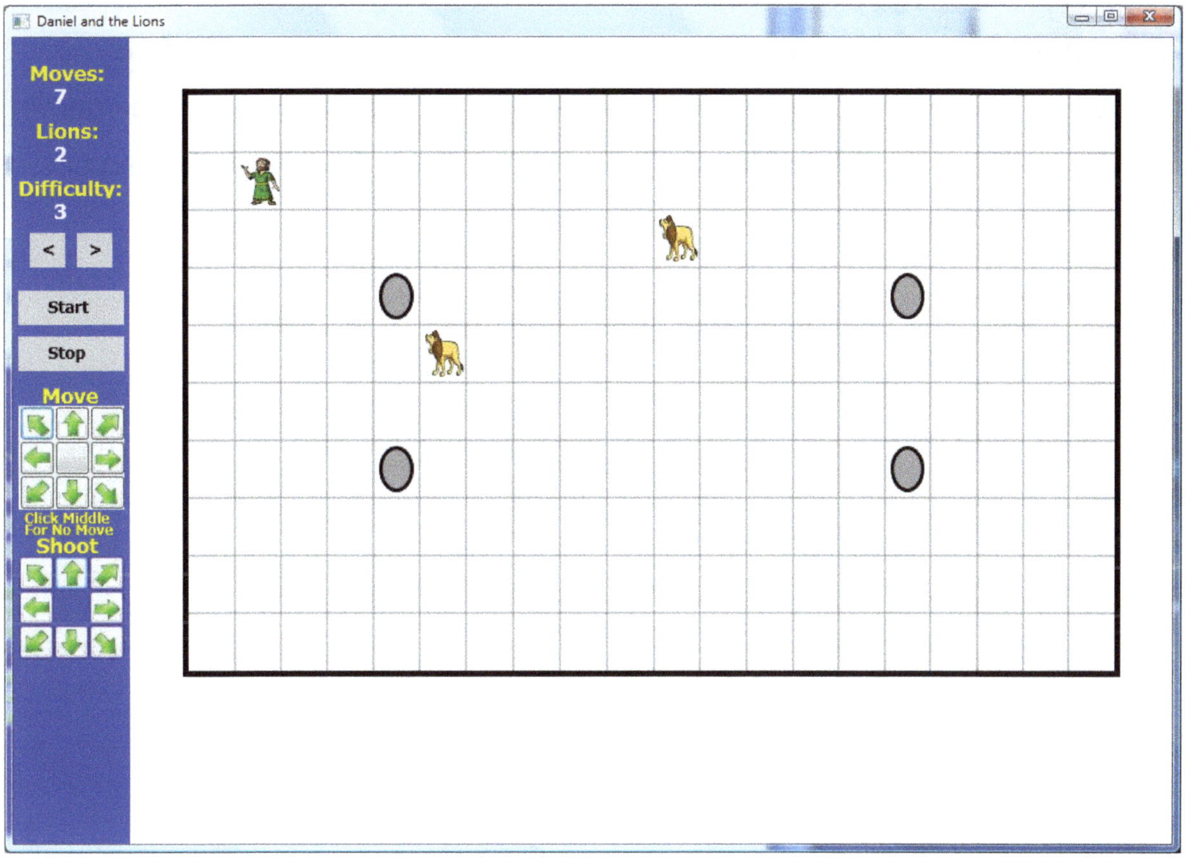

I continued this game and dispatched all 8 lions in 13 moves. At this point, I got this message:

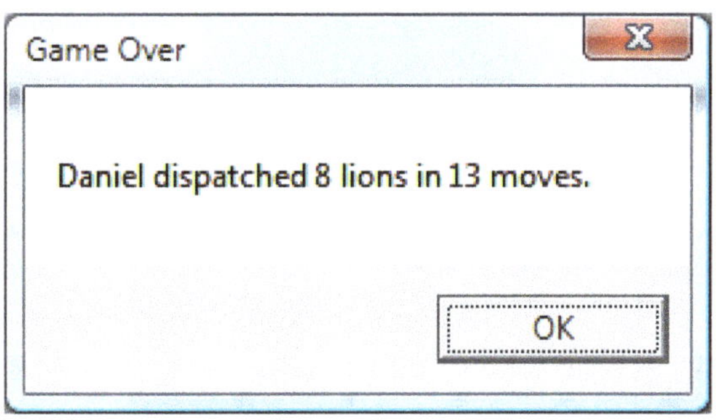

Code Design – Stop the Game

One last step and we're done. You may want to stop a game before dispatching all the lions. To do this, you can click the **Stop** button while the game is in "**DanielMove**" or "**LionsMove**" status. Recall this is the **Stop** button and its location and dimensions:

button; located at (5, 260), width 90, height 30

The code here is simple. Add the few shaded lines near the end of the **MouseDownEvent** subroutine (we've not shown a lot of code here):

```
Sub MouseDownEvent
  X = GraphicsWindow.MouseX
  Y = GraphicsWindow.MouseY
  If (GameStatus = "Initial") Then
      .
      .
  ElseIf (GameStatus = "DanielMove") Then
      .
      .
  EndIf
  If (GameStatus <> "Initial") Then
    If (Y > 260 And Y < 290) Then
      If (X > 5 And X < 95) Then
        'clicked stop while playing
        GameStatus = "Initial"
        GraphicsWindow.ShowMessage("You stopped the game.", "Game
Over")
        For i = 1 To NumberLions
          Shapes.Remove(Lion[i])
        EndFor
        Shapes.Remove(Daniel)
      EndIf
    EndIf
  EndIf
EndSub
```

Save and **Run** the program. Click **Start**, then click **Stop**. You should see this message:

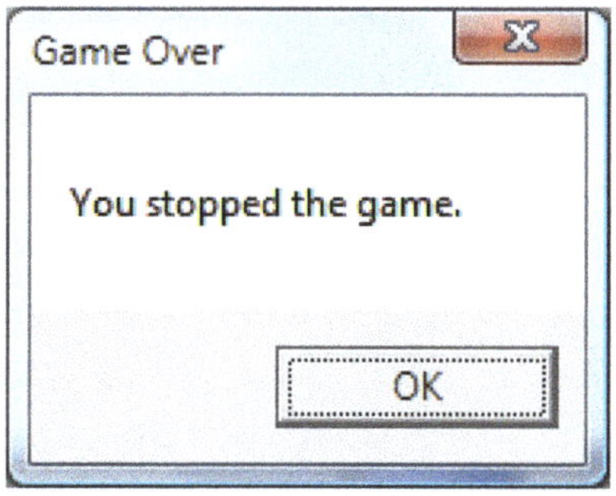

The game is now complete.

Daniel and the Lions Program Listing

Here is the complete listing of the **Daniel and the Lions** Small Basic program:

```
' Daniel and the Lions
' Small Basic Version

' Intro screen
IntroScreen:
Difficulty = 1
GameStatus = "Initial"
GraphicsWindow.Show()
GraphicsWindow.Title = "Daniel and the Lions"
GraphicsWindow.BackgroundColor = "White"
GraphicsWindow.Width = 1000
GraphicsWindow.Height = 700
GraphicsWindow.BrushColor = "Black"
GraphicsWindow.FontSize = 14
GraphicsWindow.DrawText(110, 10, "DANIEL AND THE LIONS")
GraphicsWindow.DrawText(110, 30, "In Daniel 6:16-28, King Darius
is tricked into putting Daniel into the Lions Den. Daniel prays
for God’s protection")
GraphicsWindow.DrawText(110, 50, "and God sends His Angel to shut
the Lion’s mouth.  God will protect you if you pray to Him
today.")
GraphicsWindow.DrawText(110, 180, "<-- Select Difficulty by
pressing the left button for Easy and the right button for
Harder.")
GraphicsWindow.DrawText(110, 230, "<-- Click on the Start Button
to begin.")
GraphicsWindow.DrawText(110, 270, "<-- Click on the Stop Button to
stop the program.")
GraphicsWindow.DrawText(110, 360, "<-- Use these buttons (or
keypad keys) to move Daniel.")
GraphicsWindow.DrawText(110, 490, "<-- Use these buttons to
'shoot' prayers at lions.")
GraphicsWindow.BrushColor = "Blue"
GraphicsWindow.FillRectangle(0, 0, 100, GraphicsWindow.Height)
GraphicsWindow.BrushColor = "Yellow"
GraphicsWindow.FontSize = 18
GraphicsWindow.DrawText(15, 20, "Moves:")
GraphicsWindow.DrawText(20, 70, "Lions:")
GraphicsWindow.DrawText(5, 120, "Difficulty:")
```

```
GraphicsWindow.DrawText(25, 300, "Move")
GraphicsWindow.DrawText(20, 430, "Shoot")
GraphicsWindow.FontSize = 12
GraphicsWindow.DrawText(10, 410, "Click Middle")
GraphicsWindow.DrawText(10, 420, "For No Move")
GraphicsWindow.BrushColor = "White"
GraphicsWindow.FontSize = 18
GraphicsWindow.DrawText(35, 140, Difficulty)
GraphicsWindow.BrushColor = "LightGray"
GraphicsWindow.FillRectangle(15, 170, 30, 30)
GraphicsWindow.FillRectangle(55, 170, 30, 30)
GraphicsWindow.FillRectangle(5, 220, 90, 30)
GraphicsWindow.FillRectangle(5, 260, 90, 30)
GraphicsWindow.BrushColor = "Black"
GraphicsWindow.FontSize = 14
GraphicsWindow.DrawText(25, 175, "<")
GraphicsWindow.DrawText(65, 175, ">")
GraphicsWindow.DrawText(30, 225, "Start")
GraphicsWindow.DrawText(30, 265, "Stop")
MoveImage = ImageList.LoadImage(Program.Directory +
"\MoveButtons.jpg")
MoveButtons = Shapes.AddImage(MoveImage)
Shapes.Move(MoveButtons, 5, 320)
ShootImage  = ImageList.LoadImage(Program.Directory +
"\ShootButtons.jpg")
ShootButtons = Shapes.AddImage(ShootImage)
Shapes.Move(ShootButtons, 5, 450)
GraphicsWindow.MouseDown = MouseDownEvent
GraphicsWindow.KeyDown = KeyDownEvent

Sub MouseDownEvent
  X = GraphicsWindow.MouseX
  Y = GraphicsWindow.MouseY
  If (GameStatus = "Initial") Then
    If (Y > 175 And Y < 205) Then
      If (X > 15 And X < 45) Then
        ' decrease difficulty
        Difficulty = Difficulty - 1
        If (Difficulty < 1) Then
          Difficulty = 1
        EndIf
      ElseIf (X > 55 And X < 85) Then
        'increase difficulty
        Difficulty = Difficulty + 1
        If (Difficulty > 10) Then
          Difficulty = 10
```

```
        EndIf
      EndIf
      GraphicsWindow.BrushColor = "Blue"
      GraphicsWindow.FillRectangle(0, 140, 100, 20)
      GraphicsWindow.BrushColor = "White"
      GraphicsWindow.FontSize = 18
      GraphicsWindow.DrawText(35, 140, Difficulty)
    ElseIf (Y > 220 And Y < 250) Then
      If (X > 5 And X < 95) Then
        'clicked start
        GameStatus = "DanielMove"
        GameOver = "false"
        GraphicsWindow.BrushColor = "White"
        GraphicsWindow.FillRectangle(100, 0, GraphicsWindow.Width
- 100, GraphicsWindow.Height)
        Moves = 0
        NumberLions = Difficulty + 5
        LionsLeft = NumberLions
        DisplayMovesLions()
        '  draw grid structure
        GraphicsWindow.BrushColor = "Black"
        GraphicsWindow.FillRectangle(145, 45, 810, 510)
        GraphicsWindow.BrushColor = "White"
        GraphicsWindow.FillRectangle(150, 50, 800, 500)
        GraphicsWindow.PenWidth = 1
        GraphicsWindow.PenColor = "Gray"
        For i = 1 to 9
          GraphicsWindow.DrawLine(150, (i + 1) * 50, 950, (i + 1)
* 50)
        EndFor
        For i = 1 to 19
          GraphicsWindow.DrawLine(150 + i * 40, 50, 150 + i * 40,
550)
        EndFor
        For i = 1 to 10
          For j = 1 to 20
            A[i][j] = 0
          EndFor
        EndFor
        '  Place rocks
        ' A array (0- nothing, 1-rock, 2-lion, 3-Daniel)
        A[4][5] = 1
        A[4][16] = 1
        A[7][5] = 1
        A[7][16] = 1
        GraphicsWindow.PenWidth = 3
```

```
        GraphicsWindow.PenColor = "Black"
        GraphicsWindow.BrushColor = "DarkGray"
        Rock[1] = Shapes.AddEllipse(30, 40)
        Rock[2] = Shapes.AddEllipse(30, 40)
        Rock[3] = Shapes.AddEllipse(30, 40)
        Rock[4] = Shapes.AddEllipse(30, 40)
        Shapes.Move(Rock[1], 315, 205)
        Shapes.Move(Rock[2], 755, 205)
        Shapes.Move(Rock[3], 315, 355)
        Shapes.Move(Rock[4], 755, 355)
        'Place Daniel
        DanielImage = ImageList.LoadImage(Program.Directory +
"\Daniel.jpg")
        Daniel = Shapes.AddImage(DanielImage)
        PlaceDaniel:
        Row = Math.GetRandomNumber(10)
        Column = Math.GetRandomNumber(20)
        If (A[Row][Column] = 0) Then
          A[Row][Column] = 3
          DanielRow = Row
          DanielColumn = Column
          Shapes.Move(Daniel, DanielColumn * 40 + 115, DanielRow *
50 +5)
        Else
          Goto PlaceDaniel
        EndIf
        'Place Lions
        LionImage = ImageList.LoadImage(Program.Directory +
"\Lion.jpg")
        For i = 1 To NumberLions
          Lion[i] = Shapes.AddImage(LionImage)
          PlaceLion:
          Row = Math.GetRandomNumber(10)
          Column = Math.GetRandomNumber(20)
          If (A[Row][Column] = 0) Then
            A[Row][Column] = 2
            LionRow[i] = Row
            LionColumn[i] = Column
            Shapes.Move(Lion[i], LionColumn[i] * 40 + 115,
LionRow[i] * 50 +5)
          Else
            Goto PlaceLion
          EndIf
        Endfor
      EndIf
    ElseIf (Y > 260 And Y < 290) Then
```

```
      If (X > 5 And X < 95) Then
        'clicked stop
        Program.End()
      EndIf
    EndIf
  ElseIf (GameStatus = "DanielMove") Then
    'clicks on move buttons
    MoveMade = "false"
    If (X > 5 And X < 95) Then
      If (Y > 320 And Y < 410) Then
        DeltaRow = Math.Floor((Y - 320) / 30) - 1
        DeltaColumn = Math.Floor((X - 5) / 30) - 1
        CheckMove()
      EndIf
    EndIf
    'clicks on shoot buttons
    If (X > 5 And X < 95) Then
      If (Y > 450 And Y < 540) Then
        DeltaRow = Math.Floor((Y - 450) / 30) - 1
        DeltaColumn = Math.Floor((X - 5) / 30) - 1
        If (DeltaRow <> 0 Or DeltaColumn <> 0) Then
          Moves = Moves + 1
          MoveMade = "true"
        EndIf
        PrayerRow = DanielRow
        PrayerColumn = DanielColumn
        MoveAgain:
        'check if move is okay
        PrayerRow = PrayerRow + DeltaRow
        PrayerColumn = PrayerColumn + DeltaColumn
        MoveOkay = "true"
        If (PrayerRow < 1 Or PrayerRow > 10 Or PrayerColumn < 1 Or
PrayerColumn > 20 Or (DeltaRow = 0 And DeltaColumn = 0)) Then
          ' off grid or center button area clicked
          MoveOkay = "false"
        ElseIf (A[PrayerRow][PrayerColumn] = 1) Then
          'moving to rock
          MoveOkay = "false"
        EndIf
        If (A[PrayerRow][PrayerColumn] = 2) Then
          ' dispatched a lion - find that lion
          For i = 1 to NumberLions
            If (PrayerRow = LionRow[i] And PrayerColumn =
LionColumn[i]) Then
              Goto FoundHim
            EndIf
```

```
          EndFor
          FoundHim:
          MoveOkay = "false"
          A[PrayerRow][PrayerColumn] = 0
          LionRow[i] = 0
          LionColumn[i] = 0
          Shapes.Remove(Lion[i])
          Sound.PlayChime()
          LionsLeft = LionsLeft - 1
          If (LionsLeft = 0) Then
            GameOver = "true"
          EndIf
        EndIf
        If (MoveOkay = "true") Then
          Goto MoveAgain
        Endif
      EndIf
    EndIf
    UpdateGame()
  EndIf
  If (GameStatus <> "Initial") Then
    If (Y > 260 And Y < 290) Then
      If (X > 5 And X < 95) Then
        'clicked stop while playing
        GameStatus = "Initial"
        GraphicsWindow.ShowMessage("You stopped the game.", "Game
Over")
        For i = 1 To NumberLions
          Shapes.Remove(Lion[i])
        EndFor
        Shapes.Remove(Daniel)
      EndIf
    EndIf
  EndIf
EndSub

Sub DisplayMovesLions
  GraphicsWindow.FontSize = 18
  GraphicsWindow.BrushColor = "Blue"
  GraphicsWindow.FillRectangle(0, 40, 100, 20)
  GraphicsWindow.FillRectangle(0, 90, 100, 20)
  GraphicsWindow.BrushColor = "White"
  GraphicsWindow.DrawText(35, 40, Moves)
  GraphicsWindow.DrawText(35, 90, LionsLeft)
EndSub
```

```
Sub CheckMove
  Moves = Moves + 1
  MoveMade = "true"
  'check if move is okay
  NewRow = DanielRow + DeltaRow
  NewColumn = DanielColumn + DeltaColumn
  MoveOkay = "true"
  If (NewRow < 1 Or NewRow > 10 Or NewColumn < 1 Or NewColumn >
20) Then
    ' off grid
    MoveOkay = "false"
  ElseIf (A[NewRow][NewColumn] = 1) Then
    'moving to rock
    MoveOkay = "false"
  ElseIf (A[NewRow][NewColumn] = 2) Then
    'moving to lion
    MoveOkay = "false"
    GameOver = "true"
    Shapes.Remove(Daniel)
  EndIf
  If (MoveOkay = "true") Then
    Shapes.Animate(Daniel, NewColumn * 40 + 115, NewRow * 50 +5,
200)
    A[DanielRow][DanielColumn] = 0
    DanielRow = NewRow
    DanielColumn = NewColumn
    A[DanielRow][DanielColumn] = 3
  EndIf
EndSub

Sub KeyDownEvent
  If (GameStatus = "DanielMove") Then
    'Daniel options - move using keypad
    MoveMade = "false"
    K = GraphicsWindow.LastKey
    If (K = "NumPad7") Then
      DeltaRow = -1
      DeltaColumn = -1
      CheckMove()
    EndIf
    If (K = "NumPad8") Then
      DeltaRow = -1
      DeltaColumn = 0
      CheckMove()
    EndIf
    If (K = "NumPad9") Then
```

```
      DeltaRow = -1
      DeltaColumn = 1
      CheckMove()
    EndIf
    If (K = "NumPad4") Then
      DeltaRow = 0
      DeltaColumn = -1
      CheckMove()
    EndIf
    If (K = "NumPad5") Then
      DeltaRow = 0
      DeltaColumn = 0
      CheckMove()
    EndIf
    If (K = "NumPad6") Then
      DeltaRow = 0
      DeltaColumn = 1
      CheckMove()
    EndIf
    If (K = "NumPad1") Then
      DeltaRow = 1
      DeltaColumn = -1
      CheckMove()
    EndIf
    If (K = "NumPad2") Then
      DeltaRow = 1
      DeltaColumn = 0
      CheckMove()
    EndIf
    If (K = "NumPad3") Then
      DeltaRow = 1
      DeltaColumn = 1
      CheckMove()
    EndIf
    UpdateGame()
  EndIf
EndSub

Sub UpdateGame
  DisplayMovesLions()
  If (MoveMade = "true" And GameOver = "false") Then
    'move lions
    MoveLions()
  EndIf
  If (GameOver = "true") Then
    'game is over
```

```
    GameOverMessage()
  EndIf
EndSub


Sub MoveLions
  GameStatus = "LionsMove"
  For i = 1 To NumberLions
    If (A[LionRow[i]][LionColumn[i]] = 2) Then
      If (LionRow[i] > DanielRow) Then
        DeltaRow = -1
      ElseIf (LionRow[i] < DanielRow) Then
        DeltaRow = 1
      Else
        DeltaRow = 0
      EndIf
      If (LionColumn[i] > DanielColumn) Then
        DeltaColumn = -1
      ElseIf (LionColumn[i] < DanielColumn) Then
        DeltaColumn = 1
      Else
        DeltaColumn = 0
      EndIf
      NewRow = LionRow[i] + DeltaRow
      NewColumn = LionColumn[i] + DeltaColumn
      MoveOkay = "true"
      If (NewRow < 1 Or NewRow > 10 Or NewColumn < 1 Or NewColumn
> 20) Then
        ' off grid
        MoveOkay = "false"
      ElseIf (A[NewRow][NewColumn] = 1) Then
        'moving to rock
        MoveOkay = "false"
      ElseIf (A[NewRow][NewColumn] = 2) Then
        'moving to another lion
        MoveOkay = "false"
      EndIf
      If (MoveOkay = "true") Then
        If (A[NewRow][NewColumn] = 3) Then
          'moving to Daniel
          GameOver = "true"
          Shapes.Remove(Daniel)
        EndIf
        Shapes.Animate(Lion[i], NewColumn * 40 + 115, NewRow * 50
+5, 500)
        A[LionRow[i]][LionColumn[i]] = 0
```

```
        LionRow[i] = NewRow
        LionColumn[i] = NewColumn
        A[LionRow[i]][LionColumn[i]] = 2
      EndIf
    EndIf
  EndFor
  GameStatus = "DanielMove"
EndSub

Sub GameOverMessage
  GameStatus = "Initial"
  If (LionsLeft > 0) Then
    GraphicsWindow.ShowMessage("Daniel met a lion but God shut the
mouth of the lion at the last minute and King Darius released
Daniel from the Lion's Den.", "Game Over")
    For i = 1 To NumberLions
      Shapes.Remove(Lion[i])
    EndFor
  Else
    GraphicsWindow.ShowMessage("Daniel dispatched " + NumberLions
+ " lions in " + Moves + " moves.", "Game Over")
    Shapes.Remove(Daniel)
  EndIf
EndSub
```

Daniel and the Lions Program Review

The **Daniel and the Lions** program is now complete. **Save** and **Run** the program and make sure it works as promised. Check that all options work correctly.

If there are errors in your implementation, go back over the steps of window and code design. Go over the developed code – make sure you understand how different parts of the program were coded. As mentioned in the beginning of this chapter, the completed program is saved as **Daniel** in the **BeginSB\BSB Codes\Daniel** folder.

12

Elijah and the Ravens Project

Preview

In I Kings 17:1-6, God sends ravens to drop bread for Elijah while he hides from King Ahab. In this game, you try to catch as many falling loaves of bread as possible to feed Elijah. God always provides for our needs.

Elijah and the Ravens Program Preview

In this chapter, we will build the **Elijah and the Ravens** game. Flying ravens drop loaves of bread from the sky. You position Elijah under the falling loaves to catch them for food.

The finished program is saved as **Elijah** in the **BeginSB\BSB Code \Elijah** folder. Start Small Basic and open the finished program. Run the program (click the **Run** toolbar button or press <**F5**>). The game will appear in its 'initial' state. A game description and program instructions are given. At this point, you can click the **Start** button to start the game, click arrow buttons to change the game difficulty or click **Stop** to stop the program.

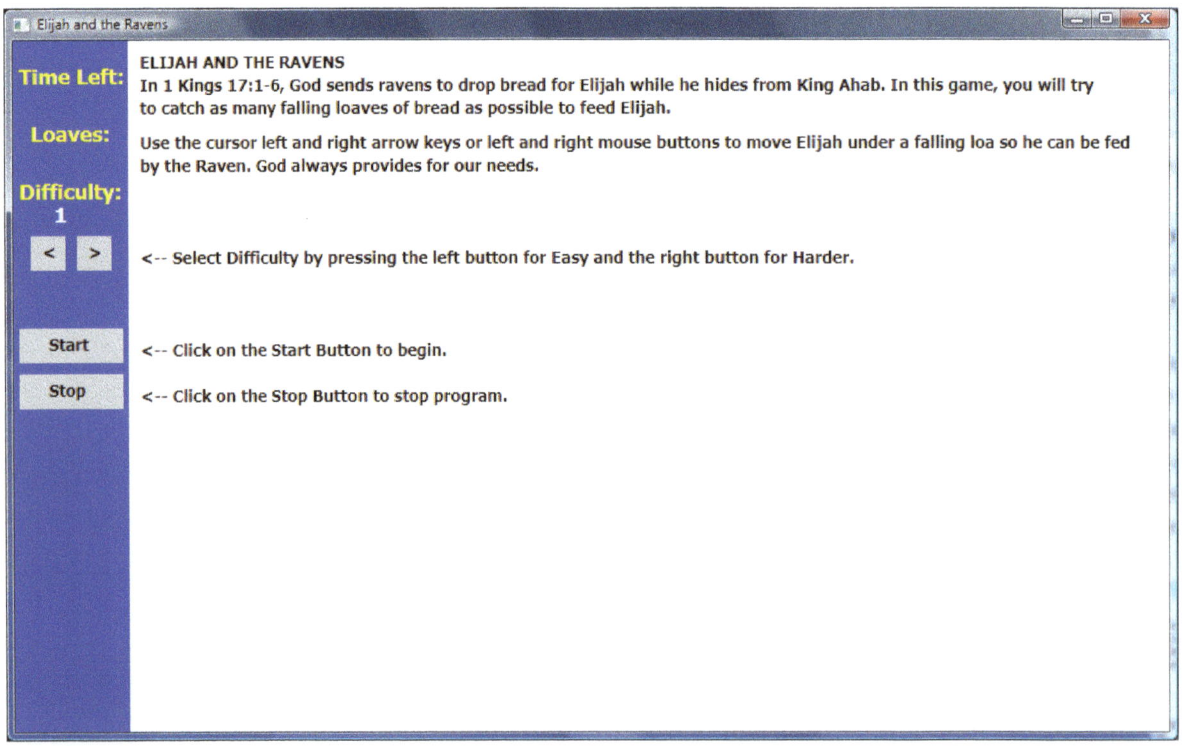

Change the difficulty if you want (I picked 3) by clicking the little arrows under **Difficulty**. Click the **Start** button to start playing. The program instructions disappear. A raven appears at the top of the screen holding a loaf of bread. Elijah is at the bottom of the screen. The loaf of bread will start falling. This is the game's 'playing' state:

You move Elijah under the falling loaf to catch it. You can move Elijah using the cursor arrow keys or by holding down the left or right mouse button. When the loaf reaches Elijah, you score a point (under **Loaves**). If the loaf passes without catching it, you score nothing. Either way, another raven appears dropping another loaf.

Here's a screen where Elijah is about to catch a loaf of bread:

The game continues for 60 seconds. The remaining time is shown under **Time Left**. You are given your final score at this point. Here's mine:

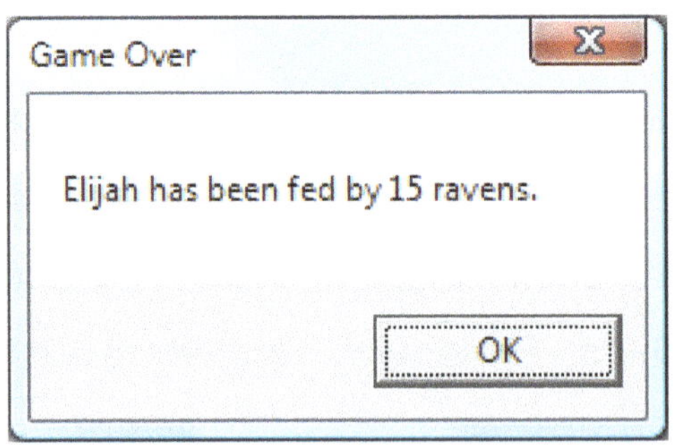

Next, if you want, you can change the difficulty – higher difficulties give you faster dropping bread. You can also click **Start** to race again or click **Stop** to stop the program. Continue playing the game to understand its operation.

You will now build this program in stages. As you build Small Basic programs, we always recommend taking a slow, step-by-step process. It minimizes programming errors and helps build your confidence as things come together in a complete program. We address **window design**. And, we address **code design**. We discuss how to use the 'buttons', how to display the raven, the bread and Elijah, and how to move the different graphic images and detect whether a loaf of bread has been caught.

Elijah and the Ravens Window Design

Here is a sketch for the window layout of the **Elijah and the Ravens** game:

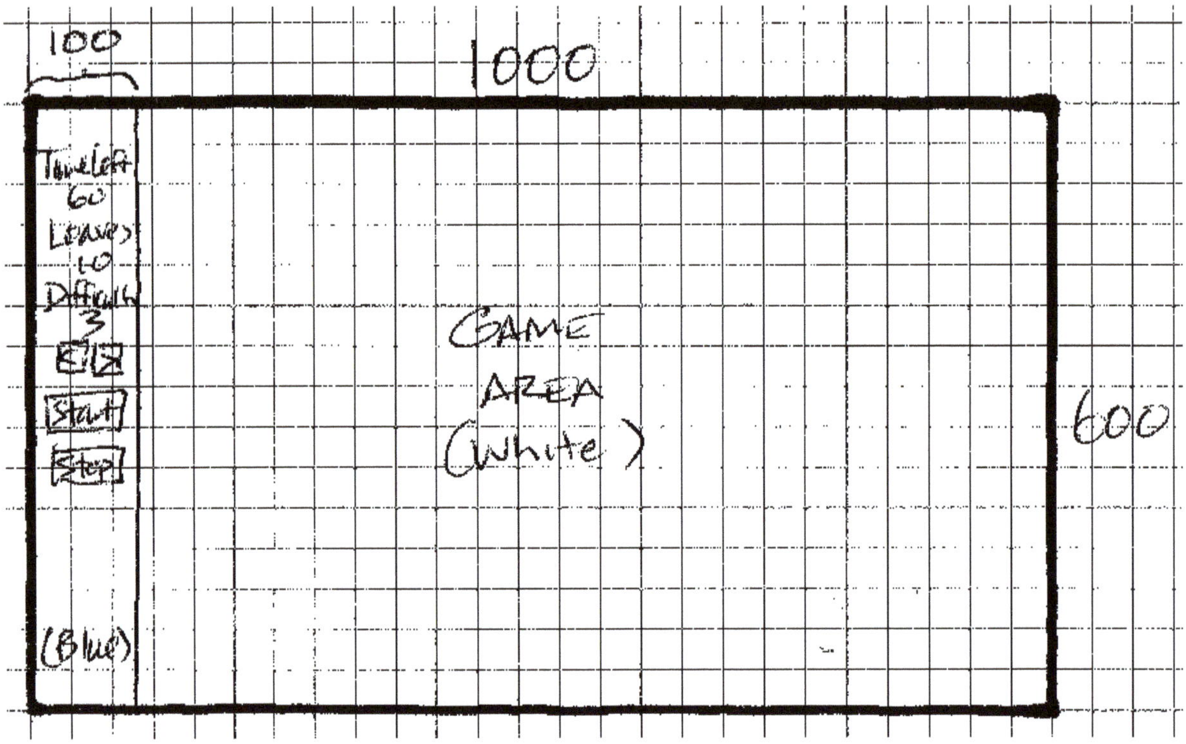

The graphics window is 1000 pixels wide and 600 pixels high. The blue background area on the left (100 pixels wide) is used to control game play. The white area on the right (900 pixels wide) displays game instructions when the program first begins and shows the game with Elijah and the ravens. In the area on the left indicators of the time remaining (**Time Left**), the number of loaves caught (**Loaves**), and the game difficulty (**Difficulty**). Under these are gray rectangles used to represent clickable game control buttons. Four 'buttons' are used: two to change the difficulty, one to start the game, and one to stop the program.

We now begin writing code for the **Elijah and the Ravens** game. We will write the code in several steps. As a first step, we will write the code that draws the window and establishes its 'initial' state. Then, we look at how to go to 'playing' state (positioning all the graphics elements) following clicking of the **Start** button. We then write code to move the bread down the screen, move Elijah (using mouse clicks or keyboard presses), and check for caught loaves of bread. During the code development process, recognize you may modify a particular procedure several times before arriving at the finished product.

Start a new program in Small Basic. Once started, we suggest you immediately save the program with a name you choose. This sets up the folder and file structure needed for your program.

Code Design – Initial State (Instructions)

Any time we start a program, there are certain initializations that must take place. Let's look at the initializations needed in the **Elijah and the Ravens** game. When the program first begins, we want to display the game instructions, any needed titling and the control buttons. We also initialize the difficulty (**Difficulty**) and the game status (**GameStatus**). We set up the game screen and display the instructions first.

Add this code to your empty code window:

```
' Elijah and the Ravens
' Small Basic Version

' Intro screen
Difficulty = 1
GameStatus = "Initial"
GraphicsWindow.Show()
GraphicsWindow.Title = "Elijah and the Ravens"
GraphicsWindow.BackgroundColor = "White"
GraphicsWindow.Width = 1000
GraphicsWindow.Height = 600
GraphicsWindow.BrushColor = "Black"
GraphicsWindow.FontSize = 14
GraphicsWindow.DrawText(110, 10, "ELIJAH AND THE RAVENS")
GraphicsWindow.DrawText(110, 30, "In 1 Kings 17:1-6, God sends
ravens to drop bread for Elijah while he hides from King Ahab. In
this game, you will try")
GraphicsWindow.DrawText(110, 50, "to catch as many falling loaves
of bread as possible to feed Elijah.")
GraphicsWindow.DrawText(110, 80, "Use the cursor left and right
arrow keys or left and right mouse buttons to move Elijah under a
falling loaf so he can be fed")
GraphicsWindow.DrawText(110, 100, "by the Raven. God always
provides for our needs.")
GraphicsWindow.DrawText(110, 180, "<-- Select Difficulty by
pressing the left button for Easy and the right button for
Harder.")
GraphicsWindow.DrawText(110, 260, "<-- Click on the Start Button
to begin.")
```

```
GraphicsWindow.DrawText(110, 300, "<-- Click on the Stop Button to
stop program.")
GraphicsWindow.BrushColor = "Blue"
GraphicsWindow.FillRectangle(0, 0, 100, GraphicsWindow.Height)
```

As mentioned, we set **Difficulty** to **1** and the **GameStatus** to "**Initial**". Next, after setting up the **GraphicsWindow**, using a series of **DrawText** statements, we write out the game instructions. **Save** and **Run** the program to see:

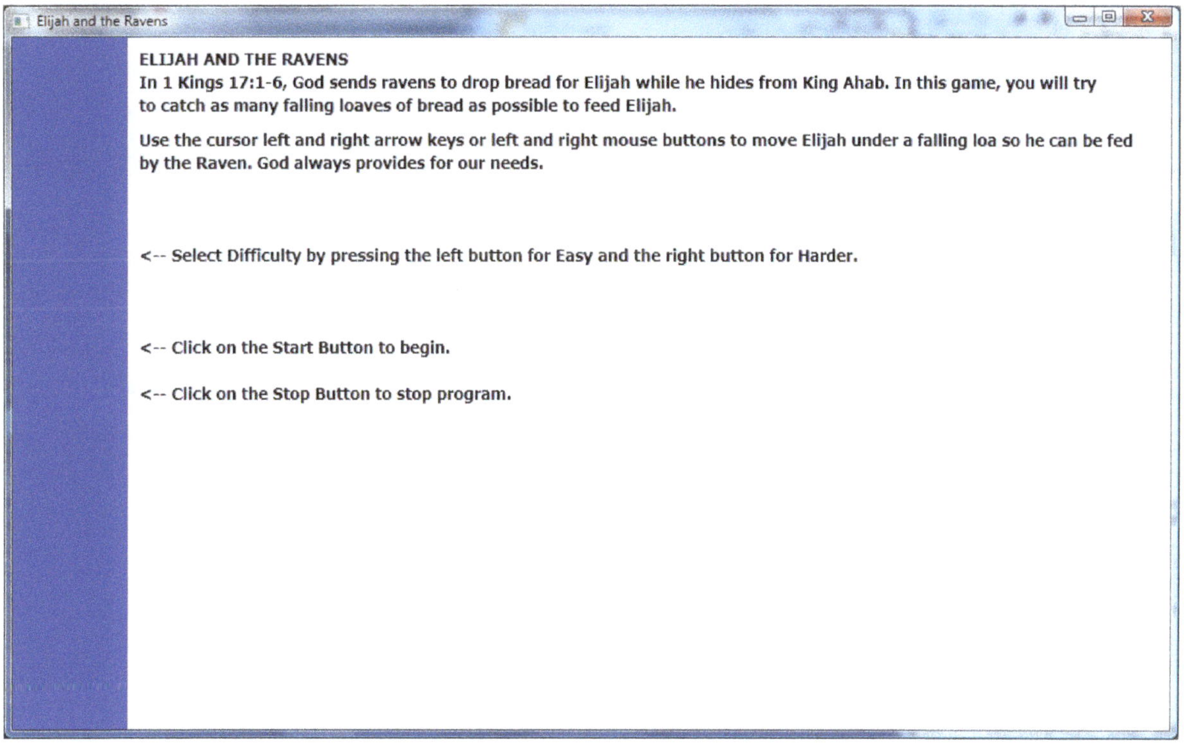

You may wonder how we came up with all the position numbers in the **DrawText** statements. They were set by trial and error. You do this a lot in Small Basic. Try some values and see how they look. Make corrections until things appear as you desire.

Code Design – Initial State (Titling and Buttons)

The other element we need when the program begins are the 'buttons' used to control the game. Each button is a gray rectangular area that can be clicked with the mouse. We will detect these clicks using the **GraphicsWindow MouseDown** event. For now, let's just draw the buttons (and titling information for the number of turtles).

Add this code to your program:

```
GraphicsWindow.BrushColor = "Yellow"
GraphicsWindow.FontSize = 18
GraphicsWindow.DrawText(5, 20, "Time Left:")
GraphicsWindow.DrawText(15, 70, "Loaves:")
GraphicsWindow.DrawText(5, 120, "Difficulty:")
GraphicsWindow.BrushColor = "White"
GraphicsWindow.DrawText(35, 140, Difficulty)
GraphicsWindow.BrushColor = "LightGray"
GraphicsWindow.FillRectangle(15, 170, 30, 30)
GraphicsWindow.FillRectangle(55, 170, 30, 30)
GraphicsWindow.FillRectangle(5, 250, 90, 30)
GraphicsWindow.FillRectangle(5, 290, 90, 30)
GraphicsWindow.BrushColor = "Black"
GraphicsWindow.FontSize = 14
GraphicsWindow.DrawText(25, 175, "<")
GraphicsWindow.DrawText(65, 175, ">")
GraphicsWindow.DrawText(30, 255, "Start")
GraphicsWindow.DrawText(30, 295, "Stop")
```

Each button is a gray rectangle with black text. There are two buttons (**<** and **>**) used to change the difficulty. There are two buttons (**Start** and **Stop**) used to control the game. Like the game instructions, the size and position for each of these elements were arrived at by trial and error. You can change any values you want. Just make sure to note where each button is located – you will need this information when writing the code to detect mouse clicks.

Save and **Run** the program to see the finished initial game screen:

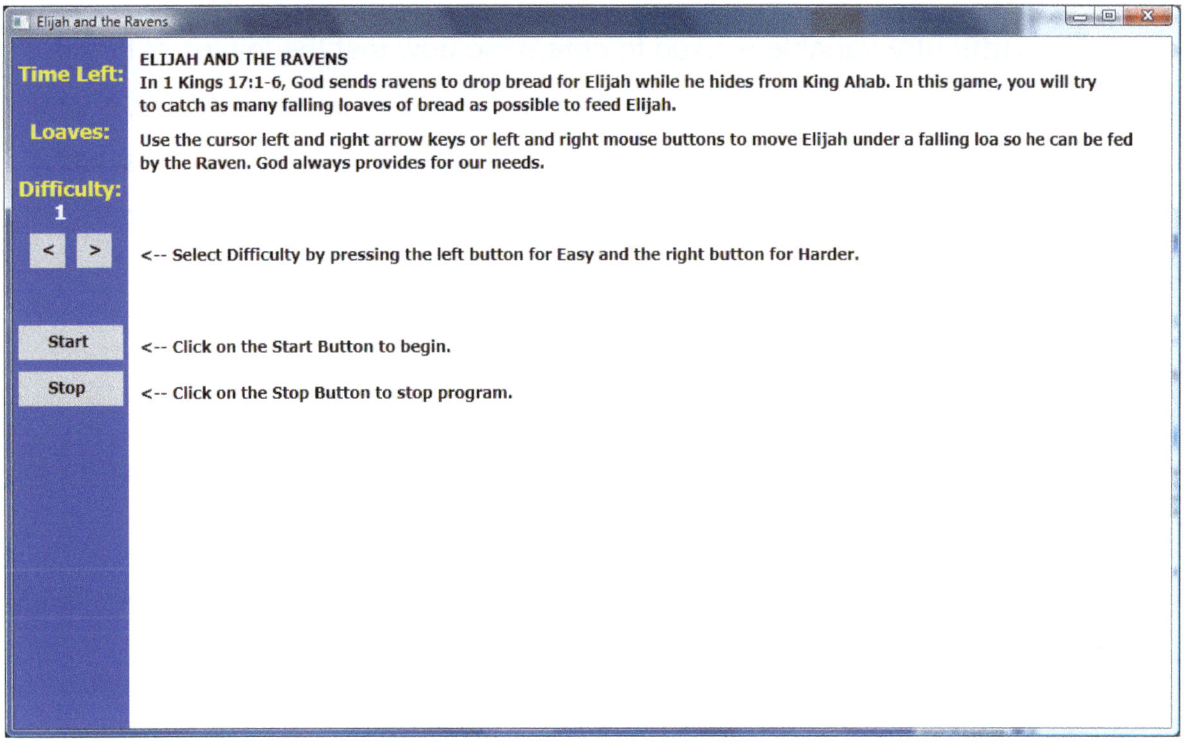

Notice the added buttons and the heading information for the **Time Left** and **Loaves**.

Code Design – Select Difficulty

The **Difficulty** variable is used to determine how fast the loaves of bread drop (the higher the difficulty, the faster they fall). To change the difficulty, a user clicks on either of the two arrow buttons. To detect clicks on these buttons, we need to know their location and size in the window. Looking back at the code, you can see:

button; located at (15, 170), width 30, height 30

button; located at (55, 170), width 30, height 30

We write code to see if a user clicks within the region defined by the buttons. If so, we take the necessary action of changing the difficulty.

We need to detect mouse clicks, so add this line of code to your program:

```
GraphicsWindow.MouseDown = MouseDownEvent
```

With this line, each time a mouse button is pressed (a **MouseDown** event) the subroutine **MouseDownEvent** is called. Let's do the code for changing the difficulty.

Add this subroutine at the end of your program:

```
Sub MouseDownEvent
  If (GameStatus = "Initial") Then
    If (GraphicsWindow.MouseY > 175 And GraphicsWindow.MouseY < 205) Then
      If (GraphicsWindow.MouseX > 15 And GraphicsWindow.MouseX < 45) Then
        ' decrease difficulty
        Difficulty = Difficulty - 1
        If (Difficulty < 1) Then
          Difficulty = 1
        EndIf
      ElseIf (GraphicsWindow.MouseX > 55 And GraphicsWindow.MouseX < 85) Then
        'increase difficulty
        Difficulty = Difficulty + 1
        If (Difficulty > 10) Then
          Difficulty = 10
        EndIf
      EndIf
      GraphicsWindow.BrushColor = "Blue"
      GraphicsWindow.FillRectangle(0, 140, 100, 20)
      GraphicsWindow.BrushColor = "White"
      GraphicsWindow.FontSize = 18
      GraphicsWindow.DrawText(35, 140, Difficulty)
    EndIf
  EndIf
EndSub
```

The code is straightforward. The difficulty can only be changed when the game is in "**Initial**" state. We look to see if the clicked coordinate (**X, Y**) is within the regions of the two arrow buttons. If the **<** button is clicked, we decrease the difficulty by one (minimum of 1). If the **>** button is clicked, we increase the difficulty (maximum of 10). The new value for the difficulty is then displayed (after first clearing the area with the previous value).

Save and **Run** the program. Make sure the arrow buttons work – make sure the difficulty is always between 1 and 10. Here's my run where I changed the difficulty to three:

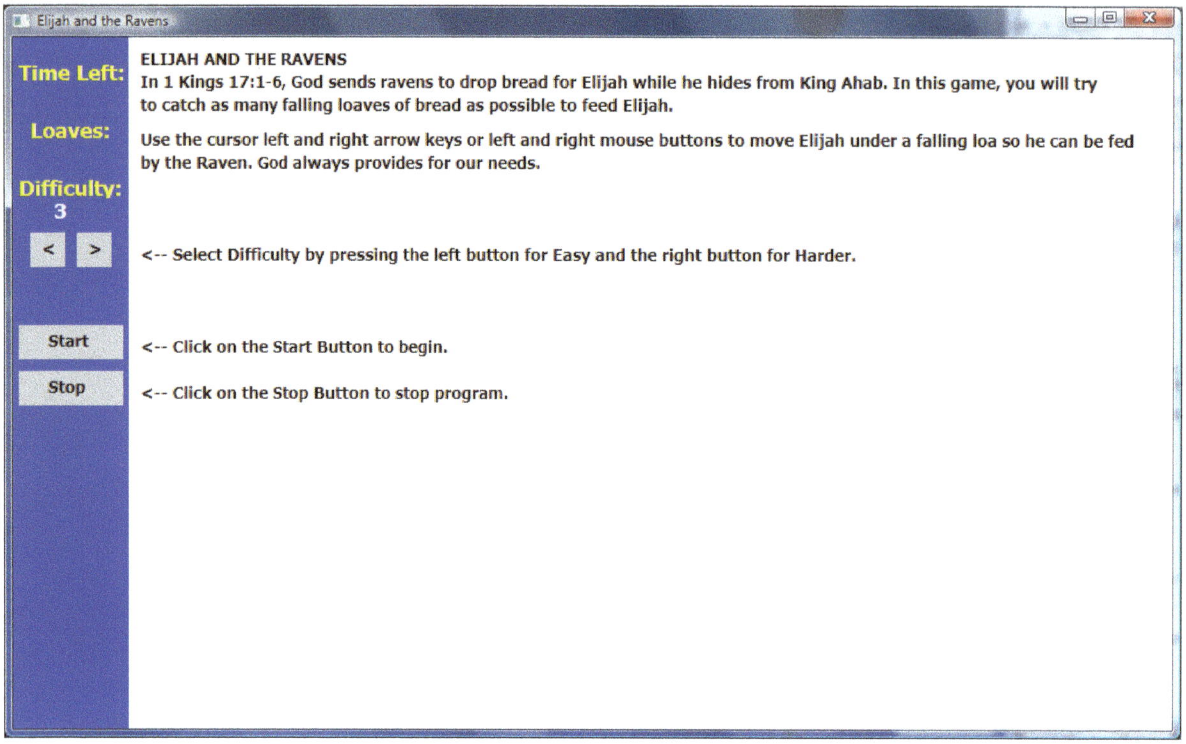

Code Design – Position Elijah

Once the difficulty is set, the next step is to click the **Start** button to allow the game to begin. Hence, we need code to move from the "**Initial**" state to what we'll call "**Playing**" state. Like the arrow buttons, to detect clicks on the **Start** button, we need to know its location and size in the window. From the code, we see:

button; located at (5, 250), width 90, height 30

When the **Start** button is clicked in "**Initial**" state, we need to take the following steps:

- Change **GameStatus** to "**Playing**"
- Clear the screen.
- Initialize score and time left.
- Place Elijah at bottom of screen
- Randomly place Raven and bread at top of screen
- Start dropping bread

There is a lot to do here, so we will take it in steps. First, we'll initialize variables and position Elijah at the bottom of the screen.

Two variables are used in game control. **TimeLeft** is an integer value telling us how much time is left in the game (in milliseconds). We choose to let a game last 60 seconds. **Score** tells us how many loaves of bread have been caught by **Elijah**.

A **Shapes** object is used for Elijah (and the raven and bread) and is represented by the graphics file:

Elijah.gif

Copy this file to your program folder. In the code, we determine both the width (**ElijahW**) and height of this graphic (**ElijahH**). Elijah is positioned at the bottom of the screen, near the middle. The variables **ElijahX** and **ElijahY** tell us where Elijah is. **ElijahDeltaX** is used to tell us how much to move Elijah with each button click or mouse press. All of these variables will be helpful when checking to see if Elijah catches or misses falling bread.

Add the shaded code to the **MouseDownEvent** subroutine:

```
Sub MouseDownEvent
  If (GameStatus = "Initial") Then
    If (GraphicsWindow.MouseY > 175 And GraphicsWindow.MouseY < 
205) Then
      If (GraphicsWindow.MouseX > 15 And GraphicsWindow.MouseX < 
45) Then
        ' decrease difficulty
        Difficulty = Difficulty - 1
        If (Difficulty < 1) Then
          Difficulty = 1
        EndIf
      ElseIf (GraphicsWindow.MouseX > 55 And GraphicsWindow.MouseX 
< 85) Then
        'increase difficulty
        Difficulty = Difficulty + 1
        If (Difficulty > 10) Then
          Difficulty = 10
```

```
          EndIf
        EndIf
        GraphicsWindow.BrushColor = "Blue"
        GraphicsWindow.FillRectangle(0, 140, 100, 20)
        GraphicsWindow.BrushColor = "White"
        GraphicsWindow.FontSize = 18
        GraphicsWindow.DrawText(35, 140, Difficulty)
      ElseIf (GraphicsWindow.MouseY > 250 And GraphicsWindow.MouseY
< 280) Then
        If (GraphicsWindow.MouseX > 5 And GraphicsWindow.MouseX <
95) Then
          'clicked start
          GameStatus = "Playing"
          'clear screen
          GraphicsWindow.BrushColor = "White"
          GraphicsWindow.FillRectangle(100, 0, 900,
GraphicsWindow.Height)
          'time/score        'time/score
          TimeLeft = 60 * 1000 ' milliseconds remaining
          Score = 0
          DisplayTimeScore()
          'Elijah
          ElijahImage = ImageList.LoadImage(Program.Directory +
"\Elijah.gif")
          ElijahW = ImageList.GetWidthOfImage(ElijahImage)
          ElijahH = ImageList.GetHeightOfImage(ElijahImage)
          Elijah = Shapes.AddImage(ElijahImage)
          ElijahDeltaX = 5
          ElijahX = 375
          ElijahY = GraphicsWindow.Height - ElijahH
          Shapes.Move(Elijah, ElijahX, Elijahy)
        EndIf
      EndIf
    EndIf
EndSub
```

You should be able to identify each step in this new code. We clear the instructions and set variables. We create the image for Elijah and position the resulting **Shapes** object.

Notice this line of code:

```
DisplayTimeScore()
```

This line calls a subroutine that updates the displayed value for **TimeLeft** and **Score**. Add this subroutine at the end of your program:

```
Sub DisplayTimeScore
  GraphicsWindow.FontSize = 18
  GraphicsWindow.BrushColor = "Blue"
  GraphicsWindow.FillRectangle(0, 40, 100, 20)
  GraphicsWindow.FillRectangle(0, 90, 100, 20)
  GraphicsWindow.BrushColor = "White"
  GraphicsWindow.DrawText(35, 40, Math.Floor(TimeLeft / 1000))
  GraphicsWindow.DrawText(35, 90, Score)
EndSub
```

Here, we clear out previous vaues for **TimeLeft** and **Score** and draw the new values (using **DrawText**). Note how we convert milliseconds to seconds.

Save and **Run** the program. Choose a difficulty (I picked 3). Click **Start** and you should see:

Notice the displayed values for **Time Left** and **Loaves**. Notice Elijah down there waiting for bread to fall. Let's get a raven and loaf of bread on the screen.

Code Design – Position Raven and Bread

The last initialization step is to randomly place the raven and bread at the top of the screen. **Shapes** objects are used for the raven and the bread and are represented by the two graphics files:

Raven.gif

Bread.gif

Copy both of these graphics files to your program folder. Once loaded, we determine the width and height of the raven (**RavenW** and **RavenH**) and the width and height for the bread (**BreadW** and **BreadH**). These help in determining if Elijah catches a loaf of bread.

Add the shaded code to the **MouseDownEvent** subroutine:

```
Sub MouseDownEvent
  If (GameStatus = "Initial") Then
    If (GraphicsWindow.MouseY > 175 And GraphicsWindow.MouseY <
205) Then
      If (GraphicsWindow.MouseX > 15 And GraphicsWindow.MouseX <
45) Then
        ' decrease difficulty
        Difficulty = Difficulty - 1
        If (Difficulty < 1) Then
          Difficulty = 1
        EndIf
      ElseIf (GraphicsWindow.MouseX > 55 And GraphicsWindow.MouseX
< 85) Then
        'increase difficulty
        Difficulty = Difficulty + 1
        If (Difficulty > 10) Then
          Difficulty = 10
```

```
          EndIf
        EndIf
        GraphicsWindow.BrushColor = "Blue"
        GraphicsWindow.FillRectangle(0, 140, 100, 20)
        GraphicsWindow.BrushColor = "White"
        GraphicsWindow.FontSize = 18
        GraphicsWindow.DrawText(35, 140, Difficulty)
      ElseIf (GraphicsWindow.MouseY > 250 And GraphicsWindow.MouseY
< 280) Then
        If (GraphicsWindow.MouseX > 5 And GraphicsWindow.MouseX <
95) Then
          'clicked start
          GameStatus = "Playing"
          'clear screen
          GraphicsWindow.BrushColor = "White"
          GraphicsWindow.FillRectangle(100, 0, 900,
GraphicsWindow.Height)
          'time/score
          TimeLeft = 60 * 1000 ' milliseconds remaining
          Score = 0
          DisplayTimeScore()
          'Elijah
          ElijahImage = ImageList.LoadImage(Program.Directory +
"\Elijah.gif")
          ElijahW = ImageList.GetWidthOfImage(ElijahImage)
          ElijahH = ImageList.GetHeightOfImage(ElijahImage)
          Elijah = Shapes.AddImage(ElijahImage)
          ElijahDeltaX = 5
          ElijahX = 375
          ElijahY = GraphicsWindow.Height - ElijahH
          Shapes.Move(Elijah, ElijahX, Elijahy)
          'Raven
          RavenImage = ImageList.LoadImage(Program.Directory +
"\Raven.gif")
          RavenW = ImageList.GetWidthOfImage(RavenImage)
          RavenH = ImageList.GetHeightOfImage(RavenImage)
          Raven = Shapes.AddImage(RavenImage)
          'Bread
          BreadImage = ImageList.LoadImage(Program.Directory +
"\Bread.gif")
          BreadW = ImageList.GetWidthOfImage(BreadImage)
          BreadH = ImageList.GetHeightOfImage(BreadImage)
          Bread = Shapes.AddImage(BreadImage)
          PositionRavenAndBread()
        EndIf
      EndIf
```

```
  EndIf
EndSub
```

The above code uses a separate subroutine (**PositionRavenAndBread**) to randomly place the raven and bread on the screen. Add this subroutine to your program:

```
Sub PositionRavenAndBread
  RavenX = Math.GetRandomNumber(GraphicsWindow.Width - RavenW -
100) + 100
  Shapes.Move(Raven, RavenX, 0)
  BreadX = RavenX + 0.5 * (RavenW - BreadW)
  BreadY = RavenH - 20
  Shapes.Move(Bread, BreadX, BreadY)
EndSub
```

Notice how the random horizontal position is selected. The coordinates **BreadX** and **BreadY** let us know where a falling loaf of bread is at all times.

Save and **Run** the program. Set the **Difficulty** (I used 3). Click **Start**. The complete initialized game is now seen:

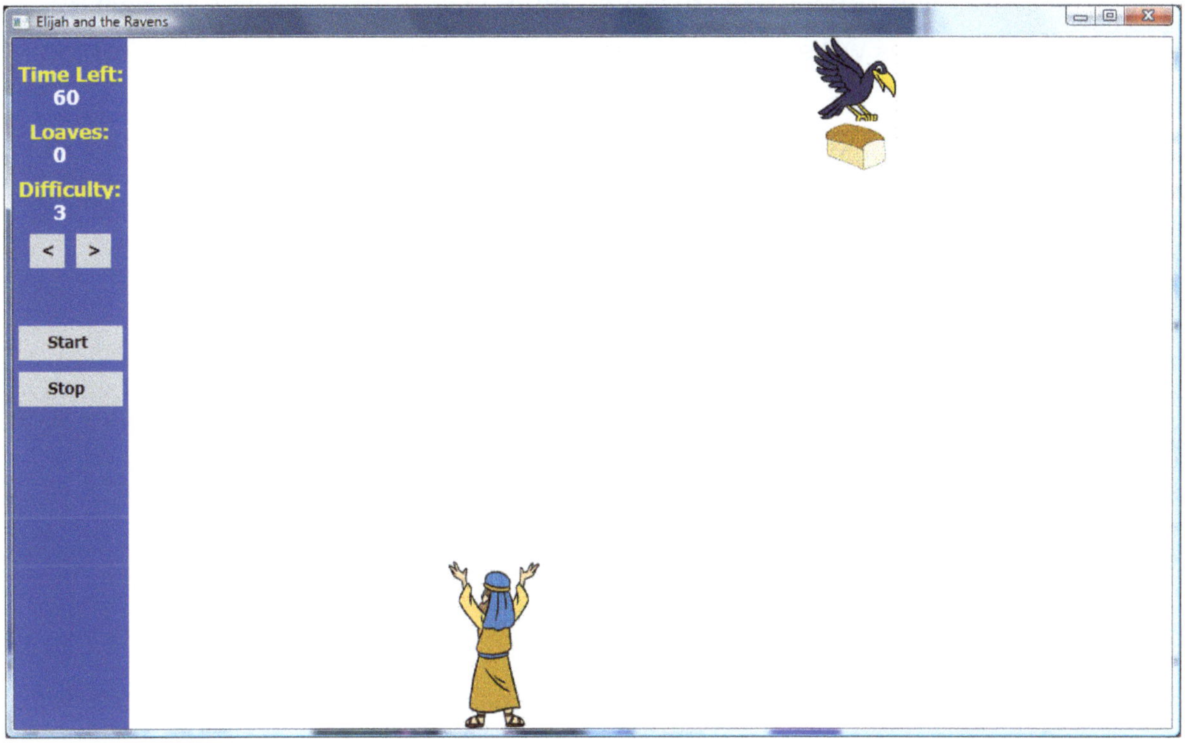

We still need to code to get the bread to drop and to move Elijah along the bottom of the screen. We write code to do these steps soon. But first, let's take care of one last thing you can do while in "**Initial**" state – stop the program.

Code Design – Stop the Program

One last thing you can do while the game is in "**Initial**" state is to click on the **Stop** button. This will stop the program. The location and size of this button are (from code):

button; located at (5, 290), width 90, height 30

The code here is simple. Add the few shaded lines in the **MouseDownEvent** subroutine:

```
Sub MouseDownEvent
  If (GameStatus = "Initial") Then
    If (GraphicsWindow.MouseY > 175 And GraphicsWindow.MouseY <
205) Then
      If (GraphicsWindow.MouseX > 15 And GraphicsWindow.MouseX <
45) Then
        ' decrease difficulty
        Difficulty = Difficulty - 1
        If (Difficulty < 1) Then
          Difficulty = 1
        EndIf
      ElseIf (GraphicsWindow.MouseX > 55 And GraphicsWindow.MouseX
< 85) Then
        'increase difficulty
        Difficulty = Difficulty + 1
        If (Difficulty > 10) Then
          Difficulty = 10
        EndIf
      EndIf
      GraphicsWindow.BrushColor = "Blue"
      GraphicsWindow.FillRectangle(0, 140, 100, 20)
      GraphicsWindow.BrushColor = "White"
      GraphicsWindow.FontSize = 18
      GraphicsWindow.DrawText(35, 140, Difficulty)
    ElseIf (GraphicsWindow.MouseY > 250 And GraphicsWindow.MouseY
< 280) Then
```

```
      If (GraphicsWindow.MouseX > 5 And GraphicsWindow.MouseX <
95) Then
        'clicked start
        GameStatus = "Playing"
        'clear screen
        GraphicsWindow.BrushColor = "White"
        GraphicsWindow.FillRectangle(100, 0, 900,
GraphicsWindow.Height)
        'time/score
        TimeLeft = 60 * 1000 ' milliseconds remaining
        Score = 0
        DisplayTimeScore()
        'Elijah
        ElijahImage = ImageList.LoadImage(Program.Directory +
"\Elijah.gif")
        ElijahW = ImageList.GetWidthOfImage(ElijahImage)
        ElijahH = ImageList.GetHeightOfImage(ElijahImage)
        Elijah = Shapes.AddImage(ElijahImage)
        ElijahDeltaX = 5
        ElijahX = 375
        ElijahY = GraphicsWindow.Height - ElijahH
        Shapes.Move(Elijah, ElijahX, Elijahy)
        'Raven
        RavenImage = ImageList.LoadImage(Program.Directory +
"\Raven.gif")
        RavenW = ImageList.GetWidthOfImage(RavenImage)
        RavenH = ImageList.GetHeightOfImage(RavenImage)
        Raven = Shapes.AddImage(RavenImage)
        'Bread
        BreadImage = ImageList.LoadImage(Program.Directory +
"\Bread.gif")
        BreadW = ImageList.GetWidthOfImage(BreadImage)
        BreadH = ImageList.GetHeightOfImage(BreadImage)
        Bread = Shapes.AddImage(BreadImage)
        PositionRavenAndBread()
      EndIf
    ElseIf (GraphicsWindow.MouseY > 290 And GraphicsWindow.MouseY
< 320) Then
      If (GraphicsWindow.MouseX > 5 And GraphicsWindow.MouseX <
95) Then
        'clicked stop
        Program.End()
      EndIf
    EndIf
  EndIf
EndSub
```

As desired, if the **Stop** button is clicked, the program ends.

Save and **Run** the program. Make sure the **Stop** button works. This completes the code for moving from "**Initial**" game status to "**Playing**" status. Now, let's look at code to move Elijah along the bottom of the screen.

Code Design – Dropping Bread

Once the game begins, the loaf of bread will drop. You move Elijah along the bottom of the screen to try and catch the dropping bread. Here we do the code that drops the bread. A variable **BreadSpeed** will determine how fast the bread drops down the screen. We assign **BreadSpeed** based on the value of **Difficulty**:

```
BreadSpeed = 0.5 * Difficulty + 3
```

Note, the higher the difficulty, the faster the speed. You can change this if you like.

We will use a timer object to control bread motion. Add these lines to assign the subroutine **TimerTickEvent** to the **Tick** event and establish the **Interval** property:

```
Timer.Tick = TimerTickEvent
Timer.Interval = 50
Timer.Pause()
```

Notice we also make sure the timer is initially paused. Add the shaded lines to the **MouseDownEvent** subroutine to turn on the timer and set the value for **BreadSpeed**:

```
Sub MouseDownEvent
  If (GameStatus = "Initial") Then
    If (GraphicsWindow.MouseY > 175 And GraphicsWindow.MouseY <
205) Then
      If (GraphicsWindow.MouseX > 15 And GraphicsWindow.MouseX <
45) Then
        ' decrease difficulty
        Difficulty = Difficulty - 1
        If (Difficulty < 1) Then
          Difficulty = 1
```

```
        EndIf
      ElseIf (GraphicsWindow.MouseX > 55 And GraphicsWindow.MouseX
< 85) Then
        'increase difficulty
        Difficulty = Difficulty + 1
        If (Difficulty > 10) Then
          Difficulty = 10
        EndIf
      EndIf
      GraphicsWindow.BrushColor = "Blue"
      GraphicsWindow.FillRectangle(0, 140, 100, 20)
      GraphicsWindow.BrushColor = "White"
      GraphicsWindow.FontSize = 18
      GraphicsWindow.DrawText(35, 140, Difficulty)
    ElseIf (GraphicsWindow.MouseY > 250 And GraphicsWindow.MouseY
< 280) Then
      If (GraphicsWindow.MouseX > 5 And GraphicsWindow.MouseX <
95) Then
        'clicked start
        GameStatus = "Playing"
        'clear screen
        GraphicsWindow.BrushColor = "White"
        GraphicsWindow.FillRectangle(100, 0, 900,
GraphicsWindow.Height)
        'time/score
        TimeLeft = 60 * 1000 ' milliseconds remaining
        Score = 0
        DisplayTimeScore()
        'Elijah
        ElijahImage = ImageList.LoadImage(Program.Directory +
"\Elijah.gif")
        ElijahW = ImageList.GetWidthOfImage(ElijahImage)
        ElijahH = ImageList.GetHeightOfImage(ElijahImage)
        Elijah = Shapes.AddImage(ElijahImage)
        ElijahDeltaX = 5
        ElijahX = 375
        ElijahY = GraphicsWindow.Height - ElijahH
        Shapes.Move(Elijah, ElijahX, Elijahy)
        'Raven
        RavenImage = ImageList.LoadImage(Program.Directory +
"\Raven.gif")
        RavenW = ImageList.GetWidthOfImage(RavenImage)
        RavenH = ImageList.GetHeightOfImage(RavenImage)
        Raven = Shapes.AddImage(RavenImage)
        'Bread
```

```
        BreadImage = ImageList.LoadImage(Program.Directory +
"\Bread.gif")
        BreadW = ImageList.GetWidthOfImage(BreadImage)
        BreadH = ImageList.GetHeightOfImage(BreadImage)
        Bread = Shapes.AddImage(BreadImage)
        PositionRavenAndBread()
        'start timer
        BreadSpeed = 0.5 * Difficulty + 3 ' base on difficulty
        Timer.Resume()
      EndIf
    ElseIf (GraphicsWindow.MouseY > 290 And GraphicsWindow.MouseY
< 320) Then
      If (GraphicsWindow.MouseX > 5 And GraphicsWindow.MouseX <
95) Then
        'clicked stop
        Program.End()
      EndIf
    EndIf
  EndIf
EndSub
```

The bread position is updated in the **TimerTickEvent** subroutine. Add this subroutine to you program:

```
Sub TimerTickEvent
  ' move bread
  BreadY = BreadY + BreadSpeed
  Shapes.Move(Bread, BreadX, BreadY)
EndSub
```

With each **Tick** event, the bread vertical position changes and the Shapes object is moved.

Save and **Run** the program. Click **Start**. The bread is falling:

But it just keeps on falling! We need to add two more pieces of code – one to move Elijah under the bread and one to determine whether Elijah has caught the bread.

Code Design – Moving Elijah

The object of the game is to move Elijah under falling bread so he can catch the loaves for food. Elijah can be moved using two different methods. First, he can be moved by using the left and right arrow buttons on the keyboard. This is easy to code. Since we are looking for key presses, add this line of code in the 'main' part of your program:

```
GraphicsWindow.KeyDown = KeyDownEvent
```

When a key is pressed, the **KeyDownEvent** subroutine is called. Add this subroutine to your program:

```
Sub KeyDownEvent
  ' check for left or right cursor key to move Elijah
  If (GameStatus = "Playing") Then
    If (GraphicsWindow.LastKey = "Left") Then
      ElijahX = ElijahX - ElijahDeltaX
    ElseIf (GraphicsWindow.LastKey = "Right") Then
      ElijahX = ElijahX + ElijahDeltaX
    EndIf
  EndIf
EndSub
```

When the left or right arrow key is pressed, Elijah is moved in the correct direction (changed by **ElijahDeltaX**). This updates his position.

Add the shaded line to **TimerTickEvent** to periodically redraw Elijah (also checking to make sure Elijah has not moved to far in either direction):

```
Sub TimerTickEvent
  ' move bread
  BreadY = BreadY + BreadSpeed
  Shapes.Move(Bread, BreadX, BreadY)
  ' move elijah
  If (ElijahX < 100) Then
    ElijahX = 100
  ElseIf (ElijahX > GraphicsWindow.Width - ElijahW) Then
    ElijahX = GraphicsWindow.Width - ElijahW
  EndIf
  Shapes.Move(Elijah, ElijahX, ElijahY)
EndSub
```

Save and **Run** the program. Click **Start**. Try moving Elijah using the left and right arrow keys:

Here I've moved him far to the left.

When we started this section, we said there were two ways to move Elijah. Let's write code for the second method – using the left and mouse button keys. It's an easy change. Add the shaded code to the **TimerTickEvent** subroutine:

```
Sub TimerTickEvent
  ' move bread
  BreadY = BreadY + BreadSpeed
  Shapes.Move(Bread, BreadX, BreadY)
  'check if mouse button is down
  If (Mouse.IsLeftButtonDown) Then
    ElijahX = ElijahX - ElijahDeltaX
  ElseIf (Mouse.IsRightButtonDown) Then
    ElijahX = ElijahX + ElijahDeltaX
  EndIf
  ' move elijah
  If (ElijahX < 100) Then
    ElijahX = 100
  ElseIf (ElijahX > GraphicsWindow.Width - ElijahW) Then
    ElijahX = GraphicsWindow.Width - ElijahW
  EndIf
  Shapes.Move(Elijah, ElijahX, ElijahY)
EndSub
```

In this code, if the left mouse button is being held down, Elijah moves to the left. Similarly, if the right mouse button is being held down, Elijah moves to the right. This code simply replicates the code we used for the arrow keys.

Save and **Run** the program. Make sure you can move Elijah with both the arrow keys and by using the mouse buttons.

Code Design – Catching Bread

When the bread approaches the bottom of the screen, we need to see if Elijah catches it. The code to do this check is in the **TimerTickEvent**. We need to do two things:

- Check to see if the bread has been caught. If so, make the bread disappear, increment score and make raven and bread reappear at a random location at the top of the screen.
- Check to see if bread has reached the same vertical position of Elijah without being caught. If so, start a new raven and bread.

How do we know if Elijah catches the bread? We want to see if the Elijah graphic collides with the bread graphic. The check cannot be made until the bread passes the top of Elijah. This happens when:

```
BreadY + BreadH > ElijahY
```

We will use a boolean variable (**Passed**) to see if this is true. Once this condition is met, we can see that Elijah collides with bread (or catches it) when:

```
ElijahX + ElijahW > BreadX And ElijahX < BreadX + BreadW
```

This says that the right side of Elijah must be "farther right" than the left side of the bread and the left side of Elijah must be "farther left" than the right side of the bread. Another boolean variable (**Collision**) is used to check this condition.

Add the shaded code to the **TimerTickEvent** subroutine:

```
Sub TimerTickEvent
  ' move bread
  BreadY = BreadY + BreadSpeed
  Shapes.Move(Bread, BreadX, BreadY)
  'check if mouse button is down
  If (Mouse.IsLeftButtonDown) Then
    ElijahX = ElijahX - ElijahDeltaX
  ElseIf (Mouse.IsRightButtonDown) Then
    ElijahX = ElijahX + ElijahDeltaX
  EndIf
  ' move elijah
  If (ElijahX < 100) Then
    ElijahX = 100
  ElseIf (ElijahX > GraphicsWindow.Width - ElijahW) Then
    ElijahX = GraphicsWindow.Width - ElijahW
  EndIf
  Shapes.Move(Elijah, ElijahX, ElijahY)
  ' check for bread collision or passed elijah
  Passed = "false"
  Collision = "false"
  If (BreadY + BreadH > ElijahY) Then
    Passed = "true"
    If (ElijahX + ElijahW > BreadX And ElijahX < BreadX + BreadW)
Then
      Collision = "true"
    EndIf
  EndIf
  If (Passed = "true") Then
    If (Collision = "true") Then
      Score = Score + 1
    EndIf
    PositionRavenAndBread()
  EndIf
  DisplayTimeScore()
EndSub
```

You should see how the listed steps are implemented. In particular, note how a new raven is positioned once **Passed** is "**true**" (and how the score is incremented if **Collision** is also "**true**".

Save and **Run** the program. Change **Difficulty** if you want (I used 3). Click **Start**. Now when you move Elijah under a falling loaf, the score will increment and another raven will appear. If Elijah misses a loaf, the score will not increment and another raven will appear. Here's my screen after catching five loaves and waiting on another:

Code Design – Stop the Game

We're almost done. With the current code, you can play the game as long as you like – notice the displayed **Time Left** is always 60. We need to implement the logic that ends the game after 60 seconds (and updates the time display). To do this, add the shaded code to the **TimerTickEvent** subroutine:

```
Sub TimerTickEvent
  ' move bread
  BreadY = BreadY + BreadSpeed
  Shapes.Move(Bread, BreadX, BreadY)
  'check if mouse button is down
  If (Mouse.IsLeftButtonDown) Then
    ElijahX = ElijahX - ElijahDeltaX
  ElseIf (Mouse.IsRightButtonDown) Then
    ElijahX = ElijahX + ElijahDeltaX
  EndIf
  ' move elijah
  If (ElijahX < 100) Then
    ElijahX = 100
  ElseIf (ElijahX > GraphicsWindow.Width - ElijahW) Then
    ElijahX = GraphicsWindow.Width - ElijahW
  EndIf
  Shapes.Move(Elijah, ElijahX, ElijahY)
  ' check for bread collision or passed elijah
  Passed = "false"
  Collision = "false"
  If (BreadY + BreadH > ElijahY) Then
    Passed = "true"
    If (ElijahX + ElijahW > BreadX And ElijahX < BreadX + BreadW)
Then
      Collision = "true"
    EndIf
  EndIf
  If (Passed = "true") Then
    If (Collision = "true") Then
      Score = Score + 1
    EndIf
    PositionRavenAndBread()
  EndIf
   'update time
  TimeLeft = TimeLeft - Timer.Interval
```

```
  DisplayTimeScore()
  If (TimeLeft = 0) Then
    Shapes.Remove(Raven)
    Shapes.Remove(Bread)
    Shapes.Remove(Elijah)
    Timer.Pause()
    GraphicsWindow.ShowMessage("Elijah has been fed by " + Score +
" ravens.", "Game Over")
    GameStatus = "Initial"
  EndIf
EndSub
```

In this new code, with each **Tick** event, the **TimeLeft** is decremented by **Interval**. Once **TimeLeft** is zero, the graphic elements (raven, bread, Elijah) are removed from the screen, the timer object is turned off and the results displayed.

Save and **Run** the program. Click **Start**. The time will count down. Here's my game in the middle:

And here's my final result:

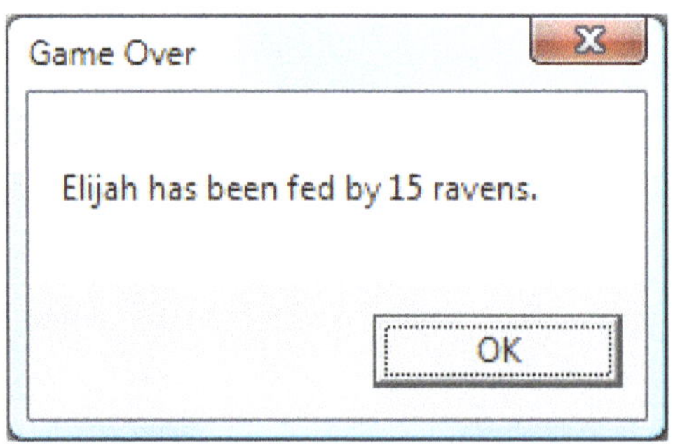

Just one last change. You may want to stop a game before 60 seconds goes by. To do this, you can click the **Stop** button while the game is in "**Playing**" status. Recall this is the **Stop** button and its location and dimensions:

button; located at (5, 290), width 90, height 30

The code here is simple. Add the few shaded lines at the end of the **MouseDownEvent** subroutine:

```
Sub MouseDownEvent
  If (GameStatus = "Initial") Then
    If (GraphicsWindow.MouseY > 175 And GraphicsWindow.MouseY <
205) Then
      If (GraphicsWindow.MouseX > 15 And GraphicsWindow.MouseX <
45) Then
        ' decrease difficulty
        Difficulty = Difficulty - 1
        If (Difficulty < 1) Then
          Difficulty = 1
        EndIf
      ElseIf (GraphicsWindow.MouseX > 55 And GraphicsWindow.MouseX
< 85) Then
        'increase difficulty
        Difficulty = Difficulty + 1
        If (Difficulty > 10) Then
          Difficulty = 10
        EndIf
      EndIf
      GraphicsWindow.BrushColor = "Blue"
      GraphicsWindow.FillRectangle(0, 140, 100, 20)
      GraphicsWindow.BrushColor = "White"
      GraphicsWindow.FontSize = 18
      GraphicsWindow.DrawText(35, 140, Difficulty)
    ElseIf (GraphicsWindow.MouseY > 250 And GraphicsWindow.MouseY
< 280) Then
      If (GraphicsWindow.MouseX > 5 And GraphicsWindow.MouseX <
95) Then
        'clicked start
        GameStatus = "Playing"
        'clear screen
        GraphicsWindow.BrushColor = "White"
```

```
        GraphicsWindow.FillRectangle(100, 0, 900,
GraphicsWindow.Height)
        'time/score
        TimeLeft = 60 * 1000 ' milliseconds remaining
        Score = 0
        DisplayTimeScore()
        'Elijah
        ElijahImage = ImageList.LoadImage(Program.Directory +
"\Elijah.gif")
        ElijahW = ImageList.GetWidthOfImage(ElijahImage)
        ElijahH = ImageList.GetHeightOfImage(ElijahImage)
        Elijah = Shapes.AddImage(ElijahImage)
        ElijahDeltaX = 5
        ElijahX = 375
        ElijahY = GraphicsWindow.Height - ElijahH
        Shapes.Move(Elijah, ElijahX, Elijahy)
        'Raven
        RavenImage = ImageList.LoadImage(Program.Directory +
"\Raven.gif")
        RavenW = ImageList.GetWidthOfImage(RavenImage)
        RavenH = ImageList.GetHeightOfImage(RavenImage)
        Raven = Shapes.AddImage(RavenImage)
        'Bread
        BreadImage = ImageList.LoadImage(Program.Directory +
"\Bread.gif")
        BreadW = ImageList.GetWidthOfImage(BreadImage)
        BreadH = ImageList.GetHeightOfImage(BreadImage)
        Bread = Shapes.AddImage(BreadImage)
        PositionRavenAndBread()
        'start timer
        BreadSpeed = 0.5 * Difficulty + 3 ' base on difficulty
        Timer.Resume()
      EndIf
    ElseIf (GraphicsWindow.MouseY > 290 And GraphicsWindow.MouseY
< 320) Then
      If (GraphicsWindow.MouseX > 5 And GraphicsWindow.MouseX <
95) Then
        'clicked stop
        Program.End()
      EndIf
    EndIf
  EndIf
  If (GameStatus = "Playing") Then
    If (GraphicsWindow.MouseY > 290 And GraphicsWindow.MouseY <
320) Then
```

```
      If (GraphicsWindow.MouseX > 5 And GraphicsWindow.MouseX <
95) Then
        'clicked stop while playing
        Shapes.Remove(Raven)
        Shapes.Remove(Bread)
        Shapes.Remove(Elijah)
        Timer.Pause()
        GraphicsWindow.ShowMessage("You stopped the game.", "Game
Over")
        GameStatus = "Initial"
      EndIf
    EndIf
  Endif
EndSub
```

Here, when stopped is pressed the game screen is cleared and a message displayed.

Save and **Run** the program. Click **Start**, then click **Stop**. You should see this message:

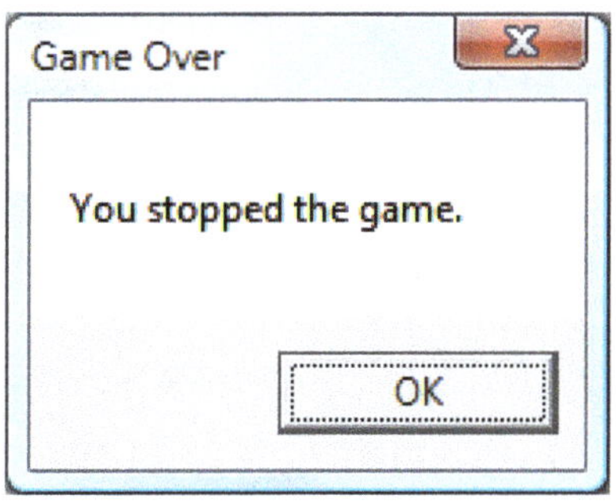

The game is now complete.

Elijah and the Ravens Program Listing

Here is the complete listing of the **Elijah and the Ravens** Small Basic program:

```
' Elijah and the Ravens
' Small Basic Version

' Intro screen
Difficulty = 1
GameStatus = "Initial"
GraphicsWindow.Show()
GraphicsWindow.Title = "Elijah and the Ravens"
GraphicsWindow.BackgroundColor = "White"
GraphicsWindow.Width = 1000
GraphicsWindow.Height = 600
GraphicsWindow.BrushColor = "Black"
GraphicsWindow.FontSize = 14
GraphicsWindow.DrawText(110, 10, "ELIJAH AND THE RAVENS")
GraphicsWindow.DrawText(110, 30, "In 1 Kings 17:1-6, God sends
ravens to drop bread for Elijah while he hides from King Ahab. In
this game, you will try")
GraphicsWindow.DrawText(110, 50, "to catch as many falling loaves
of bread as possible to feed Elijah.")
GraphicsWindow.DrawText(110, 80, "Use the cursor left and right
arrow keys or left and right mouse buttons to move Elijah under a
falling loa so he can be fed")
GraphicsWindow.DrawText(110, 100, "by the Raven. God always
provides for our needs.")
GraphicsWindow.DrawText(110, 180, "<-- Select Difficulty by
pressing the left button for Easy and the right button for
Harder.")
GraphicsWindow.DrawText(110, 260, "<-- Click on the Start Button
to begin.")
GraphicsWindow.DrawText(110, 300, "<-- Click on the Stop Button to
stop program.")
GraphicsWindow.BrushColor = "Blue"
GraphicsWindow.FillRectangle(0, 0, 100, GraphicsWindow.Height)
GraphicsWindow.BrushColor = "Yellow"
GraphicsWindow.FontSize = 18
GraphicsWindow.DrawText(5, 20, "Time Left:")
GraphicsWindow.DrawText(15, 70, "Loaves:")
GraphicsWindow.DrawText(5, 120, "Difficulty:")
```

```
GraphicsWindow.BrushColor = "White"
GraphicsWindow.DrawText(35, 140, Difficulty)
GraphicsWindow.BrushColor = "LightGray"
GraphicsWindow.FillRectangle(15, 170, 30, 30)
GraphicsWindow.FillRectangle(55, 170, 30, 30)
GraphicsWindow.FillRectangle(5, 250, 90, 30)
GraphicsWindow.FillRectangle(5, 290, 90, 30)
GraphicsWindow.BrushColor = "Black"
GraphicsWindow.FontSize = 14
GraphicsWindow.DrawText(25, 175, "<")
GraphicsWindow.DrawText(65, 175, ">")
GraphicsWindow.DrawText(30, 255, "Start")
GraphicsWindow.DrawText(30, 295, "Stop")
GraphicsWindow.MouseDown = MouseDownEvent
Timer.Tick = TimerTickEvent
Timer.Interval = 50
Timer.Pause()
GraphicsWindow.KeyDown = KeyDownEvent

Sub MouseDownEvent
  If (GameStatus = "Initial") Then
    If (GraphicsWindow.MouseY > 175 And GraphicsWindow.MouseY <
205) Then
      If (GraphicsWindow.MouseX > 15 And GraphicsWindow.MouseX <
45) Then
        ' decrease difficulty
        Difficulty = Difficulty - 1
        If (Difficulty < 1) Then
          Difficulty = 1
        EndIf
      ElseIf (GraphicsWindow.MouseX > 55 And GraphicsWindow.MouseX
< 85) Then
        'increase difficulty
        Difficulty = Difficulty + 1
        If (Difficulty > 10) Then
          Difficulty = 10
        EndIf
      EndIf
      GraphicsWindow.BrushColor = "Blue"
      GraphicsWindow.FillRectangle(0, 140, 100, 20)
      GraphicsWindow.BrushColor = "White"
      GraphicsWindow.FontSize = 18
      GraphicsWindow.DrawText(35, 140, Difficulty)
    ElseIf (GraphicsWindow.MouseY > 250 And GraphicsWindow.MouseY
< 280) Then
```

```
      If (GraphicsWindow.MouseX > 5 And GraphicsWindow.MouseX <
95) Then
        'clicked start
        GameStatus = "Playing"
        'clear screen
        GraphicsWindow.BrushColor = "White"
        GraphicsWindow.FillRectangle(100, 0, 900,
GraphicsWindow.Height)
        'time/score
        TimeLeft = 60 * 1000 ' milliseconds remaining
        Score = 0
        DisplayTimeScore()
        'Elijah
        ElijahImage = ImageList.LoadImage(Program.Directory +
"\Elijah.gif")
        ElijahW = ImageList.GetWidthOfImage(ElijahImage)
        ElijahH = ImageList.GetHeightOfImage(ElijahImage)
        Elijah = Shapes.AddImage(ElijahImage)
        ElijahDeltaX = 5
        ElijahX = 375
        ElijahY = GraphicsWindow.Height - ElijahH
        Shapes.Move(Elijah, ElijahX, Elijahy)
        'Raven
        RavenImage = ImageList.LoadImage(Program.Directory +
"\Raven.gif")
        RavenW = ImageList.GetWidthOfImage(RavenImage)
        RavenH = ImageList.GetHeightOfImage(RavenImage)
        Raven = Shapes.AddImage(RavenImage)
        'Bread
        BreadImage = ImageList.LoadImage(Program.Directory +
"\Bread.gif")
        BreadW = ImageList.GetWidthOfImage(BreadImage)
        BreadH = ImageList.GetHeightOfImage(BreadImage)
        Bread = Shapes.AddImage(BreadImage)
        PositionRavenAndBread()
        'start timer
        BreadSpeed = 0.5 * Difficulty + 3 ' base on difficulty
        Timer.Resume()
      EndIf
    ElseIf (GraphicsWindow.MouseY > 290 And GraphicsWindow.MouseY
< 320) Then
      If (GraphicsWindow.MouseX > 5 And GraphicsWindow.MouseX <
95) Then
        'clicked stop
        Program.End()
      EndIf
```

```
    EndIf
  EndIf
  If (GameStatus = "Playing") Then
    If (GraphicsWindow.MouseY > 290 And GraphicsWindow.MouseY <
320) Then
      If (GraphicsWindow.MouseX > 5 And GraphicsWindow.MouseX <
95) Then
        'clicked stop while playing
        Shapes.Remove(Raven)
        Shapes.Remove(Bread)
        Shapes.Remove(Elijah)
        Timer.Pause()
        GraphicsWindow.ShowMessage("You stopped the game.", "Game
Over")
        GameStatus = "Initial"
      EndIf
    EndIf
  Endif
EndSub

Sub DisplayTimeScore
  GraphicsWindow.FontSize = 18
  GraphicsWindow.BrushColor = "Blue"
  GraphicsWindow.FillRectangle(0, 40, 100, 20)
  GraphicsWindow.FillRectangle(0, 90, 100, 20)
  GraphicsWindow.BrushColor = "White"
  GraphicsWindow.DrawText(35, 40, Math.Floor(TimeLeft / 1000))
  GraphicsWindow.DrawText(35, 90, Score)
EndSub

Sub PositionRavenAndBread
  RavenX = Math.GetRandomNumber(GraphicsWindow.Width - RavenW -
100) + 100
  Shapes.Move(Raven, RavenX, 0)
  BreadX = RavenX + 0.5 * (RavenW - BreadW)
  BreadY = RavenH - 20
  Shapes.Move(Bread, BreadX, BreadY)
EndSub

Sub TimerTickEvent
  ' move bread
  BreadY = BreadY + BreadSpeed
  Shapes.Move(Bread, BreadX, BreadY)
  'check if mouse button is down
  If (Mouse.IsLeftButtonDown) Then
    ElijahX = ElijahX - ElijahDeltaX
```

```
  ElseIf (Mouse.IsRightButtonDown) Then
    ElijahX = ElijahX + ElijahDeltaX
  EndIf
  ' move elijah
  If (ElijahX < 100) Then
    ElijahX = 100
  ElseIf (ElijahX > GraphicsWindow.Width - ElijahW) Then
    ElijahX = GraphicsWindow.Width - ElijahW
  EndIf
  Shapes.Move(Elijah, ElijahX, ElijahY)
  ' check for bread collision or passed elijah
  Passed = "false"
  Collision = "false"
  If (BreadY + BreadH > ElijahY) Then
    Passed = "true"
    If (ElijahX + ElijahW > BreadX And ElijahX < BreadX + BreadW)
Then
      Collision = "true"
    EndIf
  EndIf
  If (Passed = "true") Then
    If (Collision = "true") Then
      Score = Score + 1
    EndIf
    PositionRavenAndBread()
  EndIf
   'update time
  TimeLeft = TimeLeft - Timer.Interval
  DisplayTimeScore()
  If (TimeLeft = 0) Then
    Shapes.Remove(Raven)
    Shapes.Remove(Bread)
    Shapes.Remove(Elijah)
    Timer.Pause()
    GraphicsWindow.ShowMessage("Elijah has been fed by " + Score +
" ravens.", "Game Over")
    GameStatus = "Initial"
  EndIf
EndSub

Sub KeyDownEvent
  ' check for left or right cursor key to move Elijah
  If (GameStatus = "Playing") Then
    If (GraphicsWindow.LastKey = "Left") Then
      ElijahX = ElijahX - ElijahDeltaX
    ElseIf (GraphicsWindow.LastKey = "Right") Then
```

```
      ElijahX = ElijahX + ElijahDeltaX
    EndIf
  EndIf
EndSub
```

Elijah and the Ravens Program Review

The **Elijah and the Ravens** program is now complete. **Save** and **Run** the program and make sure it works as promised. Check that all options work correctly.

If there are errors in your implementation, go back over the steps of window and code design. Go over the developed code – make sure you understand how different parts of the program were coded. As mentioned in the beginning of this chapter, the completed program is saved as **Elijah** in the **BeginSB\BSB Code\Elijah** folder.

13

MORE COMPUTER BIBLE GAMES AND LEARNING GAMES

Preview

By now, you should feel pretty comfortable with the steps involved in building a Small Basic program. In this last chapter, we give you more programs you can build and try. We'll present the steps involved in building each program - **Program Design**, **Program Development**, **Run the Program**, and **Other Things to Try**. But, we won't give you detailed discussion of what's going on in the code. We will just give you the code listing and point out any new ideas. You should be able to figure that out by now (with the help of the code comments). Actually, a very valuable programming skill to have is the ability to read and understand someone else's code.

The programs included are: Computer Stopwatch, Loan Calculator, Unit Conversions, Times Tables, State Capitals, Bible Book Scramble, Memory Game, The Prodigal Son, Decode, The Good Shepherd, and The Lost Coin. The first five programs will be text based applications and the last six programs will use the graphics window.

Program 1 - Computer Stopwatch

Program Design

In this program, we build a computer stopwatch that measures elapsed time in seconds (to three decimal places). When <Enter> is pressed, the stopwatch will start. When <Enter> is pressed again, the stopwatch will stop and display elapsed time. The program is saved in the **Stopwatch** folder in the program folder (**\BeginSB\BSB Code**).

Program Development

Start Small Basic. Start a new program and save it as **Stopwatch**. Type in (or copy and paste from these notes) the complete **Stopwatch** Small Basic code:

```
'
'  Stopwatch Program
'  Beginning Small Basic
'
TextWindow.Title = "Stopwatch"
Start:
TextWindow.WriteLine("")
TextWindow.Write("Press <Enter> to start stopwatch (enter a 0 to
stop the program). ")
Stop = TextWindow.Read()
If Stop <> "0" Then
  TextWindow.WriteLine("Stopwatch is running ...")
  GetSeconds()
  StartTime = Seconds
  TextWindow.Write("Press <Enter> to stop stopwatch. ")
  StopIt = TextWindow.Read()
  GetSeconds()
  EndTime = Seconds
  TextWindow.WriteLine("Elapsed time is " + (EndTime - StartTime)
+ " seconds.")
  Goto Start
EndIf
```

```
Sub GetSeconds
  Seconds = Clock.Hour * 3600 + Clock.Minute * 60 + Clock.Second +
Clock.Millisecond / 1000
EndSub
```

Let's discuss this code.

We have three variables: **StartTime** (starting time in seconds), **EndTime** (ending time in seconds) and **Stop**, used to see if we should stop the program. Ask the user to press <Enter> to start and stop the stopwatch and display the results. To stop the program, the user is asked to enter a 0 (zero) when starting the stopwatch. The timing code repeats as long as the **Stop** string is "not equal" to 0. The code logic is very straightforward. The only part of this code that might be difficult to understand is computing the times. This is done in the subroutine **GetSeconds**:

```
Sub GetSeconds
  Seconds = Clock.Hour * 3600 + Clock.Minute * 60 + Clock.Second +
Clock.Millisecond / 1000
EndSub
```

This routine uses the Small Basic **Clock** object which holds the current time in different parts (Hour, Minute, Second, and Millisecond). This routine converts each to seconds and adds them up.

Run the Program

Save your work. Run the program. Press <**Enter**> to start the stopwatch. Press <**Enter**> to stop the stopwatch. Make sure you understand how the elapsed time is computed and displayed. Here's a few of my example runs:

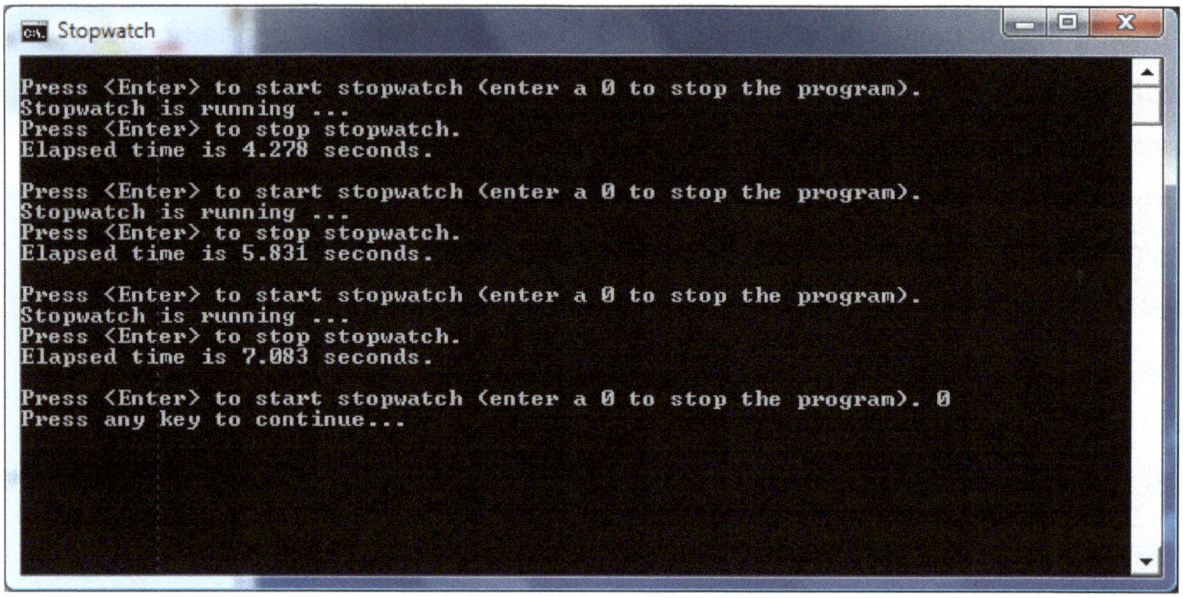

Stop the program when you get bored (enter a 0, instead of pressing <Enter> when asked to start the stopwatch).

Other Things to Try

Many stopwatches allow you to continue timing after you've stopped one or more times. That is, you can measure total elapsed time in different segments. You'll need a variable to keep track of total elapsed time and a way to tell the stopwatch you are done timing (use some other **Stop** value). Add a "lap timing" feature by displaying the time measured in each segment (a segment being defined as the time between each Start and Stop press of <Enter>).

Program 2 - Loan Calculator

Program Design

Do you want to know how much that new car will cost each month or how long it will take to pay off a credit card? This program will do the job. You enter a loan amount, a yearly interest, and a number of months, and the program computes your monthly payment. The program is saved in the **Loan** folder in the program folder (**\BeginSB\BSB Code**).

Program Development

Start Small Basic, create a new program and save it as **Loan**. Type in (or copy and paste from these notes) the complete **Loan** Small Basic code:

```
'
'  Loan Program
'  Beginning Small Basic
'
TextWindow.Title = "Loan Calculator"
GetInputs:
TextWindow.Write("Enter loan amount (enter 0 to stop): ")
Loan = TextWindow.ReadNumber()
If (Loan <> 0) Then
  TextWindow.Write("Enter yearly interest rate:  ")
  Interest = TextWindow.ReadNumber()
  TextWindow.Write("Enter number of months to pay back loan: ")
  Months = TextWindow.ReadNumber()
  ' Compute interest multiplier
  Multiplier = Math.Power((1 + Interest / 1200), Months)
  ' Compute payment
  Payment = Loan * Interest * Multiplier / (1200 * (Multiplier -
1))
  TextWindow.WriteLine("Your monthly payment is $" + Payment)
  TextWindow.WriteLine("")
  Goto GetInputs
EndIf
```

The code is pretty straightforward. The user is asked for loan amount, yearly interest and number of months. The values are input and the payment is computed (using a standard financial formula) and displayed.

Run the Program

Save your work. Run the program. Provide a loan amount, an interest, and a number of months. Press <Enter> to determine and display the monthly payment. Try a loan amount of $5,000 (don't type in the comma), an interest rate of 18%, and 24 months. Your payment should be $249.62:

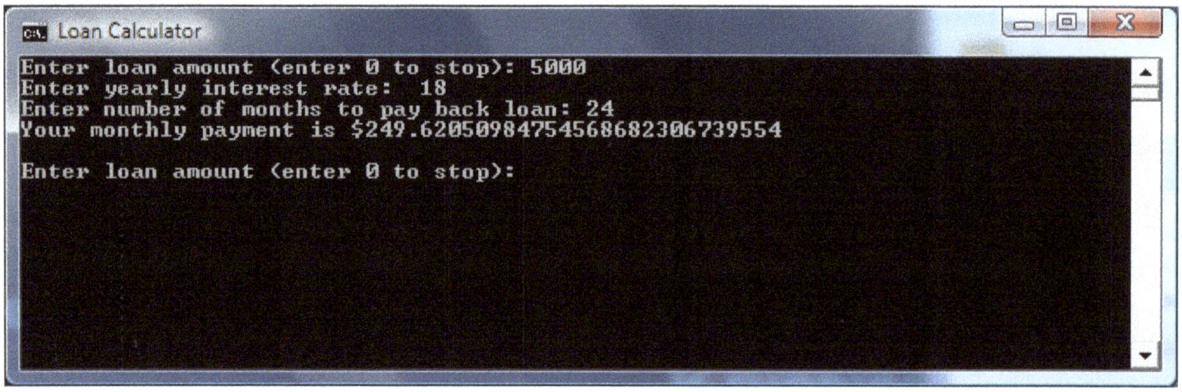

What can you do with this? Well, you can find monthly payments like we just did. Or, try this. Say you have a credit card balance of $2,000. The interest rate is 15% and you can make $100 payments each month. Use 2000 as the loan amount box, and 15 as the interest. Then, try different numbers of months until the computed payment is close to $100. This will tell you how many months it will take you to pay off the credit card. I got 23 months with payments of $100.59 each month.

Other Things to Try

This program is pretty complete. One thing to fix though - what if the interest rate is zero (a very nice bank!)? The program won't work (try it). You'll need a way to compute payments with zero interest. Also can you figure out how to display the payment amounts with exactly two numbers after the decimal point?

Program 3 – Units Conversion

Program Design

In this program, we will build a program that converts length from one unit of measure (inch, foot, yard, mile, centimeter, meter, kilometer) to another. The program is saved in the **Convert** folder in the program folder (**\BeginSB\BSB Code**).

Program Development

Start Small Basic, start a new program and save it as **Convert**. Type in (or copy and paste from these notes) the complete **Convert** Small Basic code:

```
'
'  Convert Program
'  Beginning Small Basic
'
TextWindow.Title = "Units Conversions"
' Establish conversion factors - stored in two dimensional array
' or table - the first number is the table row, the second number
' the table column
Conversions[1][1] = 1.0 ' in to in
Conversions[1][2] = 1.0 / 12.0 ' in to ft
Conversions[1][3] = 1.0 / 36.0 ' in to yd
Conversions[1][4] = (1.0 / 12.0) / 5280.0 ' in to mi
Conversions[1][5] = 2.54 ' in to cm
Conversions[1][6] = 2.54 / 100 ' in to m
Conversions[1][7] = 2.54 / 100000 ' in to km
For i = 1 To 7
  Conversions[2][i] = 12.0 * Conversions[1][i]
  Conversions[3][i] = 36.0 * Conversions[1][i]
  Conversions[4][i] = 5280.0 * (12.0 * Conversions[1][i])
  Conversions[5][i] = Conversions[1][i] / 2.54
  Conversions[6][i] = 100.0 * Conversions[1][i] / 2.54
  Conversions[7][i] = 100000.0 * (Conversions[1][i] / 2.54)
```

```
EndFor

' Initialize variables
Units[1] = "inches (in)"
Units[2] = "feet (ft)"
Units[3] = "yards (yd)"
Units[4] = "miles (mi)"
Units[5] = "centimeters (cm)"
Units[6] = "meters (m)"
Units[7] = "kilometers (km)"

StartLoop:
TextWindow.Write("Enter a value to convert (enter 0 stop): ")
FromValue = TextWindow.ReadNumber()
If (FromValue <> 0) Then
  For i = 1 To 7
    TextWindow.WriteLine(i + " - " + Units[i])
  EndFor
  GetFromUnits:
  TextWindow.Write("What units is the value in? ")
  FromUnits = TextWindow.ReadNumber()
  If (FromUnits < 1 Or FromUnits > 7) Then
    Goto GetFromUnits
  EndIf
  ' Do unit conversion
  TextWindow.WriteLine("")
  TextWindow.WriteLine(FromValue + " " + Units[FromUnits] + " 
is:")
  For i = 1 To 7
    TextWindow.WriteLine(FromValue * Conversions[FromUnits][i] + " 
" + Units[i])
  EndFor
  TextWindow.WriteLine("")
  Goto StartLoop
EndIf
```

The idea of the program is simple. Type a value and choose its units. Display that value converted to several other units. Note how the conversion factors are stored in a two-dimensional array (table).

Run the Program

Save your work. Run the program. Type in a value, select its units. Make sure all the options work as designed. Here's what I got for 5280 feet:

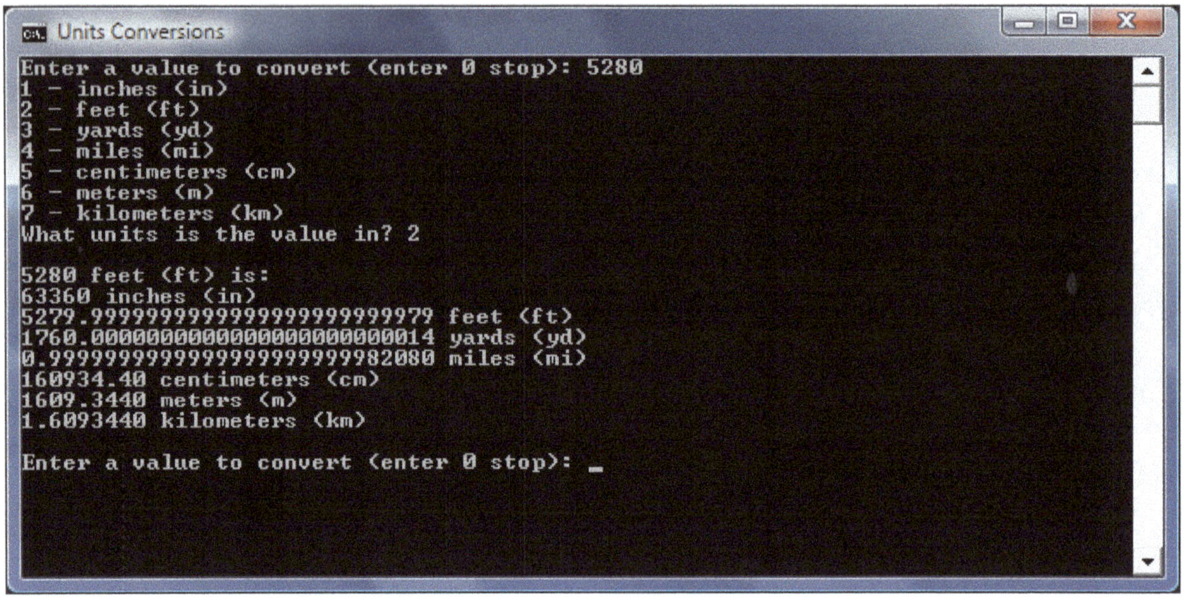

Other Things to Try

The most obvious change to this program is to include other units of measure. You could build a general purpose units conversion program that converts not only length, but weight, volume, density, area, temperature and many others. Such a program would be invaluable.

Program 4 – Times Tables

Program Design

In this program, you can give a child practice with the times tables using the numbers from 0 to 9. The computer generates a random problem. The child answers and the computer evaluates the performance. The child is given 10 problems to try. The program is saved in the **TimesTables** folder in the program folder (**\BeginSB\BSB Code**).

Program Development

Start Small Basic, start a new program and save it as **TimesTables**. Type in (or copy and paste from these notes) the complete **TimesTables** Small Basic code:

```
'
'  Times Tables Program
'  Beginning Small Basic
'
TextWindow.Title = "Times Tables"
NumProb = 0
NumRight = 0
' display the problem
For i = 1 To 10
  NumProb = NumProb + 1
  ' Generate random numbers for factors
  Number1 = Math.GetRandomNumber(10) - 1
  Number2 = Math.GetRandomNumber(10) - 1
  ' Find product
  Product = Number1 * Number2
  TextWindow.WriteLine("")
  TextWindow.WriteLine("Problem " + NumProb + ":")
  TextWindow.Write("What is " + Number1 + " x " + Number2 + " = ")
  YourAnswer = TextWindow.ReadNumber()
  ' Check answer and update score
```

```
  If (YourAnswer = Product) Then
    NumRight = NumRight + 1
    TextWindow.WriteLine("That's correct!")
  else
    TextWindow.WriteLine("Answer is " + Product)
  EndIf
  TextWindow.WriteLine("Score: " + 100.0 * NumRight / NumProb +
"%")
EndFor
```

The computer generates and displays a multiplication problem. The user types an answer and presses **<Enter>.** If correct, you are told so. If incorrect, the correct answer is given. In either case, the score is updated. Continue answering until 10 problems (a For loop is used) have been answered.

Run the Program

Save your work. Run the program. A multiplication problem will be displayed. Type an answer and press <Enter>. If correct, that's great. If not, you will be shown the correct answer. Continue for 10 problems. Try for a high score. Here's what I got for one round of problems:

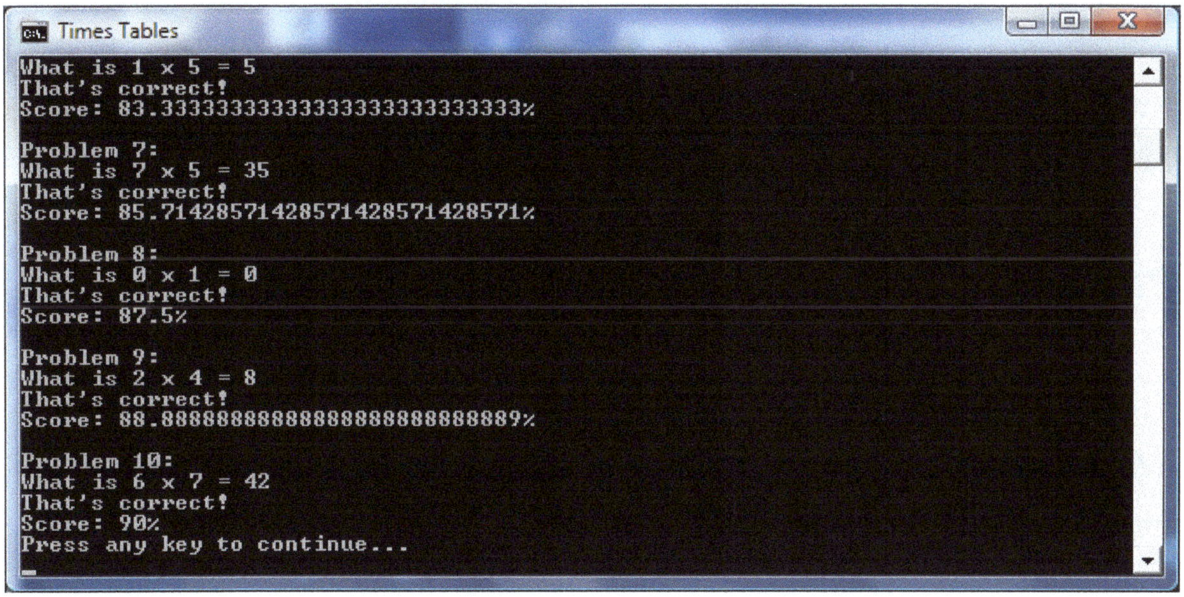

Other Things to Try

Some suggested changes to make this a more useful program are: (1) make the range of factors an option (small numbers for little kids, large numbers for older kids), (2) allow practice with a specific factor only, (3) give the user more chances at the correct answer with a decreasing score for each try, (4) set up a timer so the faster the user answers, the higher the score, (5) remove the 10 problem limit – allow the user to answer until they decide to quite and (6) expand the program to include other operations such as addition, subtraction and division.

Program 5 – State Capitals

Program Design

In this program, we build a fun game for home and school. You will be given the name of a state in the United States and four possible choices for its capital city. You enter the guess of your choice to see if you are right. (We apologize to our foreign readers – perhaps you can modify this program to build a similar multiple choice type game). The program is saved in the **StateCapitals** folder in the program folder (**\BeginSB\BSB Code**).

Program Development

Start Small Basic, start a new program and save it as **StateCapitals**. Type in (or copy and paste from these notes, especially for the state and capital names) the complete **StateCapitals** Small Basic code:

```
'
'  State Capitals Program
' Beginning Small Basic
'
TextWindow.Title = "State Capitals"
' initialize arrays
State[1] = "Alabama"
Capital[1] = "Montgomery"
State[2] = "Alaska"
Capital[2] = "Juneau"
State[3] = "Arizona"
Capital[3] = "Phoenix"
State[4] = "Arkansas"
Capital[4] = "Little Rock"
State[5] = "California"
Capital[5] = "Sacramento"
State[6] = "Colorado"
Capital[6] = "Denver"
```

```
State[7] = "Connecticut"
Capital[7] = "Hartford"
State[8] = "Delaware"
Capital[8] = "Dover"
State[9] = "Florida"
Capital[9] = "Tallahassee"
State[10] = "Georgia"
Capital[10] = "Atlanta"
State[11] = "Hawaii"
Capital[11] = "Honolulu"
State[12] = "Idaho"
Capital[12] = "Boise"
State[13] = "Illinois"
Capital[13] = "Springfield"
State[14] = "Indiana"
Capital[14] = "Indianapolis"
State[15] = "Iowa"
Capital[15] = "Des Moines"
State[16] = "Kansas"
Capital[16] = "Topeka"
State[17] = "Kentucky"
Capital[17] = "Frankfort"
State[18] = "Louisiana"
Capital[18] = "Baton Rouge"
State[19] = "Maine"
Capital[19] = "Augusta"
State[20] = "Maryland"
Capital[20] = "Annapolis"
State[21] = "Massachusetts"
Capital[21] = "Boston"
State[22] = "Michigan"
Capital[22] = "Lansing"
State[23] = "Minnesota"
Capital[23] = "Saint Paul"
State[24] = "Mississippi"
Capital[24] = "Jackson"
State[25] = "Missouri"
Capital[25] = "Jefferson City"
State[26] = "Montana"
Capital[26] = "Helena"
State[27] = "Nebraska"
Capital[27] = "Lincoln"
State[28] = "Nevada"
Capital[28] = "Carson City"
State[29] = "New Hampshire"
Capital[29] = "Concord"
```

```
State[30] = "New Jersey"
Capital[30] = "Trenton"
State[31] = "New Mexico"
Capital[31] = "Santa Fe"
State[32] = "New York"
Capital[32] = "Albany"
State[33] = "North Carolina"
Capital[33] = "Raleigh"
State[34] = "North Dakota"
Capital[34] = "Bismarck"
State[35] = "Ohio"
Capital[35] = "Columbus"
State[36] = "Oklahoma"
Capital[36] = "Oklahoma City"
State[37] = "Oregon"
Capital[37] = "Salem"
State[38] = "Pennsylvania"
Capital[38] = "Harrisburg"
State[39] = "Rhode Island"
Capital[39] = "Providence"
State[40] = "South Carolina"
Capital[40] = "Columbia"
State[41] = "South Dakota"
Capital[41] = "Pierre"
State[42] = "Tennessee"
Capital[42] = "Nashville"
State[43] = "Texas"
Capital[43] = "Austin"
State[44] = "Utah"
Capital[44] = "Salt Lake City"
State[45] = "Vermont"
Capital[45] = "Montpelier"
State[46] = "Virginia"
Capital[46] = "Richmond"
State[47] = "Washington"
Capital[47] = "Olympia"
State[48] = "West Virginia"
Capital[48] = "Charleston"
State[49] = "Wisconsin"
Capital[49] = "Madison"
State[50] = "Wyoming"
Capital[50] = "Cheyenne"

' begin questioning Loop
BeginLoop:
' Generate the next question at random
```

```
Answer = Math.GetRandomNumber(50)
' Display selected state
TextWindow.WriteLine("")
TextWindow.WriteLine("State is: " + State[Answer])
TextWindow.WriteLine("")
' CapitalUsed array is used to see which state Capitals have
'been selected as possible answers
For i = 1 To 50
  CapitalUsed[i] = 0
EndFor
' Pick four different state indices (j) at random
' These are used to set up multiple choice answers
' Stored in the ListedCapital array
For i = 1 To 4
  'Find value not used yet and not the answer
  GetJ:
  j = Math.GetRandomNumber(50)
  If (CapitalUsed[j] <> 0 Or j = Answer) Then
    Goto GetJ
  EndIf
  CapitalUsed[j] = 1
  ListedCapital[i] = j
EndFor
' Now replace one item (at random) with correct answer
ListedCapital[Math.GetRandomNumber(4)] = Answer
' Display multiple choice answers
For i = 1 To 4
  TextWindow.WriteLine(i + " - " + Capital[ListedCapital[i]])
EndFor
TextWindow.WriteLine("")
TextWindow.Write("What is the Capital? (Enter 0 to Stop) ")
CapitalSelected = TextWindow.ReadNumber()
' check answer
If (CapitalSelected <> 0) Then
  If (ListedCapital[CapitalSelected] = Answer) Then
    TextWindow.WriteLine("That's it ... good job!")
  Else
    TextWindow.WriteLine("Sorry, the answer is " + Capital[Answer]
+".")
  EndIf
  Goto BeginLoop
EndIf
```

A state (**Answer**) is picked at random, then four distinct capital cities for the multiple choice answers (no repeated values). Check the loop that picks these answers. Next, the questioning loop is completed with code to check the user answer (only one try is given):

Run the Program

Save your work. Run the program. A state name and four possible capital cities will be displayed. (Study the code used to choose and sort the possible answers – this kind of code is very useful.) Choose an answer. If correct, an encouraging message is printed and another state is displayed. If incorrect, you will be told the correct answer. Keep playing – enter a 0 as your answer to stop the program. One of my runs looks like this:

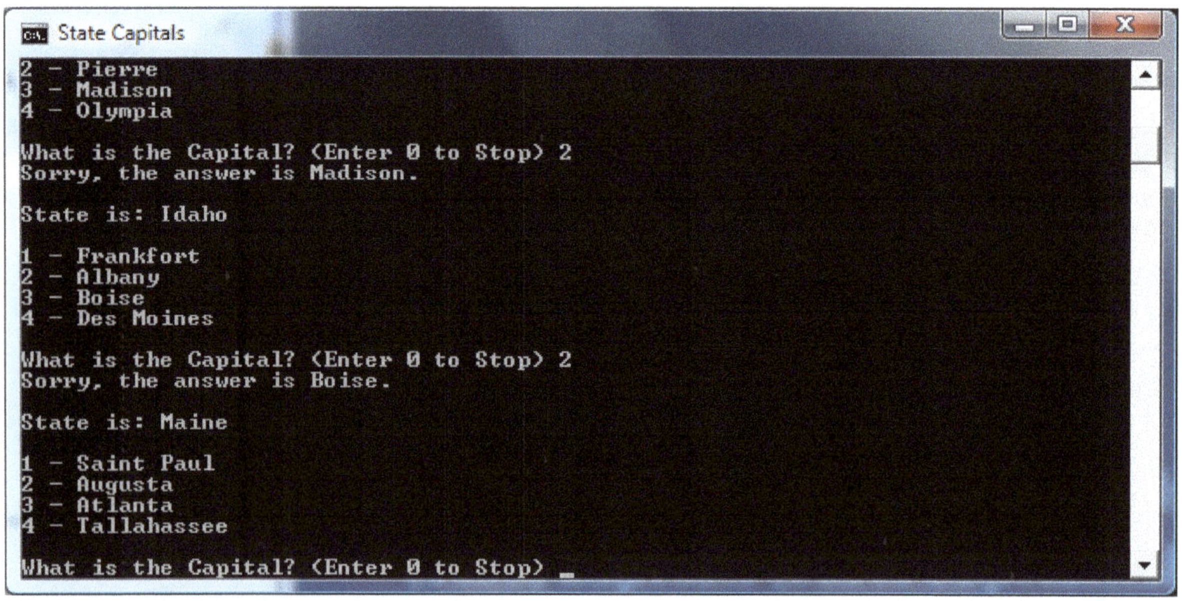

Other Things to Try

This would be a fun program to modify. How about changing it to display a capital city with four states as the multiple choices? Or, allow the user to type in the answer instead of picking from a list. Typing the answer brings up a host of programming problems – if not capitalized correctly, is the answer wrong? If slightly misspelled, is the answer wrong? Add some kind of scoring system. Allow more than one chance at the answer. Notice when selecting a multiple choice answer, if you pick something other than 0 through 4, an error will occur. Can you think of a way to fix this?

This program could also be used to build general multiple choice tests from any two lists. You could do language translations (given a word in English, choose the corresponding word in Spanish), given a book, choose the author, or given an invention, name the inventor. Use your imagination.

Program 6 – Bible Book Scramble

Program Design

This program is a classic Bible Book Scramble Game. The program is saved in the **Scramble** folder in the program folder (**\BeginSB\BSB Code**.

Program Development

Start Small Basic, start a new program and save it as **Scramble**. Type in (or copy and paste from these notes) the complete **Scramble** Small Basic code.

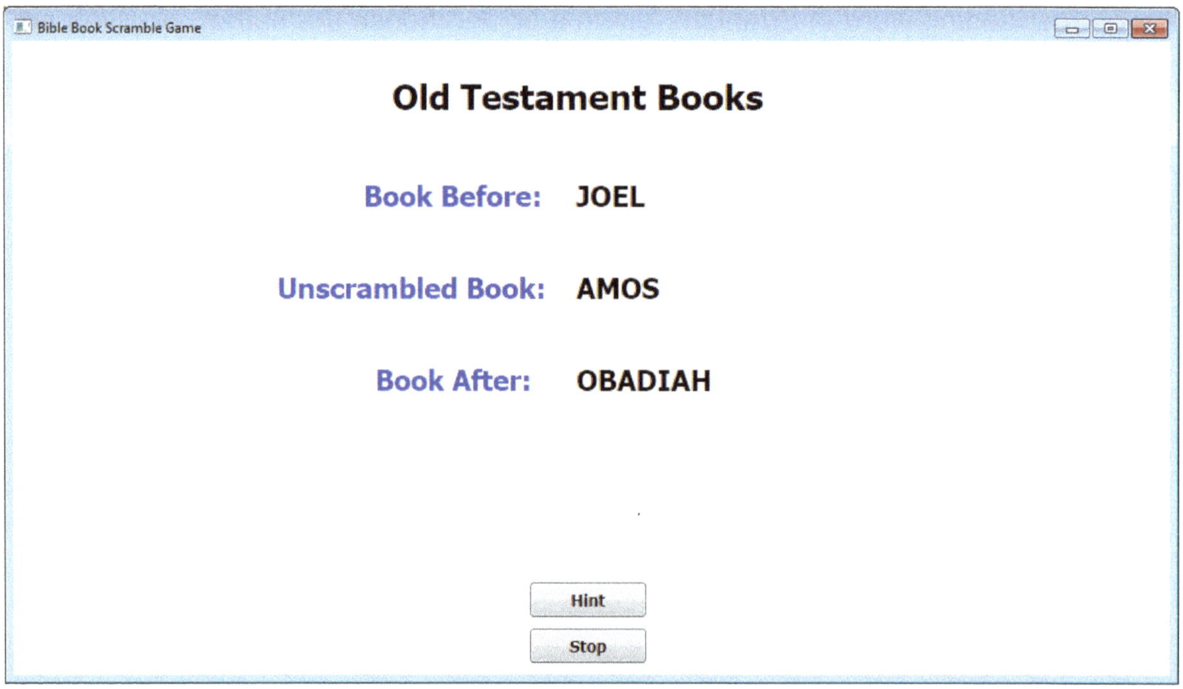

```
' Bible Book Scramble Game
' Small Basic Version
'
' Intro screen
DisplayIntroScreen()
Controls.ButtonClicked = ButtonClickedEvent
GraphicsWindow.KeyDown = KeyDownEvent
GraphicsWindow.TextInput = TextInputEvent

Sub ButtonClickedEvent
  B = Controls.LastClickedButton
  If (GameStatus <> "ChoosingGame") Then
    If (B = StopButton) Then
      'clicked stop
      DisplayIntroScreen()
    EndIf
  EndIf
  If (GameStatus = "GettingBooks") Then
    If (B = HintButton) Then
      'clicked hint - give next letter if what's there already is
correct
      If (EnteredBook = "") Then
        'no entry yet - give first letter
        EnteredBook = Text.GetSubText(Book[BookPicked +
BookEntering], 1, 1)
        GraphicsWindow.ShowMessage("I'll give you the first
letter.", "Let's start ...")
      ElseIf (EnteredBook = Text.GetSubText(Book[BookPicked +
BookEntering], 1, Text.GetLength(EnteredBook))) Then
        'what has been entered so far is correct
        If (EnteredBook = Book[BookPicked + BookEntering]) Then
          'forgot enter
          GraphicsWindow.ShowMessage("Your answer is correct. You
just forgot to press <Enter> - I'll do it for you.", "Correct
Answer!")
        ElseIf (EnteredBook = Text.GetSubText(Book[BookPicked +
BookEntering], 1, Text.GetLength(Book[BookPicked + BookEntering])
- 1)) Then
          'missing last letter
          EnteredBook = Book[BookPicked + BookEntering]
          GraphicsWindow.ShowMessage("You're just missing the last
letter. I'll add it for you.", "Close ...")
        Else
```

```
          EnteredBook = Text.GetSubText(Book[BookPicked +
BookEntering], 1, Text.GetLength(EnteredBook) + 1)
          GraphicsWindow.ShowMessage("What you have so far is
correct - I'll give you the next letter.", "Nice start ...")
        EndIf
      Else
        'count correct letters
        For i = 1 To Text.GetLength(EnteredBook)
          If (Text.GetSubText(EnteredBook, i, 1) <>
Text.GetSubText(Book[BookPicked + BookEntering], i, 1)) Then
            Goto ShowCorrect
          EndIf
        EndFor
        ShowCorrect:
        EnteredBook = Text.GetSubText(Book[BookPicked +
BookEntering], 1, i)
        If (EnteredBook = Book[BookPicked + BookEntering]) Then
          'typed too many letters
          EnteredBook = Book[BookPicked + BookEntering]
          GraphicsWindow.ShowMessage("You have the correct answer,
but typed too many letters. I will remove the extra letters and
show the correct answer.", "Correct Answer!")
        Else
          GraphicsWindow.ShowMessage("What you have typed so far
is incorrect.  I will give you the next letter after the letters
you have typed correctly. Continue typing from there.", "Incorrect
answer ...")
        EndIf
      EndIf
      DisplayEnteredBook()
      'if getting a hint, completed the book, go to next book if
there is one
      If (EnteredBook = Book[BookPicked + BookEntering]) Then
        CheckEnteredBook()
      EndIf
    EndIf
  EndIf
EndSub

Sub KeyDownEvent
  'Choosing Game Screen
  If (GameStatus = "ChoosingGame") Then
    'looking for a 1 or a 2
    If (GraphicsWindow.LastKey = "D1" Or GraphicsWindow.LastKey =
"NumPad1") Then
      GameTitle = "Old Testament Books"
```

```
        GameStatus = "PickingLetters"
        NumberBooks = 36
        Book[0] = "NONE"
        Book[1] = "GENESIS"
        Book[2] = "EXODUS"
        Book[3] = "LEVITICUS"
        Book[4] = "NUMBERS"
        Book[5] = "DEUTERONOMY"
        Book[6] = "JOSHUA"
        Book[7] = "JUDGES"
        Book[8] = "RUTH"
        Book[9] = "SAMUEL"
        Book[10] = "KINGS"
        Book[11] = "CHRONICLES"
        Book[12] = "EZRA"
        Book[13] = "NEHEMIAH"
        Book[14] = "ESTHER"
        Book[15] = "JOB"
        Book[16] = "PSALMS"
        Book[17] = "PROVERBS"
        Book[18] = "ECCLESIASTES"
        Book[19] = "SONGOFSOLOMON"
        Book[20] = "ISAIAH"
        Book[21] = "JEREMIAH"
        Book[22] = "LAMENTATIONS"
        Book[23] = "EZEKIEL"
        Book[24] = "DANIEL"
        Book[25] = "HOSEA"
        Book[26] = "JOEL"
        Book[27] = "AMOS"
        Book[28] = "OBADIAH"
        Book[29] = "JONAH"
        Book[30] = "MICAH"
        Book[31] = "NAHUM"
        Book[32] = "HABAKKUK"
        Book[33] = "ZEPHANIAH"
        Book[34] = "HAGGAI"
        Book[35] = "ZECHARIAH"
        Book[36] = "MALACHI"
        Book[37] = "MATTHEW"
    ElseIf (GraphicsWindow.LastKey = "D2" Or
GraphicsWindow.LastKey = "NumPad2") Then
        GameTitle = "New Testament Books"
        GameStatus = "PickingLetters"
        NumberBooks = 21
        Book[0] = "MALACHI"
```

```
    Book[1] = "MATTHEW"
    Book[2] = "MARK"
    Book[3] = "LUKE"
    Book[4] = "JOHN"
    Book[5] = "ACTS"
    Book[6] = "ROMANS"
    Book[7] = "CORINTHIANS"
    Book[8] = "GALATIANS"
    Book[9] = "EPHESIANS"
    Book[10] = "PHILIPPIANS"
    Book[11] = "COLOSSIANS"
    Book[12] = "THESSALONIANS"
    Book[13] = "TIMOTHY"
    Book[14] = "TITUS"
    Book[15] = "PHILEMON"
    Book[16] = "HEBREWS"
    Book[17] = "JAMES"
    Book[18] = "PETER"
    Book[19] = "JOHN"
    Book[20] = "JUDE"
    Book[21] = "REVELATION"
    Book[22] = "NONE"
  EndIf
  If (GameStatus <> "ChoosingGame") Then
    'Draw initial screen
    GraphicsWindow.Clear()
    'create buttons
    GraphicsWindow.BrushColor = "Black"
    GraphicsWindow.FontSize = 14
    HintButton = Controls.AddButton("Hint", 450, 470)
    Controls.SetSize(HintButton, 100, 30)
    StopButton = Controls.AddButton("Stop", 450, 510)
    Controls.SetSize(StopButton, 100, 30)
    Controls.HideControl(HintButton)
    GraphicsWindow.BrushColor = "Black"
    GraphicsWindow.FontSize = 30
    GraphicsWindow.DrawText(330, 30, GameTitle)
    GraphicsWindow.BrushColor = "Blue"
    GraphicsWindow.FontSize = 24
    GraphicsWindow.DrawText(265, 200, "Scrambled Book:")
    GraphicsWindow.DrawText(160, 240, "Letters Left to Guess:")
    GraphicsWindow.BrushColor = "Black"
    For i = 1 To 26
      LetterSelected[i] = 0
    EndFor
    DrawLetters()
```

```
      BookPicked = Math.GetRandomNumber(NumberBooks)
      ScrambledWord = ""
      NumberLetters = Text.GetLength(Book[BookPicked])
    EndIf
  EndIf
EndSub

Sub TextInputEvent
  ' Picking Letters for Book
  If (GameStatus = "PickingLetters") Then
    LetterPicked =
Text.ConvertToUpperCase(GraphicsWindow.LastText)
    LetterCode = Text.GetCharacterCode(LetterPicked)
    If ((LetterCode >= Text.GetCharacterCode("A") And LetterCode
<= Text.GetCharacterCode("Z")) And LetterSelected[LetterCode - 64]
= 0) Then
      LetterSelected[LetterCode - 64] = 1
      DrawLetters()
      'see if it is in word
      For i = 1 to NumberLetters
        If (LetterPicked = Text.GetSubText(Book[BookPicked], i,
1)) Then
          ScrambledWord = ScrambledWord + LetterPicked
        EndIf
      EndFor
      GraphicsWindow.BrushColor = "White"
      GraphicsWindow.FillRectangle(490, 200, 300, 30)
      GraphicsWindow.BrushColor = "Black"
      GraphicsWindow.DrawText(490, 200, ScrambledWord)
      If (Text.GetLength(ScrambledWord) = NumberLetters) Then
        GameStatus = "GettingBooks"
        GraphicsWindow.BrushColor = "White"
        GraphicsWindow.FillRectangle(0, 200, 1000, 100)
        GraphicsWindow.BrushColor = "Blue"
        GraphicsWindow.DrawText(230, 200, "Unscrambled Book:")
        GraphicsWindow.DrawText(260, 240, "Scrambled Book:")
        GraphicsWindow.BrushColor = "Black"
        GraphicsWindow.DrawText(490, 240, ScrambledWord)
        Controls.ShowControl(HintButton)
        BookEntering = 0 '0 unscramble, -1 before book, 1 after
book
        BookName = Book[BookPicked]
        EnteredBook = ""
      EndIf
    EndIf
  ElseIf (GameStatus = "GettingBooks") Then
```

```
    LetterPicked =
Text.ConvertToUpperCase(GraphicsWindow.LastText)
    LetterCode = Text.GetCharacterCode(LetterPicked)
    If ((LetterCode >= Text.GetCharacterCode("A") And LetterCode
<= Text.GetCharacterCode("Z"))) Then
      EnteredBook = EnteredBook + LetterPicked
      DisplayEnteredBook()
     ElseIf (LetterCode = 8 And Text.GetLength(EnteredBook) <> 0)
Then
      'Backspace
      EnteredBook = Text.GetSubText(EnteredBook, 1,
Text.GetLength(EnteredBook) - 1)
      DisplayEnteredBook()
    ElseIf (LetterCode = 13) Then
      CheckEnteredBook()
    EndIf
  EndIf
EndSub

Sub DisplayIntroScreen
  GameStatus = "ChoosingGame"
  GraphicsWindow.Clear()
  GraphicsWindow.Title = "Bible Book Scramble Game"
  GraphicsWindow.BackgroundColor = "White"
  GraphicsWindow.Width = 1000
  GraphicsWindow.Height = 550
  GraphicsWindow.BrushColor = "Black"
  GraphicsWindow.FontSize = 24
  GraphicsWindow.DrawText(330, 30, "Bible Book Scramble Game")
  GraphicsWindow.FontSize = 18
  GraphicsWindow.DrawText(330, 60, " © BIBLEBYTE BOOKS, 1982-
2010")
  GraphicsWindow.DrawText(380, 100, "1 - Old Testament Books")
  GraphicsWindow.DrawText(380, 130, "2 - New Testament Books")
  GraphicsWindow.FontSize = 16
  GraphicsWindow.DrawText(250, 200, "Rules: The computer has
chosen one of the books from the Bible.")
  GraphicsWindow.DrawText(250, 230, "You must guess which book it
is by first guessing the correct letters.")
  GraphicsWindow.DrawText(250, 260, "You then unscramble the book
name from these letters.  After that,")
  GraphicsWindow.DrawText(250, 290, "you must name the book before
and after the unscrambled book. ")
  GraphicsWindow.DrawText(250, 320, "Spell Song of Solomon as one
word.  Also, consider 1 & 2 Kings")
```

```
  GraphicsWindow.DrawText(250, 350, "as just Kings. Do the same
for Samuel, Chronicles, Peter, Timothy,")
  GraphicsWindow.DrawText(250, 380, "Corinthians, Thessalonians
and John.")
  GraphicsWindow.DrawText(250, 450, "To Begin, Press 1 for the Old
Testament or Press 2 for the New Testament")
EndSub

Sub DrawLetters
  'draw available letters
  LM = 440
  GraphicsWindow.BrushColor = "White"
  GraphicsWindow.FillRectangle(LM, 240, 500, 30)
  Letters = ""
  For i = 1 To 26
    If (LetterSelected[i] = 0) Then
      Letters = Letters + Text.GetCharacter(64 + i)
    EndIf
  EndFor
  GraphicsWindow.BrushColor = "Black"
  GraphicsWindow.DrawText(LM, 240, Letters)
EndSub

Sub CheckEnteredBook
  If (EnteredBook = Book[BookPicked + BookEntering]) Then
    'correct entry - move on to next book
    If (BookEntering = 0) Then
      'move to before book
      BookEntering = -1
      'clear scrambled word and setup for before book
      GraphicsWindow.BrushColor = "White"
      GraphicsWindow.FillRectangle(100, 240, 900, 30)
      GraphicsWindow.FontSize = 24
      GraphicsWindow.BrushColor = "Blue"
      GraphicsWindow.DrawText(305, 120, "Book Before:")
      'if bookpicked is 1 - there may  be no before book
      If (BookPicked = 1 And Book[0] = "NONE") Then
        GraphicsWindow.BrushColor = "Black"
        GraphicsWindow.DrawText(490, 120, "NONE")
        Goto DoAfterBook
      EndIf
      BookName = Book[BookPicked - 1]
      EnteredBook = ""
    ElseIf (BookEntering = -1) Then
      DoAfterBook:
      'move to after book
```

```
      BookEntering = 1
      GraphicsWindow.FontSize = 24
      GraphicsWindow.BrushColor = "Blue"
      GraphicsWindow.DrawText(315, 280, "Book After:")
      'if bookpicked is Numberbooks - there may  be no afer book
      If (BookPicked = NumberBooks And Book[NumberBooks + 1] =
"NONE") Then
        GraphicsWindow.BrushColor = "Black"
        GraphicsWindow.DrawText(490, 280, "NONE")
        Goto Done
      EndIf
      BookName = Book[BookPicked + 1]
      EnteredBook = ""
    Else
      Done:
      'done - erase  buttons
      GraphicsWindow.BrushColor = "White"
      GraphicsWindow.FillRectangle(440, 460, 120, 90)
      Sound.PlayChime()
      GraphicsWindow.ShowMessage("Now, share the importance of " +
Book[BookPicked] + " with your friends and family.", "Good Job!")
      DisplayIntroScreen()
    EndIf
  Else
    EnteredBook = ""
    DisplayEnteredBook()
  EndIf
EndSub

Sub DisplayEnteredBook
  GraphicsWindow.BrushColor = "White"
  GraphicsWindow.FillRectangle(490, 200 + BookEntering * 80, 500,
30)
  If (Text.GetLength(EnteredBook) <> 0) Then
    GraphicsWindow.FontSize = 24
    GraphicsWindow.BrushColor = "Black"
    GraphicsWindow.DrawText(490, 200 + BookEntering * 80,
EnteredBook)
  EndIf
EndSub
```

Program 7 – Memory Game

Program Design

In this Small Basic game for little kids, ten squares are used to hide five different pairs of shapes. The player (using the mouse) chooses two squares on the board and the shapes behind them are revealed. If the shapes match, those squares are removed from the board. If there is no match, the shapes are recovered and the player tries again. The play continues until all five pairs are matched up. The program is saved in the **Memory** folder in the program folder (**\BeginSB\BSB Code**).

Program Development

Start Small Basic, start a new program and save it as **Memory**. Type in (or copy and paste from these notes) the complete **Memory** Small Basic code:

```
'
'  Memory Game
' Beginning Small Basic
'
' create window
GraphicsWindow.Show()
GraphicsWindow.Title = "Memory"
GraphicsWindow.Width = 410
GraphicsWindow.Height = 220
' randomly sort integers from 1 to 10
NumberOfIntegers = 10
NIntegers()
Behind = NumberList
' initialize available array to true
' any numbers greater than 5, reduce by 5 for matched set
For i = 1 To 10
  Available[i] = "true"
  If (Behind[i] > 5) Then
```

```
    Behind[i] = Behind[i] - 5
  EndIf
EndFor
' pick five random colors for the shapes
For i =1 To 5
  MyColor[i] = Graphicswindow.GetRandomColor()
EndFor
' draw boxes
x = 10
y = 50
BoxColor = GraphicsWindow.GetRandomColor()
GraphicsWindow.BrushColor = BoxColor
For i = 1 To 10
  GraphicsWindow.FillRectangle(x, y, 70, 70)
  x = x + 80
  If (x > 330) Then
    x = 10
    y = y + 80
  EndIf
EndFor
' set to first choice - we're ready to go
Choice = 1
GraphicsWindow.MouseDown = MouseDownEvent
Timer.Interval = 1000
Timer.Tick = TimerTickEvent
Timer.Pause()

Sub MouseDownEvent
  Temp = 0
  ' make sure clicked in box area
  ClickX = GraphicsWindow.MouseX
  ClickY = GraphicsWindow.MouseY
  If (ClickX > 10 And ClickX < 400 And ClickY > 50 And ClickY <
200) Then
    ' figure out which box was clicked
    If (ClickY > 130) Then
      ' second row (6 to 10)
      Temp = Math.Floor(6 + (ClickX - 5) / 80)
    Else
      ' first row (1 to 5)
      Temp = Math.Floor(1 + (ClickX - 5) / 80)
    EndIf
  EndIf
  If (Temp <> 0) Then
    Picked[Choice] = Temp
    ' only execute following code:
```

```
    ' if box is  still available
    ' and not picking same box with second choice
    If (Available[Temp] = "true" And (Choice = 1 Or (Choice = 2
And Picked[1] <> Picked[2]))) Then
      ' draw selected shape
      Shape = Behind[Picked[Choice]]
      Box = Picked[Choice]
      DrawShape()
      If (Choice = 1) Then
        ' first choice - just display
        Choice = 2
      Else
        ' turn on timer to check results
        Timer.Resume()
      EndIf
    Endif
  EndIf
EndSub

Sub TimerTickEvent
  ' check for match once timer event occurs
  Timer.Pause()
  If (Behind[Picked[1]] = Behind[Picked[2]]) Then
    ' If match, remove shapes
    Available[Picked[1]] = "false"
    Available[Picked[2]] = "false"
    Shape = -2
    Box = Picked[1]
    DrawShape()
    Box = Picked[2]
    DrawShape()
  Else
    ' If no match, restore boxes
    Shape = -1
    Box = Picked[1]
    DrawShape()
    Box = Picked[2]
    DrawShape()
  EndIf
  Choice = 1
EndSub

Sub DrawShape
  'Draw Shape in Box
  ' get coordinates of Box
  If (Box > 5) Then
```

```
    yBox = 130
    xBox = 10 + (Box - 6) * 80
  Else
    yBox = 50
    xBox = 10 + (Box - 1) * 80
  EndIf
  ' Clear Box
  GraphicsWindow.BrushColor = GraphicsWindow.BackgroundColor
  GraphicsWindow.FillRectangle(xBox, YBox, 70, 70)
  ' draw shape (do nothing if Shape = -2; it just erases box)
  If (Shape = -1) Then
    'Shape = -1, draw covered box
    GraphicsWindow.BrushColor = BoxColor
    GraphicsWindow.FillRectangle(xBox, YBox, 70, 70)
  ElseIf (Shape = 1) Then
    ' circle
    GraphicsWindow.BrushColor = MyColor[1]
    GraphicsWindow.FillEllipse(xBox, yBox, 70, 70)
  ElseIf (Shape = 2) Then
    ' plus sign
    GraphicsWindow.BrushColor = MyColor[2]
    GraphicsWindow.FillRectangle(xBox, yBox + 25, 70, 20)
    GraphicsWindow.FillRectangle(xBox + 25, yBox, 20, 70)
  ElseIf (Shape = 3) Then
    ' open square
    GraphicsWindow.BrushColor = MyColor[3]
    GraphicsWindow.FillRectangle(xBox, YBox, 70, 70)
    GraphicsWindow.BrushColor = GraphicsWindow.BackgroundColor
    GraphicsWindow.FillRectangle(xBox + 20, yBox + 20, 30, 30)
  ElseIf (Shape = 4) Then
    ' rectangle
    GraphicsWindow.BrushColor = MyColor[3]
    GraphicsWindow.FillRectangle(xBox + 20, yBox, 30, 70)
  ElseIf (Shape = 5) Then
    ' ellipse
    GraphicsWindow.BrushColor = MyColor[5]
    GraphicsWindow.FillEllipse(xBox + 20, yBox, 30, 70)
  EndIf
EndSub

Sub NIntegers
  'One card shuffle code
  'Initialize NumberList
  For LoopCounter = 1 to NumberOfIntegers
    NumberList[LoopCounter] = LoopCounter
  EndFor
```

```
  'Work through Remaining values
  'Start at NumberOfItems and swap one value
  'at each For loop step
  'After each step, Remaining is decreased by 1
  For Remaining = NumberOfIntegers to 2 Step -1
    'Pick item at random
    ItemPicked = Math.GetRandomNumber(Remaining)
    'Swap picked item with bottom item
    TempValue = NumberList[Remaining]
    NumberList[Remaining] = NumberList[ItemPicked]
    NumberList[ItemPicked] = TempValue
  EndFor
EndSub
```

This code sets up the graphics window and event subroutines for mouse presses and timer events (used to implement a delay after displaying shapes). Variables are established to keep track of what shape is behind what box, whether a box has been selected and colors. Notice the hidden shapes are specified by an array of random integers. This computation uses the **NIntegers** subroutine developed back in Class 7. The **MouseDown** event method is used to select boxes (each box is 70 pixels by 70 pixels in size) for display of shapes. The **DrawShape** subroutine is used to draw a particular shape at a particular location. Finally, the timer's subroutine is where we check for a match between selected shapes. The timer is used in the program to insert a one second delay (**Interval** of 1000) between the time the last shape selected is displayed and a decision is made about a match. See if you can follow the code that implements all these steps.

Run the Program

Save your work. Run the program. Ten boxes appear. Click on one and view the shape. Click on another. If there is a match, the two shapes are removed (after a delay). If there is no match, the boxes are restored (also after a delay). The game stops when all matching shape pairs have been found. Here's what the window looks like in the middle of a game:

Other Things to Try

Some things to help improve or change this game: add a scoring system to keep track of how many tries you took to find all the matches, make it a two player game where you compete against another player or the computer, or set it up to match other items (colors, upper and lower case letters, numbers and objects, etc.). You might also add logic to let you play again (without rerunning the program), once a game is finished. And, the colors selected are random – what happens if white is selected? See if you can figure out a way to avoid choosing colors that don't look good on a white background.

Program 8 – The Prodigal Son Game

Program Design

This program is the classic Lost Coin Game. The program is saved in the **Prodigal** folder in the program folder (**\BeginSB\BSB Code**.

Program Development

Start Small Basic, start a new program and save it as **Prodigal**. Type in (or copy and paste from these notes) the complete **Prodigal** Small Basic code.

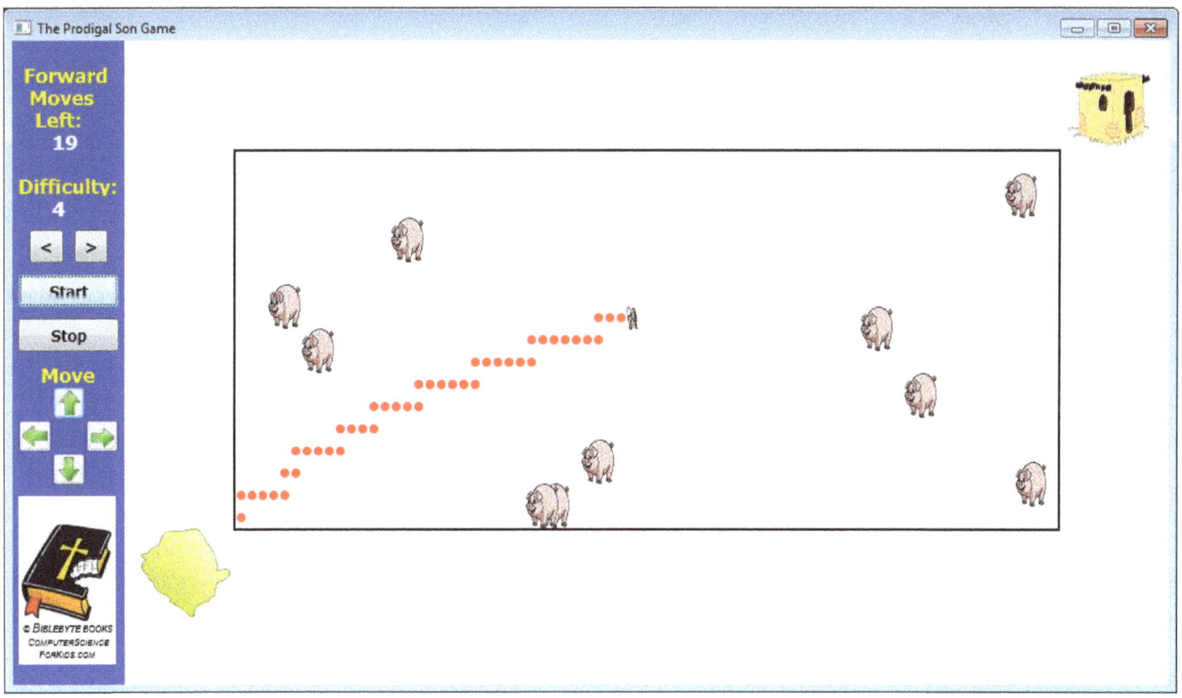

```
' The Prodigal Son Game
' Small Basic Version
'
' Intro screen
IntroScreen:
Difficulty = 1
GameStatus = "Selecting"
GraphicsWindow.Show()
GraphicsWindow.Title = "The Prodigal Son Game"
GraphicsWindow.BackgroundColor = "White"
GraphicsWindow.Width = 1040
GraphicsWindow.Height = 580
GraphicsWindow.BrushColor = "Black"
GraphicsWindow.FontSize = 14
GraphicsWindow.DrawText(110, 10, "THE PRODIGAL SON GAME")
GraphicsWindow.DrawText(110, 30, "In Luke 15:11-32, Jesus tells a parable about a prodigal son who foolishly leaves home and squanders his inheritance")
GraphicsWindow.DrawText(110, 50, "in a distant land.  After he runs out of money he has to work by feeding pigs.  When he comes to his senses he returns")
GraphicsWindow.DrawText(110, 70, "home to his father where his father has a large party to celebrate his sons return.  No matter how far we wander from God")
GraphicsWindow.DrawText(110, 90, "he always welcomes us home and forgives us of our sins.")
GraphicsWindow.DrawText(110, 130, "Help the prodigal son find his way home from the distant land all the way back to his father. To help him survive, ")
GraphicsWindow.DrawText(110, 150, "the prodigal son must find pig feeding jobs every 25 moves along the way so he can eat and eventually make his way home.")
GraphicsWindow.DrawText(110, 180, "<-- Select Difficulty by pressing the left button for Easy and the right button for Harder.")
GraphicsWindow.DrawText(110, 220, "<-- Click on the Start Button to begin.")
GraphicsWindow.DrawText(110, 260, "<-- Click on the Stop Button to stop the program.")
GraphicsWindow.DrawText(110, 360, "<-- Use these buttons (or arrow keys) to move the prodigal son.")
GraphicsWindow.DrawText(110, 550, "Find more Computer Programming Tutorials @ http://www.BibleByteBooks.com or http://www.ComputerScienceForKids.com")
```

```
GraphicsWindow.BrushColor = "Blue"
GraphicsWindow.FillRectangle(0, 0, 100, GraphicsWindow.Height)
GraphicsWindow.BrushColor = "Yellow"
GraphicsWindow.FontSize = 18
GraphicsWindow.DrawText(10, 20, "Forward")
GraphicsWindow.DrawText(15, 40, "Moves")
GraphicsWindow.DrawText(20, 60, "Left:")
GraphicsWindow.DrawText(5, 120, "Difficulty:")
GraphicsWindow.DrawText(25, 290, "Move")
GraphicsWindow.BrushColor = "White"
GraphicsWindow.FontSize = 18
GraphicsWindow.DrawText(35, 140, Difficulty)
MoveImage = ImageList.LoadImage(Program.Directory +
"\FourArrows.jpg")
MoveButtons = Shapes.AddImage(MoveImage)
Shapes.Move(MoveButtons, 5, 310)
LogoImage = ImageList.LoadImage(Program.Directory +
"\LogoHolder.jpg")
Logo = Shapes.AddImage(LogoImage)
Shapes.Move(Logo, 5, 410)
'add button controls
GraphicsWindow.BrushColor = "Black"
GraphicsWindow.FontSize = 14
DecreaseButton = Controls.AddButton("<", 15, 170)
Controls.SetSize(DecreaseButton, 30, 30)
IncreaseButton = Controls.AddButton(">", 55, 170)
Controls.SetSize(IncreaseButton, 30, 30)
StartButton = Controls.AddButton("Start", 5, 210)
Controls.SetSize(StartButton, 90, 30)
StopButton = Controls.AddButton("Stop", 5, 250)
Controls.SetSize(StopButton, 90, 30)
Controls.ButtonClicked = ButtonClickedEvent
GraphicsWindow.MouseDown = MouseDownEvent
GraphicsWindow.KeyDown = KeyDownEvent

Sub ButtonClickedEvent
  BBB = Controls.LastClickedButton
  If (GameStatus = "Selecting") Then
    If (BBB = DecreaseButton) Then
      ' decrease difficulty
      Difficulty = Difficulty - 1
      If (Difficulty < 1) Then
        Difficulty = 1
      EndIf
      GraphicsWindow.BrushColor = "Blue"
      GraphicsWindow.FillRectangle(0, 140, 100, 20)
```

```
      GraphicsWindow.BrushColor = "White"
      GraphicsWindow.FontSize = 18
      GraphicsWindow.DrawText(35, 140, Difficulty)
    ElseIf (BBB = IncreaseButton) Then
      'increase difficulty
      Difficulty = Difficulty + 1
      If (Difficulty > 10) Then
        Difficulty = 10
      EndIf
      GraphicsWindow.BrushColor = "Blue"
      GraphicsWindow.FillRectangle(0, 140, 100, 20)
      GraphicsWindow.BrushColor = "White"
      GraphicsWindow.FontSize = 18
      GraphicsWindow.DrawText(35, 140, Difficulty)
    ElseIf (BBB = StopButton) Then
      'clicked stop
      Program.End()
    ElseIf (BBB = StartButton) Then
      'clicked start
      GraphicsWindow.BrushColor = "White"
      GraphicsWindow.FillRectangle(100, 0, GraphicsWindow.Width -
100, GraphicsWindow.Height)
      Moves = 0
      DisplayMoves()
      '  draw game area structure
      GraphicsWindow.BrushColor = "Black"
      GraphicsWindow.FillRectangle(198, 98, 744, 344)
      GraphicsWindow.BrushColor = "White"
      GraphicsWindow.FillRectangle(200, 100, 740, 340)
      ' A array (0-nothing, <> 0 - pig number)
      For i = 1 to 17
        For j = 1 to 74
          A[i][j] = 0
        EndFor
      EndFor
      'add house and country
      HouseImage = ImageList.LoadImage(Program.Directory +
"\House.jpg")
      House = Shapes.AddImage(HouseImage)
      Shapes.Move(House, 945, 20)
      CountryImage = ImageList.LoadImage(Program.Directory +
"\Country.jpg")
      Country = Shapes.AddImage(CountryImage)
      Shapes.Move(Country, 115, 440)
      'setup pig image
```

```
      PigImage = ImageList.LoadImage(Program.Directory +
"\Pig.gif")
      'animate son
      SonImage = ImageList.LoadImage(Program.Directory +
"\Son.jpg")
      Son = Shapes.AddImage(SonImage)
      SonRow = 1
      SonColumn = 74
      Shapes.Move(Son, SonColumn * 10 + 190, SonRow * 20 + 80)
      SonRow = 17
      SonColumn = 1
      Shapes.Animate(Son, SonColumn * 10 + 190, SonRow * 20 + 80,
2000)
      GameStatus = "SonMove"
      GameOver = "false"
      BackwardMovesTaken = 0
      ForwardMovesLeft = 25
      NumberPigs = 0
      DisplayMoves()
    EndIf
  EndIf
  If (GameStatus <> "Selecting") Then
    If (BBB = StopButton) Then
      'clicked stop while playing
      GameStatus = "Selecting"
      GraphicsWindow.ShowMessage("You stopped the game.", "Game
Over")
      Shapes.Remove(Son)
      Shapes.Remove(House)
      Shapes.Remove(Country)
      'remove pigs
      If (NumberPigs <> 0) Then
        For i = 1 to NumberPigs
          Shapes.Remove(Pig[i])
        EndFor
      EndIf
    EndIf
  EndIf
EndSub

Sub MouseDownEvent
  If (GameStatus = "SonMove") Then
    'Move staff
    'clicks on move buttons
    If (GraphicsWindow.MouseX > Shapes.GetLeft(MoveButtons) And
GraphicsWindow.MouseX < Shapes.GetLeft(MoveButtons) + 90) Then
```

```
      If (GraphicsWindow.MouseY > Shapes.GetTop(MoveButtons) And
GraphicsWindow.MouseY < Shapes.GetTop(MoveButtons) + 90) Then
        DeltaRow = Math.Floor((GraphicsWindow.MouseY -
Shapes.GetTop(MoveButtons)) / 30) - 1
        DeltaColumn = Math.Floor((GraphicsWindow.MouseX -
Shapes.GetLeft(MoveButtons)) / 30) - 1
        'check if move is okay
        CheckMove()
      EndIf
    EndIf
    DisplayMoves()
    IsGameOver()
  EndIf
EndSub

Sub CheckMove
  NewRow = SonRow + DeltaRow
  NewColumn = SonColumn + DeltaColumn
  MoveOkay = "false"
  If (DeltaRow = 0 And DeltaColumn = 1) Then
    ' right arrow - forward move
    MoveOkay = "true"
    ForwardMovesLeft = ForwardMovesLeft - 1
  ElseIf (DeltaRow = 0 And DeltaColumn = -1) Then
    'left arrow - backward move
    MoveOkay = "true"
    BackwardMovesTaken = BackwardMovesTaken + 1
  ElseIf (DeltaRow = 1 And DeltaColumn = 0) Then
    'down arrow - backward move
    MoveOkay = "true"
    BackwardMovesTaken = BackwardMovesTaken + 1
  ElseIf (DeltaRow = -1 And DeltaColumn = 0) Then
    'up arrow - forward move
    MoveOkay = "true"
    ForwardMovesLeft = ForwardMovesLeft - 1
  EndIf
  If (NewRow < 1 Or NewRow > 17 Or NewColumn < 1 Or NewColumn >
74) Then
    ' off  grid
    MoveOkay = "false"
  EndIf
  If (MoveOkay = "true" And A[NewRow][NewColumn] <> 0) Then
    MoveOkay = "true"
    'got a pig - add moves
    If (FoundPig[A[NewRow][NewColumn]] = "false") Then
      Shapes.Remove(Pig[A[NewRow][NewColumn]])
```

```
      FoundPig[A[NewRow][NewColumn]] = "true"
      ForwardMovesLeft = 60 - (Difficulty - 1) * 5
    EndIf
  EndIf
  If (MoveOkay = "true") Then
    Shapes.Move(Son, NewColumn * 10 + 190, NewRow * 20 + 80)
    GraphicsWindow.BrushColor = "Red"
    GraphicsWindow.FillEllipse(SonColumn * 10 + 191, SonRow * 20 +
86, 8, 8)
    SonRow = NewRow
    SonColumn = NewColumn
    'do we add a pig?
    PigRow = 1 + Math.GetRandomNumber(15)
    PigColumn = 1 + Math.GetRandomNumber(200 + Difficulty * 15)
    'make sure on grid
    If (PigColumn > 72) Then
      Goto NoPig
    EndIf
    'make sure not covering son
    If (SonRow = PigRow Or SonRow = PigRow + 1 Or SonColumn =
PigColumn Or SonColumn = PigColumn + 1 Or SonColumn = PigColumn +
2) Then
      Goto NoPig
    EndIf
    NumberPigs = NumberPigs + 1
    Pig[NumberPigs] = Shapes.AddImage(PigImage)
    Shapes.Move(Pig[NumberPigs], PigColumn * 10 + 190, PigRow * 20
+ 80)
    FoundPig[NumberPigs] = "false"
    A[PigRow][PigColumn] = NumberPigs
    A[PigRow + 1][PigColumn] = NumberPigs
    A[PigRow][PigColumn + 1] = NumberPigs
    A[PigRow + 1][PigColumn + 1] = NumberPigs
    A[PigRow][PigColumn + 2] = NumberPigs
    A[PigRow + 1][PigColumn + 2] = NumberPigs
   NoPig:
  EndIf
 ' forward/backward move checks
  If (ForwardMovesLeft = 0) Then
    GameOver = "true"
    GameOverReason = "NoMoreForwardMoves"
  ElseIf (BackwardMovesTaken > 50) Then
    GameOver = "true"
    GameOverReason = "NoMoreBackwardMoves"
  EndIf
  If (NewRow = 1 And NewColumn = 74) Then
```

```
    'got home
    GameOver = "true"
    GameOverReason = "GotHome"
  EndIf
EndSub

Sub IsGameOver
  If (GameOver = "true") Then
    'game is over
    GameStatus = "Selecting"
    If (GameOverReason = "GotHome") Then
      Sound.PlayChimes()
      GraphicsWindow.ShowMessage("You made it all the way back
home to your father. Praise the Lord!", "Game Over")
    ElseIf (GameOverReason = "NoMoreForwardMoves") Then
      GraphicsWindow.ShowMessage("You ran out of forward moves -
the game has stopped.", "Game Over")
    Else
      GraphicsWindow.ShowMessage("You backtracked too much - the
game has stopped.", "Game Over")
    EndIf
    Shapes.Remove(Son)
    Shapes.Remove(House)
    Shapes.Remove(Country)
    'remove pigs
    If (NumberPigs <> 0) Then
      For i = 1 to NumberPigs
        Shapes.Remove(Pig[i])
      EndFor
    EndIf
  EndIf
EndSub



Sub DisplayMoves
  GraphicsWindow.FontSize = 18
  GraphicsWindow.BrushColor = "Blue"
  GraphicsWindow.FillRectangle(0, 80, 100, 20)
  GraphicsWindow.BrushColor = "White"
  GraphicsWindow.DrawText(35, 80, ForwardMovesLeft)
EndSub

Sub KeyDownEvent
  If (GameStatus = "SonMove") Then
    K = GraphicsWindow.LastKey
```

```
    DeltaRow = 0
    DeltaColumn = 0
    If (K = "NumPad8" Or K = "Up") Then
      DeltaRow = -1
      DeltaColumn = 0
    EndIf
    If (K = "NumPad4" Or K = "Left") Then
      DeltaRow = 0
      DeltaColumn = -1
    EndIf
    If (K = "NumPad6" Or K = "Right") Then
      DeltaRow = 0
      DeltaColumn = 1
    EndIf
    If (K = "NumPad2" Or K = "Down") Then
      DeltaRow = 1
      DeltaColumn = 0
    EndIf
    CheckMove()
    DisplayMoves()
    IsGameOver()
  EndIf
EndSub
```

Program 9 - Decode

Program Design

This program is a classic computer game. The computer generates a four-color code using six possible colors (with no repeating colors). You guess at the code. The computer then tells you how many colors in your guess are correct and how many colors are in the correct location. Based on these clues, you make a new guess. You continue guessing until you have cracked the code. The program is saved in the **Decode** folder in the program folder (**\BeginSB\BSB Code**.

Program Development

Start Small Basic, start a new program and save it as **Decode**. Type in (or copy and paste from these notes) the complete **Decode** Small Basic code:

```
'
'  Decode Program
'  Beginning Small Basic
'
' create frame
GraphicsWindow.Show()
GraphicsWindow.Width = 820
GraphicsWindow.Height = 460
GraphicsWindow.Title = "Decode Colors: R-Red, B-Blue, G-Green, P-Purple, W-White, Y-Yellow"
GraphicsWindow.BackgroundColor = "Gray"
CurrentX = 10
CurrentY = 40
PositionNumber = 1
GameOver = "false"

' put four random digits in array
```

```
' use NIntegers method
'we randomize 6 integers, but use first 4, one for each color
NumberOfIntegers = 6
NIntegers()
ComputerCode = NumberList
' drawBlank ovals, give form focus
DrawBlanks()
GraphicsWindow.KeyDown = KeyDownEvent

Sub KeyDownEvent
  If (gameOver = "true") Then
    Goto ExitSub
  EndIf
  If (GraphicsWindow.LastKey = "R") Then
    'red
    EllipseColor = "Red"
    ColorNumber = 1
  ElseIf (GraphicsWindow.LastKey = "B") Then
    'blue
    EllipseColor = "Blue"
    ColorNumber = 2
  ElseIf (GraphicsWindow.LastKey = "G") Then
    'green
    EllipseColor = "Green"
    ColorNumber = 3
  ElseIf (GraphicsWindow.LastKey = "P") Then
    'purple
    EllipseColor = "Magenta"
    ColorNumber = 4
  ElseIf (GraphicsWindow.LastKey = "W") Then
    'white
    EllipseColor = "White"
    ColorNumber = 5
  ElseIf (GraphicsWindow.LastKey = "Y") Then
    'yellow
    EllipseColor = "Yellow"
    ColorNumber = 6
  Else
    'some other key
    Goto ExitSub
  EndIf
  If (PositionNumber > 1) Then
    ' make sure it is a unique choice
    For i = 1 To PositionNumber - 1
      If (YourGuess[i] = ColorNumber) Then
        ' if already used, exit the subroutine
```

```
        Goto ExitSub
      EndIf
    EndFor
  EndIf
  GraphicsWindow.BrushColor = EllipseColor
  GraphicsWindow.FillEllipse(CurrentX + (PositionNumber - 1) * 30,
CurrentY, 20, 40)
  YourGuess[PositionNumber] = ColorNumber
  PositionNumber = PositionNumber + 1
  ' if 4 colors have been enter - check the guess
  If (PositionNumber = 5) Then
    NumberInCode = 0
    NumberInCorrectPosition = 0
    For i = 1 To 4
      For j = 1 To 4
        If (YourGuess[i] = ComputerCode[j]) Then
          NumberInCode = NumberInCode + 1
          If (i = j) Then
            NumberInCorrectPosition = NumberInCorrectPosition + 1
          EndIf
        EndIf
      EndFor
    EndFor
    ' print score
    GraphicsWindow.BrushColor = "White"
    GraphicsWindow.DrawText(CurrentX + 120, CurrentY + 25,
NumberInCode + "/" + NumberInCorrectPosition)
    If (NumberInCorrectPosition = 4) Then
      ' game over
      GameOver = "true"
      GraphicsWindow.Title = "You got the code ... the game is
over!"
    Else
      ' set up for next guess
      CurrentY = CurrentY + 60
      If (CurrentY > 400) Then
        CurrentY = 40
        CurrentX = CurrentX + 200
      EndIf
      PositionNumber = 1
      DrawBlanks()
    EndIf
  EndIf
ExitSub:
EndSub
```

```
Sub DrawBlanks
  ' draw four blank ovals at current position
  GraphicsWindow.PenColor = "White"
  For i = 1 to 4
    GraphicsWindow.DrawEllipse(CurrentX + (i - 1) * 30, CurrentY,
20, 40)
  EndFor
EndSub

Sub NIntegers
  'One card shuffle code
  'Initialize NumberList
  For LoopCounter = 1 to NumberOfIntegers
    NumberList[LoopCounter] = LoopCounter
  EndFor
  'Work through Remaining values
  'Start at NumberOfItems and swap one value
  'at each For loop step
  'After each step, Remaining is decreased by 1
  For Remaining = NumberOfIntegers to 2 Step -1
    'Pick item at random
    ItemPicked = Math.GetRandomNumber(Remaining)
    'Swap picked item with bottom item
    TempValue = NumberList[Remaining]
    NumberList[Remaining] = NumberList[ItemPicked]
    NumberList[ItemPicked] = TempValue
  EndFor
EndSub
```

Most of the code in this program is involved with generating a four-color computer code and checking the guess you input. Once the window is established, a code is selected (using a variation of the **NIntegers** random integer method we use). You choose colors by typing one of six keys:

R-Red
B-Blue
G-Green
P-Purple (really magenta)
W-White
Y-Yellow

Make sure you understand the code in the **KeyDownEvent** subroutine. See, too, how we make sure the colors selected have not already been used. Once the user selects four colors, their choices are compared to the computer's code. The score is printed out as a text string in the form:

```
NumberInCode/NumberInCorrectPosition
```

Once the code is guessed (NumberInCorrectPosition = 4), the game is over and a message is printed in the window title bar area.

Run the Program

Save your work. Run the program. Type a guess for the four-color code (the title bar lists the color choices). Note the computer will not let you type an illegal guess (non-distinct color). After choosing four colors, the computer will tell you how many colors are correct and how many are in the correct location. The score is displayed as two numbers separated by a slash. The first number is the number of correct colors, the second the number in the correct location. The game stops once you guess the computer's code. Here's a game I played:

Other Things to Try

You can give this game a variable difficulty by allowing the user to choose how many colors are in the code, how many colors are used to generate the code, and whether colors can repeat. See if you can code up and implement some of these options. You might also implement a "play again" logic or also give the player the option to "give up" and see the correct code.

Lastly, many mathematical papers have been written on developing a computer program that can decode the kinds of codes used here. Do you think you could write a computer program to determine a four color code you make up? The program would work like this: (1) computer makes a guess, (2) you tell computer how many colors are correct and how many are in correct locations, then, (3) computer generates a new guess. The computer would continue guessing until it gave up or guessed your code.

Program 10 – The Good Shepherd Game

Program Design

This program is the classic Good Shepherd Game. The program is saved in the **Shepherd** folder in the program folder (**\BeginSB\BSB Code**.

Program Development

Start Small Basic, start a new program and save it as **Shepherd**. Type in (or copy and paste from these notes) the complete **Shepherd** Small Basic code.

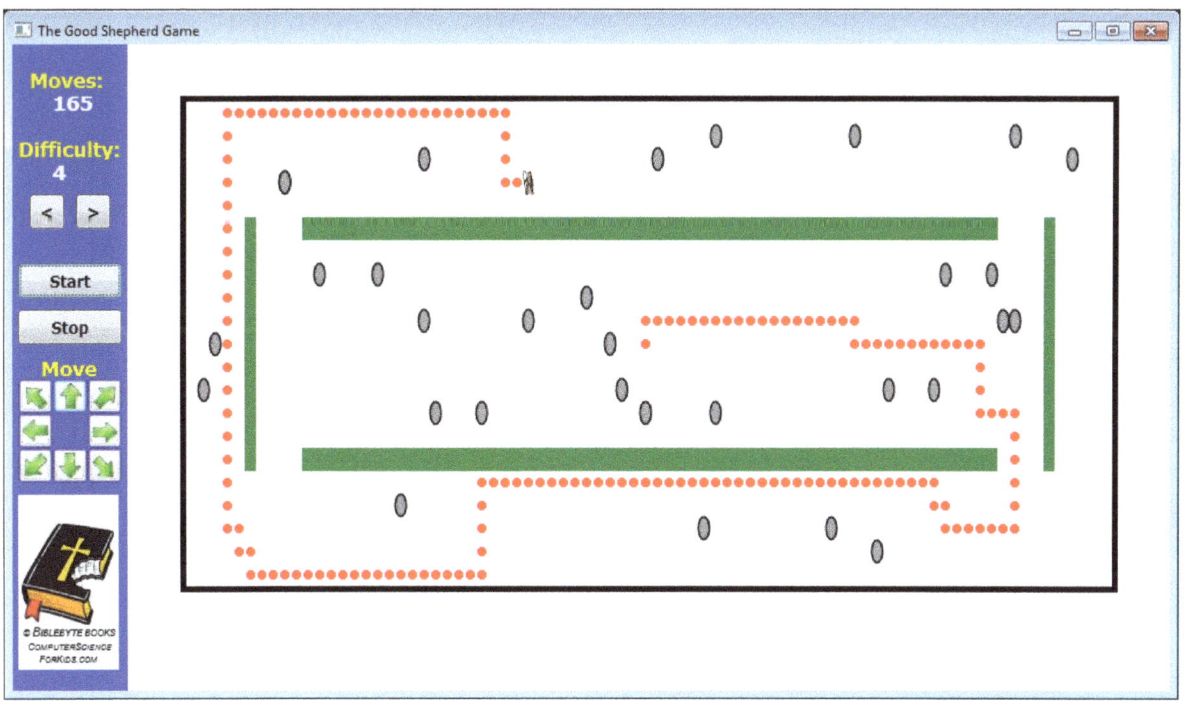

```
' The Good Shepherd Game
' Small Basic Version
'
' Intro screen
IntroScreen:
Difficulty = 1
GameStatus = "Selecting"
GraphicsWindow.Show()
GraphicsWindow.Title = "The Good Shepherd Game"
GraphicsWindow.BackgroundColor = "White"
GraphicsWindow.Width = 1000
GraphicsWindow.Height = 560
GraphicsWindow.BrushColor = "Black"
GraphicsWindow.FontSize = 14
GraphicsWindow.DrawText(110, 10, "THE GOOD SHEPHERD GAME")
GraphicsWindow.DrawText(110, 30, "In Luke 15:1-7, Jesus tells a
parable about a lost sheep.  The shepherd leaves the 99 sheep to
look for the one lost sheep.")
GraphicsWindow.DrawText(110, 50, "Once he finds the lost sheep he
rejoices!  Jesus says, in the same way, there will be more joy in
heaven over one sinner who ")
GraphicsWindow.DrawText(110, 70, "repents than over ninety-nine
righteous persons who need no repentance.  Are you the lost sheep
Jesus is looking for?")
GraphicsWindow.DrawText(110, 90, "Take the shepherd's staff and
carry it through the wilderness to find the lost sheep in the
least amount of moves.")
GraphicsWindow.DrawText(110, 110, "Hint: Look by a rock.  Sheep
feel safer around rocks.")
GraphicsWindow.DrawText(110, 140, "<-- Select Difficulty by
pressing the left button for Easy and the right button for
Harder.")
GraphicsWindow.DrawText(110, 200, "<-- Click on the Start Button
to begin.")
GraphicsWindow.DrawText(110, 240, "<-- Click on the Stop Button to
stop the program.")
GraphicsWindow.DrawText(110, 330, "<-- Use these buttons (or
keypad keys) to move the staff.")
GraphicsWindow.DrawText(110, 530, " Find more Computer Programming
Tutorials @ www.BibleByteBooks.com or
www.ComputerScienceForKids.com")
GraphicsWindow.BrushColor = "Blue"
GraphicsWindow.FillRectangle(0, 0, 100, GraphicsWindow.Height)
GraphicsWindow.BrushColor = "Yellow"
```

```
GraphicsWindow.FontSize = 18
GraphicsWindow.DrawText(15, 20, "Moves:")
GraphicsWindow.DrawText(5, 80, "Difficulty:")
GraphicsWindow.DrawText(25, 270, "Move")
GraphicsWindow.BrushColor = "White"
GraphicsWindow.FontSize = 18
GraphicsWindow.DrawText(35, 100, Difficulty)
MoveImage = ImageList.LoadImage(Program.Directory +
"\ShootButtons.jpg")
MoveButtons = Shapes.AddImage(MoveImage)
Shapes.Move(MoveButtons, 5, 290)
LogoImage = ImageList.LoadImage(Program.Directory +
"\LogoHolder.jpg")
Logo = Shapes.AddImage(LogoImage)
Shapes.Move(Logo, 5, 390)
'add button controls
GraphicsWindow.BrushColor = "Black"
GraphicsWindow.FontSize = 14
DecreaseButton = Controls.AddButton("<", 15, 130)
Controls.SetSize(DecreaseButton, 30, 30)
IncreaseButton = Controls.AddButton(">", 55, 130)
Controls.SetSize(IncreaseButton, 30, 30)
StartButton = Controls.AddButton("Start", 5, 190)
Controls.SetSize(StartButton, 90, 30)
StopButton = Controls.AddButton("Stop", 5, 230)
Controls.SetSize(StopButton, 90, 30)
Controls.ButtonClicked = ButtonClickedEvent
GraphicsWindow.MouseDown = MouseDownEvent
GraphicsWindow.KeyDown = KeyDownEvent

Sub ButtonClickedEvent
  BBB= Controls.LastClickedButton
  If (GameStatus = "Selecting") Then
    If (BBB = DecreaseButton) Then
      ' decrease difficulty
      Difficulty = Difficulty - 1
      If (Difficulty < 1) Then
        Difficulty = 1
      EndIf
      GraphicsWindow.BrushColor = "Blue"
      GraphicsWindow.FillRectangle(0, 100, 100, 20)
      GraphicsWindow.BrushColor = "White"
      GraphicsWindow.FontSize = 18
      GraphicsWindow.DrawText(35, 100, Difficulty)
    ElseIf (BBB = IncreaseButton) Then
      'increase difficulty
```

```
      Difficulty = Difficulty + 1
      If (Difficulty > 10) Then
        Difficulty = 10
      EndIf
      GraphicsWindow.BrushColor = "Blue"
      GraphicsWindow.FillRectangle(0, 100, 100, 20)
      GraphicsWindow.BrushColor = "White"
      GraphicsWindow.FontSize = 18
      GraphicsWindow.DrawText(35, 100, Difficulty)
    ElseIf (BBB = StopButton) Then
      'clicked stop
      Program.End()
    ElseIf (BBB = StartButton) Then
      'clicked start
      GameStatus = "StaffMove"
      GameOver = "false"
      StaffRow = 11
      StaffColumn = 40
      GraphicsWindow.BrushColor = "White"
      GraphicsWindow.FillRectangle(100, 0, GraphicsWindow.Width -
100, GraphicsWindow.Height)
      Moves = 0
      DisplayMoves()
      '  draw game area structure
      GraphicsWindow.BrushColor = "Black"
      GraphicsWindow.FillRectangle(145, 45, 810, 430)
      GraphicsWindow.BrushColor = "White"
      GraphicsWindow.FillRectangle(150, 50, 800, 420)
      ' A array (0-nothing, 1-barricade/rock, 2-sheep)
      For i = 1 to 21
        For j = 1 to 80
          A[i][j] = 0
        EndFor
      EndFor
      ' Barricade
      GraphicsWindow.BrushColor = "Green"
      GraphicsWindow.FillRectangle(200, 150, 10, 220)
      GraphicsWindow.FillRectangle(890, 150, 10, 220)
      For Row = 6 to 16
        A[Row][6] = 1
        A[Row][75] = 1
      EndFor
      GraphicsWindow.FillRectangle(250, 150, 600, 20)
      GraphicsWindow.FillRectangle(250, 350, 600, 20)
      For Column = 11 to 70
        A[6][Column] = 1
```

```
        A[16][Column] = 1
      EndFor
      '  Place rocks
      NumberRocks = 1 + (Difficulty - 1) * 10
      For i = 1 To NumberRocks
        GetAnother:
        Row = Math.GetRandomNumber(19) + 1
        Column = Math.GetRandomNumber(78) + 1
        ' can't be around barricades or at staff location
        If (Row = 5 Or Row = 6 Or Row = 7 Or Row = 15 Or Row = 16
Or Row = 17) Then
          Goto GetAnother
        ElseIf (Column = 5 or Column = 6 or Column = 7 or Column =
74 or Column = 75 or Column = 76) Then
          Goto GetAnother
        ElseIf (Row = StaffRow And Column = StaffColumn) Then
          Goto GetAnother
        EndIf
        RockRow[i] = Row
        RockColumn[i] = Column
        A[Row][Column] = 1
        GraphicsWindow.PenWidth = 3
        GraphicsWindow.PenColor = "Black"
        GraphicsWindow.DrawEllipse(Column * 10 + 141, Row * 20 +
31, 8, 18)
        GraphicsWindow.BrushColor = "DarkGray"
        GraphicsWindow.FillEllipse(Column * 10 + 141, Row * 20 +
31, 8, 18)
      EndFor
      'place sheep next to random rock
      PlaceSheep:
      NextToRock = Math.GetRandomNumber(NumberRocks)
      Direction = Math.GetRandomNumber(9) - 1
      DeltaRow = Math.Floor(Direction / 3) - 1
      DeltaColumn = Math.Remainder(Direction, 3) - 1
      SheepRow = RockRow[NextToRock] + DeltaRow
      SheepColumn = RockColumn[NextToRock] + DeltaColumn
      If (A[SheepRow][SheepColumn] = 1 Or (SheepRow = StaffRow And
SheepColumn = StaffColumn)) Then
        Goto PlaceSheep
      Else
        A[SheepRow][SheepColumn] = 2
      EndIf
      'Place staff
      StaffImage = ImageList.LoadImage(Program.Directory +
"\shepherd.gif")
```

```
      Staff = Shapes.AddImage(StaffImage)
      Shapes.Move(Staff, StaffColumn * 10 + 140, StaffRow * 20 +
30)
    EndIf
  EndIf
  If (GameStatus <> "Selecting") Then
    If (BBB = StopButton) Then
      'clicked stop while playing
      GameStatus = "Selecting"
      GraphicsWindow.ShowMessage("You stopped the game.", "Game
Over")
      Shapes.Remove(Staff)
    EndIf
  EndIf
EndSub
Sub MouseDownEvent
  If (GameStatus = "StaffMove") Then
    'Move staff
    'clicks on move buttons
    If (GraphicsWindow.MouseX > Shapes.GetLeft(MoveButtons) And
GraphicsWindow.MouseX < Shapes.GetLeft(MoveButtons) + 90) Then
      If (GraphicsWindow.MouseY > Shapes.GetTop(MoveButtons) And
GraphicsWindow.MouseY < Shapes.GetTop(MoveButtons) + 90) Then
        DeltaRow = Math.Floor((GraphicsWindow.MouseY -
Shapes.GetTop(MoveButtons)) / 30) - 1
        DeltaColumn = Math.Floor((GraphicsWindow.MouseX -
Shapes.GetLeft(MoveButtons)) / 30) - 1
        'check if move is okay
        NewRow = StaffRow + DeltaRow
        NewColumn = StaffColumn + DeltaColumn
        CheckMove()
      EndIf
    EndIf
    DisplayMoves()
    IsGameOver()
  EndIf
EndSub

Sub CheckMove
  If (DeltaRow <> 0 Or DeltaColumn <> 0) Then
    Moves = Moves + 1
    Sound.PlayClick()
  EndIf
  MoveOkay = "true"
  If (NewRow < 1 Or NewRow > 21 Or NewColumn < 1 Or NewColumn > 80
Or (DeltaRow = 0 And DeltaColumn = 0)) Then
```

```
    ' off grid or clicked center area
    MoveOkay = "false"
  ElseIf (A[NewRow][NewColumn] = 1) Then
    'moving to rock
    MoveOkay = "false"
  ElseIf (A[NewRow][NewColumn] = 2) Then
    'moving to sheep
    MoveOkay = "false"
    GameOver = "true"
  EndIf
  If (MoveOkay = "true") Then
    Shapes.Move(Staff, NewColumn * 10 + 140, NewRow * 20 + 30)
    GraphicsWindow.BrushColor = "Red"
    GraphicsWindow.FillEllipse(StaffColumn * 10 + 141, StaffRow *
20 + 36, 8, 8)
    StaffRow = NewRow
    StaffColumn = NewColumn
  EndIf
EndSub
Sub IsGameOver
  If (GameOver = "true") Then
    'game is over
    GameStatus = "Selecting"
    If (Moves < 500) Then
      GraphicsWindow.ShowMessage("You found the lost sheep in " +
Moves + " moves.", "Game Over")
    Else
      GraphicsWindow.ShowMessage("You seem lost - the game has
stopped.", "Game Over")
    EndIf
    Shapes.Remove(Staff)
  EndIf
EndSub
Sub DisplayMoves
  GraphicsWindow.FontSize = 18
  GraphicsWindow.BrushColor = "Blue"
  GraphicsWindow.FillRectangle(0, 40, 100, 20)
  GraphicsWindow.BrushColor = "White"
  GraphicsWindow.DrawText(35, 40, Moves)
EndSub
Sub KeyDownEvent
  If (GameStatus = "StaffMove") Then
    K = GraphicsWindow.LastKey
    DeltaRow = 0
    DeltaColumn = 0
    If (K = "NumPad7") Then
```

```
      DeltaRow = -1
      DeltaColumn = -1
    EndIf
    If (K = "NumPad8" Or K = "Up") Then
      DeltaRow = -1
      DeltaColumn = 0
    EndIf
    If (K = "NumPad9") Then
      DeltaRow = -1
      DeltaColumn = 1
    EndIf
    If (K = "NumPad4" Or K = "Left") Then
      DeltaRow = 0
      DeltaColumn = -1
    EndIf
    If (K = "NumPad6" Or K = "Right") Then
      DeltaRow = 0
      DeltaColumn = 1
    EndIf
    If (K = "NumPad1") Then
      DeltaRow = 1
      DeltaColumn = -1
    EndIf
    If (K = "NumPad2" Or K = "Down") Then
      DeltaRow = 1
      DeltaColumn = 0
    EndIf
    If (K = "NumPad3") Then
      DeltaRow = 1
      DeltaColumn = 1
    EndIf
    'check if move is okay
    NewRow = StaffRow + DeltaRow
    NewColumn = StaffColumn + DeltaColumn
    CheckMove()
    DisplayMoves()
    IsGameOver()
  EndIf
EndSub
```

Program 11 – The Lost Coin Game

Program Design

This program is the classic Lost Coin Game. The program is saved in the **LostCoin** folder in the program folder (**\BeginSB\BSB Code**.

Program Development

Start Small Basic, start a new program and save it as **LostCoin**. Type in (or copy and paste from these notes) the complete **LostCoin** Small Basic code.

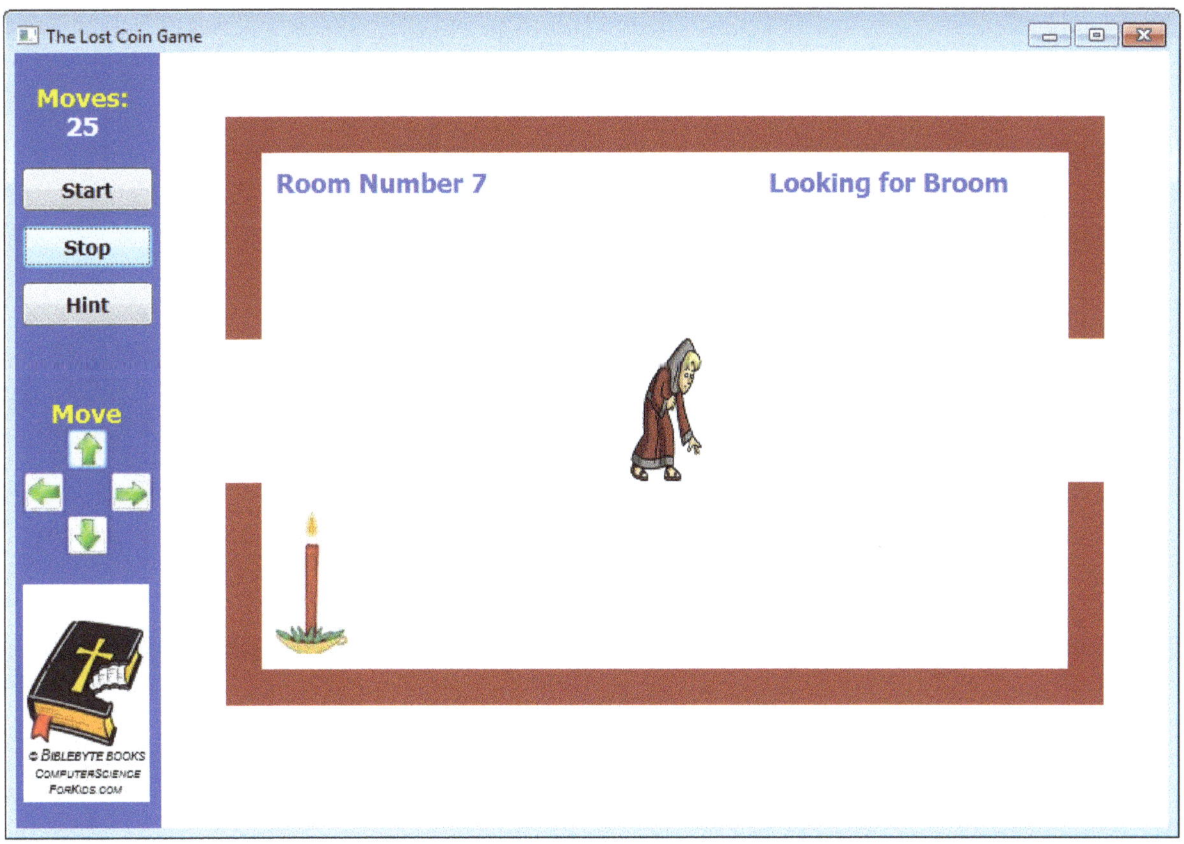

```
' The Lost Coin Game
' Small Basic Version
'
' Intro screen
IntroScreen:
Difficulty = 1
GameStatus = "Selecting"
GraphicsWindow.Show()
GraphicsWindow.Title = "The Lost Coin Game"
GraphicsWindow.BackgroundColor = "White"
GraphicsWindow.Width = 800
GraphicsWindow.Height = 540
GraphicsWindow.BrushColor = "Black"
GraphicsWindow.FontSize = 14
GraphicsWindow.DrawText(110, 10, "THE LOST COIN GAME")
GraphicsWindow.DrawText(110, 30, "In Luke Chapter 15: 8-10, Jesus tells a parable about a woman who loses a coin.  She lights a")
GraphicsWindow.DrawText(110, 50, "candle and sweeps her house to find the lost coin.  When found, she rejoices!  In the same way,")
GraphicsWindow.DrawText(110, 70, "there will be rejoicing in heaven when one sinner repents.  Help find the candle, broom and coin.")
GraphicsWindow.DrawText(110, 90, "<-- Click on the Start Button to begin.")
GraphicsWindow.DrawText(110, 130, "<-- Click on the Stop Button to stop the program.")
GraphicsWindow.DrawText(110, 170, "<-- Click here for a hint if you can't seem to locate the candle, broom or the lost coin. The hint ")
GraphicsWindow.DrawText(110, 190, "       will indicate the general direction to go to find the next item you need.  You may have to")
GraphicsWindow.DrawText(110, 210, "       change directions a few times to get through the right set of doors to reach the next item. ")
GraphicsWindow.DrawText(110, 230, "       You can click on the Hint Button as many times as you need to as it is easy to get very lost")
GraphicsWindow.DrawText(110, 250, "       in the large maze of rooms. ")
GraphicsWindow.DrawText(110, 300, "<-- Use these buttons (or arrow keys) to move the woman.")
GraphicsWindow.DrawText(110, 480, "Find more Computer Programming Tutorials @ http://www.BibleByteBooks.com and ")
```

```
GraphicsWindow.DrawText(110, 500,
"http://www.ComputerScienceForKids.com")
GraphicsWindow.BrushColor = "Blue"
GraphicsWindow.FillRectangle(0, 0, 100, GraphicsWindow.Height)
GraphicsWindow.BrushColor = "Yellow"
GraphicsWindow.FontSize = 18
GraphicsWindow.DrawText(15, 20, "Moves:")
GraphicsWindow.DrawText(25, 240, "Move")
MoveImage = ImageList.LoadImage(Program.Directory +
"\FourArrows.jpg")
MoveButtons = Shapes.AddImage(MoveImage)
Shapes.Move(MoveButtons, 5, 260)
LogoImage = ImageList.LoadImage(Program.Directory +
"\LogoHolder.jpg")
Logo = Shapes.AddImage(LogoImage)
Shapes.Move(Logo, 5, 370)
Message[1] = "Looking for Candle"
Message[2] = "Looking for Broom"
Message[3] = "Looking for Coin"
Message[4] = "Found Lost Coin"
'add button controls
GraphicsWindow.BrushColor = "Black"
GraphicsWindow.FontSize = 14
StartButton = Controls.AddButton("Start", 5, 80)
Controls.SetSize(StartButton, 90, 30)
StopButton = Controls.AddButton("Stop", 5, 120)
Controls.SetSize(StopButton, 90, 30)
HintButton = Controls.AddButton("Hint", 5, 160)
Controls.SetSize(HintButton, 90, 30)
Controls.ButtonClicked = ButtonClickedEvent
GraphicsWindow.MouseDown = MouseDownEvent
GraphicsWindow.KeyDown = KeyDownEvent

Sub ButtonClickedEvent
  BBB = Controls.LastClickedButton
  If (GameStatus = "Selecting") Then
    If (BBB = StopButton) Then
      'clicked stop
      Program.End()
    ElseIf (BBB = StartButton) Then
      'clicked start
      Shapes.Remove(Woman)
      Shapes.Remove(FoundItem[1])
      Shapes.Remove(FoundItem[2])
      Shapes.Remove(FoundItem[3])
      GameStatus = "WomanMove"
```

```
      GameOver = "false"
      GraphicsWindow.BrushColor = "White"
      GraphicsWindow.FillRectangle(100, 0, GraphicsWindow.Width -
100, GraphicsWindow.Height)
      Moves = 0
      DisplayMoves()
      'Get room, position candle, broom, coin
      RoomNumber = Math.GetRandomNumber(50)
      Location[1] = -1
      Location[2] = -2
      Location[3] = -3
      For i = 1 To 3
        GetLocations:
        Location[i] = Math.GetRandomNumber(50)
        If (Location[i] = RoomNumber Or Location[1] = Location[2]
Or Location[1] = Location[3] Or Location[2] = Location[3]) Then
          Goto GetLocations
        EndIf
      EndFor
      'Load images and shapes
      CandleImage = ImageList.LoadImage(Program.Directory +
"\Candle.jpg")
      FoundItem[1] = Shapes.AddImage(CandleImage)
      BroomImage = ImageList.LoadImage(Program.Directory +
"\Broom.jpg")
      FoundItem[2] = Shapes.AddImage(BroomImage)
      CoinImage = ImageList.LoadImage(Program.Directory +
"\Coin.jpg")
      FoundItem[3] = Shapes.AddImage(CoinImage)
      Shapes.HideShape(FoundItem[1])
      Shapes.HideShape(FoundItem[2])
      Shapes.HideShape(FoundItem[3])
      Finding = 1
      DrawRoom()
      'Place woman
      WomanImage = ImageList.LoadImage(Program.Directory +
"\Woman.gif")
      Woman = Shapes.AddImage(WomanImage)
      Shapes.Move(Woman, 425, 200)
    EndIf
  EndIf
  If (GameStatus = "WomanMove") Then
    'clicks on hint button
    If (BBB = HintButton) Then
      ' woman row/column
      WomanRow = Math.Floor((RoomNumber - 1) / 10) + 1
```

```
      WomanColumn = RoomNumber - 10 * (WomanRow - 1)
      'finding row/column
      LocationRow = Math.Floor((Location[Finding] - 1) / 10) + 1
      LocationColumn = Location[Finding] - 10 * (LocationRow - 1)
      GraphicsWindow.FontSize = 14
      GraphicsWindow.BrushColor = "White"
      If (WomanRow > LocationRow) Then
        Hint = "Move Up"
      ElseIf (WomanRow < LocationRow) Then
        Hint = "Move Down"
      Else
        Hint = ""
      EndIf
      GraphicsWindow.DrawText(8, 195, Hint)
      If (WomanColumn > LocationColumn) Then
        Hint = "Move Left"
      ElseIf (WomanColumn < LocationColumn) Then
        Hint = "Move Right"
      Else
        Hint = ""
      EndIf
      GraphicsWindow.DrawText(8, 215, Hint)
    EndIf
    IsGameOver()
  EndIf
  If (GameStatus <> "Selecting") Then
    If (BBB = StopButton) Then
      'clicked stop while playing
      GameStatus = "Selecting"
      GraphicsWindow.ShowMessage("You stopped the game.", "Game
Over")
    EndIf
  EndIf
EndSub


Sub MouseDownEvent
  If (GameStatus = "WomanMove") Then
    'Move staff
    'clicks on move buttons
    If (GraphicsWindow.MouseX > Shapes.GetLeft(MoveButtons) And
GraphicsWindow.MouseX < Shapes.GetLeft(MoveButtons) + 90) Then
      If (GraphicsWindow.MouseY > Shapes.GetTop(MoveButtons) And
GraphicsWindow.MouseY < Shapes.GetTop(MoveButtons) + 90) Then
        'clear hint area
        ClearHint()
```

```
        Row = Math.Floor((GraphicsWindow.MouseY -
Shapes.GetTop(MoveButtons)) / 30)
        Column = Math.Floor((GraphicsWindow.MouseX -
Shapes.GetLeft(MoveButtons)) / 30)
        CheckMove()
      EndIf
    EndIf
    IsGameOver()
  EndIf
EndSub

Sub ClearHint
  GraphicsWindow.BrushColor = "Blue"
  GraphicsWindow.FillRectangle(5, 195, 90, 40)
EndSub

Sub CheckMove
  MoveOkay = "false"
  If (Row = 0 And Column = 1 And ClickUp) Then
    MoveOkay = "true"
    DeltaRoom = -10
  ElseIf (Row = 1 And Column = 0 And ClickLeft) Then
    MoveOkay = "true"
    DeltaRoom = -1
  ElseIf (Row = 1 And Column = 2 And ClickRight) Then
    MoveOkay = "true"
    DeltaRoom = 1
  ElseIf (Row = 2 And Column = 1 And ClickDown) Then
    MoveOkay = "true"
    DeltaRoom = 10
  EndIf
  If (MoveOkay = "true") Then
    Moves = Moves + 1
    DisplayMoves()
    Sound.PlayClick()
    RoomNumber = RoomNumber + DeltaRoom
    If (RoomNumber > 0 And RoomNumber < 51) Then
      DrawRoom()
      If (RoomNumber = Location[Finding]) Then
        'found something
        Shapes.ShowShape(FoundItem[Finding])
        Shapes.Move(FoundItem[Finding], (Finding - 1) * 60 + 180,
320)
        Finding = Finding + 1
        DrawRoom()
        If Finding = 4  Then
```

```
          GameOver = "true"
        EndIf
      EndIf
    Else
      GameOver = "true"
    EndIf
  EndIf
EndSub

Sub IsGameOver
  If (GameOver = "true") Then
    'game is over
    GameStatus = "Selecting"
    If (Finding = 4) Then
      GraphicsWindow.ShowMessage("You found the lost coin in " +
Moves + " moves.", "Game Over")
    Else
      GraphicsWindow.ShowMessage("You left the house without
finding the coin.", "Game Over")
    EndIf
  EndIf
EndSub


Sub DisplayMoves
  GraphicsWindow.FontSize = 18
  GraphicsWindow.BrushColor = "Blue"
  GraphicsWindow.FillRectangle(0, 40, 100, 20)
  GraphicsWindow.BrushColor = "White"
  GraphicsWindow.DrawText(35, 40, Moves)
EndSub

Sub DrawRoom
  '  draw Room
  GraphicsWindow.BrushColor = "Brown"
  GraphicsWindow.FillRectangle(145, 45, 610, 410)
  GraphicsWindow.BrushColor = "White"
  GraphicsWindow.FillRectangle(170, 70, 560, 360)
  ' print room number and message
  GraphicsWindow.BrushColor = "Blue"
  GraphicsWindow.FontSize = 18
  GraphicsWindow.DrawText(180, 80, "Room Number " + RoomNumber)
  GraphicsWindow.DrawText(520, 80, Message[Finding])
  'Decide where doors are based on RoomNumber
  r = RoomNumber
  ClickUp = "false"
```

```
  ClickRight = "false"
  ClickDown = "false"
  ClickLeft = "false"
  If (r = 1 Or r = 40) Then
    ClickDown ="true"
  ElseIf (r = 31 Or r = 43) Then
    ClickRight = "true"
  ElseIf (r = 4 Or r = 12 Or r = 16 Or r = 21 Or r = 24 Or r = 28
Or r = 35 Or r= 39 Or r = 41 Or r = 44 Or r = 46 Or r = 48 Or r =
49) Then
    ClickUp = "true"
    ClickRight = "true"
  ElseIf (r = 11 Or r = 13 Or r = 18 Or r = 22 Or r = 27 Or r = 30
Or r = 33 Or r= 36) Then
    ClickUp = "true"
    ClickDown = "true"
  ElseIf (r = 2 Or r = 7 Or r = 8 Or r = 9 Or r = 15 Or r = 19 Or
r = 25 Or r= 34 Or r = 38 Or r = 42 Or r = 45 Or r = 47 Or r = 50)
Then
    ClickRight = "true"
    ClickLeft = "true"
  ElseIf (r = 3 Or r = 5 Or r = 6 Or r = 10 Or r = 14 Or r = 17 Or
r = 20 Or r= 23 Or r = 26 Or r = 29 Or r = 32 Or r = 37) Then
    ClickDown = "true"
    ClickLeft = "true"
  EndIf
  'Draw doors
  GraphicsWindow.BrushColor = "White"
  If (ClickUp) Then
    GraphicsWindow.FillRectangle(400, 45, 100, 25)'up
  EndIf
  If (ClickRight) Then
    GraphicsWindow.FillRectangle(730, 200, 25, 100) ' right
  EndIf
  If (ClickDown) Then
    GraphicsWindow.FillRectangle(400, 430, 100, 25)'down
  EndIf
  If (ClickLeft) Then
    GraphicsWindow.FillRectangle(145, 200, 25, 100) ' Left
  EndIf
EndSub

Sub KeyDownEvent
  If (GameStatus = "WomanMove") Then
    K = GraphicsWindow.LastKey
    Row = 0
```

```
    Column = 0
    If (K = "NumPad8" Or K = "Up") Then
      Row = 0
      Column = 1
    EndIf
    If (K = "NumPad4" Or K = "Left") Then
      Row = 1
      Column = 0
    EndIf
    If (K = "NumPad6" Or K = "Right") Then
      Row = 1
      Column = 2
    EndIf
    If (K = "NumPad2" Or K = "Down") Then
      Row = 2
      Column = 1
    EndIf
  EndIf
  ClearHint()
  CheckMove()
  IsGameOver()
EndSub
```

The **Computer Bible Games** class is over. You've come a long way. Remember back in the first class when you first learned about coding? You're a coding expert by now. But, that doesn't mean you know everything there is to know about programming. Computer programming is a never-ending educational process. There are always new things to learn - ways to improve your skills.

What is your next step for improvement? We offer an intermediate level course called ***Programming Games with Microsoft Small Basic*** which will teach you program design, using Small Basic objects (including button controls), many new elements of the Small Basic language, and how to debug and share finished programs. Game skills learned include handling multiple players, scoring, graphics, animation, and sounds.

One other thing to consider is moving on to a more advanced programming environment like Microsoft Visual Basic. You can build professional looking programs complete with GUI controls using this product. And, Microsoft offers a free version of the program called Visual Basic Express. If you want to give this a try, take a look at our http://www.BibleByteBooks.com website for the latest download link to our ***Computer Bible Games with Visual Basic*** tutorial.

Our company offers tutorials that cover Visual Basic for both beginners and more advanced programmers. These tutorials are self-paced, study guides that provide an overview of Microsoft Visual Basic for building GUI applications. What would you gain from these tutorials? Here are a few new things you would learn:

- Visual Basic and how to build detailed GUI applications that use controls
- How to distribute your programs to other users
- How to read and write files to disk (this could be used to save high scores in games)
- How to do more detailed animations
- How to play elaborate sounds (the chime and ring are pretty boring)
- How to use your printer
- How to create your own on-line help system

Contact us if you want more information. Or, visit our website - the address is on the title page for this course.

Appendix I. Small Basic Colors

Color	Name	RGB Value
	AliceBlue	#F0F8FF
	AntiqueWhite	#FAEBD7
	Aqua	#00FFFF
	Aquamarine	#7FFFD4
	Azure	#F0FFFF
	Beige	#F5F5DC
	Bisque	#FFE4C4
	Black	#000000
	BlanchedAlmond	#FFEBCD
	Blue	#0000FF
	BlueViolet	#8A2BE2
	Brown	#A52A2A
	BurlyWood	#DEB887
	CadetBlue	#5F9EA0
	Chartreuse	#7FFF00
	Chocolate	#D2691E
	Coral	#FF7F50
	CornflowerBlue	#6495ED

	Cornsilk	#FFF8DC
	Crimson	#DC143C
	Cyan	#00FFFF
	DarkBlue	#00008B
	DarkCyan	#008B8B
	DarkGoldenrod	#B8860B
	DarkGray / DarkGrey†	#A9A9A9
	DarkGreen	#006400
	DarkKhaki	#BDB76B
	DarkMagenta	#8B008B
	DarkOliveGreen	#556B2F
	DarkOrange	#FF8C00
	DarkOrchid	#9932CC
	DarkRed	#8B0000
	DarkSalmon	#E9967A
	DarkSeaGreen	#8FBC8F
	DarkSlateBlue	#483D8B
	DarkSlateGray / DarkSlateGrey†	#2F4F4F
	DarkTurquoise	#00CED1
	DarkViolet	#9400D3
	DeepPink	#FF1493

	DeepSkyBlue	#00BFFF
	DimGray / DimGrey†	#696969
	DodgerBlue	#1E90FF
	FireBrick	#B22222
	FloralWhite	#FFFAF0
	ForestGreen	#228B22
	Fuchsia	#FF00FF
	Gainsboro	#DCDCDC
	GhostWhite	#F8F8FF
	Gold	#FFD700
	Goldenrod	#DAA520
	Gray / Grey†	#808080
	Green	#008000
	GreenYellow	#ADFF2F
	Honeydew	#F0FFF0
	HotPink	#FF69B4
	IndianRed	#CD5C5C
	Indigo	#4B0082
	Ivory	#FFFFF0
	Khaki	#F0E68C
	Lavender	#E6E6FA

	LavenderBlush	#FFF0F5
	LawnGreen	#7CFC00
	LemonChiffon	#FFFACD
	LightBlue	#ADD8E6
	LightCoral	#F08080
	LightCyan	#E0FFFF
	LightGoldenrodYellow	#FAFAD2
	LightGreen	#90EE90
	LightGray† / LightGrey	#D3D3D3
	LightPink	#FFB6C1
	LightSalmon	#FFA07A
	LightSeaGreen	#20B2AA
	LightSkyBlue	#87CEFA
	LightSlateGray / LightSlateGrey†	#778899
	LightSteelBlue	#B0C4DE
	LightYellow	#FFFFE0
	Lime	#00FF00
	LimeGreen	#32CD32
	Linen	#FAF0E6
	Magenta	#FF00FF
	Maroon	#800000

	MediumAquamarine	#66CDAA
	MediumBlue	#0000CD
	MediumOrchid	#BA55D3
	MediumPurple	#9370DB
	MediumSeaGreen	#3CB371
	MediumSlateBlue	#7B68EE
	MediumSpringGreen	#00FA9A
	MediumTurquoise	#48D1CC
	MediumVioletRed	#C71585
	MidnightBlue	#191970
	MintCream	#F5FFFA
	MistyRose	#FFE4E1
	Moccasin	#FFE4B5
	NavajoWhite	#FFDEAD
	Navy	#000080
	OldLace	#FDF5E6
	Olive	#808000
	OliveDrab	#6B8E23
	Orange	#FFA500
	OrangeRed	#FF4500
	Orchid	#DA70D6

	PaleGoldenrod	#EEE8AA
	PaleGreen	#98FB98
	PaleTurquoise	#AFEEEE
	PaleVioletRed	#DB7093
	PapayaWhip	#FFEFD5
	PeachPuff	#FFDAB9
	Peru	#CD853F
	Pink	#FFC0CB
	Plum	#DDA0DD
	PowderBlue	#B0E0E6
	Purple	#800080
	Red	#FF0000
	RosyBrown	#BC8F8F
	RoyalBlue	#4169E1
	SaddleBrown	#8B4513
	Salmon	#FA8072
	SandyBrown	#F4A460
	SeaGreen	#2E8B57
	Seashell	#FFF5EE
	Sienna	#A0522D
	Silver	#C0C0C0

	SkyBlue	#87CEEB
	SlateBlue	#6A5ACD
	SlateGray / SlateGrey†	#708090
	Snow	#FFFAFA
	SpringGreen	#00FF7F
	SteelBlue	#4682B4
	Tan	#D2B48C
	Teal	#008080
	Thistle	#D8BFD8
	Tomato	#FF6347
	Turquoise	#40E0D0
	Violet	#EE82EE
	Wheat	#F5DEB3
	White	#FFFFFF
	WhiteSmoke	#F5F5F5
	Yellow	#FFFF00
	YellowGreen	#9ACD32

Appendix II.
Classic Small Basic Computer Games

PREVIEW

Back in the early 1980's, there were many computers introduced to the market through such mass retailers as Sears, K Mart and JC Penneys. Names like Texas Instruments, Atari, Sinclair, Commodore, VIC and Coleco Adam appeared everywhere. Each of these computers was programmed in the BASIC language. Each computer also had monthly magazines being published containing BASIC programs you could type into your computer and play. Users eagerly awaited for each issue to have more programs for their computer. Many of these programs had roots back to the 1960's, when the BASIC language first appeared.

This chapter contains three Small BASIC computer games originally published using BASIC in the classic programming book called "101 Basic Computer Games" edited by David Ahl and published by DEC. The book was re-published several times as "BASIC Computer Games" by David Ahl for several different hardware platforms. Most recently, we republished this classic programming book with David Ahl's permission as "Basic Computer Games: Small Basic 2010 Edition". The original games were simple 'text-only' programs. They had no fancy graphics and no sound. You had to use your imagination a lot back in those days. Much of the code is structured just like original BASIC programs. The original games were written long before the days of structured programs.

However, the games are still fun and invoke a nostalgic feeling in many of us older programmers. Many of us stayed up very late at night typing in all these BASIC games on our computers just so we could learn how to program. BASIC Computer Games made learning the BASIC computer language fun and rewarding.

BIBLEBYTE BOOKS also produces beginning programming tutorials for Visual Basic, Visual C# and Java so you can study and learn how to program in these popular programming languages. The most popular feature of our tutorials is that you develop the exact same games and applications in four different programming languages. This consistent and repetetive multi-language programing technique accelerates the time to learn a new programming langauge.

Special permission was granted by David H. Ahl to port and re-publish all these classic BASIC Computer Games in Microsoft Small Basic.

SMALL BASIC PROGRAM OPERATION INSTRUCTIONS

The Small Basic program files for this chapter are in a separate directory. The program files are found in the \SBGames folder. In this folder are three other folders. These folders contain the files needed for each game:

EvenWins - Even Wins files
Mugwump - Mugwump files
LunarLander - Lunar Lander files

In your Small Basic environment, just open and run the desired SMALL BASIC COMPUTER GAMES program file. Running instructions for the three classic Small BASIC Computer games are below:

EVEN WINS (Original Author: Eric Peters of Digital Equipment Corporation)
BASIC COMPUTER GAMES, Edited by David H. Ahl, Published in 1978

EVEN WINS is a game between you and the computer. To play, an odd number of markers are displayed on the screen. You take turns with the computer removing between one and four markers each turn. The game ends when there are no markers left and the winner is the one with an even number of markers removed.

When the game begins, the markers (asterisks) are displayed and the computer takes the first turn, removing from one to four markers. Then, on your turn, do the same. Remove from one to four markers by entering 1, 2, 3 or 4 key on your keyboard and pressing <Enter>. After each turn, you are shown how many markers you and the computer have. Continue alternating turns until all markers are gone. You win if you are left with an even number of markers. The computer wins if its score is an even number.

This is an interesting version of this game. The computer starts out only knowing the rules of the game and doesn't play very well. Using simple techniques of artificial intelligence, the computer gradually learns to play from its mistakes until it plays a very good game. After 20 games, the computer is a challenge to beat. Variation in your style of play seems to make the computer learn more quickly. I personally don't know how this code works - maybe you can figure it out. I just typed the code from a magazine - a technique used by many programmers (code 'borrowing').

EVEN WINS – SMALL BASIC SOURCE CODE

```
'
' Even Wins
' Original Author: Bill Palmby, Prairie View, Illinois
' BASIC COMPUTER GAMES,  Edited by David H. Ahl, Published in 1978
' Ported with Permission to Small Basic by Philip Conrod
'
'
TextWindow.Title = "Even Wins"
TextWindow.WriteLine("Take turns with the computer removing
markers (1 to 4).")
TextWindow.WriteLine("You win if you finish with an even number of
markers.")
'  Variables to help teach computer
For i = 0  to 5
  r[1][i] = 4
  r[0][i] = 4
EndFor

'  Start new game loop
GameLoop:
  gameOver = "false"
  '  number of markers, an odd number
  p = (Math.GetRandomNumber(9) + 3) * 2 + 1
  '  a is your score, b is computer score
  a = 0
  b = 0
  '  Start alternating turn loop
  While (gameOver = "false")
    TextWindow.WriteLine("")
    TextWindow.WriteLine("Computer's turn:")
    drawMarkers()
    ' computers choice and check for win
    e1 = e
    l1 = l
    e = (a / 2 - Math.Floor(a / 2)) * 2
    l = Math.Floor((p / 6 - Math.Floor(p / 6)) * 6 + 0.5)
    if (r[e][l] >= p) then
      '  took last one, game over
      gameOver = "true"
      r[e][l] = p
      m = p
      b = b + p
    else
      gameOver = "false"
      m = r[e][l]
```

```
      b = b + m
    EndIf
    TextWindow.WriteLine("I take " + m + " markers.")
    p = p - m
    if (gameOver = "false") then
      TextWindow.WriteLine("")
      TextWindow.WriteLine("Your turn:")
      ' your turn
      drawMarkers()
      if (p > 4) then
        numberToRemove = 4
      Else
        numberToRemove = p
      EndIf
      GetInput:
      TextWindow.Write("How many markers do you want to remove (1 
to " + numberToRemove + ")? ")
      m = TextWindow.ReadNumber()
      If (m <= 0 or m > numberToRemove) Then
        Goto GetInput
      EndIf
      a = a + m
      p = p - m
      if (p = 0) then
        gameOver = "true"
      EndIf

  EndIf

  endwhile

  TextWindow.WriteLine("Game is over. I have " + b + " markers. 
You have " + a + " markers.")
  '  find winner
  if (b / 2 = Math.Floor(b / 2)) Then
    TextWindow.WriteLine("I won!!!")
  else
    TextWindow.WriteLine("You won!!!")
    '  computer knowledge gained by you winning
    if (r[e][l] = 1) then
      if (r[e1][l1] <> 1) then
        r[e1][l1] = r[e1][l1] - 1
      endif
    else
      r[e][l] = r[e][l] - 1
    EndIf
```

```
endif


 TextWindow.Write("Play again? (enter a y for yes) ")
Answer = TextWindow.Read()
If (Answer = "y") Then
  Goto GameLoop
EndIf


 sub drawMarkers
    N = p
    TextWindow.WriteLine("There are " + N + " markers
remaining:")
    for i = 1 to N
      TextWindow.Write("* ")
    EndFor
    TextWindow.WriteLine("")
    TextWindow.WriteLine("I have " + b + " markers.")
    TextWindow.WriteLine("You have " + a + " markers.")
  EndSub
```

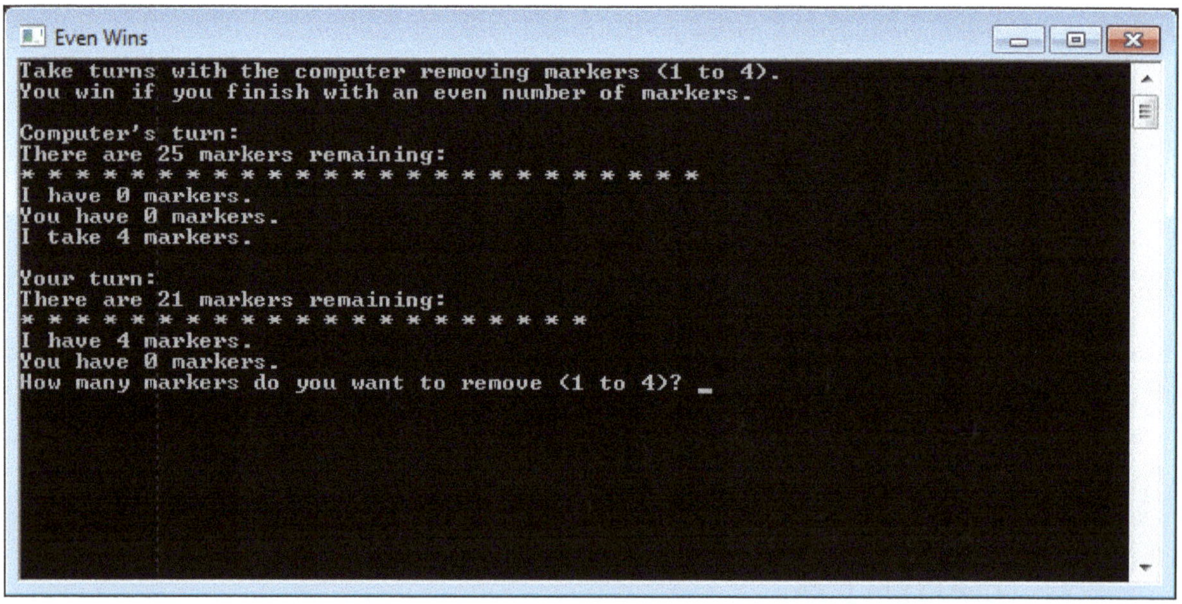

MUGWUMP (Original Author: Bob Albrecht of Peoples Computer Company)

BASIC COMPUTER GAMES, Edited by David H. Ahl, Published in 1978

The objective in this game is to find the four Mugwumps hiding on various squares of a 10 x 10 grid. After guessing a location, the computer gives you distance clues on how far you are from each Mugwump.

At the beginning of each game, a blank grid is shown. Choose a square to guess the location of a Mugwump. To choose a square, you are asked to enter the row (0 to 9) and column (0 to 9) of the selected square. After your guess, you are told how far (the famous Pythagorean triangle formula is used) you are from each remaining Mugwump. Use this information for your next guess. The program tells you how many Mugwumps are remaining and how many guesses you have taken. The game ends when all the Mugwumps have been found.

Playing the game with aid of graph paper and a compass should allow you to find all the Mugwumps in six or seven moves using triangulation similar to old Loran radio navigation (do some research to find out what this is).

```
'
' Mugwump
' Original Author: Bob Albrecht of Peoples Computer Company
' BASIC COMPUTER GAMES,  Edited by David H. Ahl, Published in 1978
' Ported with Permission to Small Basic by Philip Conrod
'
'
TextWindow.Title = "Mugwump"
TextWindow.WriteLine("Find the four Mugwumps hidden on a 10 x 10 
grid.")
TextWindow.WriteLine("After each guess, you are told how far you 
are from each Mugwump.")
TextWindow.WriteLine("")

'  Start new game loop
GameLoop:
  remaining = 4
  tries = 0
  '  hide mugwumps
  for i = 0 to 9
    for j = 0 To 9
      map[i][j] = 0
    EndFor
  EndFor
  for i = 0 To 3
    HideHim:
      for j = 0 to 1
        p[i][j] = Math.GetRandomNumber(10) - 1
      endfor
      If (map[p[i][0]][p[i][1]] <> 0) Then
        Goto HideHim
      EndIf
      map[p[i][0]][p[i][1]] = 1
  EndFor
  for i = 0 To 3
    map[p[i][0]][p[i][1]] = 0
  EndFor
  '  Next turn loop
  While(remaining > 0)
    ' draw current game board grid
    TextWindow.WriteLine("Current grid (O-Guess, X-Last Guess, M-
Mugwump):")
    TextWindow.WriteLine("  0 1 2 3 4 5 6 7 8 9")
    for i = 0 To 9
      TextWindow.Write((i) + "|")
```

```
    For j = 0 To 9
      if (map[i][j] = 0) Then
        TextWindow.Write(" |")
      elseif (map[i][j] = 1) Then
        TextWindow.Write("O|")
      elseif (map[i][j] = 2) Then
        TextWindow.Write("X|")
        map[i][j] = 1
      Else
            TextWindow.Write("M|")
      EndIf
    EndFor
    TextWindow.WriteLine("")
  EndFor
  GetInput:
  TextWindow.Write("What row? ")
  m = TextWindow.ReadNumber()
  TextWindow.Write("What column? ")
  n = TextWindow.ReadNumber()
  if (m < 0 or m > 9 or n <0 Or n > 9) then
    Goto GetInput
  EndIf
  if (map[m][n] = 1) Then
    TextWindow.WriteLine("You already looked there!")
  elseif (map[m][n] = 2) Then
    TextWindow.WriteLine("You already looked there!")
  elseif (map[m][n] = 3) Then
    TextWindow.WriteLine("You already found this Mugwump!")
  Else
    tries = tries + 1
    found = "false"
    for i = 0 to 3
      if (p[i][0] <> -1) then
        if (p[i][0] <> m or p[i][1] <> n) Then
          map[m][n] = 2
          d = Math.SquareRoot((p[i][0] - m) * (p[i][0] - m) +
(p[i][1] - n) * (p[i][1] - n))
          TextWindow.WriteLine("You are " + d + " units from
Mugwump " + (i + 1))
        Else
          found = "true"
         p[i][0] = -1
          TextWindow.WriteLine("You found Mugwump " + (i + 1) +
"!")
          remaining = remaining - 1
        EndIf
```

```
          Endif
        if (found = "true") then
            map[m][n] = 3
          EndIf
        EndFor
      endif

    EndWhile



TextWindow.Write("Play again? (enter a y for yes) ")
Answer = TextWindow.Read()
If (Answer = "y") Then
  Goto GameLoop
EndIf
```

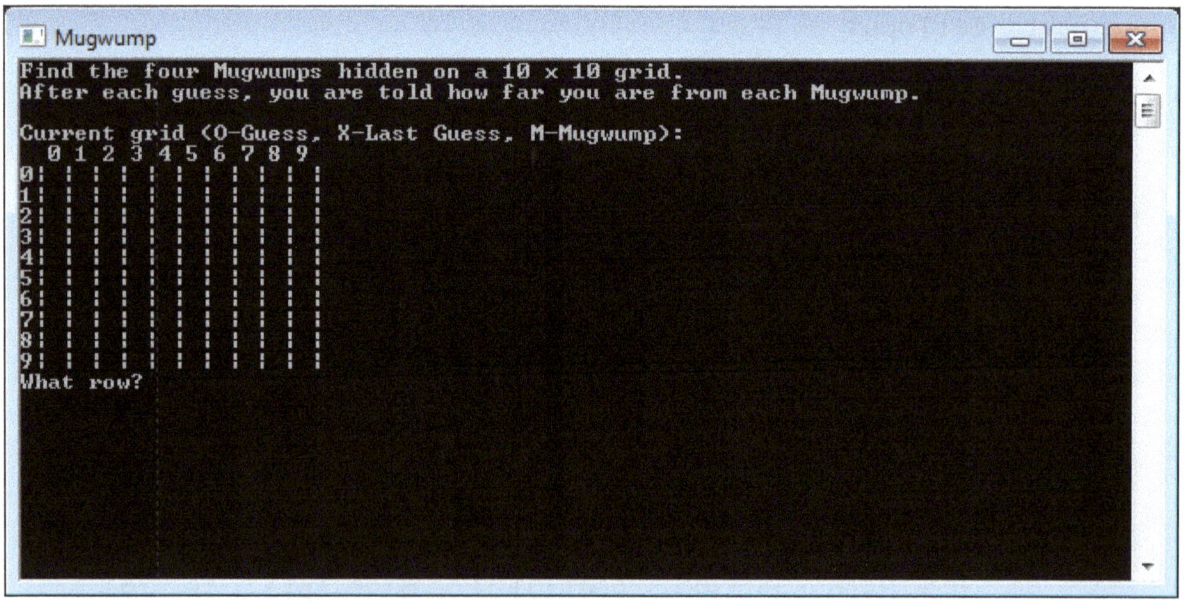

LUNAR LANDER (Original Author: Eric Peters of DEC)
BASIC COMPUTER GAMES, Edited by David H. Ahl, Published in 1978

This has been called the single most popular computer game ever. It was one of the first games written by little Billy Gates in his early programming days. You are hovering over the moon in your lunar module. You must land it safely by controlling the retrorocket burns.

When the game begins, you are 500 feet above the lunar surface and control the rocket burns in 1-second bursts. Displayed on the screen are Time, Altitude, Speed and Fuel Remaining. Each unit of fuel used slows your descent by 1 ft/sec. The maximum burn is 30 units of fuel in one second. To slow the module, enter the amount of fuel you want to burn over the next second (0 accelerates the module toward the lunar surface). Press the <Enter> key and the screen is updated with the latest data. A safe landing is achieved with final speeds less than 10 ft/sec.

The biggest mistake people make playing this game is yielding to the temptation of slowing the module much too soon. With this strategy, you run out of fuel for the lower part of the journey and the resulting tree-fall is disastrous! Use small burns early on to slow slight or maintain speed (a burn of 5 units does this). Then, really crank it on near the surface. You'll find some burn rates that work well.

LUNAR LANDER – SMALL BASIC SOURCE CODE

```
'
' Lunar Lander
' Original Author: Eric Peters of Digital Equipment Corporation
' BASIC COMPUTER GAMES,  Edited by David H. Ahl, Published in 1978
' Ported with Permission to Small Basic by Philip Conrod
'
'
TextWindow.Title = "Lunar Lander"
TextWindow.WriteLine("You are landing on the moon and have taken
manual control")
TextWindow.WriteLine("of the lunar module.  Your are 500 feet
above a good landing")
TextWindow.WriteLine("spot.  Good luck!!")
TextWindow.WriteLine("")

'  Start new game loop
GameLoop:
  gameOver = "false"
  T = 0.0     ' time
  H = 500.0   ' altitude
  V = 50.0    ' velocity
  F = 150.0   ' fuel
  '  Next turn loop
  While (gameOver = "false")
    TextWindow.WriteLine("")
    TextWindow.WriteLine("Module Status:")
    TextWindow.WriteLine("Time:      " + T)
    TextWindow.WriteLine("Altitude:  " + H)
    TextWindow.WriteLine("Velocity:  " + V)
    TextWindow.WriteLine("Fuel:      " + F)
 GetInput:
    TextWindow.Write("How much fuel to you want to burn? ")
    B = TextWindow.ReadNumber()
    If (B < 0 or B > 30 or B > F) then
      Goto GetInput
    EndIf
    T = T + 1.0
    V1 = V - B + 5.0
    F = F - B
    H = H - 0.5 * (V + V1)
    if (H > 0) then
      V = V1
      if (F <= 0) then
        TextWindow.WriteLine("")
```

```
        TextWindow.WriteLine("Out of fuel!  In free-fall!")
            While (H > 0)
          T = T + 1.0
        V1 = V + 5.0
        H = H - 0.5 * (V + V1)
        V = V1
        EndWhile
        gameOver = "true"
      endif
    else
      ' Landed
      gameOver = "true"
    endif
  EndWhile

TextWindow.WriteLine("")
TextWindow.WriteLine("Touchdown at " + T + " seconds.")
TextWindow.WriteLine("Landing velocity is " + V1 + " ft/sec.")
TextWindow.WriteLine(F + " units of fuel remain.")
if (V1 <= 2.0) then
  TextWindow.WriteLine("Congratulations! A perfect landing!")
elseif (Math.abs(V1) <= 10) then
  TextWindow.WriteLine("You inflicted some craft damage.")
  TextWindow.WriteLine("You are stranded until a rescue ship
arrives.")
else
  TextWindow.WriteLine("You blew it!")
  TextWindow.WriteLine("Condolences will be sent to the next of
kin.")
endif

TextWindow.Write("Play again? (enter a y for yes) ")
Answer = TextWindow.Read()
If (Answer = "y") Then
  Goto GameLoop
EndIf
```

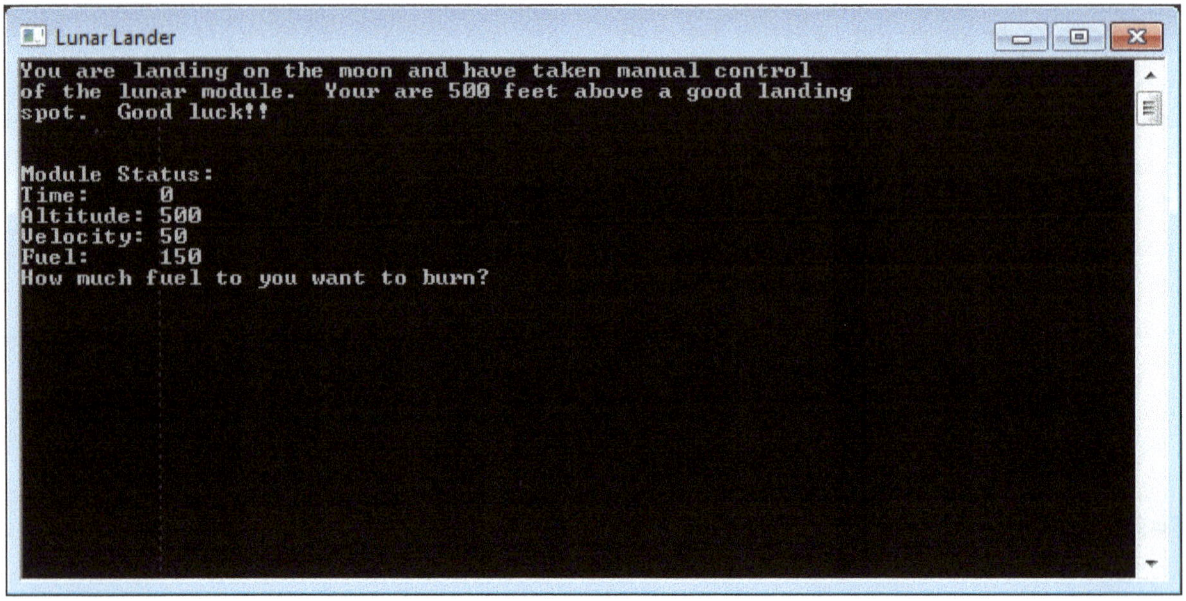
Lunar Lander
You are landing on the moon and have taken manual control
of the lunar module. Your are 500 feet above a good landing
spot. Good luck!!
Module Status:
Time: 0
Altitude: 500
Velocity: 50
Fuel: 150
How much fuel to you want to burn?

Other Self-Study and/or Instructor-Led Programming Tutorials By BibleByte Books

Computer Bible Games for Microsoft Small Basic is a self-paced "beginner" programming tutorial for Middle-School students. This tutorial consists of 13 chapters explaining (in simple, easy-to-follow terms) how to build Computer Bible Games in Small Basic. It also includes the Small Basic source code for the several of the original Computer Bible Games. The Computer Bible Games built include: Noah's Ark, Daniel and the Lions, Elijah and the Ravens, The Good Shepherd, The Prodigal Son, The Lost Coin, and Bible Scramble. Other learning projects include a card game, an allowance calculator, a drawing program, a state capitals game, and a video game.

Computer Bible Games with Visual Basic® Express is a self-paced semester long self-study "beginner" programming tutorial consisting of 13 chapters explaining (in simple, easy-to-follow terms) how to build a Visual Basic Express Windows application and Computer Bible Games. The Computer Bible Games built include: Noah's Ark, Elijah & the Ravens, and Daniel & the Lions. Other learning projects include a card game, an allowance calculator, a drawing program, a state capitals game, and a video game. We also include several college prep bonus projects including a loan calculator, portfolio manager, and checkbook balancer.

Computer Bible Games with Visual C#® Express is a semester long self-paced "beginning "programming tutorial consisting of 13 chapters explaining (in simple, easy-to-follow terms) how to build a C# Express Windows applications and Computer Bible Games. The Computer Bible Games built include: Noah's Ark, Elijah & the Ravens, and Daniel & the Lions. Other learning projects include a card game, an allowance calculator, a drawing program, a state capitals game, and a video game. We also include several college prep bonus projects including a loan calculator portfolio manager, and checkbook balancer.

Computer Bible Games with Java™ is a semester long self-paced programming tutorial consisting of 7 chapters explaining (in simple, easy-to-follow terms) how to build a Java® Computer Bible Games. This Tutorial requires a complete understanding of the Java Swing Control Library before attempting so it is an Advanced 3rd Semester Java Tutorial. The Computer Bible Games built include: Noah's Ark, Elijah & the Ravens, and Daniel & the Lions, Bible Safecracker, Bible Match, and Bible Trivia Tic-Tac-Toe. **We have also bundled our Beginning Java and Learn Java GUI Applications tutorials in this 1 year Java tutorial bundle.**

www.ingramcontent.com/pod-product-compliance
Ingram Content Group UK Ltd.
Pitfield, Milton Keynes, MK11 3LW, UK
UKHW051935071026
15590UKWH00017B/2239

9 781937